HALLELUJAH

Born and raised in New England, John Adams was exposed to both classical music and jazz from an early age. After graduating from Harvard during the tumultuous period of the late sixties he moved to San Francisco and has lived in northern California ever since. Adams's music, rooted in the driving pulses and emotional directness of American popular music, was instrumental in a historical shift of style away from the cool abstractions of dissonant modernism that had come to dominate the contemporary scene during the latter half of the twentieth century. As a composer of richly scored and expressive symphonic works (*Harmonium, Harmonielehre, Shaker Loops, Naïve and Sentimental Music, Scheherazade.2*) and creator of some of the most controversial and successful operas and oratorios in recent memory (*Nixon in China, The Death of Klinghoffer, El Niño, Doctor Atomic, The Gospel According to the Other Mary*), he has established a compelling new voice for contemporary music in our time. Composer, conductor and creative thinker, Adams is a musical polymath, active in all areas of his art. In addition to conducting the world's major symphony orchestras and conceiving and curating highly successful international festivals, he is also one of our most incisive commentators on the state of contemporary culture and the arts.

Further praise for *Hallelujah Junction*:

'*Hallelujah Junction* radiates a calm, Californian confidence, letting its ideas unfold at a gentle pace. I'm actually describing the piano piece that the American composer wrote in 1977, but I could be talking equally well about his memoir. Adams's unique touch finds its literary analogue in a style of rare precision . . . One of [his] purposes in writing this engaging book is to clarify his intentions, and in this he has admirably succeeded.'
Independent

'Confirms that Adams is not in the least self-regarding; he is a populist in the most disciplined and widely read sense. The reader needs to look no further than the significant episodes in American twentieth-century history that have formed the backbone of his compositions to appreciate the breadth and significance of his works . . . this exciting text should turn the reader back to the music.' *Classical Music*

'Absorbing, frank and often amusing.' *BBC Music Magazine*

'Adams is affable and opinionated; a serious composer embraced by the mainstream and an optimist attracted to the dark side for his operatic subjects. Great artists are defined by contradictions and *Hallulujah Junction* revels in the aesthetic cross-wires that have formed the US's most successful contemporary composer.' *Classic FM Magazine*

'A lively, witty prose writer . . . It's the range of Adams's musical appetites and intellectual hunger that leaves the strongest impression. This is a man who swallows whole new worlds with every fresh project he takes on – and makes his discoveries new for the rest of us.' *Seattle Times*

'Engrossing . . . Like his music, Adams's voice in *Hallelujah Junction* is both playful and thoughtful, unafraid of making big emotional statements but obsessed with making sure those statements are precisely crafted . . . An original and inspired book.' Wynne Delacoma, *Chicago Sun-Times*

'John Adams is the voice of America . . . thoughtful, amusing, analytical – and a good writer . . . To read something so intelligent, reasoned, and caring sure feels good these days.' Mark Swed, *Los Angeles Times*

'Among the most readably incisive autobiographies of major musical figures.' David Hajdu, *New York Times Book Review*

HALLELUJAH JUNCTION

COMPOSING AN AMERICAN LIFE

JOHN ADAMS

FABER & FABER

IN MEMORY OF HER MEMORY:
ELINORE ADAMS, BORN 1914

AND FOR MICHAEL STEINBERG

———————————————————————

First published in the United Kingdom in 2008
by Faber and Faber Limited,
Bloomsbury House
74–77 Great Russell Street, London, WC1B 3DA
This paperback edition first published in 2016

First published in the United States in 2008
by Farrar, Straus and Giroux
18 West 18th Street, New York 10011

Printed and bound by CPI Group (UK) Ltd, Croydon, CR0 4YY

A CIP record for this book
is available from the British Library

ISBN 978–0–571–23116–4

2 4 6 8 10 9 7 5 3 1

AFTER DEAD SOULS

Where O America are you
going in your glorious
automobile, careening
down the highway
toward what crash
in the deep canyon
of the Western Rockies,
or racing the sunset
over Golden Gate
toward what wild city
jumping with jazz
on the Pacific Ocean!

—ALLEN GINSBERG

CONTENTS

FOREWORD TO THE PAPERBACK EDITION

Writing *Hallelujah Junction* was a great pleasure, but as anyone who writes a memoir knows, you can only do it once. And the problem of producing an autobiography at late mid-career is that there's a built-in suggestion that what followed in the succeeding years was perhaps not as interesting or critical. That may or may not be the case. Certainly a lot of staves have been filled with "objects" (as my copyist calls the hundreds of thousands of sharps, flats, dots, fortes, pianos and meter markings that he patiently enters by the hundreds of thousands into his musical software program on my behalf).

Pieces written during this time include three works for string quartet, the First Quartet from 2008, the Second Quartet from 2014 and *Absolute Jest*, a wild twenty-five-minute essay for string quartet and orchestra based on fragments from the late Beethoven quartets. I composed all three of these pieces for the St Lawrence String Quartet, a group whose flexibility and willingness to experiment gave me the luxury of using these remarkable players as a laboratory for my imagination.

Gustavo Dudamel, who figures so prominently in the chapter about the creation of *A Flowering Tree*, became music director of the Los Angeles Philharmonic, an event that gave a thrilling buzz to the West Coast cultural scene. For Gustavo and the Philharmonic I composed two radically different pieces. The first was *City Noir* (2009), an imaginary score for an imagined "noir" film, a tribute to the dark, restless, jazz-inflected ambience of celluloid fantasy. The other was *The Gospel According to the Other Mary* (2012), a Passion oratorio that flips back and forth between the Biblical past and present-day urban America with its violent social contrasts and the immanence of grace in the face of poverty, suffering and violence. *The Other Mary* must be the only Passion oratorio to begin with the description of an agonized woman in a jail cell enduring the torture of heroin withdrawal.

Another large-scale work about a mythic woman, *Scheherazade.2* (2014–15), is a "dramatic symphony" for violin and orchestra. I wrote it for that young woman of indomitable spirit, Leila Josefowicz, who more than any other artist I know, embodies the sense of freedom and fearlessness that a modern, "empowered" Scheherazade might possess.

All of these works, I'm proud to say, have been given memorable UK performances – in the case of the orchestral pieces – by Michael Tilson Thomas and Gustavo Dudamel on tour with their own orchestras and by the London Symphony, with myself conducting; and by English National Opera, who gave my great collaborator Peter Sellars all the support and freedom he needed to realize his memorable operatic version of *Other Mary*. And the BBC Symphony Orchestra and Chorus in 2012 "caught every gesture and every word" of *Nixon in China* in a Proms concert that remains in memory as one of the highpoints of my life as a composer and conductor.

I'm keenly aware of all the stresses that an increasingly volatile market economy places on the arts, and on classical contemporary music in particular. What we do is not considered to have a high market value. No crafty speculator is going to buy *Shaker Loops* or *El Niño* for $25 million and warehouse it in a vault in Abu Dhabi. We hope that the fruits of our labours will ripen with the years and be valued by future generations as testaments of our time and our lives. This is what gives the *longa* to *ars*. To be privileged to present my very American music to the musically literate, brilliantly eccentric, unashamedly fanatic British audiences is a defining part of my life as an artist.

J.A.

PREFACE

omposing an American Life would not be the same were it not for the enormous influence that British music and musicians have had on me over the years. Several close London friends who read early drafts of this book commented on my oversight in not acknowledging my debt to the British music world, from its widely knowledgeable and endlessly adventurous audiences to its great orchestras, conductors and composers. In truth, I couldn't imagine my American life without British music and musicians.

The very first notes of a live symphony orchestra I heard as a child were those of the Boston Symphony playing the Vaughan Williams Tallis Fantasia, an experience that imprinted me for life. The Beatles and the Rolling Stones framed my college years. In the early 1970s Gavin Bryars opened up for me the eccentric world of British experimental music (a debt I was later able to repay by giving the US premieres of *Jesus Blood* and *The Sinking of the Titanic*). And Brian Eno produced my very first appearance on LP—on the appropriately named Obscure label.

Simon Rattle, later to become a close family friend, first introduced my orchestral music to England in the late 1980s with his performance of *Harmonium* at the Proms and in Barrie Gavin's film *Adams in Eden*. The fact that Simon has gone from strength to strength throughout his estimable career, demonstrating a depth of understanding and skills that range from the early Baroque through to the most recent and complex of contemporary scores is a perfect illustration of what makes British musical life so unique. It is a culture based on the enthusiastic embrace of a huge diversity of styles, but grounded in an educational philosophy that produces artists of singular flexibility and astonishingly quick learning curves. Indeed—unlike in the United States, where an aspiring classical musician must fight just to be heard above the general din—in England, when a young Rattle, or a Knussen or an Adès appears on the horizon, there is already waiting for that artist a well-developed support system ready to nurture the talent and help it blossom.

While the British may argue about and even lament their much-maligned BBC, we Americans are in awe of an institution that continues to treat its audience as grown-up, literate and educated human beings. The "Beeb" has been for this American composer a source of support and dissemination of new music that makes our dismal US "culture" channels pale in comparison.

Even a short list of the friends and supporters with whom I've had unforgettable experiences would be all too long. Suffice it to mention just a few: Tony Fell and Janis Susskind of my London-based publisher Boosey & Hawkes, who have happily made serious music thrive in a business climate presumably only interested in pop; Nicholas Kenyon, Paul Hughes and Rosemary Gent, who saw to it that virtually my entire catalog of orchestral music was heard at the Royal Albert Hall; Paul Crossley, who first invited me to conduct my own and other American music at the Queen Elizabeth Hall; the players of the London Sinfonietta, the London Symphony Orchestra and the BBC Symphony Orchestra, all of whom shared with me memorable concerts and recording sessions over a period of nearly twenty-five years; Jane Brown, my longtime conducting agent and consultant on Lake District hiking; Colin Matthews and Ollie Knussen, both composers and teachers (and in the case of Ollie a conductor) of enormous sophistication and enviable accomplishment; and Penny Woolcock and Jan Younghusband, the women who brought *Klinghoffer* to the screen. Last but possibly most critical for the project at hand, I should acknowledge Belinda Matthews, my publisher at Faber, who with her enthusiasm and good humor was among the very first to spur me on in the writing of this book.

J.A.

HALLELUJAH JUNCTION

WINNIPESAUKEE GARDENS

Weirs Beach, New Hampshire, lies on the southwestern corner of Lake Winnipesaukee in the central part of the state, just south of the White Mountains. For much of the earlier part of the last century it was a summer resort, receiving vacationers, many of whom arrived via the Boston and Maine Railroad as it passed through on its way to destinations farther north. A modest New England resort in the 1930s, Weirs Beach was no Coney Island, but it nevertheless featured a boardwalk, several small hotels, a boat marina, and—its prized possession—a dance hall built on pilings that extended out over the waters of the lake. It was here in this dance hall, Irwin's Winnipesaukee Gardens, that my father and mother met in the summer of 1935.

I have undated pictures of them from that period: Carl Adams, born Carl John Vincent Adams in Shrewsbury, Massachusetts, in 1911; and Elinore Mary Coolidge, born in 1914 in Roxbury, Massachusetts. In the photo of my father you see him seated, straddling his clarinet between his legs, one of ten members of a band identified on the picture as Ed Murphy and His Orchestra. The players are dressed nattily in dark blazers with handkerchiefs in the breast pockets, brilliant white slacks, and white wing-tip shoes. Standing to the side is the only female, the vocalist who my father later identified to me as Fredda Gibbons, at the time no more than seventeen, but later to become a hugely successful pop singer in the 1950s better known as Miss Georgia Gibbs, a regular on the Jimmy Durante *Camel Caravan*, and whose hits included "Kiss of Fire" and "Seven Lonely Days."

The band is posing for its picture on what looks like a lazy summer afternoon or early evening. It is the deep middle of the Great Depression, and big band jazz is one of the few sources of solace for a population ground down by a dysfunctional economy and massive unemployment. Everyone in the photo looks tanned and youthful and in good humor, a testament to the summer employment of a jazz musician with its leisurely unoccupied days and long nights of music, dancing, gin, and cigarettes. Three of the band members are holding clarinets. It is the era of the clarinet in American music: Artie Shaw and Benny Goodman play the instrument for its raunchy, high-register sassiness and coax out of it a provocative and licentious squeal. In these days before the advent of amplification, the sound of the clarinet carries over the clamor of a fully crowded dance floor. My father's instrument, it will also become mine, taught to me by him. By the time I am twenty-one the clarinet will have vanished from popular music. The Beatles will bring it back for a moment in 1968 in *Sgt Peppers Lonely Hearts Club Band* to summon up a sentimental, doddering oldster singing "When I'm Sixty-four."

The picture of my mother may be from the same summer of 1935, or possibly even earlier. She too is seated with a jazz band, a quintet identified only by the name Russ Cole. She wears a cotton summer dress with diagonal stripes, and her dark blond hair is pulled gently back from her bright, expressive face. She looks at the camera intently, self-conscious and a bit stagy, far more self-aware than the men in the band. Of my mother's forays into professional jazz singing I know next to nothing. She may have sung on occasion for the sheer fun of it, but it's unlikely that Russ Cole was a paying gig for her. Nevertheless, it's a pity that no recording survives of her singing from around the time this picture was taken. She couldn't have been more than nineteen, and despite a complete lack of formal training, she had a commanding stage presence and a rich, powerful voice. I suspect she was attractive and sexy. Even in her sixties, she could stop a noisy party of celebrators in its tracks with a gutsy rendition of "Won't You Come Home, Bill Bailey?"

The Irwin of Irwin's Winnipesaukee Gardens was my mother's stepfather, James Irwin, born sometime in the early 1890s in South Boston of Irish Catholic and English immigrant parents, an energetic and self-congratulatory entrepreneur who over a forty-year period became the Lakes Region's most successful businessman. Jim Irwin first visited central New Hampshire in the summer of 1914, playing cornet in a small band. Of his eventual acquisition of the choice properties of Weirs Beach much is left to rumor and legend. In his old age he liked to say, "The first time I visited I played in the band. Then I came back as a leader of the band. And finally I owned the place." The neat progression of status and ownership fits perfectly the model of self-esteem and self-initiative that he cultivated throughout his life. In fact his first purchase was a small boat marina at Weirs Beach where summer visitors could dock their pleasure crafts. As a businessman he appears to have been endlessly creative in his ideas about developing the lakefront. He was instrumental in introducing the first motorized speedboats to the area, initiated the annual Miss Winnipesaukee beauty contest, and even brought in the region's first seaplanes, offering pleasure rides over the beautiful, pine-studded lake.

By 1924 my grandfather had made enough money to build a dance hall over his very successful boat marina, modeling it after a similar one he'd seen while on a tour of Florida. It opened on Memorial Day 1925, and by the middle of the 1930s, Irwin's Winnipesaukee Gardens had become a major stop on the line for touring big bands, and throughout the Swing Era all but the most famous appeared there regularly. Even in the 1960s, when I was a teenager, bands continued to pass through, including on several occasions Duke Ellington and His Orchestra. A photo supposedly existed of one of my uncles, then a four-year-old, seated on the lap of the great stride pianist Fats Waller while both float in the waters of the lake on an inner tube.

My mother grew up with a station in life somewhere between a stepchild and an orphan. Her mother, born Ella Henry, had deep brunette hair, a commanding physical presence, and a personality that was both engaging and at times violent and tormented. Although born near Boston, she spoke with a slight Irish lilt. Pictures of her from the 1920s confirm her great physical beauty. Her first marriage was to a man named Thomas Coolidge. I know nothing about him other than he lived into his mid-nineties and that my grandmother Ella divorced him sometime around 1920 to marry Jim Irwin.

In order to accomplish this divorce, no small thing for an Irish Catholic in the Boston of 1920, my grandmother took my mother out of school—she must have been between six and eight at the time—and placed her temporarily in a Catholic convent. My mother was kept in the dark as to the reason for this sudden forced removal from her friends and teachers. All she recalls of the terrible six-month period of virtual incarceration was the strictness and prudery of the nuns and the fact that she was told to wear a T-shirt when bathing so as not to shame the Virgin Mary. Her memories of the convent as a dark, foreboding labyrinth of corridors and candles, statues of suffering saints, and the regimen of strictly observed rituals never left my mother's unconscious, and as an adult her natural sensuality and openness of character fought constant dark battles with a recurring sense of guilt and remorse.

Then one day, after six months of convent life had passed, her mother suddenly reappeared with an unknown man. "This is your new father," she informed my mother. Not long after, they all moved into a large house in Lakeport, New Hampshire, not far from Weirs Beach. Within a few short years my mother found herself caring for a new family of three half brothers and a half sister. James Irwin had meanwhile become a stunning business success. He traveled on the Boston and Maine Railroad to Boston during the workweek to do business and was rumored to have partaken in the surreal financial killings that abounded in the stock market euphoria of the 1920s. After establishing Irwin's Winnipesaukee Gardens, he concurrently worked the real estate market of the area while continuing his successful business of selling pleasure boats. His crowning achievement was the establishment of Irwin Marine, a boathouse and marina, at the time the largest of its kind in the country, that stretched nearly a quarter of a mile along Paugus Bay on the south shore of Lake Winnipesaukee. One of my first memories is of riding in a sleek, elegant Chris-Craft, one of many speedboats that my grandfather sold to his wealthy customers. On these outings the Chris-Crafts were from time to time piloted by one of my uncles. My grandfather, who never seemed to do anything other than talk business, could sell a pleasure boat, but I never saw him pilot one.

While Jim Irwin ascended in the small world of New Hampshire business, his wife began a long descent into alcoholism and depression. She gave birth to a sixth child, a Down syndrome baby who died as an infant. She suffered painful spine and back problems and was prescribed drugs. Her drinking, combined with fits of temper and physical violence, left her at times unable to care for her new children, and my mother, by then a teenager, was forced to pick up the pieces. Still bearing her original name, Elinore Coolidge—her new stepfather would not let her change it to become more officially a part of his family—she found herself bringing up her own half siblings. If there had been even the glimmer of hope in her mind that she might study acting or learn from a professional how to exploit her generous and beautiful voice, that hope would surely have been doused by the hard realities of her family duties. Elinore Coolidge never took a singing lesson at any point in her childhood, nor was there ever a mention of her attending college. Even so, her talents as a singing actress managed to survive to the point where, in her late thirties and forties, she stunned local audiences in Concord, New Hampshire, with her performances in *Carousel*, *Oklahoma!*, *The King and I*, and other Broadway classics. In *South Pacific* she stole the show with her salty portrayal of Bloody Mary. The sailors surrounded her, singing, "Bloody Mary is the girl I love . . . now ain't that too damn bad!"

My father and mother met in the summer of 1935 and soon eloped and were married in Hanover, New Hampshire. Certainly neither had the money for even a modest honeymoon. Not long after that the couple resurfaced in Worcester, Massachusetts. My sister, Carol—now Carol Dunning—was born in 1936, my only sibling. The new family spent the remainder of the Depression years and the years of World War II living mostly in the Worcester area, near where my father had been born and where his Swedish immigrant parents still lived. His father, born John Adamson in Ryd, Sweden, had come to America around the end of the previous century, the first of a large family who left the southern province of Småland during a period of especially severe agricultural hardships in the 1890s. He anglicized his name after his arrival, but I don't know if when he made that change he was aware of the famous political predecessors in Massachusetts who had already given it a good road testing. John Adams worked as a baker and eventually had his own restaurant in Shrewsbury, a town on the shore of a small lake not far from Worcester. I remember this jovial, sturdy Swede with the build of a peasant when he was in his eighties and still spoke with a thick Småland accent and called me Yannie. John Adams made a reputation for his restaurant by offering home-made bread and carrot-flavored ice cream.

Thus my name, John Coolidge Adams, so blue-bloodedly Yankee in its import, was in fact a conjunction of a Swedish paternal grandfather and a maternal grandfather I never knew.

My father had grown up in Shrewsbury and had attended Clark University in Worcester for two years before the Depression forced him to leave school. The fact that neither of my parents graduated from college may have fed the longing for knowledge and endless bibliophilia that characterized their adult lives. Neither of them had been blessed with family situations in which culture or the cultivation of the arts or higher learning of any kind was even a remote reality. Less sympathetic offspring might refer to my parents' parents as petit bourgeois or philistines. But I understand the circumstances of my grandparents' upbringing. The lives of first-generation immigrants in the early part of the twentieth century were harsh and offered few opportunities.

I was born in Worcester in 1947, which makes me a baby boomer. My father, due to a childhood bout with polio, had failed his draft physical and did not enter the armed forces. Instead he spent the war scrounging for work in Worcester. It is impossible to imagine him a soldier, so gentle and retiring was his outward persona. He was not effeminate in the least. Irresistibly handsome in his youth (as the dance-band picture corroborates), he soon became bald and carried himself in a quiet, unassuming manner. Women were instantly charmed by his self-deprecating manner and by the gentle irony of his wit. For virtually all of his adult life he held a variety of jobs in small, local businesses, never quite breaking through into any kind of palpable "success." His heart was never in it. He was more artistic than entrepreneurial, but like my mother, he lacked adequate training in both his music and his painting to attain any kind of professional mastery.

For a brief period in the early 1950s, when I was not yet three years old, he decided to take the plunge and try to survive as an artist. He and my mother moved the family from Worcester to the small Vermont town of Woodstock. It was pure inspiration. They had discovered Woodstock on a seductive autumn afternoon drive, and a fantasy of transplanting themselves became a bold reality when they made the move around 1950. On the surface Woodstock was the archetype of a New England town. With its idyllic central green surrounded by colonial-style brick and clapboard houses it could easily have doubled for the fictional Grover's Corners of the Thornton Wilder play. In fact it was somewhat of a Bohemian community, with a subculture of affluent intellectuals, aristocratic black sheep, and even a few hangover Communists from the thirties. There were brilliant and eccentric writers and artists living among the typically flinty Vermont natives.

For five years my parents lived on economic tenterhooks while becoming adopted by the arty, intellectual, heavy-drinking community of wealthy New York and Boston émigrés. My mother briefly modeled in the nude for a local painter. The Woodstock Players produced a Jean Cocteau play, *La Tour Eiffel*, a dadaist entertainment in which my mother acted and my father played in the pit orchestra. Crazy, eccentric people with extravagant personalities and, more often than not, serious drinking problems invited us to parties in their converted country farmhouses, and it was by these friends of my parents, most of them politically liberal, intellectual Jews living in rural Vermont, that I was first introduced to classical music.

But life in Woodstock was punishing for my parents. For two winter seasons they managed a bed-and-breakfast for skiers, something that at least provided a house in which to live. In the summers, however, they were forced to vacate, and at one point they found themselves with no choice but to move in with an irascible couple who ran a chicken farm many miles from the town center. I remember being four or five years old and hearing violent arguments between my parents, usually incited by one crisis or another involving money. On a roll, my mother's temper could be a thing to behold. Once, out of uncontrollable frustration, she put a hammer through a flush door that was serving as an improvised dining table. On another occasion, exasperated and overcome by the heat of an especially humid New England August day, she threw a raw steak at my father with such force that it crashed through a kitchen window and ended up on the brick patio outside.

Carl Adams's attempt to make a career as a silk-screen artist in Woodstock never bore fruit, and just to keep the family from being evicted from the houses we rented, he was forced to make long driving trips around northern New England, doing a variety of miserable traveling-salesman jobs. My sister, Carol, a teenager at the time, surely felt the brunt of these family crises much more than I. Her personality, closer in kind to our father's, was the opposite of Elinore's. I can only imagine that life for her in the presence of my mother's extroverted, dynamic flair for the theatrical must have been at times intolerable. Fortunately, soon after our arrival in Woodstock, Carol was accepted as a scholarship student into a nearby boarding school, and she soon moved out of the house. Eleven years separate us. When I was growing up she had already left home. She eventually graduated from college, married a West Point graduate, brought up four children, and devoted herself to a long and fruitful career teaching elementary school.

I first listened to music on a simple LP turntable that my father had connected to the speaker of a wood-enclosed radio receiver. A Leopold Stokowski recording of Tchaikovsky's *1812 Overture* and an album called *Bozo the Clown Conducts Favorite Circus Marches* had my undivided attention for several months. I played these recordings over and over, conducting them, following the example of the picture of Bozo the Clown on the cover, with a knitting needle for a baton. My father, when he wasn't stupefied from his exhausting drives around New England, would relax by setting up his easel or playing the clarinet in the living room. He was not as naturally talented as my mother, but he had a logical mind, could read music, and had a secure sense of rhythm. He had taken classical lessons on the instrument when he was a teenager from a high-school classmate, one Rosario Mazzeo, a polymath of a man who eventually became a member of the Boston Symphony Orchestra, invented and unsuccessfully tried to market a new "Mazzeo system" for the clarinet keys, and was a brilliant amateur photographer and friend of Ansel Adams.

In 1954, just after I had completed the first grade in the Woodstock elementary school, we moved from Vermont to the neighboring state of New Hampshire. On the map the two central New England states fit into each other almost like a yin-yang symbol. The dichotomy was not fanciful either. Vermont has always had a reputation for being more politically liberal and a welcoming home to artists and intellectuals. New Hampshire, with its "Live Free or Die" motto emblazoned on every car license plate, was decidedly more conservative, less mystically flavored in the public imagination than its neighbor to the west. But it was home to genuine and modest people, proud of their scenic lakes and craggy granite mountains.

The move to New Hampshire was prompted by my father receiving a job offer from a company that distributed industrial hardware items—"nuts and bolts," as he would say in his typically minimalist description. He and my mother had taken a map of northern New England, traced out the companies he would have to visit on a monthly basis, and found the center of that geographic circle: Concord, New Hampshire. They drove there on an exploratory expedition and found a house they could rent in the village of East Concord, several miles north on the east side of the Merrimack River.

Number 5 Mountain Road (later renumbered as 47) was owned by a ninety-year-old native who had been born in the house during the Civil War. He was half Iroquois, and to me he looked fully an "Indian" with his jet-black hair, coarse like a horse's mane, a hazel-eyed penetrating gaze, and a hooked downward curving nose in the shape of a bird of prey. He leased the house to us while he himself lived two doors away on the other side of a white Congregationalist church whose organ music I could hear on Sunday mornings. Our house had enjoyed not the slightest upgrading in the preceding forty or fifty years. Indeed, it had not even made it into the twentieth century. It lacked central heating altogether and was drafty and nasty cold from October through May. The first winter we spent in extreme discomfort, huddled around a single coal-burning cast-iron stove situated maladroitly in the middle of the dining room. There was only one tiny bathroom for the entire house, but even this appeared to be a recent, reluctant caving in to modernity, barely a historical step forward past the dual-seater privy in the adjacent barn. This bathroom was as poorly located as the coal stove, being only a few feet from the kitchen table. It was a constant embarrassment for my mother, who would try to mask the sound of a dinner guest's tinkle by breaking out into magnanimous song and rattling whatever pots or pans were within reach.

The old Indian, Scott French, lived in the basement of his own rambling house. Some forty years earlier he had had an argument with his wife, and since that day they hadn't exchanged a word, although they continued to occupy the same house. He moved to the basement, with its dirt floor and ancient coal stove, living among his sacks of potatoes and squash and reading *Reader's Digest* and the *Farm Journal* via the illumination of a neighboring streetlamp. I know that the story of this couple not speaking to each other was true because when it came time to sell the house at 5 Mountain Road to my parents, a lawyer had to be found to communicate the proposals and transactions between Scott French and his wife, even though they lived under the same roof.

But Scott French took a liking to my parents, and he honored them by sharing his seeds and spuds during planting season and by agreeing to sell the property to them—a house, a barn, and half an acre of land with a vegetable garden—for $5,000. My mother even managed to persuade him to stop using his own night soil on his potatoes in the nearby garden.

On warm summer evenings he would come to the back of our house and, standing outside, talk to us for hours through the screen door, his low, steady voice evoking events from the distant past. Having sold it to us, the house in which he'd been born was no longer his to set foot in. He always carried ninety dollars in cash in his pants pocket because, he said, he'd once lost out on a great bargain because he didn't have exactly that amount. He told stories about his youth and his job as a gravedigger in the local cemetery. The validity of these stories was certified in graphic manner one day when a man whom my father had hired to clean our chimney broke through a long-blocked-off area in the eaves to find a human skeleton in a heap on the attic floor. The condition of the bones was old, and they were lying next to a colorized map of the United States rolled up in a scroll. The map was dated 1880.

My mother, who was alone at the time of the discovery, gathered the bones and the skull into a box and took them to Mr. French's basement abode, where she found him sitting next to his stove. He told her the bones were from an old grave that he and his brother had disinterred many years ago. How the skeleton ended up in our attic he couldn't explain, although he muttered something about medical school and his long-deceased brother. My mother left the bones with him while she tried to make an arrangement with the local city hall to get them off her hands. After receiving several incredulous responses, she managed to find a town official who told her to bring them to the city hall. But when she returned to Scott French's to retrieve the bones they were gone. "I burnt 'em . . . don't worry about 'em," he told her. And she didn't. She just went home and let the bones be bones.

Shortly after, an excited German shepherd puppy knocked Mr. French over onto the sidewalk and he died, at nearly ninety-six years old, from the consequences of the fall.

.   .   .

n 1954 East Concord was still a small New England village and not just another suburban appendage to a metropolis. No interstate freeway connected it to the outside world. The only road to the state capital of Concord, a city of only 26,000, followed the railroad track for several miles and crossed a narrow steel bridge over the Merrimack River. The river was polluted, having suffered for decades from the waste dumped into it by several mills and tanneries farther north. It has since become clean enough to swim in.

East Concord had one small market that doubled as a post office. I would go there during the summer to buy baseball cards, gum, and sodas. A brook passed underneath the entrance to the store, and in the spring I learned from my friends the dubious art of spearing suckers, an ugly carp-like fish that annually swam up from the river to spawn. During the summer the local park in the village center became the site of Little League baseball games and swimming meets. On special evenings a band played concerts on a movable bandstand that was dragged around by a city truck from park to park.

It was a rural community, surrounded on all sides by woods. Hunting was popular in the autumn. Even elementary-school kids would shoot deer with .30-30 rifles. My parents would not allow a gun in the house, so I had to satisfy my atavistic curiosity by hanging around the older boys and following them on hunts. I never witnessed a deer kill, but I saw pheasants and rabbits dispatched with rifles and shotguns and I watched them be gutted, dressed, and prepared for the table.

Shortly after moving from Vermont I was enrolled in an elementary school located at the top of a small hill across the street from a Revolutionary War cemetery. Another cemetery, only a short distance up the road from our house, featured a large gravestone with the name "Pecker" on it. It commemorated the family of Jeremy Pecker, a local from the nineteenth century, whose name would surely have delighted Charles Dickens. The Pecker pedigree had died out by the time I arrived on the scene, but the gravestone continued to provide inexhaustible fodder for jokes. My school chums avowed that East Concord had originally been known as Peckerville, and that it even had played host to a baseball team, the Peckerville Moles.

About a year after moving to East Concord, while in the third grade, I began to have my first serious experiences with music. I asked to be allowed to learn the violin in the school music program, but I was too young to qualify and reluctantly had to settle for learning the clarinet from my father instead. Although this seemed to me a poor substitute, I made very fast progress. My first clarinet was not even an ebony instrument, but rather a metal version that looked somewhat like a soprano saxophone. I don't know where my father found it, because for sure the one he'd played in his jazz-band days was an ebony instrument. The only other example I ever saw of such a metal clarinet was on the cover of Jefferson Airplane's *Surrealistic Pillow* album. In that photo, an instrument very similar to my original one is being held by Marty Balin, a band member who stands next to the then-young and provocatively beautiful Grace Slick.

My father proved a methodical and patient teacher. Instructing me must have been like riding a bucking bronco. I was impatient, restless, argumentative, and precocious. Our weekly lessons in the front room remain in my mind as the only time I ever heard my father yell. But he knew exactly what to concentrate on. Somehow he impressed upon me the profound ethic, the moral imperative of playing scales and arpeggios in all keys. Mastering the remote keys and learning to play them ever faster became a kind of boy's game, and it was not long before I outstripped my father's ability to keep up with me. We played duets arranged from forgotten nineteenth-century operas: *Norma*, *Robert le Diable*, and *Zar und Zimmermann*. Somewhere I found a copy of three early duos for clarinet and bassoon by Beethoven and I transposed and copied out the bassoon part so my father could play it on the bass clarinet. I took every available opportunity to carry my clarinet to school and play it in front of the class, even if it was just a fingering etude.

In 1956, when I was nine years old, our third-grade teacher read aloud a child's biography of Mozart. This teacher, a delicate and cultivated woman in her fifties with the graceful name of Greta Swanson, loved classical music. She brought in recordings of Gieseking and Casals, but I suspect I was the only student who showed interest and appreciation and could share her passion. The story of Mozart mesmerized me. I listened to each chapter in a state of total absorption. I thought the idea of a young boy composing music not only was enchanting but was worthy of emulating. I went home one afternoon and took a pad of blank notebook paper, a ruler, and a pencil out onto the hill behind our house. I drew a staff and started to write notes. It only took a minute to realize that what Mozart had done was far more complicated and evolved than what I could do. I was bitterly let down and didn't confess my disappointment to my parents for a long time. But eventually they located a teacher of theory at Saint Paul's School, a wealthy prep school on the outskirts of the city, and I began a more-or-less orderly course in composition, harmony, and theory that went on in fits and starts for about four years.

A Magnavox cabinet-version "high fidelity" 33-rpm record player had been our family's Christmas present to itself in December 1957. No other event in my childhood changed my life as abruptly as the arrival of this piece of audio equipment. Although I was already well advanced in my clarinet playing even by the age of ten, the sudden availability of recorded music crowded out almost every other activity for most of the following two years. The old turntable-and-radio affair from Vermont had been lost in the move to New Hampshire, and in the intervening period my parents had simply never had the time or money to buy a new record player. But now the new Magnavox in the front living room quickly became Grand Central for my every uncommitted moment. We did not own a piano, so my musical experience up to then was largely melody-driven. Once we acquired the Magnavox, a new LP appeared in the house on a weekly basis, many bought at my insistent pleading: Brandenburg Concertos, Beethoven symphonies, Mozart string quintets, *Rhapsody in Blue*, and big band recordings by my parents' favorites, Benny Goodman and Duke Ellington. I had several recordings of the serene and perfect late clarinet music of Mozart, both the Concerto and the A-Major Quintet. I soon began learning both of these pieces, and I eventually performed them with local orchestras and chamber groups.

I preferred listening to music while lying on the floor directly in front of the speaker, head in hands, or, if no one was around, I would continue with my conductorial fantasies, learning much of the standard orchestral repertoire this way, by ear, without scores, purely by listening over and over. At that age the experience was akin to language acquisition, so naturally and so automatically did I absorb pieces by listening and moving my arms, giving cues and raising crescendos. Many years later, when my own son and daughter were taking their first music lessons, I read *Nurtured by Love* by the Japanese pedagogue Shinichi Suzuki. Suzuki's success in teaching very young children rested on his belief that musical skill can be acquired by everyone, regardless of supposed "talent," if music is treated in the same way that language is—as a natural, almost unconsciously acquired skill. Suzuki reasoned that since virtually every human in the world speaks his or her own language fluently there is no reason that he or she cannot play an instrument with equal fluency, given the proper environment. I find his premise believable, and although I could never quite become an unqualified fan of Suzuki's detailed curriculum, I think the way I acquired music as a child very much bears out his central thesis.

My ability with the clarinet brought both pleasure and pain. I learned it almost too quickly, and I rapidly outgrew whatever musical programs the local public schools had to offer. School bands and orchestras were simply too slow and not challenging enough for me, and I became bratty and impatient when made to sit through a slow rehearsal. This offended the music teachers and placed my parents in the delicate position of having to appease the teachers while not forcing me to waste long hours in rudimentary situations. Fortunately I was invited to join two adult ensembles at a very young age, one an orchestra and the other a concert band. These groups became my laboratories as both a performer and a composer. Without them I would never have advanced as quickly as I did.

The orchestra, my first orchestra, performed under the august name of the New Hampshire State Hospital Auxiliary Orchestra. It was a community ensemble sponsored by the main mental hospital in the state. The performers were local amateurs—businessmen, schoolteachers, a car mechanic, our family doctor (on trombone), several lawyers, and others—who enjoyed a weekly confrontation with the instruments they had learned in their youth. The repertoire was "light classics." The first rehearsal I ever played included the Schubert "Unfinished" Symphony and Grieg's *Peer Gynt* Suite. But we also played show tunes and Sousa marches. Occasionally a patient would be allowed to join the orchestra with predictably unpredictable results. Concerts were given three or four times a season for the assembled patients. These concerts were intense affairs. Nurses and guards would lead hundreds of patients in single file into the gymnasium where we in the orchestra sat, ready to play our concert. The first thing that I would notice would be the dank, suffocating odor of unwashed clothes and perspiring bodies. A constant, low-level din of talk and chaotic movement prevailed throughout the show. Patients shouted and waved. When I, the only young person in the orchestra, walked onto the stage the audience would inevitably break out into loud, wildly approving applause, and my face would go crimson with embarrassment. Intermissions were accompanied by punch and cookies, and the orchestra members were encouraged to mingle with the patients. A scarecrow of a woman in a long, faded taffeta dress would never fail to seek me out and clasp me to her bony bosom. Half of her nose was missing, sliced off in some awful event of her past. I found it impossible to extricate myself from her desperate grip until the attendants came and gently untangled us.

Another patient walked around with a harmonica stuffed into his mouth. When he smiled his face became the front grille of an automobile. He serenaded us by moving the harmonica with his lips while conducting with his free hands.

My fame among the patients peaked in my fifteenth year when I composed a suite for string orchestra with the help of my composition teacher. He conducted the premiere while I stood anxiously behind the audience, wincing at every wrong note or false entrance, of which there were many. When the conductor summoned me for a bow, the audience of patients, by then already die-hard Adams fans, went berserk.

Even more critical in my development were the summers playing in Nevers' 2nd Regiment Band. This band dated back to the Civil War and continues to exist today as a semiprofessional ensemble that gives weekly concerts in the various city parks of the Concord area and marches during all the appropriate summer holidays, from Memorial Day to Labor Day. I played in the clarinet section along with my father. Again, although playing in a group mostly comprised of adults, I quickly advanced to the position of principal clarinet, which in a band is akin to concertmaster. For me the musicianship training was excellent, as each concert usually featured some transcription of a nineteenth-century opera overture. The lead clarinet parts were in most cases simply transposed versions of the original violin parts and at times could be ferociously difficult. I ate up the *Oberon* overture, *Leonore No. 3*, *Rienzi*, and *Poet and Peasant* while the baritone horns and mellophones and bass drum struggled to stay on the beat. Every concert began and ended with a march. Although Sousa was the favorite, I learned dozens of others, many with the same florid clarinet obbligati that gave a shrill color to the final choruses of "The Washington Post March," "On the Mall," and "Thunder and Blazes." We wore absurd bright-blue uniforms with gold epaulets. Seeing my father dressed thus, I realized how ill adept a soldier he would have been had he not been granted a medical deferment and instead had been drafted into the service.

iving far enough outside the city of Concord, I got used to a solitary existence. When not in school I took to making trails of my own in the surrounding woods. I had special locations I would visit. I find it astonishing now to realize how much time I spent alone, and not unhappily so.

Bruce Craigmore is a composer not at all known to the wider public. A "New Hampshire composer," he wrote and conducted his own music and enjoyed an international career similar to Leonard Bernstein's. Among his major works were the ballet *The Legend of Sleepy Hollow*, a tone poem based on the astral constellations in the manner of Gustav Holst's *The Planets*, twelve symphonies (including a "Tragic" symphony followed by a "Spring" symphony), and numerous concertos. Bruce Craigmore did not like the operatic voice and composed no vocal music, so we will never know what an opera from him might have been like. When not guest-conducting major orchestras in his works he lived alone, Thoreau-style, in a cabin on a remote lake some sixty miles to the north of East Concord.

He was, of course, my alter ego during the more hectic period of my early adolescence. I cultivated this imagined personality with minute care for the details of his life, keeping data sheets of his opus numbers and schedules of his performances with the world's great orchestras. Apparently he was serenely celibate, for his only attachment to another being was to his dog. Why I felt constrained to create a completely alternate personality for myself, right down to the bland WASP-sounding name, is a puzzle to me. I drew pictures of him conducting and kept a list of favored pieces taped to the wall next to my bed. This all happened around the time of puberty. My bedroom had by then become the scene of feverish fantasies spurred on by the clandestinely obtained novels I had found in my parents' collection of old paperbacks. *Peyton Place* by Grace Metalious, a scurrilous best seller, featuring small-town adultery in a genuine New Hampshire setting, was the most assiduously thumbed over of my hidden collection. I later upped my literary cachet when I discovered that the likes of *Lady Chatterley's Lover* and *The Kama Sutra* could also bring on the desired rush. On the wall facing my bed I taped a page from *Life* magazine with the famous Yousuf Karsh photograph of Sibelius. I remember the caption: "With a gaze mighty enough to summon up a symphony, the Finnish master contemplates the brooding Nordic landscape." Or something like that. Between the hard-won climaxes of Sibelius and the trash-talking characters of *Peyton Place*, Portnoy would have had little to complain about.

entered my adolescence already determined to become a composer, a strange thing, it seems to me, for a boy of thirteen. No one had prodded me to imagine a life of writing music. Normal models for young boys are the standard ones of being an athlete, a soldier, or some adventurous profession like an explorer or mountain climber. I was largely a solitary child, but I still kept a few close friends, some of whom I played baseball with or did overnight hikes in the wooded areas that surround the town. Although Thoreau was a hero for me, I was not a true outsider, no Adrian Leverkühn. I wanted to be on the local Little League team, the Concord Auto-Dealers (named after their sponsors), but I didn't make the first cut. That was my only brush with team sports. Between the clarinet and my fantasy composer's life, by now crowded with international engagements and commissions to fulfill, I was comfortable spending most of my time alone. I wasn't viewed as a sissy by the other children; more likely they thought of me as remote and unapproachable. In Hermann Hesse's novel *Demian*, the young narrator tells of a bully, Franz Kromer, who terrorizes him, extorts money, and generally casts a veil over his days until he is saved by his friend, Demian. I didn't have a Franz Kromer to fear, but for a period I frequently had to cope with a rough, heavy boy who lived in a shack-like house deep in the backwoods outskirts of our village. He would lie in wait for me when I got off the school bus carrying under one arm my schoolbooks and under the other my clarinet case. I would have to submit to a routine interrogation, verbal abuse topped off by a ritual beating that, because of his size and ferocity, I was unable to protect myself against. I took to seeking out different paths home, but he always seemed to find me. Eventually he lost interest. Several years later I heard that his mother had hanged herself in the family's shack.

My father's talents as a clarinet teacher were exceptional. He discovered that he got such pleasure from teaching that he eventually had other students, all of whom loved him for his humor and his patience. But he knew when he'd given me everything he had to offer, and when

I was thirteen we began to make a biweekly ninety-minute drive to the Boston area for clarinet lessons. My new teacher was Felix Viscuglia, a relaxed and affable man who had a background in jazz as well as classical clarinet. He was the bass clarinet player in the Boston Symphony. Besides gaining from him a secure technique and a general, all-around confidence, I also came to know and understand, if only intuitively, the personality and worldview of a professional orchestra player. I know this aided me immensely in later life when I began to conduct orchestras. I learned early that orchestra players hate more than anything to have their time wasted, that they appreciate a modicum of humility in a conductor, and that they know immediately, almost instantaneously, if the conductor is prepared or merely faking knowledge of the score.

The clarinet is quite possibly the easiest of all orchestral instruments to master. The improvements on the key system made in the late nineteenth century by Theobald Boehm allowed virtually effortless movement between registers. Chromatic passages, fiendishly treacherous on the oboe and bassoon, can be easily dispatched on the Boehm-system clarinet by even a mediocre player. The main issue with the clarinet quickly becomes the sound, whether the player can produce a beautiful tone. My tone was bright and clear, but it was a bit tight, possibly because at the age of ten I had caught a baseball on my front lip, requiring surgical stitches. I never achieved the kind of liquid round tone of the best classical players. Even so, my technical abilities advanced rapidly. I devoured the standard literature for the instrument, which admittedly is not extensive. To remind me of what a proper embouchure looked like, my father placed the LP of Benny Goodman's *1938 Carnegie Hall Jazz Concert* on my music stand for me to stare at while I played through my scales and arpeggios.

A clarinetist hungry for great classical works is left with only a handful by Mozart and Brahms. In the twentieth century several of the memorable works for the instrument were the result of commissions by Benny Goodman, particularly Bartók's *Contrasts* for clarinet, violin, and piano, and the wonderful, jazzy concerto by Aaron Copland. Of lesser works, concertos by von Weber, Hindemith, Nielsen, and others, there are many, and clarinetists fight for the rare opportunities to perform them. But in no way is the literature as rich and extensive as it is for piano, violin, or cello. I mastered most of the clarinet literature and began performing some of the concertos with local orchestras. I found opportunities to play chamber music in summer camps and in seminars and workshops. Unfortunately neither my parents nor I realized until too late how important piano lessons could have been. By the time my mother arranged to have a used piano moved into the house my interests were so scattered that I had neither the time nor the inclination to start from scratch to learn a new instrument. As a result, for the rest of my life I have had to live with only the most rudimentary, self-taught mode of hunt-and-peck. But who knows what direction things might have taken had I been as good on the piano as I was on the clarinet? Sometimes creativity in the arts is born of a deep-seated sense of frustration, even of inferiority. Many composers became composers because they could not express themselves in a quicker, more easily attainable medium. I suspect my lifelong frustrations with the piano go hand in hand with the birth of many of my best musical ideas. The great Japanese composer Toru Takemitsu described a solemn ritual that he followed before beginning every new piece. He would take out the Bach *St. Matthew Passion* and play through it at the piano. "Since I was a very bad pianist, playing through the *Passion* would take a very long time, and by then I would already have a good idea of what to do in my next piece."

I continued to compose real, written pieces in addition to the "imagined" ones by Bruce Craigmore. Eventually my alter ego vanished into the mist with his dog and his cabin on the lake. I wrote fully notated pieces and heard some of them performed, including the suite for strings first heard at the State Hospital, several small pieces for winds, a great deal of solo clarinet pieces, and an *Overture in F*, which I wrote, Rilke-style, by holing up in my room for an entire weekend without coming out except for meals and to go to the bathroom. *Overture in F* was a decisive experience because I soon discovered that composing was only the first step in the creative process. What had to follow was the tedium of extracting parts, proofreading, and reproduction of the performance materials. All of this seemed so dreary and earthbound that I doubted the great composers ever submitted to its humbling necessity.

In the summer of 1962 I attended a summer music camp on the

shore of an idyllic lake in western Maine. Many things happened in the short six weeks I was there. I was nearly electrocuted paddling a canoe across the lake during a sudden thunderstorm. The weather had changed dramatically during a picnic on the far shore, and the counselors asked for volunteers to take the canoes back across the lake while the rest of the campers waited for a bus to arrive. Several of us took off in aluminum canoes, frantically thrashing the water while the sky grew purple and violent. I could smell the ozone, and as anxiety changed to true terror, I knocked off my glasses with a stroke of the paddle and had to navigate with my eyes squinting and my heart pounding.

At the camp I was allowed to conduct, not just once but many times. I conducted the Schumann Piano Concerto with the camp orchestra, and I led several pieces with the wind band. I had my first tentative sexual experiences with a pretty and sympathetic blond bassoonist, and with her, on a camp outing to a nearby town, I saw the recently released film *West Side Story*. This was not my first exposure to the overwhelming talent of Leonard Bernstein—I had already watched many of his *Young People's Concerts* on television—but it was the moment when I felt most aroused to the potential of becoming an artist who might forge a language, Whitman-like, out of the compost of American life.

At the end of that summer session I attempted to foment a rebellion among the student population, a rash act of political agitprop that resulted in my being kicked out of the camp a week before the final concert. The motives for the rebellion were not unfounded. The camp director, a tall, silver-haired martinet in his fifties with an eye for the coed counselors, had repeatedly made outlandishly false promises to both the faculty and the students. He was a pretentious and mendacious man who on the first week of the season had broken his leg frolicking in the sand with the camp's cute twenty-year-old swimming coach. By the time he made his long-awaited return from the hospital, sporting an imposing white cast from his toe to his hip and accompanied by the triumphal march from Verdi's *Aida*, the camp's activities had become a chaotic mess into which I had opportunistically inserted both myself and my conductorial aspirations. I was fifteen, but I imagined that the student population would support me in my plan to conduct the final concert of the season before the assembled parents. I couldn't conceive that "Doc," as the director preferred to be called, would shunt me aside and conduct the concert from his wheelchair with his big toe sticking out of that long plaster cast.

Rumor, nevertheless, made the wind her post-horse. The plans for my camp coup were discovered, and at dawn on a cool August morning I was awakened by the camp's embarrassed athletic director, who, on orders from Doc, frantically stuffed all my clothes and toilet articles into bags and suitcases, drove me forty miles to the nearest bus station, and bought me a one-way ticket—not to my home (which was not possible via a direct route) but to the Greyhound terminal in Boston. Upon arriving in Boston, I sat there alone, clutching my clarinet case amid the usual unsavory characters of a bus waiting room, until a family friend summoned by my alarmed and concerned parents came to my aid.

It was not my first attempt at confrontational politics but only the most disastrous to date. Two years earlier, during the presidential campaign between Nixon and Kennedy, I had insisted upon holding a debate in our eighth-grade class over the issues in the forthcoming election. The teacher, Miss Fanning, an old-school spinster much set in her ways after decades of imparting to her students the traditional versions of American history, adamantly refused. In frustration I wrote a scathing, demeaning letter to the editor of the *Concord Monitor*. The editor, for reasons known only to himself, allowed the letter to be printed under the title "Debate Denied." I suddenly found myself author of the following days' most hotly discussed news item in the entire central New Hampshire region. I no longer have a copy of the scandalous letter, but I recall a phrase of my screed: "She may think life is just a bowl of cherries, but . . ." The situation was made all the more complicated by the fact that my mother was by then working part-time as a proofreader at the *Monitor*, and she surely saw the letter and must have approved its publication. In the end, everyone regretted the affair. I was summarily yanked from Miss Fanning's class, put in a different class, and kept on a tight leash for the remainder of the school year.

Dartmouth College in Hanover, New Hampshire, is fifty miles to the northwest of Concord and is situated just east of the Connecticut River, which forms the border between Vermont and New Hampshire. For several summers in the 1960s a well-funded and adventurous music festival, the Congregation of the Arts, took over the campus. An orchestra of instrumentalists from around the country performed weekly concerts with a focus on living composers. Aaron Copland, Carlos Chávez, Henry Cowell, Vincent Persichetti, Zoltán Kodály, Elliott Carter, and many others visited the quiet college town to hear their works performed and to give master classes. I spent the last two summers of my high-school years at this festival, playing in the orchestra and studying theory and conducting. There were many prized young pupils from the Juilliard School there, but I found that, with the exception of my miserable lack of keyboard experience, I had no trouble matching them for knowledge and skills. I began rounding up students and conducting them in ensemble pieces. This time I wisely did not attempt a coup but instead rather bluntly demanded of the music director, Mario di Bonaventura, that he take me on as a conducting student and let me be his protégé. He had been trained in the severe French style of musicianship and, I suspect, enjoyed terrifying me with stories of classes with Nadia Boulanger and Igor Markevitch. But he did give me the only conducting lessons I ever took, and what I learned from him served me well in the years to come.

More important, I met two members of the Harvard music faculty who proved instrumental in getting me accepted into the undergraduate class. One was Walter Piston, by then already retired from his professorship. A droll, soft-spoken Yankee composer of genteel neoclassical works, he reminded me much of my father. He had a summerhouse near my former town of Woodstock, Vermont, and he took a liking to me with my overflowing enthusiasm for his music and my New England background.

A small, compact woman named Luise Vosgerchian, a firecracker of a personality with inexhaustible energy and an abrupt, occasionally devastating wit, taught keyboard harmony and analysis with the same devout sense of mission she had received from her own teacher, Boulanger. Luise had just begun as an instructor at Harvard, and she had come to Dartmouth to teach during the summer festival. She was able to see through the blight of my pianistic incompetence and find a way to tailor a curriculum that gave me a good grounding in harmonic practice. She remained a teacher and guiding spirit for the next four years, including the first two years of my Harvard career. I spent an unknowable number of hours at the piano, struggling over figured bass exercises, memorizing harmonic cadences and coaxing them through all keys. Because my hands, unlike those of a pianist, didn't fall naturally into position, I had to examine my fingers visually with every new chord, a tedious extra bit of work that left me deeply humbled about the complexities of harmonic practice.

One critical insight that Luise had inherited from Boulanger was that brilliant musical skills don't necessarily translate into original creative talent. The kind of gift that allows one to sight-read full scores at the piano, to transpose effortlessly into any key, or to identify the pitch of any note—all of these are enviable and endlessly useful for a musician. But for every composer such as Brahms or Mozart or Shostakovich who could do almost everything, playing on the piano anything put before them, there is a Berlioz, a Schoenberg, a Varèse, or a Cage for whom the musical imagination was not a function of vast technical facility. Luise Vosgerchian understood that. She used to distinguish between a "keen ear," one that could accurately pick pitches out of a dense chromatic cluster, and a "composer's ear," by which I think she meant an ear for new sounds, for unthought-of sonorities. Nevertheless, keen ear or composer's ear, she was hard on me, and I had to work like an ox to earn her approval.

My poison-pen letter writing and summer-camp bolshevism behind me, I spent the remainder of my high-school life more or less uneventfully. I began to teach clarinet students on school-day afternoons, and with the money I earned I paid for a weekly Saturday train trip to Boston. I would leave Concord at 6:45 a.m. and ride the Boston and Maine train along the banks of the Merrimack, the same waterway traversed by Thoreau and his brother and documented in *A Week on the Concord and Merrimack Rivers*. Upon arrival at North Station, I would take the streetcar to Boston University for morning rehearsals of the Greater Boston Youth Symphony. In the afternoons I would take a clarinet lesson with Felix Viscuglia and/or theory lessons with a graduate student in Cambridge. This routine went on for about three years, during which time I discovered that I had also inherited from my parents an addiction to reading and to loitering in bookstores. Harvard

Square provided the ideal pusher for my jones. I rarely returned from a Saturday trip without some new book, and I remember many of them: *A Farewell to Arms*, *Crime and Punishment*, *A Mencken Chrestomathy*, *The Portable Aristotle*, *The Writings of Sigmund Freud* (not as good as *Peyton Place*, I thought), William Faulkner's *Sanctuary*, Will Durant's *The Story of Philosophy*, Edith Hamilton's *The Greek Way*, and countless biographies, not only of composers but of writers, philosophers, and historical figures. When I graduated from Concord High School I was asked the usual questions to go with my yearbook picture. Under "prize possession" I wrote "my libido." The student editors printed this without looking up "libido" in the dictionary. "We thought it was a musical instrument," one of them said when she eventually found out its meaning.

2.

FROM *HELP!* TO "LET IT BE"

O n the Friday night of my first week as a Harvard freshman—in September 1965—I went to see the Beatles in their congenially madcap movie *Help!* at the Harvard Square Theater. By the time I left Harvard five and a half years later, "Let It Be," their terminal anthem of resignation and valediction, was in the stores. My college years were bracketed not only by the Beatles and all that happened to them but by the vast sea change of consciousness and political activity that erupted within a brief few years in the late 1960s. One always walks on thin ice in writing about the past. To write about the "Sixties" is all the more perilous, and one has to skirt the temptation to mythologize and to idealize. That T-shirt with the motto on the back "If you remember the Sixties you weren't there" is not without a grain of truth.

Within a span of four or five years, a cluster of signal historical and cultural events all coalesced as if in a centrifuge. Of the spasms that rocked the country at the time, the hugely unpopular and divisive Vietnam War was undoubtedly the principal catalyst. But other radical fruits of social and philosophical thought were ripening as well: feminism, African American identity, the birth control pill, the advent of ecological consciousness, and the pervasiveness of recreational drugs.

And then of course there was the music: rock music—something utterly new, Dionysian, and magnificently provocative. For several years one needed only to switch on the AM radio to find an endless sequence of pop songs, the inventiveness and inspiration of which seemed inexhaustible.

While I was driving north from Cambridge to "Live Free or Die" New Hampshire in late 1968, a beefy-looking man in a Ford Galaxy overtook me in the passing lane, made a quick evaluation, and, for no other reason than pure animosity, showed me the middle finger. My John Lennon granny glasses, and my mustache, sideburns, and long hair, not to mention the Volkswagen I was driving, were enough for him to define me as being "on the other side." The person attached to that finger was only one of many who saw in the younger generation an insult and a threat to their way of life, to democracy, freedom, and the American Way. Two years later feelings had degenerated even more. Standing along the side of Massachusetts Avenue, watching a large antiwar march go by, I suddenly found myself part of panicking crowd being attacked by club-swinging Boston police in riot gear. The helmeted cop who lunged at me with a billy club seemed genuinely delighted to have been given carte blanche to thrash away at a member of the college-educated elite. It was as if American society had been left on spin cycle with no one capable of calming the nation's anxieties. In the phrase of William Burroughs, we'd bought the ticket that exploded.

Despite graduating magna cum laude, I was far from an ideal student, ignoring or simply sleeping through many of my classes. I favored my own contrarian route through the curriculum, staying up late to listen to music or to carouse with friends and then forgoing the following morning's classes in favor of sitting alone at a piano, improvising on pop songs or lurching bar by laborious bar through *The Well-Tempered Clavier*.

I failed a course in ancient Greek in the first semester of freshman year. I had arrived with the preposterous aspiration of reading all the great works of Western literature in their original languages. But a month into a take-no-prisoners Introduction to Greek Grammar had me already on the ropes, and I avoided classical literature from then on. Nor did I excel in the classroom courses in tonal harmony, a throwback to the old days, when harmony was taught in lectures with tedious written exercises. I needed to go at my own pace and in my own peculiar manner. I found another music student, by a strange co-incidence also named John Adams, and the two of us met on early mornings in a room above the Freshman Union to give each other ear-training drills. The music community at Harvard quickly dubbed us "John C" and "F John." My first-year harmony teacher was the vener-able Elliot Forbes, a kind, gentle Boston blue blood, a Beethoven scholar whose Cambridge pedigree reached all the way back to Revo-lutionary War times. He directed the Harvard Glee Club, and my morning ear-training partner, F. John Adams, eventually became his successor.

Around that time Pierre Boulez guest-conducted the Boston Sym-phony Orchestra and made waves in the American classical music world with his punchy, polemical interviews and his evident mastery of his chosen repertoire (Berg, Debussy, Stravinsky, etc.). Not only the young composers but also the older professors in the Harvard Music Department were enchanted and doubtless a bit intimidated by the calm air of authority and self-control he radiated. Boulez seemed like the ideal hero to take us forth into the brutal, pitiless, unconquered landscape of contemporary music. I went to the library and sought out his book of lectures on contemporary music, published under the title *Penser la musique aujourd'hui*. Even in an English translation—titled *Boulez on Music Today*—the book was pretty much impenetrable. Couched in a dense thicket of procedural dicta, it was the work of a technocrat bristling with all the gleaming armaments of his specialized field. I cannot imagine how these lectures must have fallen on an audi-ence of the kind of genuinely curious intellectual generalists, the proverbial "gentle readers," who, after hearing his Boston Symphony concerts, might have tried reading this book. Nevertheless I resigned myself to accepting Boulez's machine-gun prose and his equally ag-gressive works like the Second Piano Sonata and *Le marteau sans maître* as the social contract of a new millennium in music. I began to carry his scores with me everywhere, hoping that somehow, perhaps by osmosis, they would reveal themselves to me and make me love them as I loved Mozart and Miles Davis's *Kind of Blue*.

Sometime later I read the famous 1958 article by the American serialist composer Milton Babbitt, who compared his relationship with the listener to that of one scientist reading a paper to another:

> The time has passed when the normally well-educated man without special preparation could understand the most advanced work in, for example, mathematics, philosophy, and physics. Advanced music, to the extent that it reflects the knowledge and originality of the informed composer, scarcely can be expected to appear more intelligible than these arts and sciences to the person whose musical education usually has been even less extensive than his background in other fields.

Babbitt's image of himself as a member of an elite laboratory of like-minded specialists scandalized and offended the larger classical musical community, which I suspect was his puckish intention. He was far and away better known for his essay published in *High Fidelity* magazine under the title "Who Cares if You Listen?" than he was for his original compositions. He may not have been responsible for the controversial phrase—an editor had apparently changed it without Babbitt's permission from its original title, "The Composer as Specialist"—but the fact that "Who Cares if You Listen?" lodged in people's minds like an advertising jingle confirmed a general malignant feeling about the arrogance of contemporary composers.

n the fifties and sixties composers began to adopt a posture of dispassionate scientific investigation as their operative model. The earliest photos of Karlheinz Stockhausen had him looking like a wonkish NASA engineer surrounded by oscillators and cathode tubes, clean-cut down to the white business shirt and tie (although by the time I went to hear him lecture in 1971 at the New England Conservatory of Music, Stockhausen had become a hippie with a vengeance, complete with an extraterrestrial curriculum vitae).

Babbitt didn't get me too worked up. Boulez, however, caused me endless cognitive dissonance because he was an indisputably expert musician, a gifted conductor, and an articulate apologist for serialist music, who possessed the intellectual powers to stake out and defend his positions. The language of his articles, published in a collection titled *Relevés d'apprenti* (*Stocktakings from an Apprenticeship*), was caustic, aggressive, and partisan in the classic tradition of the French polemicist. A typical volley was "Any composer who has not experienced the absolute necessity of the serial system of composition is USELESS." I nearly broke out in hives, so uncertain was I of just how seriously I should take him. But even in my relative innocence I was able to detect the fatal cul-de-sac into which the Boulezian ideology was headed. He could only see music from a dialectical point of view. A new creative idea was "useless" unless it fit into his historical tunnel vision. That particular continuum I found ridiculously exclusive, being founded on a kind of Darwinian view of stylistic evolution. If a composition's pedigree could not be traced back through the usual route of Stravinsky and/or Schoenberg it simply lacked merit. And if it didn't in some way advance the evolution of the language, yielding progress either by a technological innovation or in the increasing complexity of the discourse, it was not even worth discussing.

Despite my hunch that Boulez's was the wrong way to make art, I continued to try embracing the beast. Still in my freshman year, and by way of venting my frustration with the direction contemporary music was heading, I wrote a letter to Leonard Bernstein. I had never met him, but for some reason I felt the need to prick such a famous superstar to see if he might possibly bleed. I thought maybe that sharing my own frustration would perhaps sting him enough to elicit a response. Composed more in the negative spirit of a heckler at a baseball game than in any true seriousness, my letter to him was written on a sheet of embossed Harvard stationery so that I might better get his attention. It was prompted by my hearing his most recent piece, *Chichester Psalms*. I did not know at the time that *Chichester Psalms* was Bernstein's own cri de coeur in the midst of the crisis of serialism and atonality, which he too, at the peak of his fame, was confronting. I was appalled by the swooning sentimentality and bland tonal language of his piece. In my letter I chided him, asking, "What about Boulez?"

A week later there in my mailbox at Wigglesworth Hall was a letter—from Leonard Bernstein. He said quite simply that he had to do what he had to do. What I could not have known was the deep struggle that had preceded both the composing of *Chichester Psalms* and the writing of that letter.

I felt caught between a rock and a hard place. On the one hand was the hair shirt and bed of nails of the serialists, and on the other the gushy emotionalism of Bernstein's "Kaddish" Symphony or Samuel Barber's Violin Concerto. I watched how the works of Webern gained pride of place in composition and analysis seminars in music departments. Webern's music, with its methodological arcana and hyper-compressed expressive world, fit the prerequisites of college analysis courses to a tee. To make matters worse, Stravinsky himself had taken the veil and followed reverently in the Austrian serialist's path. Imagine me, if you will, an aspiring composer, sitting in a classroom diligently counting backward from twelve, tracing down combinatorial transformations, and trying to get a rush from a three-minute setting of a poem by Georg Trakl or Stefan George. Then imagine this same student emerging from his somber seminar, walking across the campus, and hearing from some dorm window the screaming, slashing, bending, soaring, lawless guitar of Jimi Hendrix.

The Harvard Music Department could at times be like a contentious family, but I was not unhappy there. I had too much to learn, and my teachers had much to offer. In addition to Luise Vosgerchian's grueling drills in figured bass and keyboard harmony, I took a counterpoint course with the immensely gifted David Del Tredici, and in my last years there I was admitted to the courses in analysis and composition taught by the two senior composers on the faculty, Leon Kirchner and Earl Kim. Both Kirchner and Kim had studied in California in the early 1950s with Schoenberg, who had clearly made a profound, life-altering impression on them. For reasons I never could figure out, a rather unpleasant animosity had sprung up between the two composers, a lamentable situation that was well known among the students, who joined in the partisan feelings.

Kim was a painfully slow, excruciatingly self-critical, almost self-censoring composer. Over the four or five years that I knew him he wrote only a single work, a group of vocal and instrumental settings of a Samuel Beckett text called *Exercises en Route*. They were exquisitely wrought both in sound and in their appearance on the page, an elegance that for him was nearly an obsession. The only other large-scale work I knew of his, which he wrote after I left Cambridge, was a violin concerto, which Itzhak Perlman premiered. Earl Kim was always cordial, but music was for him a kind of private devotional ritual, and one got the feeling that few—least of all he himself—were allowed into the inner sanctum of his personal pantheon. Nevertheless when, at the beginning of my first graduate year, I brought in a wild, seat-of-the-pants assemblage of musique concrète I'd made in the electronic music lab, he enthusiastically encouraged me to continue working on it.

More critical for me were my classes with Leon Kirchner. Kirchner was a tall, imposing man who even in his fifties had movie-star charisma and a handsome, brooding face that to me looked like a cross between James Dean and Jack Kerouac. Unlike Kim, who rarely (if ever) performed and whose life seemed to be confined to his home and his classroom, Kirchner was a man of the music world, friend of many of the great classical performers such as Rudolf Serkin and Leon Fleischer, and himself a pianist and conductor of considerable gifts. He lived with his beautiful, generous wife, Gertrude (née Schoenberg!), in a large, rambling house just off Harvard Square that was full of art and sculpture. I was more or less intimidated by him from the start, and it took me decades to feel comfortable in his presence.

Kirchner was one of the most intuitive musicians I ever encountered. Although highly sophisticated, immensely well-read, and a close friend and verbal sparring partner of Harvard's intellectual heavyweights, he approached music more like a jazz musician than a note-parsing analyst. Despite his studies with Schoenberg, he was entirely American educated, never having spent any formative time abroad. Although serialism, tone rows, magic squares, or other numerical processes were very à la mode at the time, Kirchner could never find a way to make his own musical instincts fit into the straitjacket of a rigorous method. He adored both Stravinsky and Schoenberg, but I never once recall him discussing their music from a methodological perspective. That made studying at Harvard substantially different from being at Columbia or Princeton, where Babbitt and his imitators ruled the roost.

Kirchner as a composer presented a problematic model for me as a student. In his love for the great masters—Bach, Beethoven, Mozart, Schubert, Brahms—he showed that his heart was in the right place.

(Interestingly, I'd noticed that these names were conspicuously missing from the Boulezian canon.) But after being around him for a while I began to notice that the act of composing for him was something akin to self-immolation. I got the feeling that composing was *meant* to be a painful activity, a ferocious wrestling match with inner demons. Alas, this nearly constant feeling of pain is not uncommon among creative people. Of course for some the creative act is as natural as eating and sleeping. One gets the feeling with Brahms, for example, that he couldn't make it through the day without writing at least a motet or an intermezzo, like a hen laying her morning egg. But then there are the Rilkes, the F. Scott Fitzgeralds, and the Schoenbergs, for whom making art comes in manic bursts only after long, painfully barren periods.

Kirchner did not have a neat, habitual way to compose, and it was his lifelong curse to be erroneously classified by careless music critics as a "twelve-tone composer." His music was hyper-expressive, emotionally hot, and formally very much sui generis. It didn't follow any of the controversial stylistic conceits of the time, but neither was it easily accessible to the average classical music listener. Like him, it was intensely serious, but not in a dry, academic way. I felt enormous respect for it, but there was something about its surrounding ambience that made me want to escape and find a less tortured way of being creative.

Despite my teenage fantasies of becoming the American Beethoven, I actually did very little composing throughout my first three years of college. My musical awareness was growing at the same time that a painful realization of my own inadequacies was dawning on me. I temporarily lost the courage and audacity to write my own music. In place of that I plunged headfirst into an intense life of performing. It was a good thing, too, because I gained enormous confidence as a conductor and in the art of relating to others, an art not universally shared among creative people.

Harvard was, and still is, exceptional in the way it affords invaluable opportunities to students who have the grit and temerity to assume positions of responsibility. I began conducting student productions during my second year. The first two undertakings were presented in the elegant dining hall of Leverett House, one of the undergraduate dorms. That particular space had the advantage of a raised dais at the end nearest the Charles River. With its chandeliers and high ceiling, the dining hall suggested a small theater in some eighteenth-century duke's or prince's estate, and the invitation to present operas there was irresistible. In the fall of 1967 we came forth with a show called "Bach and the Beatles." This was inspired by a clever album called *The Baroque Beatles Book*, the brainchild of a hip musicologist, Joshua Rifkin, who was later instrumental in the resurgence of the music of Scott Joplin. Rifkin's recording presented early Beatles songs dressed up in pseudo-Handelian drag. Accompanied by harpsichord, piccolo trumpet, and a consort of viols, songs like "Help!," "A Hard Day's Night," and "Ticket to Ride" were delivered as if they were outtakes from Handel's *Jephtha*, complete with da capo arias, choruses, and recitatives. For undergraduate savants it was the ideal mix of the demotic and wink-of-the-eye sophisticated. The Leverett House production was wittily staged, with the appropriate raunchiness and embedded double entendres, by another sophomore, Kenny McBain. It was my first taste of the greasepaint of music theater, and I found I liked it more than I wanted to admit.

Later in the same academic year, I undertook a far grander plan, six performances, also in the Leverett House dining hall, of Mozart's *Le Nozze di Figaro*. The stage director was a senior, majoring in English and well known already for his acting abilities: John Lithgow. I shudder to think how the young singers in the cast responded to my musical direction. I knew nothing about opera or about theatrical producing, nor did I have a clue about the extremely delicate instrument that is a classical singer's voice. From my vantage point in front of the orchestra, the singers never seemed loud enough, and I urged them on with hectic gesticulations as if they were a brass band. Pulling it all together took more than two months. Between auditions, scaring up an orchestra, supervising musical and staging rehearsals, and even managing the publicity I nearly lost track of my other academic responsibilities.

My clarinet provided enough casual employment to keep me in pocket money. A weekend gig with some local orchestra would pay nearly a hundred dollars, much better than a whole week of working the usual college jobs. I was occasionally called to substitute with the Boston Symphony Orchestra. In 1966, in what must have been an extremely rare event, the BSO played in the pit of the musty, dilapidated Back Bay Theater in the American premiere of the Schoenberg opera *Moses und Aron*. I was in the clarinet section for those historic performances.

On another occasion an emergency call, again from the Boston Symphony, forced me out of my dorm bunk bed on a cold November morning in order to make a 10:00 a.m. rehearsal at Symphony Hall. I had no idea what was to be rehearsed, but a rash of illness in the clarinet section had required a last-minute substitute. I arrived to find the stage absolutely crammed with players. The rehearsal was to begin with a scene from the late Richard Strauss opera *Daphne*, which, needless to say, was unknown to me. At the time the music director of the BSO was Erich Leinsdorf, a knowledgeable and imaginative conductor whose talents were constantly overshadowed by his inability to rein in a withering sarcasm and showy arrogance. The orchestra members largely despised him. He began the rehearsal of *Daphne* by holding up a biography of Strauss and informing the players that, since they doubtless would not know much about this obscure opera and since they might *possibly* be keen to inform themselves about it, he was arranging to have the book placed for their perusal on a table in the musicians lounge. Shortly afterward, everyone heard a thud on the floor of the empty hall. A violinist in back of the section, unseen by Leinsdorf, had taken the book and tossed it high out into the empty hall where it crashed down amid the empty seats.

Leinsdorf, who had never seen me but obviously had been informed about my presence as a substitute, started the rehearsal with a sweeping downbeat. The orchestra launched into the typically noisy, confused first reading that often accompanies an encounter with an unfamiliar work. I realized in a minute that the principal clarinet player, a portly Neapolitan named Gino Cioffi who was still challenged by spoken English, had become seriously lost. I felt torn between staying in what I judged to be the right place or, out of stand-partner loyalty, going with him. It didn't really matter in any case, because the orchestra was wailing on overdrive, percussion was flaying, brass blaring, and a sizable number of people were already lost. With a hundred people onstage generating an acoustical maelstrom, who would even notice what I chose to play? But then Leinsdorf lowered his arms, the music gradually petered out, and I heard words that made my entrails soften, spoken in a preening Austrian accent: "I think perhaps the *second clarinet* may . . . possibly . . . have . . . shall we say . . . perhaps . . . what? . . . a 'missssssprint' on his page?" I felt the klieg lights of a hundred pairs of eyes, including the soloist, Beverly Sills, staring at me. "Perhaps the young man from *Haaaar*vard would like to check with me the notes in his part." The pronunciation of "Harvard" was drawn out with a caustic disdain. In front of the entire Boston Symphony Orchestra, not to mention "Bubbles" Sills, I was then taken through a public solfège exam, complete with transposition from A clarinet to concert pitch. Eventually Leinsdorf tired of playing the cat to my cornered mouse and went on to hunt bigger game. In the end, I was invited to go on tour with the orchestra, playing in the Strauss and other works, but fortunately my examination period was approaching and I had a good excuse for politely declining more encounters with the charms of an old-school autocrat.

A more satisfying experience, although an endlessly exhausting one, was the year and a half I spent conducting the undergraduate Bach Society Orchestra. This was, and continues to be, a unique institution, a chamber orchestra made up of talented players from Harvard and many other surrounding colleges and conducted by an undergraduate who is chosen yearly by audition. It provides on-the-job training in every sense of the word, and my college dorm room quickly was converted into a hub of nervous activity with a constantly ringing telephone, irritated roommates, and piles of orchestra rental materials, scores, tapes, and disks scattered over my desk and bed. The quality of the orchestra is largely the result of the campaigning that the conductor has to undertake at the beginning of the year to coax good players into the group. For a college junior I had better than average judgment about these matters, and my professional forays around Boston commanded some respect among the students, so I was able to put together an estimable group of players. I remember all of my programs and their performance with great clarity even now. I opened in the fall of 1967 with Haydn's Symphony No. 99, Stravinsky's *Danses concertantes*, Milhaud's *La Création du monde*, and a Mozart piano concerto. By the end of the first season the Bach Society Orchestra had become dangerously high profile among campus activities, and the inevitable journalistic comeuppance was awaiting me. This came in the form of a review in *The Harvard Crimson* that marched me to the scaffold for my overreaching programming:

> The Bach Society Orchestra concert was the major disappointment of last week's musical offerings. Many heads could roll when a collective effort like this goes awry, but the conductor, John Adams, is the one who must stand in the dock.
>
> The program Adams chose for the group demanded a far higher level of musical competence than one can reasonably expect of any undergraduate organization—even one as fine as BSO. The works, Mozart's overture to "The Abduction from the Seraglio," Beethoven's Symphony No. 2, the Adagio from Mahler's Symphony No. 5, and Debussy's "L'Apres Midi d'une Faune," would trip up even the most agile professionals.
>
> But let this pass: set aside the slurred inner voices in the Mozart, the gaping holes in the Beethoven where one fully expects to hear second violins and violas, the cracking and blasting brass, the consistently out-of-tune winds. These are the agonized sounds (or silences) of musicians stretched beyond their capabilities . . .
>
> The winds were always successful in outblasting the strings and often completely obliterated the fiddlers who seemed in particular to be their mortal enemies. The leather-lunged trumpets vandalized the two outer movements of the Beethoven, while percussionists ran roughshod over the Mozart overture . . .
>
> A special citation for insubordination and vulgarity beyond the control of any conductor is in order. This to the tympanist who, juggling his sticks with the dexterity of a weightlifter, produced a sustained, and equally unwanted cannonade, the likes of which has not been heard since the retreat from Dunkirk.

The *Crimson* critic's complaints were doubtless accurate, but they missed the palpable enthusiasm and unbuttoned pleasure that both the orchestra members and their conductor and possibly even the audience were experiencing. The Beethoven symphony's exuberant aggressiveness shocked and delighted me. Listening to recordings or even a live performance could never have prepared me for the surge of energy that I felt from the podium. With its blindingly bright D major clanging against the plaster walls of Paine Hall, it introduced me firsthand to the sheer radicalism and manic drive of Beethoven's early music.

Back in the dorm room and at all-night parties of pot, scotch whiskey, and unfiltered Lucky Strikes, we bored like weevils through the harmonic changes and textual minutiae of albums by the Paul Butterfield Blues Band, Rahsaan Roland Kirk, Bob Dylan, Cream, Jefferson Airplane, the Electric Flag, Country Joe and the Fish, the Beach Boys, the Doors, and of course, Jimi Hendrix. I would fall asleep on the hardwood floor of a friend's room with my head wedged between a pair of stereo speakers as if they were headphones, and I would wake up in sweaty clothes, smelling gamey, my glasses bent out of shape, and find that I was already late for class. I made more progress in my command of harmonic practice by reproducing these pop songs from memory at the piano than I ever did by my forced marches through the figured bass treatises. More than any other social phenomenon of a socially phenomenal era, rock music was the fulcrum of a culture. Young people communicated to each other through the medium of its lyrics, especially those by Bob Dylan and John Lennon, and its intense emotionalism seemed to speak for our common experience and what we imagined to be our universally held beliefs.

What particularly enchanted me about the popular music of the time was its harmonic ingenuity, something that was fresh and inventive in the late sixties, although it would soon become routine and predictable within a short span of five or ten years. A song like Brian Wilson's "Good Vibrations" took the standard pop song through a tonal hall of mirrors, moving into remote keys with an effortlessness that gave the music its feeling of endless delight. "Wouldn't It Be Nice," another Beach Boys song by Wilson, begins with an eight-beat introduction in A major played on the harp, which is then followed, after a single thwop on the drum, by the main tune in the remote flat submediant key of F. This kind of tonal surprise was nothing new in

the classical or jazz world, but appearing here in the context of a standard rock-and-roll song it felt novel and fresh. More than any other
songwriter of that era, Brian Wilson understood the value of harmonic
surprise.

The Beatles too, even from their earliest days, demonstrated an exceptional harmonic imagination, and as their message matured, their
vision became increasingly complex and shaded, their harmonic world
ever richer. Songs on what we knew as the White Album and on *Abbey
Road* went deeper in every sense—emotionally, psychologically, harmonically, textually, and in the incredible wit and invention of their
sound world. The LP album went from being a simple reproduction of
a live performance (as it generally was in the jazz and classical tradition) to a studio creation, a virtual thing in itself. The final song on the
Sgt Pepper album, beginning with John Lennon's world-weary "I read
the news today, oh boy," ends with a swirling vortex of electronically
manipulated sound that suggests the planetary visions of Stockhausen's *Hymnen*. These Beatles albums significantly altered the notion
of what a "recording" was about, and they proposed that the studio
itself, with all its technological powers of transformation, could be a
locus of artistic creation, representing a new reality, just as the film-
editing studio had become in the hands of the great directors. We
listened to the George Martin–produced albums in a state of astonishment. The sound world was completely new, with its close-miked, un-
characteristic instruments like the scraping, hacking cello of "I Am the
Walrus," the chirping piccolo trumpet of "Penny Lane," and the chugging string quartet behind "Eleanor Rigby."

The emotional intensity of rock seemed to fly in the face of the
studied coolness of "serious" contemporary music. While I admired
the audacity of the seventy-five-year-old Stravinsky suddenly taking
up serialism (and doing it with what I thought was more imagination
and appeal than Webern), most of his late works still struck me as arid
and ritualistic, especially when compared with the vital life force of his
earlier music. *Requiem Canticles*, which I first heard live in a performance at Harvard's Sanders Theatre in 1968, felt appropriately solemn
and oracular, like those Old Testament stories that the octogenarian
composer loved so much. But it was hard to imagine that even as in-

ventive and polymorphous a mind as Stravinsky's could eventually run out of inspiration and require daily injections of a severe and rigorous method to give one last stir to the creative juices.

At around the same time the Harvard Music Department reluctantly submitted to fashion and purchased a modular synthesizer and two half-track Scully tape recorders to make up what would become the Electronic Music Studio, housed in a stuffy room on the top floor of the department building. Leon Kirchner had already blazed the first trail by having composed a string quartet accompanied by taped electronic music, a work that won him the Pulitzer Prize. The synthesizer attracted attention from everyone in the department, even the musicologists, with its amusingly sci-fi appearance. It entertained the staff and the students for a while, but eventually only a handful of zealots, myself included, spent any serious time exploring its strange and new musical possibilities.

My senior year as an undergraduate at Harvard was a year of real crisis. The Vietnam War was no longer just a remote event or a moral abstraction; it was a frightening reality. Every male college student was faced with the challenge of what to do about the inevitable letter from his local draft board that would be awaiting him on graduation day. One of the bitterest criticisms of the war was that it was fought on the basis of class. Young men who did not have the advantages of a college deferment were automatically drafted and sent to fight. We students knew that a college deferment was something to be grateful for, but we were also aware that it was patently unfair and discriminatory. This was brought home to me one cold afternoon in November on a trip back to East Concord for Thanksgiving. I took a walk through the local cemetery with no particular goal in mind, only to be shocked and numbed to find the fresh gravestone of a former playmate, a boy who had come from a poor family and had enlisted straight out of high school. Lt. Ronald Roach, who as a boy rode the school bus with me for years and loved to reach over and give me a "noogie" (a sharp, stinging rap on the head with his knuckles), had been killed in action while I stayed sheltered within the security of my college deferment.

A dorm mate and I took a wild, Kerouac-inspired drive south during the spring break of 1968. In less than a week, fueled by coffee, cigarettes, and junk food, we drove from Boston to Key West and back.

On the return trip, passing through Washington, D.C., we found ourselves caught in traffic during a dangerously angry urban riot that followed on the heels of the assassination of Martin Luther King Jr. Only
a few nights earlier, while driving through a humid South Carolina
night, we had heard on the car radio the shockingly unexpected announcement by Lyndon Baines Johnson that he would not seek another term in office. The country, its fabric rent by the war and racism,
was simply more than he could govern.

By 1969, the year of my graduation, the war had gone from noble
endeavor to unwinnable mess. Not only had it prematurely ended
Johnson's presidency, causing a meltdown in the Democratic Party, but
it also had brought Richard Nixon back into our lives. A quick end to
the war was not foreseeable, and the political sentiment among young
people in their twenties was rapidly turning from indignation to something darker and more sinister. Huge antiwar protests turned ugly and
violent. The public demand for a withdrawal was growing. "Nixon's
dad should have pulled out early" was a popular graffiti slogan. In
April, right before the beginning of my very last exam period as an undergraduate, a group of activist students allied with SDS (Students for
a Democratic Society) walked into the dean's office, physically ejected
the school's administration, and began a sit-in to protest what they
construed to be the university's complicity in the war effort. The action
was meant to upset the community, and it succeeded. The president of
the university, a quiet former classics professor named Nathan Pusey,
made the momentous and regrettable decision to invite the Middlesex
County police into Harvard Yard to forcibly remove the protesters. The
cops came at dawn in buses, dressed for business with riot gear and
clubs. The symbolism of that invasion into the very heart of the university's inner sanctum was more shattering than either Pusey or any
of his defenders could have imagined. What followed was a solid year
of rage. The university became nearly ungovernable. I and most of the
rest of the class of '69 wore red protest armbands with our traditional
gowns on the day we graduated. One student speaker during the com-
mencement ceremony launched an impassioned tirade against the war,
the government, the university administration, and other implicated
parties and had to be forcibly pushed off the podium by several student marshals. On one occasion, probably a year later, I heard several

student friends of mine talking about the planning of an "action" at Yale that would involve the use of firearms and arson.

The U.S. Armed Forces did not spare me the customary grace period that the others received. Instead, my first draft notice arrived nearly two months before my graduation. My father called with the unsettling news that I was to appear on an early morning in May at the Concord, New Hampshire, Selective Service Board to submit to a physical examination in preparation for being inducted. Being drafted for two years of service in Vietnam was not something anyone I knew considered a promising postgraduate option. The rumor mill was rife with stories, some of them wildly fantastical, of ways to beat the draft. Among the hundreds of friends and acquaintances I had, I can think of only one or two who, like John Kerry, actually enlisted and went to fight. I prepared for my preinduction physical examination by laying waste to my nervous system and cardiopulmonary functions through a combination of forced sleeplessness and over-the-counter drugs. I artificially jacked up my pulse rate and blood pressure and the pupils of my eyes became dilated. This ruse failed to impress the army doctor who examined me, and he responded by forcing me to undergo the same test twice a day for two weeks, a total of fourteen separate visits to get my pulse read and blood pressure taken. While other friends of mine were suddenly becoming Quakers, pondering exile in Canada or Sweden, discovering previously undetected symptoms of insanity, gender confusion, or homicidal tendencies, I walked around during the week before final exams cranked up on coffee, No-Doz, sinus sprays (good for a quick jolt of the blood pressure), and a few other less official substances, my mouth parched and my breath smelling like a cadaver. No one was fooled. The draft board called me back yet another time in July. I distinctly recall returning to East Concord, staying up the entire night of the first moon landing to prepare myself for another physical exam. My mental faculties were by now fried to a crisp. With my heart pounding and my pulse racing, I listened again at 2:00 a.m. from the family living room to Neil Armstrong declaiming something about a giant step for mankind.

In the end, the draft board simply gave up and gave me a 1-Y, a provisional medical deferment. Thus, in July 1969 I found myself graduated from college, freed of the long-standing anxiety of having to fight in a war that I thought was wrong. I was suddenly able to do anything, but so unexpected was the freedom I didn't have a clue as to where to begin.

On a quiet Sunday morning in August a close friend called me and said, "Adams, you want to take some mescaline?" I had absolutely nothing to do. I was free of the long juggernaut of the draft board. I had graduated and was working a menial summer job just to stay afloat. What was billed as "mescaline" was more likely LSD bought on the street, but the effect was powerful. No doubt about it. I had read Aldous Huxley's rather clinical account in *The Doors of Perception*, and of course I knew all the silly Timothy Leary books with their naïve utopian declarations of free love and eternal laughter. Life in Cambridge was full of the lore of good trips and bad trips, how to do it, how to go up and come down, how to avoid a "bummer." My friend, a wry and verbally agile classmate, had "scored" the acid.

For the better part of sixteen hours he and I did nothing outwardly special. We simply walked around the town, viewing familiar sights, places we'd walked by hundreds of times in the past, but this time we saw them as vibrating, pulsing constellations of energy. Colors were so vivid that they seemed to speak their nature to you—"I am GREEN"— so saturated were they with their own essence. I was astonished at how the acid did not appear to alter my personal interchanges with people. I didn't become giddy or palpably "stoned" or garrulous or any of the qualities I'd been led to expect. Instead I felt serenely in control, finding great humor in the way the cosmos seemed to be revealing itself. The trip was symphonic in form, with an exposition, development, and recap. Or maybe it was a rondo . . . I forget. There were plateaus of steady state consciousness followed by dips and then ascents to soaring heights that could be a bit frightening, so ecstatic was the feeling. It was reassuring to travel with a partner. We were in close sync and enjoyed each other's quips and observations. At the very zenith I had a perception about the absolute nature of reality, life, and death that was immensely calming. This is doubtless the danger zone of psychedelic drug-taking where the tripper can make the fatal assumption that he or she is immortal. But I remained sitting safely on a patch of fresh grass in the summer twilight of Harvard Yard, glowing with a feeling of immense well-being.

Fully aware that there is nothing so boring as suffering through someone's account of an acid trip, I kept my revelations to myself as much as I could. I certainly didn't want to become an acid child, barefoot on the street with a chronic cough and bad teeth. But I thought that LSD did open what Huxley (and Jim Morrison) called the "doors" and give a hint of the universe as it might be if only I could shed my habitual way of being in the world. Of course the next step was a choice between more drugs and more trips or taking the slow, laborious road of mental and spiritual discipline offered by religion, specifically Tibetan or Zen Buddhism. Over the next year I took six or seven more excursions, never with quite the same results. One was the proverbial bad trip, a mindless Saturday-night dalliance that became a descent into hell, offering up a vision worthy of Rimbaud of a nothingness and nonbeing that went to the darkest outpost of despair. A long walk home at midnight through sinister back streets launched a six-hour state of paranoid panic that was the complete antipode of the first trip's bliss. I crawled under the sheets and stared for a very long time at a spot on the rug that periodically morphed into a beast by Hieronymus Bosch.

The last of my trips was pure Monty Python. It took place a year later in the idyllic surroundings of the Marlboro Music Festival in Vermont. I wandered into a rehearsal of Beethoven's *Choral Fantasy* and watched the great Austrian pianist Rudolf Serkin play a gleaming black Steinway that stretched out in front him from nine feet to twelve feet, and then to twenty feet and so on, à la R. Crumb, until it became the world's longest stretch limousine. That image may have been what gave birth years later to my piece *Grand Pianola Music*. By the following year, 1971, I more or less gave up all psychedelic encounters, including marijuana. They seemed tied to a time and place, and I felt that getting to the truly important spiritual and mental "there" would require a more serious and arduous journey.

3

FREE RADICALS

A series of dilapidated houses in the environs of Cambridge were home for my last three years there. I shared a three-story, Archie Bunker–style duplex near Porter Square with four other students in 1968 and early 1969. The escape from the protective womb of the campus was exciting, but chaos and distraction were always threatening. The house soon became a way station on the route of many young wanderers, dropouts, draft resisters, dope dealers, and the like. All the bedrooms were full, and most mornings some unfamiliar body could be found stretched out on the pockmarked sofa in the living room. I moved a spinet piano into the cellar and played at odd hours. A friend brought a large collection of jazz LPs, and I began to listen intently, learning by ear how Coltrane or Miles or Eric Dolphy would move through the fast, fearsome harmonic structures of a bop tune. I found an old tenor saxophone and played along, trying to ape the open, throaty sound of "Trane" or Sonny Rollins, but I soon found that the skill required to move effortlessly through the complex chromatic changes of a song like "Giant Steps" would be no quick, casual acquisition. On the contrary, this was a highly evolved, immensely complex art form.

I made two decisions during that year that helped frame my future. The first was to decline an invitation to attend the conducting program at Tanglewood, and the second was to petition the Harvard Music Department to allow me to submit an original composition in lieu of a senior thesis.

I suspected that a high-energy summer of being around superstar classical musicians at Tanglewood might prove a fatal distraction to my embryonic creative life. I knew that it had been the launchpad for many stellar conducting careers, from Bernstein's to Seiji Ozawa's and Michael Tilson Thomas's. It was a difficult offer to turn down, coming via close advisers to Bernstein himself who taught there every year. There was nothing to prevent me from having a success at Tanglewood as a conductor and then returning to my composing, but I already had a negative intuition from examining both Bernstein's and Boulez's careers. More than likely, a full-blown life as a conductor was seriously threatening to one's private muse. Something about the extrovert, political behavior required of a conductor ran against the grain of the more meditative, imaginative existence of a composer. I was not in the least surprised to hear of the agonies that Bernstein was facing on the occasions when he attempted to remove himself from the buzz and commotion of his public life in order to rediscover his natural, unblocked creative self.

In the days of Wagner or Berlioz the distinction between performer and composer was less sharply defined. The personality cult of the music director was a twentieth-century invention. What mattered most to nineteenth-century audiences was the novelty of the music they were hearing. In Handel's and Mozart's time the public was annoyed *not* to hear a new work. But with the advent of the "maestro," particularly beginning with conductors like Mahler, Toscanini, Stokowski, and Koussevitzky, the authority figure at the center of the stage assumed a magisterial glow that captivated the attention of the listeners.

Starting with the era of Wagner, the art of the conductor evolved enormously in response to the ever-increasing rhythmic and ensemble demands of the music. Any work by Mozart or Haydn can be kept together serviceably by a simple time beater. But an opera like *Tristan und Isolde*, or any one of Mahler's symphonies, requires a conductor with vastly greater technical skills, someone who can negotiate constant changes of tempi and shifts of timbre and dynamics among an ensemble of some hundred players. Most of the orchestral music from the time of Wagner to the present is unthinkable without a commanding technical and interpretive presence on the podium. In a work like *Le Sacre du printemps*, a single miscue with the baton can easily throw the tightly aligned organization of the music off-kilter, causing the performance to go instantaneously slack and out of control. There is an aspect of spectator sport in watching a physically gifted, musically innate conductor leading a committed performance of a demanding work. Bernstein was the consummate master of making the podium the expressive nucleus of the live performance. He brought to his art the perfect mixture of intellectual preparation and readiness for the unexpected, spontaneous gesture.

I always felt comfortable on the podium. Even when very young I often experienced music through the motions of my arms and upper body. As an adolescent I would wait until no one was in the house, and then put on a recording and stand in front of the record player conducting all the details of the music in rapt attention. It is a paradox that I am a terrible dancer, inept and painfully self-conscious, but as a conductor I have always been able to move more or less effortlessly. I was never able to make the two activities—dancing and conducting—inform each other, to the point where, whenever a late-night party gave way to dancing, I would always make noises about a speedy departure.

In the spring of 1969, during my final undergraduate year, I labored mightily on my first full-length piece, *The Electric Wake*. The origins of the title to this piece are lost in the backwaters of my memory. I suspect that it owes something to the influence of beat poetry and the legions of psychedelic bands that sported non sequitur names like the Strawberry Alarm Clock, the Electric Flag, and Cream. *The Electric Wake* was a "wake" because the music was a setting of poetry about a psychedelic nymphet/goddess named Talley who consumes herself in a burning drug-induced ecstasy somewhere in a London park. The poetry was the work of a classmate, a premed student and ardent nocturnal poet. The psychotropic themes of his work reflected both the times and an aspiring clinician's fascination with pharmacology. He wrote a great deal of poetry—reams of it. Somewhere in the bowels of the university's Weidner Library the score to *The Electric Wake* lies in its richly deserved solitude. Of its content all that I can recall is that most of the poems were apostrophes declaimed in an elevated tone of Byronic rapture. I set them for "electric" (that is, amplified) soprano and an ensemble of "electric" strings, keyboards, harp, and percussion. The main influences were Bartók's Music for Strings, Percussion, and Celesta and Messiaen's *Chronochromie*. Because the campus disturbances of that year were so upsetting to the usual rhythms of college life, I never had a chance to hear my piece performed. Nevertheless, composing *The Electric Wake* under the enormous pressure of a deadline, not to mention the spotlight status of being the first composition to qualify as a senior thesis, was a healthy provocation to my sensibilities and a goad to my sluggish sense of self-discipline. I sat in a tiny practice room at the Hilles Library at Radcliffe College for months, filling it with cigarette smoke, coffee cups, and half-eaten sandwiches while I plugged away, trying not just to compose a piece but to form a brand-new original voice that was mine and mine only. Had not the panic over the military draft intervened to turn the rest of my semester into chaos, I might have had the opportunity to put together a group of musicians and hear what I'd written. Doubtless I would have learned much if I'd attempted to bring the piece from the written page to the reality of a live performance. The real importance of *The Electric Wake* was that it signaled my serious intention to become a composer.

lost interest in playing the clarinet. I'd mastered the existing repertoire for that instrument even before I was out of high school, and all that was left was playing the same handful of good pieces over and over again. Weekend jobs with local orchestras had been a good source of income, but I didn't take the instrument out of the case from one week to the next, and I began to lose my facility and my sound. In the spring of my senior year, just before the calamity of the draft, I played the clarinet concerto by Walter Piston at Carnegie Hall in a concert presented by the Harvard-Radcliffe Orchestra. By then I was already out of shape as a clarinetist, and my performance, although capable, was not inspired. The last public concert on the instrument I can recall was at a celebration for Aaron Copland's seventieth birthday presented by the Brandeis University Music Department. I played the tricky, rhythmically treacherous Sextet by Copland and had the pleasure of meeting its composer after the concert, who commented in his thick Brooklyn accent, "Yeah, the kid knows his stuff."

My grandfather James Irwin died in 1966. On a bleak, frigid March day I took the bus from Cambridge to Laconia, New Hampshire, to attend his funeral. Only several weeks earlier, well into his seventies, he had remarried; she was a woman some twenty or more years his junior. On their honeymoon in the Caribbean he had suffered a heart attack and collapsed. The funeral back in Laconia was strange beyond belief. The new wife's family, totally unknown to all of my mother's siblings, wandered through Grandfather's big house, eating and drinking and looking very comfortable, as if they'd grown up there. My grandfather's will included a large cash settlement for his bride of a week. The rest of his estate was apportioned among his natural children. My mother was to receive a small bequest of $5,000, but in the end the estate's cash reserve ran out and she never received anything. Irwin's Winnipesaukee Gardens struggled on for a few more years, still presenting some big bands for an aging audience. Eventually my uncles shut down the whole enterprise, and not long afterward the beautiful old dance hall, site of so many summer memories, was covered with Astroturf and made into a miniature golf course.

Fortunately, before the demise of the dance hall, I was able to hear Duke Ellington and His Orchestra there twice. The second time, in the summer of 1966, he was touring with selections from his Shakespeare suite, *Such Sweet Thunder*. I knew this album as well as any Beethoven symphony, and I knew the names and unique musical styles of every member of that great ensemble. The band had the unmistakable look of being in the middle of a long, mind-numbing summer tour, and the players were tired and distracted. The Duke officiated in his classically elegant manner, introducing the numbers with whimsical little verbal riffs. The crowd on the dance floor was noisy and paid not the least attention either to what he was saying or to what the band was playing. They would only register if they heard "Mood Indigo" or "Sophisticated Lady." *Such Sweet Thunder* was as unfamiliar to them as Webern.

People sat around small tables, drinking highballs and gin and tonics. I watched while a boozed-up middle-aged woman in a party dress and high heels climbed unsteadily onto the dais and sat down next to Ellington on his piano bench. The silly baby grand piano was painted an atrocious white, and it sounded as pathetic as it looked. Ellington, with a serene aplomb I had seen only once before in my life—when Ted Williams played one of his last games in Fenway Park—took everything in stride. Even this brash physical invasion of his personal space by an obnoxious drunk failed to ruffle him. He was the master of indefatigable charm and contained elegance. Who could possibly know what this great composer had been forced to suffer over decades of racial slights from a population that wanted to be thrilled by his talent but was not willing to grant him full status as a human?

I was most likely the only person in the crowded dance hall who knew the numbers the band was playing. Only later when they launched into the obligatory "Take the 'A' Train," the song that customarily signaled the end of their set, could one detect a rustle of recognition and pleasure from the crowd on the dance floor. I waited until the drunken woman meandered off into the crowd, and I quickly eased myself down into her place on the piano bench next to the Duke. I didn't know what to say, so shocked was I to be sitting next to one of my greatest heroes. I bleated out, "I'm writing my thesis on you!" This was a complete fabrication, of course. I couldn't think of any other reason to justify my impulsive decision to sit next to this tired, infinitely patient man and impose myself on him. I watched his hands on the keyboard of that hideous out-of-tune instrument and noticed the almost imperceptible communication he maintained with certain key players—Johnny Hodges, the moody, mercurial lead alto sax; Cat Anderson, with his screeching stratospheric trumpet; Harry Carney, the baritone sax player with a sound as big as a freight train. They had the glazed eyes of oxen laboring in the midday sun. The slightest movement of an eyebrow could indicate a change of soloist, a sudden shift of key, or the abrupt launching of an up-tempo.

Ellington's piano style was effective and unobtrusive. He would at times jab or even punch out the chords, alternating them with descending cascades in the right hand, coming down the keys in ripples. He was in no way a virtuoso of the caliber of Art Tatum or Fats Waller. But the piano was nevertheless a key ingredient in the Ellington sound. I went and stood directly in front of the band, only a foot or two from the saxophones and trumpets. The sound was immense. The Ellington saxophones blew with a full-throated, raw power that needed no help from electronic amplification. In a moderately large dance hall the music filled the space with an astonishing power and energy. Hearing the band in what I suppose could be described as its "natural setting," with the sound of a raucous and largely inattentive crowd, complete with clinking glasses and loud bursts of laughter, was an overwhelming emotional and acoustical experience. The signature jabs and "bullets" of the Ellington brass made an indelible impression on me, and now I hear them throughout my own orchestral works, from *Short Ride in a Fast Machine* to *Nixon in China* and even later pieces like *Naive and Sentimental Music* and *Doctor Atomic*.

Although it was the season of the Beatles' White Album, and of the great first album by the Band, I gradually ceased to listen to rock, becoming more serious in my study of jazz, an art form that to me seemed more musically involving and meaningful. In urban areas throughout the country African Americans were finding a new voice. A mixture of pride, anger, and indignation was prompted by the Martin Luther King assassination the previous year. I read Eldridge Cleaver's scabrous *Soul on Ice*, a cultural call to arms written from prison in the tonality of a searing, scathing jazz riff. The Black Panthers, before the FBI systematically infiltrated and destroyed them, tried to lift the blighted inner cities out of their dolorous cycle of poverty and despair. Black radicals found that they had an appreciative audience among the white college population, probably because many of us felt discriminated against in our own fashion. But the comparison was risible, because the true situation for most urban blacks bordered on the hopeless, and in the intervening forty years it has improved very little.

John Coltrane's last albums seemed much in tune with the chaotic nature of those years. They were wild, free-form expressions of raw emotion and barely controlled energy that utterly abandoned the formal rigor of classical jazz. I wasn't sure that I really liked repeated listenings, but somehow the radical nature of the expression seemed appropriately attuned to the times. It was indeed a time of pushing the limits. One wanted to see where the breaking points lay.

Someone loaned me a copy of *Naked Lunch* by William Burroughs. It was my initiation into the crazed intoxication of beat literature. The wild, off-the-wall sexual and drug-laden fantasias of Dr. Benway and the surrounding cast of junkies, small-time crooks, and deadbeat cops were like a beat version of Rabelais, only better. More than any other writer of the era—more than Norman Mailer, or Allen Ginsberg, or Jean Genet—Burroughs was the voice of the antiestablishment. He was funny and morally shocking, and he was boldly experimental in what he did with literary form and structure. I also detected in his books an underlying honesty about the human condition, a brutal candor that had first seen the light during the blandest period of the Eisenhower years and now more than ever held up a mirror to the cultural values of the Nixon era with all its fatuous appeals to the paranoias and pieties of the American middle class.

In the middle of August 1969 things changed abruptly. I decided to hang on for another few years at Harvard, accepting a last-minute opening in the graduate school as a composition student. The Music Department accepted me without my even making a formal application. I entered as a graduate student with full scholarship and a monthly living stipend. The idea was that I would take classes for two years and then repay my debt through several more years as a teaching assistant, on track to receive a doctoral degree in music composition. I lasted only two years.

Graduate school was largely unstructured. With only a few required classes to attend, I was able to work hard at composing, and I could spend hundreds of hours alone in the Electronic Music Studio. The scene was loose and no one really seemed to care. But I must have had an intuition from the start that I would never be able to endure the long grind that traditionally culminates years later with the awarding of a doctorate. I knew that life in academia would wear me down for certain. I saw young men and women in their thirties still awaiting the big moment. For musicologists, for scholars of all sorts, this slow maturing seemed appropriate. But for someone trying to stake out a personal language, a genuine creative voice, a long period of graduate servitude seemed counterproductive. I thought that then, and thirty-five years later my opinion has not changed.

The last two years in Cambridge were enlivened immeasurably by being married to Hawley Currens. She is the youngest of a family of four irresistibly attractive blond sisters. Their father, a cardiologist originally from Illinois, worked at Massachusetts General Hospital and speculated in real estate on the side. He and his wife had moved from Newton, where the girls grew up, to a town house on Beacon Hill in Boston. The family also owned a rambling house on the seashore in Wareham, just north of the Cape Cod canal. We spent some of our best times at this classic old New England summerhouse with its immense screened porch, wicker furniture, and sparse bedrooms smelling of sea air and pine.

Hawley played the violin and loved black soul music. My life was suddenly full of Otis Redding, Marvin Gaye, Valerie Simpson, the Supremes, Stevie Wonder, and Ray Charles. She worked as a music teacher in the Boston inner-city schools for the two years I spent in graduate school. Many of her students were African American children with whom she struck up trusting, confident friendships.

We might not have decided to marry at all, but our sharing a flat in Cambridge caused palpable anxiety for some members of Hawley's family, so on February 1, 1970, in the Church of the Advent, not far from her family's house on Beacon Hill, we did the ritual ceremony with many family and friends in attendance. The marriage lasted until the fall of 1974, and it was a source of much pleasure and enjoyment until it went into a tailspin during the final year. Unlike me, Hawley was always comfortable meeting others, and she complemented my stubborn personality with her readiness to go anywhere and befriend just about anyone. We knew jazz musicians, street poets, Boston Brahmins, Boston Symphony members, drug dealers, a friend who I suspected was an ex-con, and another, Jack Kornfield, who years later founded the Buddhist meditation center Spirit Rock in northern California.

Given that her other sisters were married and all but one of them lived in the Boston area, I suddenly became part of a large extended family. That was a change for someone like me who had grown up virtually an only child in a very small town. Her family worked hard to tolerate my leftist politics and my espousal of avant-garde musical ideas. One uncle, a retired Massachusetts superior court judge, enjoyed teasing me with graphic descriptions of the electrocutions he'd witnessed during his years on the bench. Sucking on an after-dinner cigar, Uncle Harry would elaborate on the final moments of some miserable defendant he'd personally sent to the chair.

Hawley's parents could well have desired a more conservative, economically upscale mate for their daughter, but if they did, they never revealed any chagrin about her choice of a husband.

y mother had given me a copy of John Cage's book *Silence* as a graduation present in 1969. It was fitting that this book, which was to make such an impression upon me, should come from her, and that she should have found it in the Manchester, New Hampshire, art museum bookstore where she worked. It's doubtful that a music store would have stocked *Silence*, at least in Cambridge in 1969. And for sure no faculty member would have recommended my reading it. Such a book was simply off the radar of music professors and university composers at that time.

Cage, especially the Cage of the short anecdotes and lectures written in a deceptively simple style that echoed Gertrude Stein, spoke to me in terms both radical and illuminating. He was a philosophical optimist, part Zen adept and part American maverick inventor, and for me what he represented stood in sharp contrast to the depressing tone of the postwar European avant-garde and the pseudoscience of serialism. I read *Silence* and its sequel, *A Year from Monday*, and I kept going back to them almost as if they were sacred texts. The personal style of Cage's prose was refreshing, inviting, and inclusive. *Silence* documented Cage's philosophical and stylistic journey from the era of the percussion and prepared music of the 1930s and 1940s to the aleatoric works of the 1950s. One lecture in particular, "Composition as Process," given at Darmstadt in the early 1950s, and reprinted in several crammed pages of minuscule font, was a marvel of clarity and analytic reasoning. No one before had illuminated for me so well the essentials of the compositional process. When I read Cage's description of form as "the morphology of the continuity" and structure as "the division of the whole into parts," I felt for the first time that I understood the essence of what these elements of musical architecture were.

Unlike Schoenberg or Webern, Cage didn't mind repeating himself, either for symmetry, for rhetorical emphasis, or just for the fun of it. I later discovered that Cage had provided many of the crucial ideas that took hold among the European avant-garde, and that Stockhausen, Boulez, Berio, and Kagel had borrowed heavily from him, only later to obfuscate about their debt to him. The generally held impression, the "received knowledge" in the music world, was that Cage was a jovial finger painter, a renegade who reveled in chaos and created not "music" but "noise," and that his was an approach to art that purposefully abdicated responsibility in matters of taste and aesthetic judgment. I found these casual put-downs far off the mark. Instead of an anarchist clown, he seemed more to be a thoughtful radical, logical and rigorous almost to the point of absurdity. He was a man of immense generosity and warmth, but he also possessed the stubborn self-discipline that allowed him to take his observations to what Paul Klee called "the farthest reaches of the fertile territory" and even beyond.

Cage was one of the first artists in any field to acknowledge the existence of chance and uncertainty, and he surely was the first to attempt to bring their effects into the creative act. In the post-Heisenberg universe, this was bound to happen anyway. Physics had been revolutionized by the acknowledgment of quantum behavior and its inherent unpredictability. In the 1950s and 1960s the trend among composers was to follow the cues of scientists very carefully, whether it was Iannis Xenakis's musical analogues of mathematical formulas, Babbitt's number theories, or Stockhausen's laboratory experiments with organized sound. Cage, however, came to his new aesthetic of chance music from other sources, particularly from Zen, which he had studied with D. T. Suzuki, the master who had done so much to explain and expose the principles of Buddhist practice to Americans.

I was quickly won over by Cage's avuncular personality, a mixture of gentle humor and guileless simplicity that was ever so refreshing after what I'd been getting from the European avant-garde. *A Year from Monday* was infused with the utopian optimism of Buckminster Fuller, a philosopher, architect, and inventor whose Yankee practicality and playful approach to problem solving was much beloved by Cage. The truth is that, despite the Vietnam War and all the malaise of the times, the late 1960s and early 1970s in the United States was also a period of tremendous optimism. The first Earth Day was celebrated on April 22, 1970. Organic foods, vegetarianism, recycling, and the concept of sustainable exploitation of natural resources—all of these new modes of awareness came into the public consciousness during these years. Cage's proselytizing went far beyond a new approach to music. With his infectious laughter and beaming smile he became a latter-day Thoreau, only not quite so abstemious.

So how did I make Cageian thought cohabit in my head with bebop, Beethoven, John Lennon, and Stravinsky? The answer is: I didn't. I remarked very soon after discovering him that Cage was apparently deaf or at least monumentally indifferent to all kinds of music, including most classical and virtually all jazz and popular music. His was an art that went to extremes to avoid the "ego" in musical expression. As he tells us in "Composition as Process," part of the reason he adopted chance procedures was to take himself and his prejudices out of the creative act. Taste, desire, passion, and even personality were all manifestations of the "ego" that Cage considered as corrupting our appreciation of sound in its natural, virgin state. If I understood him correctly, he wanted to allow the sounds to "just be sounds" and nothing more. He went to great lengths to devise procedures to ensure that he the composer was not abusing the existing sounds by forcing them to behave according to his ego. He tossed coins and subjected the result to hexagrams of the *I Ching*. In one piece, *Atlas Eclipticalis*, Cage placed a map of the celestial firmament over a sheet of manuscript paper and let the various stars and constellations determine the pitches, durations, and amplitudes of the music. Later, in the late 1960s, he utilized a mainframe computer (in the days long before personal laptops) to generate random musical decisions. All of this he did with an exceptional flair that never failed to capture the attention of his audiences and the press, even if they were scandalized by the results.

For a while I wrongly imagined that Cage's theory was the Magna Carta of a new millennium in the arts. It seemed to me that by being utterly indifferent to the hierarchies of tonality and deaf to the traditions of the past, Cage was leading us into a new era of democracy among the elements of music, where any sound was of equal value and all pitches enjoyed universal suffrage. This, being both radical and antiauthoritarian, delighted me no end. I dug it, and I became a follower of John Cage for the next five years, although I had to suffer extensive cognitive dissonance over the fact that I continued to get my emotional highs from Coltrane, Beethoven, Bartók, and Joplin (Janis, not Scott).

composed two serious pieces during my two years of graduate school. The first was a quintet for piano and strings, written in the spring of 1970. I must have put Cage aside altogether to compose this piece, because it resembled Alban Berg more than anyone else. This composition, which was the first of mine to be well performed by capable, professional players, was a student piece in the sense that it was almost entirely derivative in style and idea. But it also possessed a powerful harmonic urgency and rhythmic drive that caught some listeners' attention when it was first performed in Cambridge in May of that year. My teacher, Leon Kirchner, liked its serious, *appassionata* nature, and he arranged for a second performance at the prestigious Marlboro Music Festival in Vermont. I later played a tape of the piece for Aaron Copland, who gave it his undivided attention and then pronounced it "a tough listen"—meaning, I presumed, that although he could acknowledge its unities, he was nonetheless discomfited by its dissonance and unyielding emotional intensity. If I'd learned anything from John Cage, there was certainly no evidence in my Quintet for Piano and Strings, music that sounded like it could have been composed in 1910 Vienna by a young man bent on committing a murder-suicide.

The other composition from my graduate years was far more futuristic and no less apocalyptic: a fifteen-minute tape composition called *Heavy Metal*. The title came from a character in William Burroughs's gallery of the extraterrestrial underworld, Uranian Willy, the Heavy Metal Kid. This was years before the similarly named genre of rock came into existence. For this piece, composed entirely on tape with processed prerecorded sounds melded with the gurgling sequences of the Buchla synthesizer, I recorded a friend reading the final paragraph of Burroughs's experimental novel *The Soft Machine*, a paragraph full of quintessential Burroughs phrases, part sci-fi garble, part junkie street lingo. "Think police keep all boardroom reports and we are not allowed to proffer the disaster accounts . . . a long time I held the stale overcoat in the tired subway dawn . . . migrants of ape in gasoline crack of history . . ." and so on.

I placed this text in the middle of a small universe of random sounds that included everything from the rattling of kitchen pots and pans, to radio transmissions, to clanging Peking Opera gongs I'd recorded at a dinner party given by my Chinese professor. The models for *Heavy Metal* were several classics from the era of studio tape music: *Variations IV* by Cage, and the sprawling, interplanetary electronic compositions by Stockhausen, especially *Telemusik* and *Hymnen*. (This was very likely the same music that the Beatles had listened to prior to making *Sgt Pepper*.) Unfortunately there was no one to teach me the etiquette of dealing with magnetic tape, so my editing and remixing was crude, resulting in a final version of *Heavy Metal* that suffered from hiss and frequency loss. I spliced the various segments together with a razor blade and Scotch tape. It was a funky, homemade piece, but unlike the previous year's Berg imitation, it was a genuinely original work. It sufficed for my master's thesis, although I never gave the university a copy. In the intervening years, I neglected to take care of the master tape, and it finally deteriorated from age and exposure. *Heavy Metal* is lost to the ages.

Toward the end of my second graduate year I submitted my Piano Quintet for a cash prize that was awarded to the best student composition of the year by a Harvard music major. I was reasonably confident I would win, even though I was aware that the jury was comprised of several Pulitzer Prize–winning twelve-tone composers, none of them a Harvard professor. Their verdict was a shocker. In their opinion not one of the compositions submitted by any of us student composers that year warranted the prize, so none was awarded. I was insulted and enraged, and I went on a rant worthy of the young Berlioz. Not only was the judgment a blow to my own self-esteem but it also appeared to be a general put-down of all of us who did not toe the line and write in the accepted serialist style. Already I was becoming worn down by too many years spent in the same limited environment. I had yet to travel abroad. I had not even spent a single summer outside of Cambridge, something that might have afforded me a fresh viewpoint on life and on my work. The rejection, which I took as a slap in the face, seemed like the proverbial handwriting on the wall. In fact it was unexpectedly salubrious in that it forced me for the first time to contemplate getting away from the small, constricted world of academia. As much as I had loved life in Cambridge, and for all the friends I'd made there, it was clear that I needed to take a giant step out of that milieu.

Maybe, I thought to myself, six months or even a year in California might be a good change. Neither my young wife nor I had ever been there. So after six years at Harvard, and after twenty-three years of living in New England, we packed a chronically unreliable Volkswagen Beetle with everything we owned, and on a clear, breezy August morning we drove northwest, starting from East Concord, in the direction of the Trans-Canada Highway and from there headed due west toward the Rockies and the Pacific.

4.

REGAL APPAREL

—you might throw a tire and hike to a gas station and stumble unexpectedly onto the rest of your life . . .

—DENIS JOHNSON, *Already Dead: A California Gothic*

The Volkswagen broke down not even thirty miles from home, necessitating an embarrassing return and a full day's delay while a mechanic fumbled with the aged engine. Ritual farewells and kisses were repeated and the journey begun all over again. The route passed near Lake Champlain in northwestern Vermont and on into the Canadian provinces, where the Trans-Canada Highway skirts the craggy rock-and-pine north shore of Lake Superior, eventually giving onto the prairie expanses of Manitoba and Saskatchewan. The farther we penetrated the vast middle of the continent the more I began to feel that this was not going to be a mere visit, a short trip away from home to take a break from study. Something about the immensity of the land made me feel both serious and exhilarated. Several weeks before leaving I had dreamed I was already in California, finding it a paradise of deep greens and shimmering blues, undulating mountains and powerful seacoasts. The reality would turn out to be both similar and different, but no less affecting.

Sleeping in a small tent and cooking on a hopelessly inadequate camp stove, we took turns driving the long, straight highway through small hamlets that emerged onto the horizon one by one, marked by a grain elevator or a single church steeple. At six on a Sunday morning, a million and a half miles from the nearest town or gas station in the province of Saskatchewan, the temperamental Volkswagen once again voiced its reluctance to this odyssey. Perhaps sensing it was being flogged into making this one last trip only to die in an alien land, it made a noise like a spoon caught in a Disposall and sputtered to a halt. After hours of waiting on the roadside, the prairie stretching out in all directions into nothingness, I hailed a passing truck whose driver offered a tow to a sleepy village where the locals spoke a mixture of English and German. The car repair took the rest of the day and made a painful dent in our shoestring budget.

At ten o'clock on a brilliantly clear, moonlit night I began to sense that the flatness of the prairie was changing. In the purple-black of the horizon ahead I could detect a faint shadow looming. As we moved in its direction the shadow rose into the sky: the Rockies, jagged and grand and more imposing than anything I'd ever seen in New England. In the platinum glow of the moonlight I could tell that these mountains were unlike the soft, gentle outlines of the Appalachians I'd grown up with. I knew that I had arrived in the mythic, primordial West, and I felt that a passage had been achieved, irrevocably transforming my life.

Alberta gave way to British Columbia, and we followed a road that snaked around dizzying curves beneath peaks that jutted miles up into the turbulent sky. The mountains were both wild and serene, their slopes carpeted by thick mantles of fir and pine—their regal apparel—while a scrim of light mist clung to the crevices on the highest altitudes. We made contact with the Pacific in Florence, Oregon, at dusk, eight days after leaving New Hampshire. My experiences with ocean coasts up to now had been limited to the gray-green, flinty littoral of Maine and Massachusetts with its musky, salt-scented odors and its generically picturesque coves and harbors. But this wind-buffeted Pacific escarpment was profoundly different, abutting a surf that welled up in great surges of energy and smashed with a languid and brutal majesty against the continental shelf. Years later I would gravitate to the coastline of northern Sonoma, driving the long, meandering curves of Route 1 with one eye on the ever-changing pattern of sea and sky and the other on the treacherous embankments off the highway. On one summer afternoon several years later, while driving south along the edge of a precipice skirting the cliffs, I would see a car speeding around a curve and, losing control, disappear over the narrow curb in a 500-foot death plunge to the rocks below.

This first encounter with the far coast, the Pacific and its remote landscapes, had numinous meaning for me, and I found I was ready to absorb the change and all its implications for my future. Behind me lay New England, familiar and comforting, where the landscape felt closed in like a warm family nest. Here the dome of the sky was more expansive, the sea more present, and the land more untamed and mysterious. I'd prepared myself for the trip by reading evocative descriptions of the California coast by writers such as Robinson Jeffers, Henry Miller, Jack Kerouac, Allen Ginsberg, and Gary Snyder. But nothing could summon up the constellation of emotions and sensations that this first encounter provided. In 2003, thirty-two years later, I would compose *The Dharma at Big Sur*, a dreamlike vision of the coastline, as homage to this moment of arrival.

My first view of San Francisco was from the Golden Gate Bridge on a fresh, clean August morning when the world seemed exceptionally at peace with itself. Approaching the city from the north, one passes through a tunnel in southernmost Marin County that leads onto the famous bridge. To the southeast lies the city, clustered on the peninsula between the bay to the east and the Pacific to the west. It was one of those summer mornings that I would come to know and never cease to savor over the years. The nighttime fog cools the city and the bay as far as the Oakland hills, only to burn off at midday, leaving the air and the land scrubbed clean and bathed in a shimmering, glad summer light. In 1971 you could still hear the long, plaintive moans of foghorns rolling across the nocturnal waters of the bay when the weather turned overcast. It was the mythic city of the gold rush, of Sam Spade, the Dharma Bums, and the Grateful Dead. To me, so ready for a change from the New England confines of my upbringing, it looked every bit as lovely and inviting and congenially seductive as I had imagined it would.

We entered the city in the serene morning light and drove by houses that looked friendly and eccentric. I'd never seen a Victorian house, the classic northern California wood structure with steep sloped roof, decorative detail around the edges, and tall, wood-framed windows that gave off a flavor of the previous century with its mixture of gentility and the Old West. The Mission District was waking up slowly. Latino storekeepers were hosing down their sidewalks, I could hear children speaking Spanish, and I smelled the warm, nutty aroma of fresh tortillas wafting out of the *panaderías* on the side streets.

I soon made straight for the part of town called North Beach. I wanted to see for myself if there was indeed the mythical City Lights bookstore, original stomping grounds of the beat poets where sojourners of Enlightenment were rumored to have tanked up on cheap wine and marijuana and read aloud their poetry. I found it at the corner of a raucous part of town, on the border between Chinatown and the old Italian section. Tacky, laughably hokey strip clubs lined both sides of neighboring streets, and each had its own sleazy barker, dressed in regulation loud, horrific seventies-style bell-bottoms and Hawaiian shirt. His job was to coax the reluctant tourist into the dark interior. "Come on in, sir, take a peek. It's on the house. Ladies invited, too."

I learned that North Beach was neither a beach nor was it north of anything in particular. Several months later, while sitting in a café there, I would see Allen Ginsberg himself walk in, looking avuncular and good-natured but also rather pointedly on some kind of mission. I went up to him, introduced myself, and asked him for William Burroughs's address because I wanted to send him a copy of my tape piece, *Heavy Metal.* Ginsberg peered at me quizzically through his thick eyeglasses, whipped out an old-fashioned fountain pen from his cloth book bag, tore a piece of paper from a notebook, and handed both the pen and paper to me. He dictated Burroughs's address in London. "Send it to him," he said. "He's always interested."

There was no question that I liked this new city, its mild and inviting climate and the natural flow of life it supported, neither too frantic nor too laid-back. But San Francisco was not to be home, at least not for another year. Housing was dear and our budget was tight, already compromised by the infirmities of the Volkswagen. I had neither a job nor any prospects of finding one. After several days of futile searching for a San Francisco flat that could be had for no more than $250 a month, we drove across the bay to the university town of Berkeley. Although I was not keen on living in another college town that resembled Cambridge, I felt the chances of finding a place to live would be better there. And I was right. After only a short search we moved into a nondescript modern apartment building at the corner of Dwight Way and the infamous Telegraph Avenue. I lied about my indigent status in order to get the apartment, saying that I had a teaching job at a nearby college. The building manager, himself not much older than I, took pity on me and offered me employment as his assistant, and thus, with two degrees from Harvard University, I began my professional life at $4 an hour, cleaning kitchens and toilets and chasing dope dealers from the hallways and foyers of the building.

Telegraph Avenue in Berkeley, like Haight Street in San Francisco, is one of those meccas of deeply committed oddity, and in the more than thirty years I've known it, never has it yielded up its funky weirdness, adamantly resisting gentrification and corporate crawl. Then as now, straight, squeaky-clean Cal students in slacks and Windbreakers mingled with aged hippies and burned-out street people muttering to themselves in brain-addled confusion. Adolescent runaways with sickly complexions and greasy hair lounged on the sidewalk, begging spare change, their stray mongrels sitting at their side. Street vendors sold hash pipes, tie-dyed T-shirts, and Vietcong flags that smelled of patchouli and verbena. For a buck a street poet would improvise a verse for you. Pictures of Meher Baba, the Indian avatar, or of Ram Dass, the university professor turned holy guru, lined the store windows. You could buy a bumper sticker that said WAR IS NOT HEALTHY FOR CHILDREN AND OTHER LIVING THINGS or a FRANK ZAPPA FOR PRESIDENT button. Ancient VW vans, the emblematic vehicles of the stoned generation, chugged and farted up the street, their doors and panels sporting peace symbols or Sanskrit phrases all painted in garish psychedelic hues.

For a year I walked up and down the avenue, meandering into the various bookstores such as Moe's, Cody's, and Shakespeare and Company, drinking espressos at Café Mediterranean, the grimy hangout for poets and street people, or simply meditating on the gallery of infinitely morphing faces and bodies that populated both sides of the narrow street. At the north end lay Sather Gate and the entrance to the University of California, with its Nobel scientists and the physicists who developed the atomic bomb. To the south the avenue led into

Oakland, home of Huey Newton, the Black Panthers, fabled shipyards, and dicey drug-plagued neighborhoods.

In exchange for free rent I maintained the humiliating position of assistant building manager, and not surprisingly I soon found myself in a rut, sleeping late and at night drinking the local inexpensive wine that could be purchased by the gallon. Then I found out about a job opening at a large warehouse on the Oakland waterfront not far from the Bay Bridge. In February I started working in this miserable, cold, drafty single-story building that was owned by a disreputable import company with the preposterous and grandiose name of Regal Apparel. I began my tenure there as a "lumper," part of a team of men who would climb into the back of huge containers that had been packed in Singapore or Seoul, unloading them by hand. Each was packed with hundreds of tons of dry goods, which meant cheap clothing manufactured in the Orient for American department stores. I personally handled most of the Bermuda shorts worn by Richard Nixon's Silent Majority during the summer of 1972.

My coworkers at Regal Apparel were Oakland types, some of them African Americans, others working-class white guys with barely a high-school education. I learned to be comfortable with them, sharing jokes and ironic observations about the shop steward or the buxom payroll clerk. I learned the quiet desperation of the minimum-wage earner: the long hours, the mind-numbing routine, the callous indifference of management, and the corrupt backpedaling of the union flunkies. Many of these men, although not yet thirty years old, already had behind them one or more broken marriages, problem children, arrest records, and an inventory of high-interest loans from which they would never manage to extricate themselves. Color television sets, dishwashers, stereos, a new pickup truck, or a trip to Reno— everything was bought on credit, and with each purchase they lowered themselves another foot into the black hole of debt from which they would never climb out. I could understand the desperate logic of crime, of a robbery or a burglary: it would be no different than buying a lottery ticket—laughable odds, but always that remote chance of scoring with a magic bullet, just like in the movies. Alas, it never happened for these hopeless but largely affable employees at Regal Apparel. For all of us the day was measured in chunks where the clock inched ahead between cigarette breaks, lunch under harsh fluorescent light fixtures, and the final buzzer that marked the end of the workday.

I had imagined that I could live a double life as proletarian worker during the day and avant-garde composer at night. But that was a pipe dream. In fact I was so physically and mentally worn down by evening that I would more often than not drift off to sleep by nine or ten, and the most I could accomplish was to read a few pages of one of the books I'd bought at Cody's or Moe's. Meanwhile Hawley had found a job teaching yoga and doing phone soliciting for a health club in downtown Oakland. Her boss, a jittery man who looked like and probably was a gangster, kept a loaded revolver in his office desk.

In May of that year, 1972, from the roof of our apartment building we watched an angry antiwar riot on the street below us. Four sports cars parked in the lot of a dealership facing us were torched and burst into violent flames. A riot policeman shot a canister of tear gas into our midst and the bitter, acrid fumes made us scatter. A few years earlier, a man watching an antiwar demonstration from a nearby rooftop, James Rector, had been shot dead by the police. The emotions about the Vietnam War were by now at their ugliest, and the radicals of Berkeley were old hands at street politics. But it seemed like a good idea to get off that roof as fast as possible. Real guns and real bullets were being used by the cops, and in 1972 desperate people were actually planting bombs in public buildings around the country.

I did no music for a full year. By midwinter I was falling into a depression. California was enchanting, but the prospects of surviving on a grinding minimum-wage job were enough to make me think reluctantly about returning to graduate school. I profoundly didn't want to go the route of being a university composer. Something in me railed against the notion. But I felt stuck in my situation, the romance of a proletarian existence having quickly evaporated in the harsh reality of a forty-six-hour workweek.

In the middle of all this the phone rang one afternoon. On the other end was Harry Kraut, Leonard Bernstein's personal manager, the man who had invited me to Tanglewood when I was still an undergraduate. Two years earlier I had sat next to Bernstein during a long, boring dinner of the Harvard Music Department board of overseers, and at the end of the evening Bernstein had proposed that I take some time off from school, become his personal assistant, and travel with him to Vienna and elsewhere. Now, on the phone, Harry Kraut said, "Lenny wants to know how you are. Are you still married? Yes? Well, give us a call if your situation changes." It was a blunt but realistic inquiry. No sense in hiring a young assistant to move all over the world and keep the maestro company if he had to cope with a young wife as well. Nothing more came of it, and I continued on my daily commutes to the Oakland waterfront.

Then, miraculously, a job prospect appeared out of nowhere. A friend, the only friend from back east that I'd had in California, the composer Ivan Tcherepnin, called me one day in May, right when I was on the verge of returning to Cambridge and Harvard. He told me that the San Francisco Conservatory of Music was looking for someone to teach composing and direct the school's series of New Music concerts. The two faculty members who had been organizing these concerts had made an abrupt, stagy resignation over some dispute, and the school's president was searching in a hurry to fill the post by autumn. On the way to Regal Apparel the day before, the rusted-out floor of the Volkswagen had collapsed while I was driving on the Ashby Avenue freeway ramp, and I had suddenly found my seat scraping along the pavement of Interstate 80 while I frantically searched for the emergency shoulder. It seemed as emphatic a message as any that I needed a change of station in life, another giant step.

The Conservatory was housed in what had once been a home for unwed mothers in the Sunset District. It overlooked block upon block of identical middle-class residential homes on streets that sloped gently westward from Twin Peaks to the Great Highway and the Pacific. In the summer the entire Sunset District might be cloaked in a blanket of cold, clammy fog for weeks at a time. In the winter one could see the whitecapped breakers of the Pacific as they advanced under stately cloud formations, while rainstorms made their way toward land. A streetcar line, the N-Judah, ran miles from the downtown to the outer reaches and the beach. In years to come I would live alone in a tiny, two-room cottage just two blocks from the surf.

In a city that was otherwise full of piquant character and astonishing vistas, the Sunset District was bland and ordinary. One had to know it well to ferret out a special ethnic restaurant or a hidden bookstore or secluded park. The Conservatory's historical pedigree was immediately visible upon entering the old mission-style building on the corner of Nineteenth Avenue and Ortega Street. Above the entry was a sculpted-stucco group of cherubic babies. The building, with its adobe tile roof and cupola topped by a flagpole, was in the Mexican style with a paved central courtyard. Its past as a quiet sanctuary for unwed mothers and their newborns was now given over to the Ivesian cacophony of pianos, trumpets, double basses, and singers. Students sporting wild hair and dressed in baggy jeans and sandals wandered the hallways. The sound of twenty or more grand pianos pumping out Chopin, Bach, and Rachmaninoff from all corners of the building created a constant din like a Conlon Nancarrow player-piano study, a racket that announced itself every morning at eight to the surrounding middle-class neighborhood.

I would end up teaching at this school from 1972 to 1982, during which time I slowly and haltingly found my voice as a composer. I taught a staggering number of courses in the first few years, ranging from form and analysis, to elementary composition, to orchestration, to opera (about which I knew only marginally more than my class). I even had a clarinet student until he realized that I never picked up my instrument from one lesson to the next. There was a keen interest afoot for all kinds of avant-garde music, something utterly unimaginable at any of the East Coast colleges. The general level of student ability was modest with very few on par with what might be expected of a Juilliard or a Curtis performer. I had students who could barely play their instruments at all, but who were nevertheless delighted to join me in a John Cage "event" or perform in one of Alvin Lucier's electroacoustic process pieces.

I was hired not only to teach but also to direct the school's New Music Ensemble. This group, although composed of students, had become something of a cause célèbre in the city, having for years given glamorous, attention-getting concerts of avant-garde music at the de Young Museum in Golden Gate Park. All the major names of the era from Cage, Stockhausen, and Boulez to Kagel, Ligeti, Feldman, and Ashley were presented in front of adventurous and gratefully enthusiastic audiences, and the concerts were routinely covered by three of the local newspapers—again, something unthinkable in Boston or most other U.S. cities.

Suddenly I was the new director. No one had a clue about who this twenty-four-year-old from New England was—just that he'd last worked a warehouse job in Oakland. My first concert set the tone for what would be nearly ten years of bizarre menus I would serve up in museums, gallery spaces, and park arboreta around the city: Cage, Schoenberg, Ashley, and *Messe de Nostre Dame* by the fourteenth-century French composer Guillaume de Machaut. For the Machaut, a piece whose strangeness had caught my attention and stirred my imagination, I composed a "trope" of electronic taped music, with ring-modulated bell sounds, traffic noise, and footsteps meant to provide a continuum to the live singing of the mass (which I conducted from the stage). The *San Francisco Chronicle* critic who covered the concert compared my twentieth-century surround-sound accompaniment to Machaut's mass to "someone scrawling graffiti on the walls of the Chartres Cathedral." It was the first of many delicious opportunities for bon mots that my years of alternative programming would afford local music critics grateful for an easy target. The main value of my Machaut electronic accompaniment was that it turned out to be a rough sketch of what I would do thirty years later with *On the Transmigration of Souls* by mixing ambient city sounds with live instrumentalists and singers.

In those days the Conservatory would periodically go through financial crises when, cash-strapped, it had to make do by admitting less-than-qualified students just to stay afloat. By hiring me, they also had made a compromise of sorts. I was simply not mature enough to understand the complex needs of undergraduate and graduate music students, each of whom had enrolled for very different reasons. I rambled away in my graduate analysis class about anything that happened to be on my mind—late Beethoven, Tolstoy, Debussy piano music, fin-de-siècle Vienna (after having read Carl Schorske's in-depth study of Klimt, Kokoschka, and Freud), Arnold Hauser's *Social History of Art*, Dante (in the year I discovered the *Divine Comedy*), Stockhausen, *Le Sacre du printemps*, and on and on. I taught musical analysis largely by discussing scores, trying to draw the students into dialogue and then requiring papers and written exams at the end of the semesters. This was a style of teaching better suited to a university setting, something more akin to what I had experienced in college. But for some of the pianists, instrumentalists, and voice students in the class it was tough sledding. I could at times be blithely indifferent to the fact that out of a class of some fifteen or twenty students, more than a third of them were foreign-born and still struggling desperately to get command of English. I can't begin to imagine what a panic must have seized some of them every Monday when they were made to sit in a small classroom for two hours of intensely verbal conceptualizing by a teacher only a few years older than they were, who was making up his seat-of-the-pants curriculum as he went along. At the end of one spring semester, a young graduate student of conducting from Seoul handed in his exam blue book, bowed nervously, said something I didn't understand, and quietly left the room. Later that evening I opened his exam book to find his essay answers written entirely in Korean.

Homemade, guerrilla electronics were becoming very hip among those of us who wanted to be avant-garde. Composers like David Tudor, Lucier, Ashley, and Cage were making radical compositions with Rube Goldberg–like machines of their own design and construction. In the 1970s the music world had yet to go digital, and all electronic music came either from the manipulation of tape recorders or from oscillators whose sensitivity to heat made them unreliable and capricious. It is a perfect snapshot of my life during those years to picture me talking about Beethoven's Opus 132 String Quartet in the morning to a class of glazed-eyed grad students, rehearsing the school orchestra in *Petroushka* or a Mozart symphony in the late afternoon, and then staying up nights until the building closed, huddled in my office with a soldering iron, my desktop covered with surplus resistors, capacitors, wires, and circuit-board chips that I had scrounged at a flea market near the Oakland airport.

I emerged with the "Studebaker," a clumsy, bulky homemade modular synthesizer that featured a bank of intermittently truant oscillators, filters, ring modulators, and a device with the piquantly suggestive name "sample and hold." Housed in a heavy redwood case, it was unnecessarily cumbersome due to my incompetence as an instrument designer. Even so, I composed several extremely satisfying live electronic pieces for the Studebaker (named after a recalcitrant car my family had owned during my childhood). With all guns firing, the Studebaker was capable of producing a sonic commotion audible from several zip codes away. Among the works I produced with it was a forty-minute "ritual" called *Grounding*, which I first performed with my students at the Hall of Flowers in Golden Gate Park. This piece was very much a child of the times, being a loosely structured "process piece," replete with wailing soprano saxophones (which played a movement called "Strident Bands") and a trio of aggressively amplified vocalists chanting fragments of tantric poetry and excerpts from a book on symbolic logic, *Laws of Form* by George Spencer-Brown. The Studebaker contributed to this piece a sonic retaining wall of buzzing, snarling sawtooth waves that must surely have reamed out the inner ears of the sixty or seventy brave and foolish souls who had paid five dollars for a ticket to witness this event.

At another concert, or "happening," in the same Golden Gate Park location I supervised a collaborative piece called *Lo-Fi*. The idea of this piece, suggested by a friend and fellow faculty member Alden Jenks, was to make music from junk . . . specifically from audio junk. Unlike the pretentious faux-Buddhism of *Grounding*, *Lo-Fi* was genuinely whimsical and charming even if it did, like most avant-garde pieces of the time, overstay its welcome by an hour or so. For this piece I went off with my more daring students to scavenge Salvation Army and Goodwill stores, junk antique shops, and used-audio suppliers in search of anything that was old and out-of-date but could produce sound. We found 78 and 45 rpm turntables and piles of popular music albums from the 1940s and 1950s. We surrounded the audience in the dank, cement-floored Hall of Flowers with an array of junk audio: naked speaker cones yanked from automobile dashboards, transistor panels with their winking blue-and-red diodes dangling from the ceiling, a real windup Edison Victrola, and a phalanx of pots, pans, iron brake drums, saw blades, trash cans, and alarm bells, all maniacally wired to our flimsy amplifiers and loudspeakers. We piped scratchy 78 rpm recordings of Liberace, Frank Sinatra, and the Andrews Sisters through punishing electronic circuits that turned the innocent hit-parade songs of an earlier era into a din of squeaks, scratches, chirrups, and ear-piercing feedback. The benevolent spirit of John Cage, mischievous and rigorously absurd—or absurdly rigorous—

hovered over *Lo-Fi*. One of my more skeptical students who had declined to participate in the audio love-fest of *Lo-Fi* approached me after the concert and drolly offered to give me composition lessons.

American Standard, another piece from the early 1970s, revealed an interest in trolling the backwaters of my childhood memory for musical artifacts pregnant with special meaning. It was the first of a particular family of my pieces that evoke the American-ness of my background, sometimes with wry humor and sometimes with a reserved, gentle nostalgia. Later, technically more assured examples of this kind were to include *Grand Pianola Music*, *Gnarly Buttons*, *My Father Knew Charles Ives*, and parts of my first opera, *Nixon in China*.

American Standard was composed in 1973 during that hectic first year of teaching and conducting at the Conservatory. Its genesis was in a newfound fascination with a style of "experimental music" then being practiced in England. Earlier in the year I had begun corresponding with the English composer Gavin Bryars, and then later with Cornelius Cardew, the politically radical composer and performer who had founded the Scratch Orchestra. I liked the philosophy of Scratch music, which was anti-elite and antihistorical to the max. The Scratch credo encouraged amateurs, who were welcome not only to perform, regardless of their lack of expertise, but also to engage actively in the creative process. It was somewhat of a throwback to Hindemith's *Gebrauchsmusik*, only more fun. Some of Cardew's scores, like *The Great Learning*, consisted not of musical notation so much as verbal instruction for group improvisations. Cardew's ideas from his "Scratch" period were fresh, playful, and humanistic. *American Standard*, my response to this "people's aesthetic," had three movements, each of which was a deconstruction of a "standard" American musical form. "John Philip Sousa," the first movement, was obviously a march. The centerpiece, "Christian Zeal and Activity," was a familiar hymn tune suspended in the ether. And "Sentimentals" was a trope of an old familiar jazz tune. I treated each of these forms radically. The march, for example, was stripped down to a plodding pulse with no melody or harmony. The unspecified ensemble—it was always important in Scratch aesthetic that instrumentation be drawn from whatever was at hand—played whatever pitch they wanted. The only requirements were that they stay together with the uniform pulse and that, on cue,

they move a random distance either higher or lower. The musical result sounded like the retreat from battle of a badly wounded army—
not my original intention, but in fact curiously evocative.

"Christian Zeal and Activity," the second panel of the triptych of
American Standard, was more successful. Here, a familiar four-part
hymn tune's strict homophony was dislodged, and the individual SATB
voices made to float apart from one another like slow bubbles rising in
a dense liquid. The title I found in an old revivalist hymnbook where
the individual hymns had been grouped under various headings, such
as Service, God's Love, Easter, Christ's Mission, and so on. Again, in
Scratch aesthetic, my score invited the performers to add extra-
musical material that might pertain to the mood. For the first performance, I taped a late-night AM radio talk show in which a bored,
abusive host argues "What is God?" with a patient, stubborn man who
eventually identifies himself as a preacher. This is the version that appeared on my first commercial LP, produced in England by Brian Eno.
I later composed a tape collage of an evangelical preacher telling the
story of Jesus and the man with the withered hand. This tape piece,
"Sermon," accompanied a later recording of "Christian Zeal and Activity" by the San Francisco Symphony.

The final part of *American Standard*, "Sentimentals," was a deconstruction of Duke Ellington's "Sophisticated Lady." My naïveté about
copyright issues made future use of this particular movement a problem. And perhaps it is just as well, as the humor of "Sentimentals" was
quickly lost amid a series of tiresome aleatoric manipulations of
Ellington's melody.

American Standard, along with several other pieces from the early
1970s, was self-published. I had my ink autograph score made into
offset plates by a local printer, and I bound the large pages with heavy
electrician's tape. The first performance of *American Standard* was in
March 1973 in a concert I directed at the San Francisco Museum of
Modern Art, which also included examples of British experimental
music. Scores for the British pieces had been sent to me by Bryars,
among them one by John White called *Drinking and Hooting Machine*.
The following year Bryars himself came to San Francisco, and together
we gave the first U.S. performances of his signature piece *Jesus' Blood
Never Failed Me Yet*. And Cardew contributed as well, composing a

piece for me to premiere with my students. By 1974, however, this alternately playful and stern Englishman had transformed himself into a strict Maoist ideologue, having renounced his mentors in a book with the deliciously absurd title *Stockhausen Serves Imperialism*.

When Cardew came to the West Coast in the spring of 1975, I invited him to give a talk at the Conservatory. To me he was a big name, and I worked furiously to drum up a sizable crowd of fellow composers and students to attend. But on the afternoon of his talk, he did not appear for more than an hour, and when he did finally arrive, without any apology whatsoever for his delay, the audience had all but departed, disappointed and annoyed at me. He explained that he had been at an antiwar rally and was unable to call in and advise me that he'd be late. Given that the Vietnam War had for all intents and purposes ended two years earlier, Cardew's ability to ferret out an antiwar protest in a city unfamiliar to him was impressive. At dinner, I found him intensely serious, humorless, and full of stock Marxist dicta that slammed the door shut on any and all attempts at casual conversation. There was a melancholy about him, and I could detect something of the weary, spiritually besieged missionary in his eyes. By that point in his creative life he was only writing "people's music," which largely consisted of simple diatonic settings of political prose and poetry like the Chinese Communist–inspired ensemble piece he composed for my group, *Wild Lilies Bloom Red as Flame*. Not long afterward, he was killed in a hit-and-run accident near his home in a working-class section of London.

One thing Cardew wrote in *Stockhausen Serves Imperialism* affected me deeply. Describing his earlier devotion to the avant-garde experimentalism of Cage and Stockhausen, Cardew speaks of how he faithfully and rigorously followed all the minute instructions of these process pieces, assuming the iron discipline of a Zen adept and carrying out the master's instructions, no matter how absurd they may be. It's important to understand what kinds of pieces, particularly by Cage, had become prestigious at the time. A composition like Cage's *Variations I* was in truth not a fixed work of art but rather a set of tools with instructions as to how one might make art with them. Pieces like this from the high era of chance music, if you were faithful to the rules, could be fiendishly precise in their detailed performance instructions, all in the service of yielding unpredictable and largely chaotic results.

Cardew had followed all of Cage's directions to a tee and had done so for years, believing that this discipline would help to remove the ego and let the sounds just be sounds. But now Cardew was very publicly renouncing the error of his ways, violently condemning the aesthetics of chance and indeterminacy, proclaiming that the musical, emotional, and social results of all this avant-garde activity was, in a word, a "desert." This was a brutal admission, not only because so many of us had come to revere Cage as our guru but also because Cardew's apostasy threatened to confirm what most conservative music critics had been saying all along: that the musical experiments of Cage and his school were little more than Dadaist doodling. Cardew's recanting of Cage had all the intonation of a Cultural Revolution public confession. "This was a bad thing and I will not offer excuses for it," he said.

M y brushes with radical politics peaked on a morning in April 1974 when I arrived at my local bank a block away from the Conservatory to cash a check. The bank had just announced a change in their hours, and I couldn't recall whether their new opening time was 9:30 or 10:00, so I split the difference and arrived shortly before 10 a.m. Had I come only minutes earlier I would have been caught in one of the most famous bank robberies of all time. Instead, I stood among a gathering crowd of neighbors and watched while police and paramedics loaded someone onto a stretcher and drove off in an ambulance. For a neighborhood as becalmed as the Sunset District, an armed bank robbery was the last thing one would expect.

But this was not just any heist. The small neighborhood branch of the Hibernia Bank where I kept my meager savings had been hit by the Symbionese Liberation Army, and among the robbers was nineteen-year-old publishing heiress Patty Hearst. Just two months earlier this member of perhaps the most influential newspaper publishing family in history had been kidnapped from her Berkeley apartment, and for weeks it had been impossible to avoid the daily barrage of articles speculating on her whereabouts. Now here she was on the grainy videotape of the bank's surveillance cameras, in a knee-length overcoat and cradling a machine gun. She was standing exactly in the spot where, were it not for a matter of a few minutes, I would have been waiting in line to cash my ten-buck check. Her abductors, a mixed group of political radicals and ex-convicts, had chosen her for their kidnap target, and at least temporarily they had succeeded not only in converting her to their cause but also in achieving one of the most successful publicity coups in recent history. The slogan of the SLA was "Death to the Fascist insect that preys upon the life of the people." Her abductors used her to leverage the Hearst family into giving some $6 million in food to poor inner-city families, and the blaring headlines in the Hearst papers continued the story for months until Los Angeles cops finally surrounded a house in the south of the city and burned it, killing six of the SLA members. Patty, whose nom de guerre was now "Tania," was not among those burned to death. She was later arrested and did a brief stint in prison before being pardoned by Jimmy Carter. In the years following I would occasionally see her at social functions in the city, looking ever-more matronly and conservatively attired.

My marriage went awry with alarming rapidity. Restless with our life in a rented Sunset District house, Hawley wanted to go it alone and work on her jazz violin skills, and she doubtless was anxious to get free of my zealous activities with experimental music, composing, conducting, and producing concerts. I emphatically did not want to split up, but there was no going back. What little we owned was divided, and I soon found myself living in a single rented room, with nothing more than a few books, some records, and my by now neglected pair of clarinets. For a while I was consumed in a state of morbid self-pity. I survived on boiled eggs and ramen for half a year, reading Zen stories and studying electronic circuits and sitting by myself in obscure restaurants and coffee shops like a brooding anarchist. The female graduate students at the school took pity on me and offered company, but I was, at least for the time being, savoring my pain and solitude.

Finally I snapped out of my self-imposed mourning and moved into a splendid little cottage on the remote avenues of the Sunset, one block from Golden Gate Park and two blocks from the ocean. From my bedroom I could hear the breakers hitting the seawall and smell the brackish morning air. Here in this hidden two-room beach house, which was tucked behind an art cinema, the Surf Theater, I lived alone for four years and wrote my first mature music. I had finally arrived.

5.

FAULTY WIRING

With my friends I made avant-garde music in every imaginable location throughout the city: in underground culverts, in an arboretum in Golden Gate Park, in the rotunda of the San Francisco Art Museum, in dank vacant storefronts and bookstore lofts, even in a converted Masonic temple. I lugged my ridiculously bulky Studebaker synthesizer from one event to another, and set up loudspeakers amid a nest of cables, patch cords, transformers, and various other tools of the trade. I made a piece called *Triggering*, in which I followed improvising dancers around the floor of a converted warehouse on Mission Street with a long-distance shotgun microphone. Each time a dancer hit the floor or slapped a hand or even grunted from exertion my microphone picked up the sound and caused circuits on my synthesizer to fire, emitting a loud sound. These I mixed with audio "found objects" I kept on cassette tapes—everything from the sound of insect and animal noises to passing ocean vessels, cable cars, and the jostling of a crowded city street. I vividly recall standing patiently in the park with my microphone poised above a pile of dog poop, recording the buzz of several blissed-out flies as they hovered over their find.

And then there was the Reno Hotel. For a year or more in the mid-1970s I hung out with half a dozen performance artists, filmmakers, and students from Mills College in Oakland who had moved into an abandoned transient hotel in the skid-row area known as South of Market. This was the same depressed part of town where Kerouac had weathered his crushing alcoholic benders. The Reno Hotel, on a narrow side alley called Harriet Street, had been condemned for several years and was awaiting the final stroke of the wrecking ball. But demolition had mysteriously halted, leaving one half of the structure standing and the other half a lethal pile of bombed-out debris—smashed beams, broken glass, rusted nails, and live electrical conduits. Into this absurdly dangerous, toxic shell of a building, bristling with any number of possibilities for serious bodily injury, came a bunch of artist-squatters, mostly students and hangers-on from Mills. One of them, Virginia Quesada, a graduate student filmmaker, organized "Night at the Reno," an avant-garde extravaganza unlike anything that even John Cage could have imagined. She invited electronic music composers, conceptualists, video artists, monologists, painters, and any number of other unclassifiable types to each occupy one of the fifty-odd vacant flophouse rooms in the upstairs of the Reno Hotel and "do art" there. On a Saturday night in April 1976 hundreds of people flooded the hallways of the hotel, drinking, partying, and checking out the various events in the rooms. Of course there was no electricity on the upper floors, nor was there a functioning stairway—one climbed an improvised ladder through treacherous darkness to the next floor. In preparation for the big bash, I had crawled up that ladder and threaded industrial-grade electrical conduit along the dark, vermin-filled hallways to provide electricity to the rooms. Fortunately no one walked off into the dark, demolished side of the building to plunge to his death several stories below. Amazingly, the police were never alerted. And my hazardous, untutored electrician's work did not create a short circuit and cause what would have been a catastrophic fire. Night at the Reno was spared from being the Coconut Grove of the avant-garde. In a way, that big absurdist party for all of San Francisco's leading-edge artists was both the high point and the beginning of the decline of experimental activity in the Bay Area.

———

ive-electronic" music was happening in Europe, in New York, and on college campuses throughout the country, but in San Francisco it had its own West Coast flavor. In the days before laptop computers, electronic music was a messy business, characterized by misbehaving circuits, faulty wiring, capricious oscillators, malfunctioning tape recorders, and unexpected jolts of eardrum death. Nevertheless, music of beauty and astonishing originality would now and then emerge from the chaos. One composer and close, lifelong friend, Ingram Marshall, specialized in playing a Balinese *gambuh*, a long wooden flute with a deep, throaty sound, which he would process through delay circuits that created moody dreamscapes with long, melancholy arabesques caught up in loops that folded back upon themselves. The sustained, mournful tones of the San Francisco Bay foghorns became the source for another of Ingram's pieces, *Fog Tropes*, which mixed recordings of the foghorns with plangent brass chords to create a mysterious, subtly disturbing nocturne. Ingram's work and his willingness to bare his emotional sensibilities had a huge effect on me. His live electronic performance piece *The Fragility Cycles* had a memorably haunting moment called "Sibelius in His Radio Corner," in which a repeated passage in the Sixth Symphony was spliced, electronically processed, and reconstructed to produce a delicately fractured remix of the original. *Gradual Requiem* incorporated the quiet, meditative strumming of a mandolin into a harmonic weft of slow, sequentially changing minor triads. The mandolin player for *Gradual Requiem*, Foster Reed, was Ingram's personal Count Razumovsky, functioning in the role of performer, patron, and funder for the work's recording. Foster founded a record company, New Albion Records, to make the music of Ingram and other West Coast composers more widely available. The company continues to produce albums by Lou Harrison, Daniel Lentz, Paul Dresher, Pauline Oliveros, and many other West Coast composers.

In the mid-1970s I would drive across the Bay Bridge to Mills College for Saturday afternoon concerts by Robert Ashley and his students. Ashley, a charismatic and soft-spoken Midwesterner with an infallible sense of understatement and a perfect ear for American speech, had become a guru for young aspiring experimental composers, performance artists, and filmmakers. Mills was a small, idyllic Eden on the outskirts of Oakland, a strange, isolated Arcadia surrounded by brutal freeway overpasses and acres of ugly tract housing with menacing pit bulls and abandoned car hulks rusting in the driveways. In an earlier era the French composer Darius Milhaud had taught there. He was succeeded briefly by the Italian composer Luciano Berio. The young Steve Reich and his friend Phil Lesh, later to be bass player in the Grateful Dead, had studied with Berio at Mills. But in the 1970s Ashley's loose, post-Cageian aesthetic ruled. Concerts, if they could be called that, took place with an air of studied casualness and complete indifference to formality. An audience member might have difficulty telling whether a piece was being performed or whether one had reached intermission—or indeed whether the entire event had been canceled without anyone being informed. I found most of Ashley's students, all of whom adored him and meticulously imitated his mannerisms, to be imaginative and creative. But they were by and large technical and musical amateurs. Most were cheerfully ignorant of even the rudiments of musical theory, and only a few were really adept in electronics or engineering. Ashley himself fostered the casual, low-key ambience that prevailed in the Tape Music Center at Mills. Cage and his frequent collaborator, David Tudor, were the models for the Mills aesthetic. I liked Ashley's compositions, especially the long interior monologue *Perfect Lives*, which he spoke in his soothing, bemused Midwestern voice, accompanied by the endlessly resourceful piano improvisations of his longtime musical partner, "Blue" Gene Tyranny. Ashley had found the tonality of middle-American speech, part melancholy and part whimsy, that could not be replicated either in written prose or in outright song. His art lay in between the two— meditative, seemingly improvisatory, but in fact carefully constructed. He was indeed a master, but his art fell into the cracks between poetry and song and has yet to gain the appreciation it deserves. Laurie Anderson was later to take much from Ashley's style and idea, but her performances were mixed with familiar gestures from the world of popular music and her "tech" was high tech, ingenious, and more immediately accessible, more entertaining.

I began to get restless and dissatisfied with my concerts of experimental music. Most events in which I took part were played to tiny audiences consisting largely of other composers. Boredom was a major element in many of these events, part of the rigors of the aesthetic, and Cage was the eloquent apologist for the aesthetics of patience. In 1971 while still in Cambridge I'd gone to Brandeis University one evening to attend a Cage event that he was presenting in a large hall in the student union. The tables and chairs had been cleared and the audience was clustered around on the floor, listening to Cage, who was seated at a table with nothing more than a typed manuscript, a microphone, and a reading lamp. His reading was from a long piece called *Mureau*, made by submitting passages from Thoreau's journals to chance procedures via the *I Ching*. Cage later performed similar assemblages with James Joyce's *Finnegans Wake*. In both cases the syntactic organization of the text was atomized, at times leaving only individual words and syllables floating free-form in grammatical space. Thoreau's phrases drifted in and out of comprehensibility, now and then becoming so remotely isolated from their original syntax as to be rendered into sonic objects with a possibility but not a probability of interconnectedness. At other times, the chance couplings of words would reveal unexpected new meanings. I was charmed for the first half hour, and then I became gradually bored and finally irritated, a frequent behavioral vector for audiences of avant-garde music in those days. The restlessness I was experiencing may have been in part due to the setting and in part due to my unwillingness to accept boredom as an element of the experience. At the Brandeis event Cage read into the microphone patiently and methodically for hours without taking a single pause. People twitched on the hardwood floor or wistfully eyed the exit doors. One audience member, a tall, imposing middle-aged woman with blond hair and dressed in hippie garb, for no particular reason started doing yoga exercises directly in front of Cage's desk, eventually standing on her head for half an hour. Her large upside-down figure and her dangling breasts balanced precariously in front of the undistracted composer who patiently carried on reading his text. Cage was inviting us to open our ears and minds and not to be bothered if our attention periodically wandered. Something was bound to occur that would delight us, he had often written in his books. I didn't understand the beauty and ingenuity of this performance at the time. It took me years to appreciate the special poetry Cage had derived from the simple journal entries of Thoreau.

Another Cage event, called *HPSCHD*, was an excuse for a grand "only in San Francisco" art party in the Museum of Modern Art's rotunda. For *HPSCHD* Cage had used not a literary text but rather the music of Mozart for his source material. This was less challenging but far more entertaining than the Thoreau and Joyce deconstructions, being an invitation to flood both the physical and the acoustical space with seven harpsichords and harpsichordists assembled from the local music community, all playing fragments of Mozart keyboard music which had been randomly organized by a computer algorithm. Computer-generated sound competed with short cameos of Mozart's keyboard music with the added strangeness of hearing them played on harpsichord, not piano. It was in the nature of an installation rather than a performance, and people, many dressed in outlandish outfits, packed the space, sipping wine, greeting friends, chatting, and generally having a great time. If there was a didactic point to the piece—and by then I'd learned that Cage was, next to Duchamp, the most didactic of artists—this time it eluded me.

I too produced several pieces that seriously pushed the boredom envelope. I composed *Ktaadn* for a local chorus. This piece was founded on Cageian chance principles, but they were colored by a New England exile's longing—and I was that exile. Inspired by Thoreau's description of reaching the peak of Mount Katahdin (Ktaadn) in Maine, I took a map of the area, and with a compass drew a circle with a radius of fifty miles around the summit of the mountain. This I estimated was the view on the clear day that Thoreau had described. I then made a list of all the local Abenaki place-names that I could find on the map. I set each of these names to short, modal melodies: Millinocket, Pemadumcook, Mattawamkeag, Chesuncook . . . Then, I "invited" (a key word in those days) all members of the chorus to make his or her own individual sequence of these melodies. For an indeterminate time the chorus sang these names, accompanied only by the mewing of my electronic drones in the background. The result was a congenial but more or less uneventful chaos of communal mumbling. There was no formal shape to the piece. I was hard put not to acknowledge the tedium that set in at about the fifth minute, once the audience realized that things were unlikely to change.

Another of my pieces from the same period, circa 1975, *Schedules of Discharging Capacitors*, required the performers to build tiny homemade oscillators and band pass filters. The spellbinding drama of the piece consisted in seeing the performers insert little electronic components into tiny alligator clips. The connection once made, the room would fill with a high-pitched buzzing like a swarm of cicadas on a hot night.

These pieces were playful and they gave a renegade perspective to technology in the pre-digital era. It would be unfair now to go back and dismiss them as trivial or sophomoric. They were genuine attempts to fit my individualism into what I perceived, rightly or wrongly, to be the governing aesthetic philosophy of the time. They employed chance procedures, but not with the Zen rigor that Cage practiced. They eschewed virtuosity. Pieces like *American Standard* or *Ktaadn* could be performed by amateurs. Most of all they earnestly avoided being earnest. I took Cage seriously in his admonishment about keeping the ego out of the music.

But I wasn't happy about it. I could feel a restlessness and lingering dissatisfaction with the avant-garde position. Boredom has its uses in a work of art. It can lend ballast to long, evolving structures and help to articulate and better define moments of high informational content. But the avant-garde, especially the musical version of it, brought boredom to the foreground as a fundamental aesthetic principle. Composers avoided teleological forms like the plague. A musical form was teleological if it followed a purposeful development toward an end— the "purpose-driven life," so to speak. Cage advocated an open acceptance to "whatever eventuality," and he devised games or rituals to make musical decision-making arbitrary and impersonal—tossing coins, obtaining *I Ching* hexagrams, constructing magic squares, or even using the map of the stellar constellations to derive pitches, dynamics, and durations. One could talk about this or write about it until the cows came home, but no amount of exegesis could get around the fact that, without the benevolent presence of Cage himself, the result of all the coin tossing and chance operations was more often than not emotionally cold and expressively indifferent. I didn't see that much difference between a work created American-style by tossing coins and one created Euro-style by transposing serial sets of pitches. During the early 1960s Norbert Wiener, the founder of the science of cybernetics and an expert on communications theory, wrote about the relationship between predictability and information. A comment of his kept coming up on my mental screen every time I encountered another obscure, opaque composition from that era. He'd said that there was a breaking point, a point of critical mass beyond which, if the brain is presented with too much disconnected stimulus, meaning would cease to exist. This seemed to be what I was encountering in a great deal of avant-garde experimental music.

Looking back on the era now, I am impressed that throughout the confusion and dissatisfaction and ambivalence, I never doubted that I wanted to become a composer. I simply had not found a voice, a mode of self-expression that was both original and full of enough potential on which to build a personal musical language. But I was ripe for a discovery, and just at the right moment intuitions and revelations came together to form the composer that I would become.

n Mission Street in San Francisco, Alan Scarritt and his wife, Marilyn, both conceptual artists, had opened a gallery space called Site. It was a typical converted commercial space in an old building with only a lethargic freight elevator for access. The art installations at Site were often so minimal that it was hard to tell what was "installed" and what was simply left over from the previous owners who had been vendors of some obscure industrial hardware. In the winter of 1976 I presented a one-person event before an audience of friends and gallerygoers that may have been the first real testing of my original voice as a composer. For this event I linked together a series of recent pieces, some live and some on tape, into a single, uninterrupted performance that I called Wavemaker. The choice of the title implied not only that all my music was an expression of acoustical waves but that even the formal structures, with their repeated patterns and periodic modulations, were also expressions of waveforms. Of the several tape compositions I presented, one, *Onyx*, was a four-channel study made with the Studebaker synthesizer. It flooded the room in a bath of rich, resonant, emphatically tonal chords mixed with a recording of cicadas I'd made during a nighttime walk in Switzerland the previous summer. Nothing much happened in *Onyx* other than the slow, tidal movement of those warm harmonies drifting from one key center to another. Perhaps I'd inadvertently stumbled on New Age ten years before it became a trope of its own.

The culminating moment of the evening at Site Gallery was the title composition, *Wavemaker*, for three violins that featured consonant intervals energized by fast, repeated bow strokes. Chuggah chuggah chuggah . . . the bows bounced over the strings, creating what felt like ecstatic waves of raw energy in the compressed space of the small gallery. That piece eventually became the basis for *Shaker Loops*, one of my first successful works, but it took the better part of two years and several misfires before I could perfect the idea.

Buoyed by the warm reception from the Site event, I began thinking of other ways that I could translate my fascination with the wave metaphor. A close friend, the pianist Mack McCray, proposed that I write a big solo piece for him, something grand and virtuosic that would play to his powerful hands with their subtle control of pianistic colors. To compose the piece for him I moved a battered spinet piano into my tiny cottage by the beach. The room where I worked was so small that even that little spinet sounded thunderous, and I banged away at it for months, testing out ideas for the music that would ultimately become *Phrygian Gates*, my first mature composition, my official "opus one." By the time Mack played it in March 1977 at Hellman Hall at the Conservatory, I had just turned thirty. It had taken that long to find my voice.

The enigmatic title *Phrygian Gates* reveals the music's origins. Lasting twenty-four minutes and moving through six of the twelve key centers of the circle of fifths, the piece turned out to be a behemoth: a nonstop tour of the keys—or rather half of them—that kept the pianist going at maximum concentration as the music moved back and forth from Lydian to Phrygian modes. I imagined each hand of the performer as its own wavemaker, independent of the other. The "waves" were actually repeated patterns that changed shape as the music moved along. Inserted into every new key area was an arbitrary "ping," usually a high bell-like note, which articulated an internal structure of 3–3–2–4.

Phrygian Gates and its smaller companion piece, *China Gates*, written for the pianist Sarah Cahill, were the most strictly organized, rigorously ordered works I ever composed. They also demonstrated the fruits of my initiation to Minimalism. I had first heard Terry Riley's epochal *In C* while still living in Cambridge, probably in 1971. A friend, another composition student, invited me back to his flat with the promise of introducing me to something "like you've never heard before." And he was right. What he played for me was the famous Columbia Masterworks LP of the landmark piece that announced a new style in contemporary music. Terry's *In C* may have been to contemporary American music what Ginsberg's *Howl* or Kerouac's *On the Road* were to literature. With its insistent, unyielding pulse on the high C of a piano and the sunny, upbeat fragments of melodies recirculating over and over in a loose polyphony, *In C* captured the congenial hippie spirit of the West Coast while at the same time proposing a new, slowly evolving approach to musical form. It was also marvelously provocative, giving an R. Crumb middle finger to the crabbed, pedantic world of academic modernism.

I later heard more organized, more elegant versions of the Minimalist aesthetic when Steve Reich brought his ensemble to town in 1974. Their performance of *Drumming* revealed a different but equally novel take on pulsation as the guiding principle of the music—the main event, so to speak—but compared to *In C*, Reich's materials were more fastidiously organized and the gradual process of melodic, harmonic, and timbral evolution more methodical. What also impressed me about Reich's music-making was that it was done at a high level of expertise and preparation. In contrast to the free, anarchic avant-garde "happenings" I'd been involved with, Reich's music used precision and balanced counterpoint to create a sound world that was carefully organized, musically engaging, and sensually appealing.

Not long afterward, I put together a performance of Reich's *Music for Mallet Instruments, Voices and Organ* with my students at the Conservatory, one of the first performances of his instrumental music outside of his own group. It gave me an opportunity to get inside the inner workings of a Minimalist piece.

Riley, Reich, and Glass (whose selections from *Einstein on the Beach* I also heard at the same time when Glass toured San Francisco with his group) all influenced me positively and pointed to a way out of the cul-de-sac in which I seemed to be stuck. I had grown up listening to jazz and then later found myself surrounded by the pounding, insistent rhythms and simple harmonic language of rock. That genuinely native music felt to me like my own genome, and I wanted above all to be able musically to intone those roots, just as the great American writers like Whitman, William Carlos Williams, Kerouac, and Ginsberg had found poetry in the speech of the common person. What appealed to me about these early works of Minimalism was that they did not deconstruct or obliterate the fundamental elements of musical discourse such as regular pulsation, tonal harmony, or motivic repetition. Indeed they did the opposite: they embraced pulsation and repetition with an almost childlike glee. To me, it felt like the pleasure principle had been invited back into the listening experience.

Phrygian Gates was a success, especially when Mack McCray played it. Audiences were entranced by his big, powerful body hovering over the keyboard and by his gigantic bear-paw hands that could deliver both hammer-like blows and the most delicate of caresses. We later made an LP recording of it on a local record label, 1750 Arch Records. The cover featured a black-and-white photo portrait of the composer wearing a white fedora and staring seriously into the camera while the lights of San Francisco glimmer in the distance.

My next piece, a string quartet written for the Kronos Quartet and also called *Wavemaker*, crashed and burned at its premiere. *Wavemaker* was an expanded version of the piece for three violins I'd done at Site Gallery, but my compositional thinking for it was murky and indecisive. Everything that could go wrong with a piece of music seemed to happen in this twenty-minute string quartet. I began with a weak idea of long sustained chords floating in space that neither evolved nor had any particular charm in themselves beyond the title, "Standing Waves in Mesto Affect." I also misunderstood the essentially contrapuntal nature of string-quartet writing. Rather than treating the group as four individual, independent voices, I tried to make them behave like one of my synthesizers.

The premiere of *Wavemaker* by Kronos took place in a concert at the Cabrillo Festival of Contemporary Music near Santa Cruz, California, in August 1978. The Kronos players had been vague about rehearsal schedules with me, so I hadn't heard the piece while they were learning it, a crucial mistake for a composer introducing a new work. To make matters worse, I had had too much to eat and drink the night before the premiere. The following morning, while suffering the effects of my overindulgence, I stepped on a nest of bees while walking the dog in Golden Gate Park and was stung numerous times. The bee venom brought on an anaphylactic response, causing me momentarily to lose consciousness. When I recovered I was so weak and unstable that I had to find someone to drive me to the dress rehearsal. Arriving at Santa Cruz I walked into the empty hall and heard Kronos scraping away at *Wavemaker*, futilely trying to make some kind of coherent case for it. The piece was obviously under-rehearsed, but it wouldn't have made any difference. Between the toxin of the bee stings and the shock of hearing my new quartet for the first time, my nervous system began yet again to go into red alert. An hour later I found myself on a bed in the emergency room of the Santa Cruz hospital, connected to an IV dripping adrenaline into my arm while a man who'd nearly lost a finger to a chain saw moaned in the neighboring bed.

Not all premieres involved fainting spells and trips to the hospital emergency room. A few months later, having realized what was wrong with *Wavemaker*, I completely changed it, added three more string instruments (including a crucial double bass), and renamed the piece *Shaker Loops*. This was emphatically a better piece. Expanded to seven strings, the music could sustain long harmonic pedals and produce a richer, more powerful sound. I eventually made an arrangement for string orchestra that Michael Tilson Thomas introduced with the American Composers Orchestra several years later. The version for seven solo strings, however, usually elicits the most audience excitement, perhaps because the individual players work so much harder to maintain the required intensity. *Shaker Loops* is a multifaceted title. "Shake" in string-player parlance means to move the bow rapidly across the string, thus causing a tremolo, or fast buzzing sound. But "shake" also conjures images of the Shaker sect, and particularly the shaking and trembling that accompanied their legendary sacred services. From the front window of our home in New Hampshire I could see Shaker Road, which led several miles up through the woods to a defunct Shaker colony in the nearby tiny village of Canterbury. As a child I'd heard stories, probably exaggerated, of the "shaking" ceremonies. "Shaker" had originally been a term of mockery. In fact, these church members called themselves the United Society of Believers. But the image of their shaking dance caught my attention. The idea of reaching a similar state of ecstatic revelation through music was certainly in my mind as I composed *Shaker Loops*.

San Francisco went through a menacing eclipse of its usual good humor around the time I was composing *Shaker Loops*. Late in 1978, a local Christian evangelical named Jim Jones, whose People's Temple was based in the city, used his frightening charisma and power of intimidation to take 913 of his followers to a remote jungle in Guyana and lead them in a mass ritualistic suicide by ingesting cyanide-laced Kool-Aid. Although the event itself took place thousands of miles away, many of the dead were San Franciscans and the tragedy was deeply felt in the city. Barely more than a week later, on November 27, crazed homophobic former city supervisor Dan White sneaked into city hall through an open window and shot dead Mayor George Moscone and Supervisor Harvey Milk, a leading figure in the gay community. I moved from my solitary cottage near the beach to a Victorian in the Haight-Ashbury. The Haight's "summer of love" had happened eleven years earlier. Now the area was seriously run-down. The house belonged to David Rumsey, a real estate developer and arts patron with a taste for contemporary painting and music. I shared the house with friends, including Mack McCray, Ingram Marshall, and Jennifer Culp, later cellist in the Kronos Quartet. The house was one block down from the corner of Haight and Cole where the renowned Straight Theater had once stood. In the other direction was the panhandle of Golden Gate Park. To get there one had to pass the house that was headquarters to a shadowy, paranoid group called the White Panthers, who were rumored to have a small arsenal of assault weapons stashed in their broken-down house. There was always a sentry at the window who eyeballed all passersby with cold, judgmental suspicion. I never did find out what their political pedigree was, or whether they officially aligned themselves with the Black Panthers of Oakland. Their official party statement, however, seemed clear enough: "For the first time in America there is a generation of visionary maniac white motherfucker country dope fiend rock and roll freaks who are ready to get down and kick out the jams." My neighbors.

uilding large, expressive structures by the repetition of small elements—that was the essential technique of Minimalism in music.
Several years earlier, however, on a trip to Florence, Italy, I'd had a
memorable initiation into a much older use of that technique. I'd gone
there as a coach for a summer music program for American teenagers,
all of us unsuspecting of the overwhelming sensory experience that
awaited us. What so profoundly affected me was the way the Italian
Renaissance architects and sculptors built their large public and private buildings by the use of repetition of small motifs, whether in
stone, marble, glass, or ceramics. Florence exuded a beauty that was
rational in its order and sensual in its feel for color, texture, and proportion. The perfect geometries of its architecture glowed in the warm
summer light with pale greens and salmon pinks. When I returned
from Europe I was determined to find a way to express that same combination of order and sensuality in musical terms. Minimalist procedures pointed to a way. I felt that the classics of the style were
groundbreakers for sure, but I also recognized that Minimalism as a
governing aesthetic could and would rapidly exhaust itself. Like Cubism in painting, it was a radically new idea, but its reductive worldview would soon leave its practitioners caught in an expressive
cul-de-sac. Picasso saw the value and pregnant possibility of Cubism,
but he also understood that as a unique way of seeing the world, it
must eventually be absorbed into a larger, more embracing language.
What struck me about works like Reich's *Drumming* and Glass's *Music
with Changing Parts* was that their machinery was always front and
center, the main event, as it were. Their construction, the way they operated as systems, constituted a large part of their charm.

But as much as they enchanted me, these Minimalist compositions
felt like latter-day descendants of Baroque compositions from the eigh-
teenth century. As musical organisms the pieces were largely mono-
lithic, their expressive worlds more often than not confined to a single
affect. One spoke of trances or hypnotic states. That was both the bril-
liance of the style's originality and the conundrum of how to make it
evolve into a language of greater subtlety. As enchanted as I was by
this marvelous new music, I missed the shock of the unexpected, the

possibility of a sudden revolution in mood or coloration. Over time my intuitions about Minimalism's strengths and its weaknesses would be borne out. Glass would find ways to adapt his music to any number of uses, film-scoring being perhaps the most successful. But his musical rhetoric would remain largely unchanged over a period of nearly forty years. Much of his symphonic music, such as the 1996 "Heroes" Symphony, based on songs by David Bowie and Brian Eno, moves among simple, familiar harmonies in regular symmetrical units of two and four bars, while the orchestration, once established for a movement, remains more or less unchanged. Every once in a while in Glass's music a genuinely strange and magical timbral combination will emerge, as happens intermittently in his 2007 opera *Appomattox*, but in general I have had the feeling that he rarely troubles himself much with delving into new possibilities or combinations for the many different instruments that he writes for. Perhaps this is an unfair assumption on my part, but too often the music sounds like it is hastily "scored," as if part of a postproduction compositional phase.

Glass was at his most imaginative and most powerfully original in his early operas. Certainly *Einstein on the Beach* was one of the major watershed works of the century. I also responded positively to *Akhnaten*, where his skillful use of motivic repetition, harmonic stasis, and dramatic monotony evokes the sense of deep, unknowable mystery one gets when contemplating the statues and iconography of ancient Egypt. When he applied the same musical tropes to smaller structures the results struck me as less successful. Squeezed into five- or ten-minute forms, as in the pop album *Song from Liquid Days* that he did with Paul Simon, David Byrne, Linda Ronstadt, and others, what is oracular and grand in the operas is reduced nearly to a parody of itself. Nevertheless, Glass's achievement is utterly unique, his voice immediately recognizable, and his ascension into the realms of cultural iconography has given a dose of much-needed glamour to the status of the classical composer in contemporary life. His generosity toward and support of younger composers has been exemplary, on the level of what Copland did for rising talent fifty years earlier.

I have a long-standing respect for Steve Reich, for his seriousness of purpose and his genuine desire to make his musical language reflect the deepening nature of his spiritual life. This journey has turned out

not to be an easy one, although by the 1990s Reich fortunately had
built up such goodwill for his "classics" that his public never lost faith
in him. The early works from the seventies and early eighties shimmer
and vibrate with the joy of a newfound language. *Music for 18 Musicians*, composed between 1974 and 1976, was the culmination, the
summa, of his unique musical personality. The ecstatic, driving pulse,
launched in the very first bar, never lets down. The harmonies, diatonic and largely built on sustained chords of open fourths and fifths,
are subtly poised between tension and resolution in a way that keeps
the music from ever becoming slack or tired. Most of all a wondrous
sound surface permeates the piece, a tapestry made by the most novel
mixture of clarinets (forever moving in parallel motion), women's
voices, strings, and the familiar Reichian ensemble of pianos, marim-
bas, and maracas. When I first heard *Music for 18 Musicians* I felt that
the experience of pure aural pleasure, so long absent in contemporary
classical music, had reemerged from a long, dark night of the soul.

Then came *Tehillim*, the first of Reich's pieces to announce his devotional relationship to Judaism and to the shape and sound of the Hebrew language. *Tehillim*, with the fresh, unforced sound of four female
voices and the brisk clapping and tapping of the percussionists, is a
work of optimism and youth. Reich took the syllabic structures of the
ancient Psalms as his template for the music's formal design. Instead of
short, motivic fragments, there were now full-blown melodies articulating the words of the Hebrew texts. As a result, this is metrically the
most complicated of all his scores, with units constantly shifting between groups of four, five, seven, ten, and even seventeen. Of all the
contemporary scores I conducted during those days, *Tehillim* required
the most labor and concentration to internalize.

In Reich's later music I would occasionally sense a tightness, an
unwillingness to relax the grip on the musical elements, a resistance to
letting them realize their own autonomous potential. Perhaps some of
this had to do with his adoption of speech patterns as a rhythmic basis
for his melodies. This technique began with *Different Trains*, his
somber evocation of his childhood with its quiet, disturbing references
to the Holocaust. In *Different Trains* we experience for the first time
Reich's technique of transposing a spoken phrase, "from Chicago to
New York" for instance, to instruments, creating a musical "double" of

the spoken word. In so doing, the rhythmic shape of the spoken phrase as well as its tonal inflection are imitated by the instruments. When I heard it the first time, I was not entirely certain this was a natural, effortless way to generate melody. But other aspects of *Different Trains*, from the humanity of the recorded voices to the eerie, melancholy train whistle punctuating the sound surface, all tied to the subtext of the composer's personal narrative, made listening to it an unfailingly moving experience.

In 1975 Ingram Marshall bought a small cabin in the High Sierra, some forty miles north of the town of Truckee and not far from the Nevada border. I began spending whatever free time I had in this area. The dense fir forests and craggy granite crests hiding small jewellike alpine lakes doubtless reminded me of the New Hampshire of my childhood. Several years later, with the help of a mutual friend, the same David Rumsey who owned the Victorian in the Haight-Ashbury, I was able to co-own another cabin in the same area. The route to the cabin starts in San Francisco, crosses the Bay Bridge and follows Interstate 80 into the Central Valley past Sacramento, and begins climbing into the foothills, near where Terry Riley had his Sri Moonshine Ranch. From here the road ascends ever higher, into the country where gold fever spread in the 1850s, and ends at Clark Station, at 6,000 feet above sea level on a dirt road deep in the Tahoe National Forest. In the summer the air is clear and brilliant, warm and dry. Trails wind along mountain ridges with vistas of the valley to the west and the hardpan terrain of Nevada to the east. At or near the cabin I have seen bears, spotted owls, mule deer, giant porcupines, and once, in a remote turn of high mountain trail, a large mountain lion sitting in perfect stillness, her deep, glassy eyes focused directly on me.

Ingram was a good companion. He had spent formative time in many places I hadn't: Bali, Scandinavia, SoHo in New York City, and the California Institute of the Arts outside Los Angeles. He shared my interest in electronic music and Minimalism, but he also loved Bruckner, Sibelius, Mahler, and Ives, late-Romantic composers who were not much on the radar screen of the rest of the new music community. He had friends who were part of a burgeoning movement in world music, people who knew Carnatic dance, Balinese puppet theater, and North Indian raga traditions. Virtually none of this had been available to me at Harvard. The only non-Western course I'd taken was a single semester seminar on Peking Opera and the music of the ch'in, the classical Chinese lute taught by Rulan Pian, a woman professor from the Chinese Studies program. No one in the Harvard Music Department knew much about Asian or African or Latin American music. In the sixties and seventies non-Western music was still a dark continent as far as the Ivy League colleges were concerned. On the East Coast only Wesleyan University in Connecticut took non-European musical cultures seriously and attempted to devise a practical curriculum around them.

Ingram had friends involved in every imaginable area of the arts. One, Peter Plonsky, a small, nervous, pale-featured performance artist who favored trench coats and heavy black-rimmed glasses, did "spontaneous mind emissions," a kind of glossolalia full of shouts, mumbles, trills, rolled eyeballs, and strangulation sounds that could be genuinely alarming, suggesting a choking victim or someone undergoing a petit-mal seizure. Ingram, when I first met him, lived in a drafty garage space under the Fell Street freeway ramp. Dressed in an old Marimekko striped pajama, a relic of his days at the Swedish Radio, he cooked gourmet meals for any number of guests with a wok and a green two-burner Coleman camp stove. Only a few feet away from the cooking area was his Serge modular synthesizer, his microphone, and several two-channel Revox tape recorders that constituted his studio. Nearby, next to a case of prized California wines, slept a large, phlegmatic dog of uncertain breed named Ibu. On one occasion, during my brief fling with video art, I filmed Ingram doing a Julia Child impersonation while he cooked *fonds d'artichaut farcis*, lecturing the camera at every step of the preparation while Strauss's *Ein Heldenleben* soared in the background.

Another acquaintance of Ingram's from the CalArts days was Charlemagne Palestine, a New York artist of unclassifiable genre, a strange genius—musician, painter, sculptor, and spinner of brilliant, often scabrous spoken monologues that he preferred to perform in small, cramped spaces. The physical intimacy with his audience allowed him to monitor and tweak the discomfort level in the room with uncanny, even perverse exactitude. Charlemagne's colossal narcissism was tempered by his wild humor and his prodigious energies as a performer. By the time I met him, he was already winding down the phase of his career that had been devoted to legendary multi-hour improvisations, called "Strumming Music," on the Bösendorfer grand piano. In the late seventies, when Ingram introduced him to me, Charlemagne was moving away from music toward sculptural work, much of it centered around his fetish for teddy bears. This was not as risible as it might seem.

I presented Charlemagne in concert twice over a three-year period. He first created a piece, entirely without any notation, for twelve string players from my Conservatory ensemble. It consisted of a single chord, spanning a wide tessitura with many open intervals. He gave the players directions for manipulating the sound of the chord through different unison bow strokes and preplanned gestures of other kinds. Standing in front of them, he conducted—or rather, he gesticulated—pulling and pushing the space in front of him, drawing sound from the chord, playing with it, following the results, and prodding the ensemble to take the sounds in new, unexpected directions. It was a novel idea, an extension of his own way of treating sonorities in his keyboard music. But it was a sketch of something that, with much more work and much more living with the ideas, might have produced more variation and surprise. As it was, he did not take the piece further. When he returned several years later to do the same piece in a San Francisco Symphony–sponsored New and Unusual Music concert, I could see that he'd been either unable or unwilling to develop his ideas. On that same later concert, he suddenly stopped in the middle of what was supposed to be a forty- or fifty-minute Bösendorfer improvisation, got up from the piano, and said to the puzzled audience, "I want to go home now and see who shot JR." (It was the night of the culminating *Dallas* TV episode that would reveal the identity of the notorious Texan's would-be assassin.) It was a capricious gesture by Charlemagne, a gratuitous flipping-off of the audience, alas not unknown in the avant-garde canon of aggressive behavior. It also suggested to me that Charlemagne had come to a dead end with his musical ideas and was at a loss as to where to go next. Nonetheless, Charlemagne's work was always personal and genuine, even to the point of pain, and I will always associate my memories of him with the peculiar zeitgeist of the seventies.

Another New York composer-performer who flourished at that time and whose work I found influential was Glenn Branca. Branca, somewhat like Charlemagne, worked with "walls of sound," but his work came in the form of ensembles of specially tuned electric guitars, all amplified to mind-bendingly loud volumes. Inspired by the craggy, maverick West Coast composer and inventor Harry Partch, Branca had gone deep into the world of alternate tuning, using Pythagorean ratios that, when amplified at high levels, created acoustical phantoms, sonic artifacts, impossible to achieve under normal performance conditions. The Branca event I heard at the Japan Center Theatre in San Francisco in 1982 was one of his guitar symphonies. The band looked no different than thousands of other indie or alternative rock bands of the time: guys in jeans and old T-shirts fussing with their cables while their faces maintained the de rigueur distracted look of rock musicians. Branca, thin and lean-featured, in thrift-store threads and James Dean pompadour, led with his own guitar. The tunings yanked the listener out of the comfortable, familiar world of "equal temperament." The metal strings of the guitars glistened and throbbed with an entirely new resonance, something at once alien and, at least to me, intensely stimulating. Once the drums kicked in the theater pulsed with a pounding energy, but unlike a standard high-decibel rock concert, this one was filled with astonishing, unexpected acoustical events. Several decades later I invited Branca to perform his *Symphony for 100 Guitars* at a festival I was producing for the Los Angeles Philharmonic. The event was, of course, the photo-op of all time for the West Coast avant-garde. One hundred casually dressed guitarists, each with his or her own beloved ax and amplifier, crowded the stage of Disney Hall. The doors were shut and seventy minutes of the loudest sound one might endure without permanent ear damage ensued. Earplugs were not simply "advised"; they were indispensable. Branca's music had not changed all that much over the intervening twenty-five years. It still aimed to create states of acoustical high energy and produce timbral events impossible with softer, unamplified sound. Although I had to admit that his was a high-risk art that required stoicism from the listener, I felt strongly that he was an authentic and original artist.

6.

A HARMONY LESSON

O n an early evening in the spring of 1976 I had a revelation while driving along a ridge in the Sierra foothills—not Saul on the road to Damascus, but Dogjam on the road to Downieville. At the time I listened to music on a bulky portable Sony cassette deck, a TC-158, about the size of a small satchel, with a built-in speaker and a carrying strap. With the portable Walkman still several years away, I had to laboriously make cassette tapes off my LP collection so that I could take them anywhere I went. The ever-increasing piles of plastic cassette cases comprised a scan of my musical pedigree, everything from Monteverdi's Vespers (1610) to Miles Davis's *Bitches Brew* and a piece called *Silver Apples of the Moon*, an electronic music composition for the Buchla synthesizer by Morton Subotnick.

That evening, beside me on the seat of my old Karmann Ghia convertible, the Sony was playing a recording of music from act I of *Götterdämmerung*. As I threaded the car along the sharp curves and looked out on mist lingering in the narrow ravines and riverbeds beneath the steep mountain ridges, I listened intently to the shapely ascents and descents of Wagner's melodies and the rich, constantly morphing harmonic world they described. Wagner had not much been on my mind in those days, and certainly the whole world of his dramatic theory, his mythological poems, and his long, complicated operas was far removed from my notions of cutting-edge contemporary music. But this music, especially the quiet opening bars of "Dawn and Siegfried's Rhine Journey," with its graceful leaps of sixths and sevenths and soft cushions of string chords, spoke to me. I said out loud, almost without thinking, "He cares." I was puzzled by my own statement. Who "cares"? Evidently Wagner. "What does he care about?" That was harder to answer. I was experiencing an intuition not so much about Wagner as about myself and the nature of my relationship to music. During my late teens, in the course of learning chromatic harmony, I'd been introduced to the cycles of Robert Schumann's lieder, a miniature universe of heightened emotive states and sudden bipolar eruptions of feeling-tone complexes, all expressed in a harmonic palette of the most subtle gradations of tonal ambiguity. Part of my study involved listening to a single pitch, a C sharp, for instance, and then noting carefully how the role of that C sharp changed in the course of a movement or a song. For both Wagner and Schumann any individual pitch was forever relative, being at one moment the center of gravity and then, in a flash, suddenly reduced to the status of a distant satellite, its authority robbed by the mysterious alchemy of tonal relationships. My model was "Im wunderschönen Monat Mai," the opening song of Schumann's *Dichterliebe*, that most intimate of confessional monologues set to poems by Heine. "Im wunderschönen Monat Mai" is a song in which the harmonic stasis teeters on a delicate fulcrum of ambiguity until it falls gently to a cadence of the utmost warmth and tenderness.

What was creating such a deep impression upon me in the music of these German composers was the pure expressivity of their art. What Wagner and Schumann cared about was making the intensity of their emotions palpable to the listener. The harmonies, restless and forever migrating to a new tonal center, moved between tension and resolution in an uncanny way that constantly propelled the listener forward. The melodic leaps, always singable, always perfectly vocalized, gave shape and direction to the churning harmonic movement beneath. They were lovely beyond description.

Driving still higher into the mountains, I began to think about the direction that music had taken during the elapsed time since Wagner had written those notes, how his admixture of chromatic harmonies, his liberation of the orchestra's evocative powers and the psychologically acute dream-weaving of his poetical texts had held virtually all other classical composers in thrall for more than a century. This was not just music about desire. It was desire itself. The emotional and sensual power it possessed was inescapable, and its influence reached well beyond musicians to affect other artists, intellectuals, and almost anyone with the capacity to respond to the musical mode of communication. Why had this music—despite its complexity, despite its longueurs, despite the roving, constant postponement of resolution—gained such a passionate, grateful audience? Obviously there were many reasons, but chief among them was the sincerity of the music. Wagner, like Schumann and Chopin before him, was responsible for epochal changes in the way we experience music. His harmonies were literally unchained, allowed to roam through fields of opposing polarities that produced an expressive world of constantly changing, forever ambiguous, disturbingly human yearning. His sound world was luminous and mysterious, the result of his probing, restless mind and his insatiable interest in the acoustical possibilities of orchestral instruments. No one since Beethoven had been gifted with an understanding of their expressive potential, either as individual solo voices or as massed choirs.

istorians like to see what happened to European classical music in the wake of Wagnerism as a reaction against its suffocating hegemony. They'll say that the animal energy of Stravinsky and the compressed, hyper-expressive lyricism of the Viennese School—Schoenberg, Berg, and Webern—were responses to or reactions against the vast influence that Wagner's music, indeed his whole ideology, exerted on the field of musical and dramatic aesthetics.

But it's been my experience that creative artists don't make art in the negative mode. One doesn't suffer through the agonies of forging a personal language, of wresting something out of nothing simply to react against an oppressive father figure or merely to rebel against a received way of doing things. Granted, rebellion in a young artist can be a tonic, a productive and liberating energy. But works like *Le Sacre du printemps, Pierrot Lunaire,* and Ives's Fourth Symphony emerged not because the composers were reacting against Wagner and his epigones but rather because the composers *needed* to make them, because the times had changed and a new expression, a new way of experiencing the world was called for.

Like a tree with its roots sunk deep in the most fertile soil, Wagner's art kept giving fruit long after his death. By 1911, the year my father was born, the fruit was at its ripest all over Europe, from Strauss and Mahler and the young Schoenberg to Debussy, Ravel, Elgar, and Sibelius. When its influence went into decline it did so within a flash. And that flash was World War I.

It is not a cliché to see the calamity of the First World War as reaching every corner of human consciousness in the Western world, overturning all preceding traditions. Musical style was not immune to these forces. In the immediate postwar climate, there was a hatred of all things German in France, Russia, and to a lesser extent, in England and America. This may not have been a bad thing in the short term, because the Germanic way of doing things in classical music had prevailed for so long that it threatened to choke off new ideas from other cultural sources. The interest in things exotic, folkloric, and coloristic that had begun in Paris in the immediate prewar decade reemerged once the war ended. But something about the changed psychological climate fostered a new brashness of tone that was edgier, more ironic and confrontational, even to the point of violence. Music from that postwar period often had a forcefulness that seemed born of long-suppressed atavistic energies. Bartók's shocking *Miraculous Mandarin* and pounding, muscular First Piano Concerto; Shostakovich's wry and piquant First Symphony; Prokofiev's outrageously flamboyant Second Piano Concerto and industrial-strength Third Symphony; busy, bustling, hard-edged neoclassic pieces by Hindemith and Stravinsky; the suave and sexy *Bolero* of Ravel and his two piano concertos, one jazzy and effervescent, the other brooding and mysterious—all this music moved Europe away from the iconographic expression of nineteenth-century Germanic Romanticism.

The harmonic language developed by Schumann and Wagner did not die out with the advent of Modernism. It simply moved across the Atlantic, where it was appropriated by composers, many of them

African Americans and émigré Jews, who created one of the great musical traditions of all time, the American popular song. This was a tradition that I grew up with, and when I first began to study chromatic harmony seriously I immediately noticed that what made a particular moment in Schumann's *Liederkreis* so aching and poignant was also what made the "hook," the memorable phrase that you can't get out of your head, in the best American Broadway or jazz songs.

I now realize that my moment of revelation while driving in the mountains was all about harmony. Years later, during a public discussion with the composer and conductor Esa-Pekka Salonen, a question arose about what we composers, living in the postmodern world, thought about tonal harmony. Esa-Pekka's answer was illuminating. He said that when he thought of the ten moments in music that had affected him the most, perhaps nine of those moments had to do with a change of harmony. His observation not only shed light on why tonality in the hands of a master is such a powerful emotional and intellectual tool but also hints at an explanation for why atonally conceived music proved to be so severely limiting in both its expressive range as well as in its ability to maintain large formal structures.

In 1976, while still in the process of forming my own voice, I'd had that critical encounter with Wagner, an ear-opening experience that reminded me in vivid terms of the power of tonal harmony, both as an expressive tool and as a means of achieving structural coherence. The expressive potential was obvious. But tonality also gave the composer the ability to create large, unified architectural forms whose balanced internal tensions, like the beams and supports of a grand cathedral, made possible musical statements that were both varied and unified. Thinking about things historically, I began to confirm a suspicion that I'd had for a very long time, that atonality, rather than enriching the expressive palette of the composer, in fact did just the opposite. When I surveyed the music of other cultures both geographically and historically, nowhere could I find a coherent, meaningful musical system that wasn't tonal at its root. The music of Webern, presented to me in the classroom as a paradigm of modern sensibility, was unique, original, personal. But expressively it made me feel tight and constricted, its defining characteristic an emotional parsimony that, when taken up by later practitioners of that style, was most of the time bleak and unfeeling.

I learned much about tonal harmony from listening to jazz composers and improvisers. For years, when not teaching or fussing with my synthesizers, I would sit at the piano, playing through harmonic changes drawn from famous standards, and I would work out melodic counterlines above them, often substituting closely or even distantly related chords in the place of the originals. This of course is routine practice for a good jazz musician, but most new music avant-garde composers lacked an understanding of harmony on this level. Sometimes I would find sheet music of songs by Gershwin, Richard Rodgers Ellington, W. C. Handy, or Billy Strayhorn and memorize the changes, pondering over the rightness of a particular sequence of chords. Or I would slowly, laboriously inch through a recording of a tune by Miles Davis or Charlie Parker or John Coltrane, writing down the harmonies and then trying them out in different keys. I learned much more about tonal harmony from this activity than I'd learned by sitting in a classroom and doing written exercises from a textbook.

I was struck by the fact that the harmonic essence of the early popular American composers like Gershwin, Cole Porter, Rodgers, and Ellington was not all that different from the chromaticism of the late Romantic composers. Doubtless all of these American songwriters had been brought up learning the piano music of Chopin, Schumann, Debussy, and Rachmaninoff. The half-diminished chord, a four-voiced mix of major and minor thirds, otherwise known as the Tristan chord, was the defining tool of Romantic sensibility, and it was imported into American jazz and show music with great imagination. The vaudeville and show music of the first two decades of the twentieth century, while bouncy and cheeky, was harmonically bland and lacked the power to portray any serious range of human behavior and emotion. But by the 1920s a miraculous marriage occurred that fused African American blues harmonic and melodic inflection to the tonal chromaticism of the European Romantics. Gershwin's *Rhapsody in Blue*, a work as perfect in its own genre as any that Mozart composed in his, was the product of a supremely confident twenty-four-year-old who got everything right in one stroke. Its signature motif, the "blue note" flatted seventh, is a rendering on the piano of the keening style of singing from the Negro South. Gershwin threads that motto into a harmonic web of delicious stepwise modulations that take every advantage of the discoveries from fifty or even sixty years earlier. But here, the mood is New World, high energy, with a jubilant lyricism that gives the impression of an irresistible spontaneity. In the hands of Gershwin, the ambiguity and restlessness of those potent Romantic chords is reborn to a new life, not morbidly self-aware and shaded toward the dark end of the emotional spectrum, but full of a fresh optimism, busy and brash and thoroughly at ease with itself.

Forging a personal harmonic language has always been the essential challenge for a composer. While there are many other elements that contribute to a composer's uniqueness—the rhythmic drive, the sense of color, the contrapuntal density, the ability to evoke atmosphere, even the melodic profile—none is as critical as the harmony. Therein lies a work's essential genome, the identifying DNA that gives it character and makes it special and memorable. We know almost instantaneously that we are listening to Messiaen because we recognize his unique harmonic world. Likewise, the success of early pieces by Reich and Glass had as much to do with their harmonic language as with their rhythmic manipulations.

Even as a very young listener who knew most of Schoenberg, Berg, and Webern, I didn't see atonality as a promising basis for organizing a musical structure. There was no doubting that these three Austrian masters had found ways to make memorable music from essentially atonal harmonic materials. Craggy, prickly twelve-tone pieces like Schoenberg's Violin Concerto and the Variations for Orchestra continue to give me a thrill in a similar way that paintings by Francis Bacon do. *Moses und Aron*, Schoenberg's Old Testament fable of truth and falsehood, has the implacable voice of Talmudic authority written on desert stone. Berg's *Lyric Suite* for string quartet is suffused with the restless and mercurial lyricism of an overwrought, hypersensitive lover. And Webern's hyper-compressed chamber music, small and tightly compacted like a heavy atom, seems forever on the point of vanishing into pure expressive energy.

But atonality (music that purposefully avoids a tonal center and accepts all intervals as equal in importance), rather than being the

Promised Land so confidently predicted by Schoenberg, Boulez, and Babbitt, proved to be nothing of the kind. After a heady first planting, the terrain these composers discovered was unable to reproduce its initial harvest. Could it be, as Leonard Bernstein had mused after reading the linguistic theories of Noam Chomsky, that tonality was indeed a fundamental organizational principle, and that our brains are, in a sense, hardwired to seek out and find a musical center of gravity in any complex of pitches?

The harmonic language of my earlier works like *Phrygian Gates* and *Shaker Loops* was stable and comfortably settled in distinct tonal regions. This was characteristic of the Minimalist style. I achieved variety in the design by carefully working up to the big moment of a key change. In *Phrygian Gates*, the modulations were dictated by a precompositional design, just as an architect might sketch out all the floor plans in advance of the start of construction. *Shaker Loops* attained its form in a unique way: I gave each individual player pages full of repeated musical phrases, and then, while conducting them, I spontaneously cued each player's progress through the modules. This was similar to but more complicated than what Terry Riley had done with his *In C*. However, I noticed that *Shaker Loops* only seemed to work when I was the conductor. When someone else gave the cues, the overall shape of the piece, and especially its harmonic movement, always troubled me. In the end I made a written-out version of *Shaker Loops*, locking in the harmonic and formal design in a time scale that made the most sense.

The last piece I wrote in the little cottage near the beach on Forty-sixth Avenue in San Francisco was my first orchestral essay, *Common Tones in Simple Time*. The title certainly summed up the goals of Minimalism, and in a way, this twenty-minute orchestral landscape was my adieu to the chaste, scaled-down aesthetics of that particular style. *Common Tones in Simple Time* is a "pastoral with pulse," utilizing the same brisk chugging technique that had been so successful in *Shaker Loops*. The tonal regions are stable, and harmonic change arrives only at very discrete moments, in the "gates" that I'd perfected in the earlier piano pieces. For the first half of the piece, the music stays entirely in the middle to high tessitura. When the first low bass note arrives, it is a major event, a case study of the Minimalist creed of "less is more."

If *Common Tones in Simple Time* never quite stirred the public's attention like some of my other pieces, it may be that the "less" factor never quite produced a corresponding "more." *Shaker Loops*, despite its placid harmonies, was loaded with novel, even outrageous ideas, and performing it demanded visibly strenuous activity from the players, an energy that was quickly communicated to the listener. *Common Tones*, however, used a large symphony orchestra plus two grand pianos to weave a mild and tranquil tapestry of sound that was the epitome of nonteleological form. The piece's quiet, almost passive purring through harmonic regions may have dissuaded conductors in succeeding years from programming it more. Nevertheless, it retains a small but ardent group of fans who seem to "get" the landscape conceit of the music.

n the late 1970s Seiji Ozawa left San Francisco to begin his long tenure with the Boston Symphony. A young, relatively unknown Dutch conductor, Edo de Waart, succeeded him as music director of the San Francisco Symphony. Ozawa, hip and glamorous with an athletic manner on the podium, had led the orchestra in concerts from the stage of the War Memorial Opera House. The sound of the music produced in that setting was dry and thankless, and it was hard to believe that the orchestra had enjoyed a supposedly golden era there thirty years earlier with the great French conductor Pierre Monteux. Ozawa's performances, or at least the few that I attended, amplified all the faults I attributed to the classical music industry. The concertgoing experience was largely about him, his podium exertions, and his impressive ability to conduct anything and everything from memory. De Waart, a serious Dutchman, was Ozawa's polar opposite. He cared little about onstage mannerisms, preferring instead to focus on the quality of the sound and the excellence of the individual playing among the various sections. His performances of Mahler and Bruckner were genuinely felt and could be deeply affecting. He got to the emotional core of the music not through intellectual design but through pure intuition. I began going to orchestra concerts again. Eventually we became friends, and he hired me to help him in the area of contemporary music, where he had next to no expertise. It was a good part-

nership that lasted for a long time. Edo was the first conductor to recognize my potential as an orchestra composer. He began by posing a
huge, risky challenge—that I compose a large-scale piece for chorus
and orchestra that would premiere in the inaugural season of the orchestra's new home, the Louise M. Davies Symphony Hall, due to open
in the fall of 1980. Up to this point, I was known only as a local avant-
garde composer who had written some small-scale pieces and had a
penchant for arousing the ire of the local critics. Not only did Edo de
Waart stick his neck out by commissioning a piece from me, but he
also asked me to create a whole new series of contemporary music
concerts that would be sponsored by the Symphony. I called these concerts New and Unusual Music, and in the few seasons that I curated
and conducted them, they became a cause célèbre among the San
Francisco alternative community.

Once again I found myself presenting new music in rather oddball
locations around the city. The first concerts took place in an industrial
warehouse that had been converted into a trade center for furniture
and fashion wear. Later the series moved on to a nasty, dank nightclub
venue in Japantown. There, amid the backstage detritus of clogged toilets, cigarette butts, McDonald's wrappers, and empty beer bottles, we
presented music by Anton Webern, Elliott Carter, Diamanda Galas,
Glenn Branca, Robert Ashley, Paul Dresher, and Anthony Davis.

Shortly after de Waart took over, the orchestra made the bold
stroke of hiring Peter Pastreich as executive director. Pastreich's
Brooklyn-bred mannerisms and occasionally blunt conversational style
belied an erudite and widely cultured person who seemed to love classical music as much as any composer or performer I'd ever met. Pastreich then turned around and brought Michael Steinberg from Boston
to be artistic adviser and to write notes for the San Francisco Symphony's weekly program books. Michael's ability to render, in beautiful
and uncluttered English prose, complex and subtle musical issues set
the gold standard for how one communicates about music in words. I
owe Michael an immense debt for all he illuminated and for the grace
and lack of condescension in his writing. There is no one, with the
possible exception of Donald Francis Tovey, who can write about music with the simplicity, eloquence, and capacity for revelation that
Michael possesses.

Another key ingredient of the Pastreich era at the San Francisco Symphony was his hiring of the dynamic young Deborah Borda, who joined the staff as a lowly assistant manager. Over the succeeding years Deborah would go on to become one of the major figures in American classical music life, successively taking on positions as executive director of orchestras in Saint Paul, Minneapolis, New York, and finally Los Angeles. Deborah, a close friend and coworker of my wife, became my producer for the New and Unusual Music concerts, and the experience of designing those outrageous events gave her a chance to exercise her interest in and love for the unexpected. In later years she would bring that combination of administrative expertise and artistic alacrity to her collaborations with Esa-Pekka Salonen, Frank Gehry, and Gustavo Dudamel.

I suddenly found that I'd had dropped in my lap a major commission from an "establishment" arts organization to be premiered in a high-profile setting. This was not something I had experienced before, and in truth I was not certain what I would do. To make matters more fraught, Edo de Waart decided that I should also include a chorus . . . he wanted a choral symphony, but without solo vocalists. Still living in the Haight-Ashbury house, where I had my piano crammed into a room slightly larger than a closet, I puzzled over how I might put my newly discovered musical language to use for such grand forces and how to fill a hall of more than 3,000 seats with sound. Up to that point my music had been almost entirely chamber music or electronic pieces. I could make as imposing a sound as anyone with loudspeakers, but the idea of producing a full panoply of orchestral and choral texture without resorting to synthesizers and electronics was daunting.

At first I thought I'd get around the issue by simply using the choral voices as if they were sound generators—like the oscillators in my homemade synthesizer. I wouldn't bother with a text. Instead I would make the chorus sing only sustained vowel sounds. This idea turned out to be stillborn, for I soon discovered that, short of inventing a whole language with its own sonic characteristics, the possibilities of a chorus simply making meaningless vowel and consonant sounds were surprisingly limited. Ligeti had already covered much of the available fertile ground in that region in pieces like his Requiem and *Lux aeterna*. I realized very quickly that by foreclosing on the use of a text, I was placing debilitating strictures on myself.

So I began a search for a text. I went through a lot of poetry, looking not only for good words but also for a theme that would bind the poetry into a meaningful whole. I first went to Wallace Stevens, thinking that I might share both his New England sensibilities and a common philosophical outlook. He'd published some of his first poems under the title *Harmonium*, and given that tonal harmony was very much at the forefront of my concerns, such a title seemed, well, harmonious. In the end the word "harmonium" was all that I drew from Stevens. I loved the poetry, but it didn't in any way fit my musical needs. Then I stumbled on a poem by John Donne with the intriguing title "Negative Love." The whole poem was a trope on negatives, a way of saying something ultimately positive by a curious kind of conceptual inversion. It reminded me of the *Tao Te Ching* ("the way that can be spoken of is not the true way"). But even more, in its ascending classifications of the different kinds of human love, it harkened back to Plato's *Symposium*. I saw in the poem the suggestion of a soaring arrow, a vector pointing upward, its ascent impelled by ever-increasing rhythmic and sonic energy. Thus "Negative Love" suggested a musical form for me. Later critics of my setting have complained that much of the poem's philosophical and theological subtlety is railroaded by a too-simplistic musical treatment. That may well be. Nevertheless, the blossoming of consciousness that the Donne text suggests was a launchpad for my imagination, and once I started, the ideas flowed freely.

> I never stoop'd so low, as they
> Which on an eye, cheeke, lip, can prey
>   Seldome to them, which soare no higher
>   Than vertue or the minde to 'admire,
> For sense, and understanding may
>   Know, what gives fuell to their fire:
> My love, though silly, is more brave,
> For may I misse, when ere I crave,
> If I know yet, what I would have.

If that be simply perfectest
Which can by no way be exprest
      But Negatives, my love is so.
      To All, which all love, I say no.
If any who deciphers best,
      What we know not, our selves, can know,
Let him teach mee that nothing. This
As yet my ease, and comfort is,
Though I speed not, I cannot misse.

Starting with a pulsing D natural, reiterating the syllable "no" over and over, the chorus gradually builds a large wall of consonance, accompanied by gently rippling figurations in the winds and later in the strings. The music swells to a large climax on "fuell to their fire," and then makes a sudden harmonic shift to E-flat major. The major/minor duality, oscillating back and forth with the common tone G at the top, became a characteristic signature for me. I used it again in *Grand Pianola Music* and then in *Harmonielehre*. There was no hidden significance to those particular harmonies. Rather, they seemed to demand inclusion for some mysterious reason, and I did not resist.

I once described the musical setting of "Negative Love" as a "vector pointing heavenward." The voices, pure phonics at the beginning, unite in powerful and sonorous declamations at key structural points ("Let him teach mee that nothing . . ."). This style of clear, homophonic chordal writing for chorus became a key element in my later stage works like *El Niño* and *Doctor Atomic*.

How to follow a labyrinthine, philosophically allusive text like that of Donne's without veering toward the precious? I have by now completely forgotten why I chose Emily Dickinson for the remainder of *Harmonium*. The thread that binds my choice of poetry is not obvious. Dickinson, our first great American poet (although never acknowledged during her brief lifetime), speaks in the plainest of language. Her thoughts may be subtle and lapidary, but the expression has nothing in common with the dense wordplay of Donne, the English "metaphysical" poet. One could easily feel a startling non sequitur in the way I chose to follow "Negative Love" with a slow, solemn setting of Dickinson's most celebrated piece of verse, "Because

I could not stop for Death." That poem, one of the most famous in the American canon, had already been set by Aaron Copland, who, like I, unwittingly used the smoothed-over, naturalized version (the work of a patronizing gentleman-editor and friend of the poet) and not Dickinson's more cryptic, radical original.

"Because I could not stop for Death" spoke to me probably because of memories of my own childhood. The narrator's voice comes from beyond the grave, giving us a gently elegiac panorama of what she sees from a horse-drawn hearse as it passes through the familiar places in the small town where she lived and died. In East Concord, only a few minutes' walk from our front door, there was a cemetery, and many of the graves dated from the same time that Emily Dickinson lived not far away in Amherst, Massachusetts. I treated the poem as if the images—the dignified grace of the horses, the school where children played, the fields of grain, the setting sun—were passing before the mind's eye as a vastly slowed-down film sequence. There is pulse to the music, but now the pulse is barely ticking at all. The restless energy of John Donne's "Negative Love" has by now wound down almost to a standstill. In fact the music finally does reach "negative movement," and from there it moves into what I imagined was a kind of bardo state, a transitional passage from the end of one lifetime to the dawning of a new one.

Then comes the awakening of a new motion and energy. The orchestra, heaving and surging from its very depths, gradually erupts into a frenetic stampede, hurling itself out of the darkness onto a new vista of "Wild Nights" with its bright and clangorous vibrations. To the accompaniment of a monster orchestral gamelan, the chorus shouts the second Dickinson poem:

Wild Nights—Wild Nights!
Were I with thee
Wild Nights should be
Our luxury!

Futile—the Winds—
To a Heart in port—
Done with the Compass—

Done with the Chart!
Rowing in Eden—
Ah, the sea!
Might I but moor—Tonight—
In Thee!

At the climactic point I had the temerity to launch a *Shaker Loops*–style mass accelerando. The chorus sings "Were I with thee Wild Nights should be our Luxury" over and over as the conductor drives the pulse faster and faster, forcing it virtually to the brink of chaos, at which point the entire ensemble (some 220 performers in the world premiere) come together for two gigantic, spasmodic swells, only to leave the chorus hanging, pianissimo, over empty space.

The premiere of *Harmonium*, on April 15, 1981, at Davies Hall, took almost everyone, including its composer, by surprise. The choral writing was full of unreasonable difficulties, the result of my inexperience in composing for voices. The semiprofessional San Francisco Symphony Chorus labored to follow my hand-autographed parts, struggling to cope with acres and acres of seemingly identically repeating bars, counting, looking anxiously for cues, and generally holding on for dear life. But the performance was electrifying, and the huge tsunamis of massed voices and orchestra elicited a palpable thrill among the audience, most of whom were there to hear the Austrian pianist Alfred Brendel play Beethoven's "Emperor" Concerto on the program's second half. Seated in a box behind the first violins, I was in the first line of undiminished fortissimos, and by the end of the final grand climax of "Wild Nights" I realized I'd stopped breathing several minutes before.

Harmonium is a curious piece, one of those odd birds in the classical music literature, a choral symphony. With the requisite hundred or more voices, text intelligibility is nearly impossible to attain, especially in a large hall. But issues of intelligibility aside, the sound of a many-voiced choir singing with a full symphony orchestra produces a spaciousness of resonance and a dramatic, oracular quality that can't be had with smaller forces. For all its maddening difficulties of execution, *Harmonium* caught on and gradually worked its way into the choral-orchestral repertoire. Singers continue to blanch at the challenges to their voices and my requirement that they count bars as if they were rivets in a stadium roof, but that does not seem to put them off. Once they learn to perform it, rarely will chorus members communicate to me a lingering resentment over the work's challenges.

The tape of the first performance of *Harmonium* made the rounds, not only locally but even as far as Europe. Composers and conductors visiting San Francisco would call me and ask to listen to the piece. Several others took it up for performance, including Dennis Russell Davies in Cologne, and the intrepid Leonard Slatkin, who must have sweated off several pounds conducting outdoors in Chicago's summer concerts at Grant Park in ninety-five-degree heat and 99 percent humidity. Steve Reich generously introduced the piece to Manfred Eicher, head of ECM Records, and plans for a recording started being discussed. By the time that recording happened, several years later, Eicher had changed his mind about the piece, calling it "bombastic," and he declined even to show up to produce his own very expensive recording session. Instead, he sent his second in command at the time, Bob Hurwitz. I will never know if the moody, reclusive Eicher regretted that decision, because Bob Hurwitz and I quickly became close friends, and when he took over the ailing Nonesuch Records label several years later, one of the first calls he made was to me. The result was a longstanding relationship, both personal and professional, that lasts to this day, with Nonesuch recording and releasing virtually every one of my works since 1985.

I have no memory of what kind of pieces I imagined would follow *Harmonium*. In the months preceding its premiere I had begun to receive messages from the stage director Robert Wilson. He was looking for a composer for a new idea he was hatching, an immense theatrical production called *the CIVIL warS: a tree is best measured when it is down*. I knew that Wilson had collaborated with Philip Glass on the epochal *Einstein on the Beach* and that he could claim a devoted following in Europe, but I knew little else about him other than he was the author of works with titles like *Deafman Glance* and *The Life and Times of Joseph Stalin*. Although we had yet to meet, I began receiving handwritten picture-postcards from Wilson, several of which he sent from the Bavarian town of Garmisch-Partenkirchen, a location I recognized as being the site of Richard Strauss's elegant mountain home that had been built with profits gained from *Salome* and *Der Rosenkavalier*. A mutual friend had told Wilson about me and had given him a tape of *Harmonium*. Wilson asked that I come to Munich to meet him and discuss composing the score for *the CIVIL warS*. I was still very much a young and unknown composer and hence more than a little impressed that an international figure like Wilson would, without ever having met me, be penning me picture-postcards. So partly as a means of winding down after the long pressures of composing *Harmonium*, I made the trip to Munich. I got there to find him deep into rehearsals of a new play, *The Golden Windows*. Upon arriving, I sat for several hours in the back of the Munich Kammertheater watching him agonize over the lighting of a small house, a totemic image that, when the lamps focused on it were adjusted, seemed to glow with a mysterious radiant energy. Wilson's appearance struck me as incongruous. With his horn-rimmed glasses, close-cropped hair, and Ivy League clothes, he looked more like a venture-capital consultant than an avant-garde theatrical genius. He treated me capriciously, alternating between extravagant attention and utter disinterest. He would sit with me in a *Bierstube*, sketching images with a felt-tip pen on a paper napkin, and then without explanation or apology, leave me waiting for him for four, five, or even six hours. He was adamant that I fly to Paris to meet the German Wagnerian soprano Hildegard Behrens. One night, in his hotel room at the Four Seasons in Munich, he dialed up the superstar diva Jessye Norman. After oozing into the phone for several minutes he suddenly handed it over to me, whereupon I had a halting, most embarrassing conversation with the great singer, who, doubtless equally uncomfortable, spoke to me in a polite, regal tone. I returned home with a "libretto," an elegantly bound black volume of text that made no sense no matter how I tried to parse it. It was a nonsense collage of words and short phrases that Wilson had put together, explicitly avoiding any kind of linear meaning. From my experience with Cage texts I could understand what he was aiming at, but I had little interest in trying to impose form on what was an exercise in deliberate verbal chaos.

In the end I did not participate in *the CIVIL warS*. The project eventually ballooned into a mega-production employing multiple composers, among them Glass, David Byrne, and Gavin Bryars. I could tell that Wilson was an exceptional artist, possibly a genius (as was so often said of him), but there was something grandiose about him that chafed my Yankee sensibilities. The preciousness of the title, *the Civil warS*, gave me pause to think that perhaps this was not the best collaborative step to take in my creative career.

Instead, I played the bad boy by writing *Grand Pianola Music*. Anyone who might have dismissed *Harmonium* as "bombastic" would now be blown out of the water by this one. *Grand Pianola Music* was launched by my LSD memory of Rudolf Serkin's ever-expanding Steinway as he played the Beethoven *Choral Fantasy* on a warm summer afternoon in Vermont at the Marlboro Music Festival. That memory was further amplified several years later when I had a dream that I was driving along a lonely stretch of California highway as two black Steinways loomed up from behind and zoomed by in the passing lane at breakneck speed, gushing forth volleys of E-flat and B-flat major triads as they roared past. These were the triads of the "heroic" flat keys of Beethoven—of the "Eroica," of the "Emperor" Concerto and of the "Hammerklavier" Sonata. In *Grand Pianola Music* I evoked this absurd scenario and into it mixed all kinds of other musical detritus. The first movement features the languorous cooing of three female voices, singing sweet triads over a pulsing carpet of soft pianos and woodwind staccatos. I was Ulysses, lashed to the mast, my ears bravely open to the sexual innuendo of these comely Sirens. Arousal. Climax. Thwacking bass drums. Valhalla brass. "Hammerklavier" head-to-head with Liberace cocktails. Then decompression as the woodwinds putter on congenially like Mister Natural out for a stroll.

After a reflective slow movement, the final movement of *Grand Pianola Music*, entitled "On the Dominant Divide," begins with a long, sustained dominant seventh chord that pulses and throbs for sixty bars before it finally disgorges a virtual Niagara of piano arpeggios. What follows is a melody that sounds utterly familiar, like an "Ur-melodie." You think you've heard it before but can't quite recall when or where. In fact it is an original tune. Back and forth over that most fundamental of all tonal progressions—tonic-dominant-tonic—the pianos rock and roll while the brass and drums offer increasing ballast.

It was a P. T. Barnum of a work, and on its first performance in February 1982 in the grimy Japan Center Theatre in San Francisco the befuddled audience didn't know whether to cheer or maintain a stony silence. A performance several months later at Avery Fisher Hall in New York actually did elicit some partisan boos, thereby giving the piece the luster of scandal, a value-added benefit by now rare in the otherwise tepid and polite world of contemporary art music. When I went onstage to take a bow the blood rushed to my face at the sound of the booing, but the pianist Ursula Oppens, a veteran of countless contemporary music concerts, grabbed my hand and said, "Oh my god, they're actually booing . . . don't you just love it?"

The truth is that these early performances of *Grand Pianola Music* were poor. The piece, for all its bluster and vulgarities, is for the most part quite delicately scored (for winds, brass, and percussion, without strings), and I had to revise it many times to get the balances and proportions correct. And I did not at the time understand how essential it was to obtain singers with pure voices and pinpoint intonation. So uncertain was I about the piece's value that I nearly destroyed it. Close friends who had been stirred and excited by *Shaker Loops* and *Harmonium* thought *Grand Pianola Music* was absolute shit. A publication from IRCAM, the organ of Pierre Boulez's scholarly music research institute in Paris, cited the piece as a conspicuous example of American "consumerism," and the article's author placed me in league with two other favorite icons of American culture: Disney and McDonald's. *Grand Pianola Music* proved that I was, in the Parnassian judgment of IRCAM, the fast-food king of classical music.

How could I say to the disapproving critics of the piece that in the end I loved *Grand Pianola Music* and am proud of its originality and inspiration? It is my truant child, the one that antagonizes those listeners overburdened with good taste. When I look back on it, I am struck not so much by its outrageousness (which in fact is nowhere near outrageous enough), but rather by the fact I'd managed to find musical invention in such anecdotal musical material. There is an openness about it that, for all its satire and nose-thumbing, makes me feel that it rests comfortably in the American vein.

n the early 1980s experimental music in America began to come out of its foxhole and show a more accessible public face. Although Cage was still universally recognized as the paterfamilias, younger com-

posers, those who had come of age during the late fifties and early sixties, were beginning to draw large and enthusiastic audiences. The
music they were composing signaled contemporary music's emergence
from decades of abstraction, hypertrophy, and near anarchy. To the
success of the Minimalists—Glass, Reich, and Riley—were added genuine originals like Laurie Anderson and Meredith Monk and Glenn
Branca, all artists with appealing stage personalities and strikingly
original creative visions. For several years an annual festival called
New Music America moved around the country, and it served as a kind
of grand bazaar for the latest trends, from live electronic, to multimedia, to free improvisation, to high-tech performance art.

I attended the first New Music America festival, which was held in
New York and sponsored in part by the Kitchen, a small nonprofit performance space that had been the launchpad for many of these new
composer-performers. In June 1981 New Music America chose San
Francisco for its location. I was represented, but just barely—the pianist Joe Kubera played my four-minute miniature, *China Gates*. Of far
more meaningful importance was the fact that among the people running the festival was a recent graduate from UC San Diego, Deborah
O'Grady, together with an old friend of mine, Robin Kirck. These two
intelligent and attractive young women organized and smoothly ran a
weeklong festival of what otherwise could easily have been a convention of stoned anarchists. Debbie O'Grady (born Deborah Ziegler before her mother divorced and remarried) had a subtle sense of humor
and a sweet, open personality that belied her enormous sophistication.
I found her irresistible. She had come from a large family in suburban
Detroit, where her stepfather had run a business related to the auto industry. The oil crisis of the early 1970s had left the family nearly
broke, and all but Debbie, the oldest of five, moved to Florida. Her
parents, not unlike those of my own mother and father, were slow to
recognize her artistic talent, let alone foster it, and their economic situation had forced her to fend for herself once she left home for college. She had turned out to possess a myriad of talents, from music, to
photography, to having an intuitive grasp of complex schools of philosophy and psychology. Like me, she had come to California partly in
search of a new sounding board for her ideas. She had worked as a
waitress for several years while putting herself through college. Then,

with only a smattering of conventional musical training, she had been awarded a scholarship to graduate school in music composition at the University of California in San Diego. We stayed casually in touch for the year following New Music America. We talked a lot about the Swiss psychologist Carl Gustav Jung and about politics, music, and literature. Eventually we found we were soul mates, but our first year together was fraught with indecision and ambivalence on my part, some of it due to a sudden inexplicable difficulty with composing.

Still living in the Haight-Ashbury house, I taught and conducted during the day and came home to compose at night. Shortly after finishing *Grand Pianola Music*, I was approached to compose music for a documentary film about Jung. The film, *Matter of Heart*, was the work of several devoted Jungian analysts who wanted to make something that would focus less on his theories and discoveries than on his own complex personality and his equally complex relations to the many people who surrounded him. Among the funders of the film was the painter Sam Francis, one of the few surviving artists of the great Abstract Expressionist era, and a confirmed Jungian, now living in Santa Monica.

For *Matter of Heart* I composed a score of stunning mediocrity. It was not out of lack of inspiration or any indifference to the task at hand. To the contrary: once I accepted the assignment, I became deeply involved in reading and thinking about Jung's books, even to the point of initiating what became a year and a half of Jungian therapy with a San Francisco analyst. Long talks with Debbie about Jung's theory of types had begun to lay the groundwork for a better understanding of the structure of my own artistic makeup. I even used some of my commission money to spend several weeks in Switzerland, visiting Jung's rural retreat at Bollingen on the shores of the Zürichsee. Through a friend of one of the filmmakers, I was introduced to Jung's grandson, who opened the little stone building that Jung himself had built and let me go inside and marvel at the vividly colored archetypical images which the eighty-year-old psychologist had painted on the walls.

Nevertheless, the excitement I felt upon reading those classic examinations of the psyche—dense, brilliantly intuitive revelations of human behavior—somehow failed me when it came to composing the film score. To make matters worse, the music I wrote for a "Branden-burg Sixth" ensemble of violas, celli, and basses (with added harp) was recorded in a bone-dry, sonically lifeless rock-and-roll studio. It was one of my few ventures into film music, and it was not a success. Ideas no longer seemed to be arriving with the fluency and ease that had produced *Harmonium* and *Grand Pianola Music*. I decided it was time to get away from instrumental music and go back to working with synthesizer and tape. Perhaps if I didn't have to worry about notating my ideas on music paper I might regain the old insouciance.

A chance to do this in a big way appeared almost as if by command. A new art museum, the Museum of Contemporary Art, otherwise known as MOCA, was being planned for the Bunker Hill area of downtown Los Angeles. Since the permanent home, designed by Arata Isozaki, would be years in construction, the directors found a temporary site, an old brick warehouse that had only recently been the car-repair shop for the LA Police Department. To celebrate the opening of what was dubbed the "Temporary Contemporary," the museum directors wanted a multimedia performance work that would take place right in the interior of the converted building. A young associate director of the museum, Julie Lazar, invited the great Minimalist choreographer Lucinda Childs to create a single, long choreographic piece. The set would be designed by a local architect I'd never heard of, Frank Gehry. I was invited to compose the music, even though at the time my reputation had not traveled much beyond the new music community. Lucinda Childs, quiet, calm, occasionally tense, cut a striking figure with her elegant poise, her exquisite dress, and the chiseled facial features of a high-fashion model. She was—and is—an intellectually acute artist, but a fundamental modesty, even to the point of shyness, often made her difficult for me to understand.

In our early meetings Lucinda was deferential to me about the shape and nature of what I might compose. She only wanted something that would be at least an hour long and, presumably, appropriate for dance, especially for her mathematically precise choreographic constructions. Her previous successes had been with Philip Glass, with whom she had created several works and had been a key contributor to the Wilson/Glass *Einstein on the Beach*, for which she not only did the choreography but also performed the spoken text.

Frank Gehry, well-known locally but in 1983 only at the beginning of the course that would make him the world's most famous architect, I found to be avuncular and amused to be involved in a project that didn't require him to go head-to-head with city zoning restrictions, meddlesome politicians, or anxious patrons. For Lucinda's dance, Frank constructed a two-level platform of raw wood beams and timbers, the back wall of which was covered with an industrial-grade chain-link fence, a typical Gehry touch. The piece was called *Available Light*, a suggestion by Lucinda's close friend and companion, Susan Sontag.

I literally went on a retreat to create the electronic score of *Available Light*, composing it in a converted horse barn on the seaside ranch belonging to Carl Djerassi, the Vienna-born chemist, art patron, novelist, and key figure in the development of the contraceptive pill. Djerassi's ranch sprawled over a thousand acres of coastal redwood and rolling hills that sloped down to the Pacific. Only forty minutes south of San Francisco, the ranch nevertheless felt remote from civilization, despite the fact that Silicon Valley was no more than ten miles to the east. The nearest neighbor was Neil Young, who hunkered down with his guitar, mixing board, and ranch dogs on an equally mysterious tract of land adjacent to Djerassi's. To memorialize his artist daughter, who several years earlier had committed suicide in a wooded area of this same ranch, Carl had created a foundation and a colony dedicated to giving creative artists a tranquil and physically attractive setting in which to produce new work. That winter, 1982–83, only a handful of other artists, all women, were in residence. One was an illustrator of children's books, another a French writer working on her memoirs of growing up Jewish in southern France during the war.

Storms cut the electricity for days, and I could not power up my synthesizer and tape recorders. To pass the time I walked alone through the deep, waterlogged forest terrain and studied the play of the winter light on the surface of the Pacific, only a mile to the west. Eventually the electricity came back on, and over a period of four months I created what turned out to be a moody sixty-minute sonic landscape, palpably influenced by the changing winter weather and the mysterious topography of that coastal terrain. After I was done with the electronic composing, I went back and scored music for brass instruments, music that I later recorded in a studio and mixed onto the tape of the electronic score. I called my piece *Light Over Water*, a title I thought more evocative of the music's genesis than Lucinda's title, *Available Light*, which is what the piece was called when it included the dance element.

The conditions for composing the music were crude. I was not working in a real studio but in what had just recently been a horse barn, and I was equipped with nothing more than a primitive digital keyboard, an effects processor, and a four-channel tape deck. It would still be several years before I would have the benefit of new sampling technologies and software MIDI programs. Many passages that I struggled over could have been achieved with minimal effort eight or ten years later.

Light Over Water, for all its technical limitations, established an ongoing theme in my work, that of the large-canvas landscape, the sonic evocation of wide spaces, and the slowly evolving play of light and shapes against a background of what at times can be an immense solitude. I returned to that mode in many different guises in the following years: in the 1992 *Hoodoo Zephyr* album, in the orchestral works *El Dorado* and *The Dharma at Big Sur*, and especially in the alien and volatile soundscapes of *Doctor Atomic*, music that evokes a New Mexican desert landscape on the brink of a nuclear explosion.

Although I resisted admitting it to myself, *Light Over Water* was not ideal dance music. There were some passages of easy-to-follow pulse (for which the dancers were demonstrably grateful), but much of the piece consisted of bold-stroke washes of sound with little or nothing for a choreographer to hold on to. Lucinda nonetheless listened to the music with her acute, painstakingly analytical ear, and found a way to make it work. There were difficult moments, typical of so many artistic collaborations. Choreography was a world largely unknown to me, and I had made the mistake of starting the composing without much thought of what would make good dance music. The other Minimalists, particularly Glass, always provided clear, simple structures whose easily discernible patterns fit hand in glove with the kind of formal invention Lucinda favored. Even so, while *Available*

Light did not go down in the annals of dance as an epochal event, the antithetical nature of the music may have inspired in its choreographer ideas and solutions that otherwise would not have been anticipated.

On the day that I left for Los Angeles and the preparations for *Available Light*, Debbie discovered that she was pregnant. Life would be changing radically now. The following year and a half would bring both enormous frustration and unimaginable joy.

7.

THE PEOPLE ARE
THE HEROES NOW

ometime around 1982 or 1983, while still living in the Haight-Ashbury house, I began to receive clippings from *The Boston Globe* from my mother in New Hampshire. They included glowing accounts of a controversial young Harvard student named Peter Sellars, who, still in his early twenties, had done the equivalent of throwing a live rattlesnake into the staid and conservative lawn party that was Boston's musical life. In August 1983 I went back to New Hampshire to visit East Concord and to hear a performance of *Shaker Loops* at the Monadnock Music Festival in the southern part of the state. Sellars was in residence at the festival, directing the staging of an obscure Haydn opera, *Armida*. The festival's director, James Bolle, was adamant that the two of us meet, and we did so for the first time in the cafeteria of the small rural school where the musicians were rehearsing. I arrived first that day and sat in the cafeteria carefully examining all the people as they entered, one by one, for their lunch, wondering which of them might be Peter Sellars. When the genuine article entered he came at me con moto with a knowing and open expression that made it seem as if we had known each other for years.

It was typical of his special way with everyone—warm and focused and completely at ease. His small body and extraordinarily large head crowned by a shock of coarse hair that in later years he would wear in an absurd Bart Simpson crew cut made him appear as if he were hard-wired to an electrical outlet. His expressive face and intelligent eyes zeroed in on whomever he was talking to with a wide, appreciative smile. I realized that I was in the presence of very rare spirit. Peter possessed a maturity and intrapersonal confidence far in advance of his years. I would later learn that his outré appearance and theatrically extravagant mannerisms were just a diversion, an entertainment even, concealing a man sensitive and empathetic to the extreme, one whose balance of masculine and feminine energies was keenly individuated. Already he was becoming famous for what some misinterpreted as "fast-food" productions of Mozart and Handel operas. What those who dismissed his work were missing, of course, was that hiding behind the pop playfulness of his productions was an intensely serious and sophisticated artist with the moral zeal of an abolitionist.

With the constant movement of his compact arms and hands amplifying his thoughts, he spoke with an exuberant mix of high- and lowbrow expressions, effusing not only about music (my own included) but also about literature, history, politics, and art. His words came in full paragraphs, punctuated by sudden peals of a laughter that was neither aggressive nor nervous, but rather the result of amusement at what his words had managed to conjure. I would soon come to realize that his musical sensibility was quite unlike any I'd encountered anywhere and that his extravagance was part gentle self-mockery and part the result of his profound love of music, a love that was coupled with his peculiar gift for relating musical ideas to vivid corporeal images. Peter had very little formal training in music, and he had never mastered an instrument. Nevertheless, as a youngster he had led a fantasy life similar to mine, conducting recordings of the classics, standing on a little podium built for him by his father.

Over time, one of life's great pleasures would be finding myself on the receiving end of one of Peter's monumental verbal riffs, usually a nonstop, wall-to-wall summation of a piece that he'd just heard, or a work of choreography or theater he'd witnessed. His quick, intensely reactive mind and endlessly resourceful gift for verbalization would illuminate the music of Mozart, Shostakovich, Bach, Stravinsky, Debussy, or Handel; the choreography of George Balanchine, William Forsythe, or Mark Morris; or the architecture of Philip Johnson or Frank Gehry. You would be left wondering, "How did I miss all that?"

His restless curiosity and inexhaustible powers of absorption would take him in every direction imaginable. The mention of Japan would launch a thorough disquisition on the history of that country's novel or perhaps a quick summary of its best filmmakers. Without the slightest air of pretension he could wax eloquent about Balinese puppet theater, the video art of Nam June Paik, John Cage's lithographs, the plays of the Wooster Group, or the films of Jean-Luc Godard, one of which he had actually acted in. He would not merely befriend Nubian oud players and Latino gang members, Wagnerian heldentenors and inner-city graffiti artists, but he would make serious and memorable art with all of them. He could be comfortable chatting with a member of the Saudi royal family or schmoozing in the heady company at Davos or the Kennedy Center. But then he would fly halfway around the globe to speak for a friend's high-school drama class.

On that summer day of our first meeting in 1983 Peter already knew several of my early pieces, and he wasted little time in proposing that we collaborate on making an opera. He even knew what to call it: *Nixon in China*, a wry and mischievous title, like a pop-art mangling of *Iphigenia in Tauris*. He told me he had been watching Chinese Communist political ballets, the products of Madame Mao's fevered agit-prop culture campaigns, and these, together with a reading of Henry Kissinger's pompous, self-congratulatory account of his White House years, had suggested an opera that might be a delicious "East meets West" study in modern Realpolitik. How he could have imagined me, who had never written a note for solo voice, as the ideal composer for such a project beggars understanding. Nevertheless, I was jazzed by the idea of working with him. Whereas Robert Wilson had made me feel uneasy about what role music might play in his productions, Peter's enthusiasm had the opposite effect, signaling the supreme value he placed on what I would write. I also sensed that our collaboration would be just that—a shared voyage of discovery. I returned to San Francisco agreeing to stay in touch with him, although I was uncertain if "Nixon in China" would be my choice for a theme. When I thought of what kind of opera I should like to write, what Peter was proposing only reminded me of all those bad TV comics who did Nixon impressions, hunching their shoulders and making the infamous two-handed V-for-victory sign.

Nearly two years passed before I realized not only that "Nixon in China" was a brilliant idea for an opera but that it should be composed by John Adams. How could it be otherwise?

In the meantime I was gradually drifting into a first-class funk, suffering from a perplexing and deeply disturbing creative block. It was a toxic state of mind that led to an eighteen-month dry spell and drove me to the blackest of moods. Like a baseball player falling deeper and deeper into a self-perpetuating slump, I began to spend the larger part of my energies analyzing why I could not produce. Day after day, with what I deemed Yankee rectitude and Protestant work ethic, I would lock myself in my studio and try any and all tricks to unravel the thread of what had become a perfect tangle of reasons as to why everything I was doing was wrong, "aesthetically unethical," or in bad taste, or not sophisticated enough. There were many causes for this sudden and alarming cessation of musical ideas. Even though I was in my mid-thirties, I was still a young composer and not secure enough to know that a bad spell was just that—a bad spell—and that it would eventually pass. So rather than easing up I pressed harder and harder, with the result being that I soon began to freak, fearing that I would never compose again. Added to this was the fact that I now held an actual professional position with a title: composer in residence with the San Francisco Symphony. The well-funded residency, sponsored by Exxon and the Ford Foundation, gave my soon-to-be family of four a secure salary for several years, with the proviso that I deliver a major orchestral work as the culmination of my residency. That deadline contributed an external pressure on top of the already deeply destructive internal ones I was imposing upon myself. The block went on, day after day, for those eighteen agonizing months. But it may in the end have been inevitable, a necessary backtracking to gauge my real identity and learn to be comfortable with who I really was, both as a person and as a creative artist.

Strange indeed that the path out of this terrible psychological thicket would include an encounter with that darkest and most intimidating of all the figures in my personal gallery, Arnold Schoenberg. I'd maintained a puzzled fascination for Schoenberg ever since encountering *Pierrot Lunaire* as a teenager. Like a brooding, egocentric father, impossible to please, he loomed in my consciousness, sometimes as the embodiment of a mercurial creative force and other times as a lethal defoliant, ready to kill off any and all sprouts of life that might appear in its immediate range. In a particularly revealing dream that occurred during this difficult period, I'd found myself on a dirt road in a dark, damp winter forest, not unlike that which led through the redwoods to the Djerassi ranch. I was carrying two babies in my arms, twins. Out of the damp, nocturnal gloom a malevolent-looking man in an overcoat suddenly appeared in front of me, his swarthy face half covered by a large fedora. He reached out to grab one of the babies from me. A violent struggle followed. I knew that it was Schoenberg and that he was trying to abduct my children. This image doubtless had less to do with Schoenberg than with my own anxious predicament at the time, some of which I blamed on the long shadow he cast over my thinking. As an expression of my mental and emotional state, the dream was vivid and alarming, even a bit hysterical. But it was also instructive, to say the least.

armonielehre, the forty-minute symphony that broke me out of this long creative lockdown, was a statement of belief in the power of tonality at a time when I was uncertain about its future. I needn't have worried, as the huge success of popular music and our growing awareness of other non-Western traditions were already making it clear that tonal harmony was in no danger of demise. The title of my work comes ironically from a treatise on tonal harmony that Schoenberg wrote and published at exactly the same time that his own compositions were, paradoxically, abandoning it. My decision to name my symphony *Harmonielehre* is almost impossible to explain. It was part whimsical, part an acknowledgment of my puzzling father-son relationship to the master (and by extension to my own teacher, Leon Kirchner). I also said at the time that the actual German word, roughly translated as the "theory of harmony" or "harmony lesson," might also imply a psychic quest for harmony. The shape and general expressive scenario of the piece does bear this out. The end of the last movement culminates in a vast harmonic struggle that breaks through into an emphatic release on E-flat major. I certainly was not unaware of the models that existed in earlier music, from the Beethoven "Eroica" and "Emperor" up through the Sibelius Fifth Symphony. The final eighty bars of the piece are a reworking for orchestra of the end of *Light Over Water*, an illustration of the extent to which my musical thinking easily crossbred electronic and orchestrated music.

An anecdotal but true story exists about both the first and third movements of *Harmonielehre*. At what seemed like the absolute nadir of my creative block I'd had a vivid dream in which I was crossing the San Francisco Bay Bridge. In that dream I looked out to see a huge oil tanker sitting in the water. As I watched, it slowly rose up like a Saturn rocket and blasted out of the bay and into the sky. I could see the rust-colored metal oxide of its hull as it took off. Shortly after, possibly the very next day, I sat down in my studio to find, almost as if they were waiting for me, the powerful pounding E-minor chords that launch the piece. From there it proceeded to take shape with great speed, almost as if the floodgates had been opened and nearly two years of pent-up energy and ideas came rushing forth.

Another dream provided the special ethereal atmosphere that opens the third and final movement, "Meister Eckhardt and Quackie." This was a single image: the medieval mystic floating in space and carrying on his shoulder, like a blithe and gentle homunculus, our four-month-old daughter, Emily. Because of the funny, ducklike noise she made as a baby, we'd nicknamed her "Quackie." The image, strange and whimsical and inexplicable as dreams often can be, confirmed how the birth of a child can be an event of such intense psychic power that it will cause the most insurmountable walls of psychic resistance to come tumbling down. The birth of both of our children had this kind of numinous power for me, so much so that I returned to this primal event fifteen years later and made it the theme of the Nativity oratorio, *El Niño*.

Harmonielehre was a one-of-kind, once-only essay in the wedding of fin-de-siècle chromatic harmony with the rhythmic and formal procedures of Minimalism. If it succeeded it is probably because it avoided being too rigorously bound to the practices of either tradition. The harmonies brush up against many totemic works of the preceding hundred years, from *Parsifal* and *Pelléas et Mélisande* through the Mahler of the Tenth Symphony to Sibelius (particularly his Fourth Symphony) and the luminescent, crepuscular tone-painting of Schoenberg's *Gurrelieder*. There was a playfulness, even an impudence about my ease with appropriation. The music reveled in a kind of enlightened thievery that I would never be able to commit later. I can't even find the proper term to describe my mental state while composing, so quickly did the ideas come and so free was my spirit of accepting them into the fold. Those writers who mistakenly compared *Harmonielehre* to postmodernist architecture with its self-conscious borrowings from past traditions miss the spirit in which my work was composed. I doubtless contributed to the typecasting when, a few months after the premiere, I gave an interview to Jonathan Cott, comparing the piece to Philip Johnson's recently constructed AT&T building in New York. That was an inaccurate and misleading connection, because *Harmonielehre* lacks the cool, calculated irony of Johnson's Postmodernism. In fact, while writing the piece, I felt as if I were channeling the sensibilities of those composers I loved and finding a contemporary form for their special harmonic worlds, treating them as if they had been conjured in a séance.

But too much analyzing of the piece can take away its pleasures and make one lose touch with the absolute spontaneity of its creation. Certainly, *Harmonielehre* provoked a lot of criticism from those who felt it was the work of an epigone trying to turn back the clock of music history. Others, such as one critic writing in *The New Republic*, felt that behind a sleek and suspiciously clever manipulation of the orchestra was a composer bent on perverting and cheapening an otherwise decent new musical style, Minimalism. It was for sure a dangerous way to make art, stepping on the toes of past masters while inviting charges of corruption and showboating from those of my contemporaries who were still trying to follow the straight and narrow of Modernism. But *Harmonielehre*, for all its referencing and allusions, was a genuine statement. It was a piece serious in its expressiveness, and the explosive energies and bright colors that inhabit its three movements do not strike me as anything other than the product of that particular time and place. If the work is a parody, it is a parody made lovingly and entirely without irony.

The San Francisco Symphony recorded *Harmonielehre* in the same week as its premiere. The parts hadn't been well proofed and I later had to recompose and extend the ending. But that recording, for all its minor faults, projected a sense of confidence and energy that belied the orchestra's unfamiliarity with the music. Like the tanker rising from San Francisco Bay, the piece took off, and within a few years it had become one of the very few contemporary works longer than fifteen minutes to be accepted onto the programs of American and European orchestras. Peter Sellars later used it as the score to his eerie and mysterious silent film, *The Cabinet of Doctor Ramirez*.

In early 1984, before having started *Harmonielehre*, I'd spied a stoned-out Haight-Ashbury local peeing on the steps of our rented Victorian, and I took that as a sign that this neighborhood, for all its admirable grit and scrappiness, was no place for a new baby. The year before, a police SWAT team had blocked me from getting into my house. They had cordoned off the street and, armed with sniper carbines, were perched on the surrounding rooftops because one of our neighbors across the street was holding his parole officer hostage with a shotgun. Time to move. The week after Emily was born we left San Francisco and drove our belongings across the bay to a rented house in north Berkeley. A year later we bought our own house on nearby Holly Street. Berkeley once again became my home, and it continues to be. The following year, 1985, our son, Sam, was born. At the same time I resolved to support this new family not by returning to teaching but by making my creative work provide the wherewithal for our existence. It was a conscious decision, and I made it because I knew that I responded well to the pressure of deadlines and thought that the motivation of having to provide for my family would perhaps keep a fire under me and prevent me from again falling into the anguished, overanalyzing block that I'd been victim to during the previous two years.

.   .   .

Richard Nixon had been the bogeyman of my young manhood. I first associated him with the button-down attitudes of the 1950s and the long, malignant chill of the cold war, black-and-white TVs, large cars with fins, anticommunist propaganda, and the nervous, pervasive conservatism of my childhood. My mother, an ardent liberal and tireless volunteer for the New Hampshire Democratic Party, had infected me from an early age with a fascination for politics. Since every four years New Hampshire traditionally was the site of the country's first presidential primaries, and since our town of Concord was the state's capital, politics, particularly big-time presidential politics, seized the attention of the local population for months at a time. My mother had even once hosted a ladies' tea for Rose Fitzgerald Kennedy, JFK's mother, and she kept a picture of herself seated next to that small, energetic Bostonian, serving her from an elegant silver teapot. To me, Nixon's ability to get any votes at all against the charismatic and handsome John F. Kennedy was difficult to understand. In fact Nixon's appeal was more likely the result of his being the un-Kennedy—not being a liberal Democrat, not being from a rich New England family, not being Catholic, not speaking with a Harvard-tuned, Massachusetts twang.

As a thirteen-year-old I watched the famous 1960 television debates, verbal duels in which the still-new medium of television had treated Nixon unkindly, revealing his sweaty forehead, dry mouth, and shifty eyes. Kennedy won the debates and the election, started our entanglement in Vietnam, was assassinated and followed in office by the decidedly less charismatic and unlovable Lyndon Johnson. By the time I graduated from college, Richard Nixon, stubborn and tenacious, petty and Machiavellian, had made his comeback and was now president. I was precisely the walking specimen of young punk that Nixon railed against when he addressed his imagined "silent majority," complaining about the antiwar movement's lack of patriotism, its cowardice, and its unfair gift for strident attention-getting. To our abject addiction to loud music, promiscuous sex, and political naïveté, Nixon countered with his silent, long-suffering Middle Americans—the modest, the monogamous, the shy, and the dutiful. They were the small-town businessmen with their obedient churchgoing wives and households of 2.5 children. Nixon's Quaker childhood of hardship and poverty constituted a personal history that ought to have been mythical and inspiring, especially when contrasted with Kennedy's birthright of wealth, power, and privilege. But Nixon managed to muddy the waters of his image by choosing the wrong pals, from Spiro Agnew and Bebe Rebozo to John Mitchell and the gang that bumbled the Watergate break-in. His ham-fisted plan to crush the North Vietnamese through a carrot-and-stick mix of saturation bombing and a simultaneous diplomatic "peace offensive" had only led to a humiliating collapse of the American presence in Vietnam and a decade of bitter recrimination back home.

In the winter of 1972, while still working at Regal Apparel in Oakland and living on Telegraph Avenue in Berkeley, I watched on a tiny black-and-white television while Air Force One landed on the tarmac of Peking, and Richard Nixon, followed by Pat and Secretary of State Henry Kissinger, descended the jet's ramp to be greeted by Chou Enlai, the premier of the People's Republic. It was a bold gesture, this idea of walking straight into the Communist heart of darkness and offering a good old Rotarian handshake to the natives, those same Chinese who up to then, as we'd been often warned, represented every imaginable barometer of inscrutable cunning, naked aggression, and careless affront to our cherished notions of representative democracy. But Nixon fancied himself a pragmatic businessman who listened to other businessmen, and China, give or take a few annoying issues about personal liberty and human rights, was, well, an irresistibly attractive market for our patriotically manufactured American goods. When Nixon stepped out of the plane that February day in Peking the veil of mystery that had enveloped the great Chinese continent and its billion-plus people began to part. The next day brought us the shocking images of Mao Tse-tung greeting the president—the famous handshake more earth-shattering in its import than landing a man on the moon. Lo and behold, Mao had long since ceased being the stolid, confident icon of a million posters and little red books, the Chairman and Great Helmsman whose face adorned student dorm rooms in the West and factory workplaces in the East. Rather, he was now revealed as a frail, trembling octogenarian, barely able to rise out of his chair long enough to endure the photo op with the grinning president. The Cultural Revolution, the horrific civil war—in Alice Goodman's words, a "bloodbath on Platonic principles"—that pitted young against old and son against father, remained an open wound in the nation's psyche. The memory of it was still fresh, and its most high-profile instigator, Chiang Ch'ing, aka Madame Mao, had only recently been blocked from abusing her increasingly feeble husband's bully pulpit to terrorize the cultural and political life of this very large, very poor, isolated nation.

Eleven years later, when Peter Sellars proposed an opera about the Nixon visit, my own antipathy toward that president who'd tried to draft me and send me to fight in Vietnam had not even begun to reach equanimity. In the meantime Nixon had been thoroughly disgraced by Watergate, and the American love for a good rehabilitation story had yet to be extended to him. Nixon, nevertheless, was undaunted, and he had written books attempting to establish himself as a wise elder statesman. Now Ronald Reagan was president, and it was trickle-down Morning in America. The more I thought about it, the better I liked the idea of putting Richard Nixon to music. I called Peter and told him that my preference would be a libretto by a real poet. The artifice of verse might lift the story and its characters, so numbingly familiar to us from the news media, out of the ordinary and onto a more archetypal plane. Peter called back, mentioning a classmate of his from his Harvard years. She had not written a great deal of poetry, but he had a hunch that she would be right for the project. In December 1985 Alice Goodman, Peter Sellars, and I met to begin work on *Nixon in China*. Appropriately, we met at the Kennedy Center in Washington, D.C.

We were there because Peter had just been appointed artistic director of the American National Theatre. The appointment of a radical theater director still in his twenties was controversial, the bold decision of Roger Stevens, a multimillionaire businessman and backer of Broadway shows. Stevens had recently hit showbiz gold by investing in the fantastically successful musical *Les Misérables*. He had seen Peter's work and thought that he would shake things up in a positive way at the Kennedy Center, where he was a board member and major donor. In truth, Peter lasted only a few years in Washington. The cultural climate in the nation's capital reflected the Reagans' taste, and the paucity of any really sophisticated audience made it hardly the right place for

Peter's style of theater. But being able to plan the scenario of *Nixon in China* from within the walls of one of the seats of national power was an undeniably subversive pleasure.

Alice Goodman arrived from Cambridge, England, where she had moved after graduating from Harvard. She had used her poetic gift to turn some literal translations of plays into elegant texts for several of Peter's undergraduate productions. Other than what Peter told me about her and a single original poem that I read, there was little in her curriculum vitae that might suggest she could compose an opera libretto. Her knowledge of music was about equal to my knowledge of poetry. But her love of poetry and the depth of her familiarity with everyone from Homer, Shakespeare, and Byron right up to Frank O'Hara and Allen Ginsberg gave me cause to think that her lack of track record would be offset by her high standards and evident enthusiasm for the project. In fact, what Alice ultimately produced went far beyond what is usual in opera. She turned out to have everything one could want in a librettist and then some: a natural feel for rhythms of vernacular American speech, an uncanny ear that embraced everything from the creaking solipsisms of White House speechmakers to the gnomic utterances of Mao Tse-tung. She could move from character to character and from scene to scene, alternating between diplomatic pronouncement, philosophical rumination, raunchy aside, and poignant sentiment. And she did all of this in concise verse couplets, exhibiting a talent and technique that has nearly vanished from American poetical practice.

Nixon's visit to China, itself a carefully staged media event, overflowed with an abundance of themes to pick from. On one level it signified a clash of the titans. Nixon and Mao virtually embodied the twentieth century's great agonistic struggle for human happiness: capitalism versus communism; the market economy versus the social welfare state. The lead characters were so vivid they literally cried out for operatic treatment, and Alice shrewdly caught the essence of each. Nixon's "News" aria, sung on the tarmac as he emerges from Air Force One and greets a long line of identically clad Communist dignitaries, moves from presidential *vanitas* ("when I shook hands with Chou En-lai . . . the whole world was listening"), to political visionary ("simply achieving a great human dream"), to a sudden mood swing in the direction of sour suspicion ("the rats begin to chew the sheets . . ."). Mao's apothegmatic utterances, in part inspired by Alice's careful reading of his own poetry and of course of his famous little red book, stand in stark contrast to the small-town chamber of commerce language of Nixon. In his banquet toast, the effusive president, giddy and flushed with the realization that he's pulled off the diplomatic coup of the decade, goes for the rhetorical gold:

> But let us, in these next five days
> Start a long march on new highways,
> In different lanes, but parallel
> And heading for a single goal.
> The world watches and listens. We
> Must seize the hour and seize the day.

The female roles were every bit as appealing to me as the men's. Pat Nixon, dressed in the traditional First Lady's fire-engine-red coat, is the quintessence of middle-American womanhood, obedient and submissive, bowing to the historical imperative of her husband's ego, assuaging his spontaneous eruptions of paranoia, submerging her own ego in his, and going through the ritual motions of her office while doing her best to conceal the pain that public life has visited upon her. Off camera she sneaks a cigarette and two aspirin to relieve one of her chronic splitting headaches. In a simple and immensely moving soliloquy, Alice allows Pat's fundamentally decent soul to express itself in a vision of the "heartland":

> Let lonely drivers on the road
> Pull over for a bite to eat,
> Let the farmer switch on the light
> Over the porch, let passersby
> Look in at the large family
> Around the table, let them pass.
> Let the expression on the face
> Of the Statue of Liberty

Change just a little, let her see
What lies inland: across the plain
One man is marching—the Unknown
Soldier has risen from his tomb;
Let him be recognized at home.

It was part of Alice's genius to be able to handle images of Americana—so routinely abused in magazine and television advertising—in a way that recaptured their virgin essence, making them, when Pat sings them, not clichés at all but statements of a deeply felt, unconflicted belief.

The explosive antipode to Pat's humility and selflessness was Chiang Ch'ing, Mao's wife and coconspirator, a woman inflated with power and willing to use it to accomplish her agenda of permanent revolution, no matter how many lives might be ruined in the effort. In 1981 her proud, defiant face could be seen everywhere in the media as she stood in the stocks during her trial for using her political influence to foment the Cultural Revolution and bring the entire country almost to a halt in a frenzy of violence and paranoia. Among U.S. radical feminists, Chiang Ch'ing had become a sympathetic figure, a woman who had dared to mess with the male power elite in a Communist state and then, stubbornly unapologetic at her own trial, had been condemned to death for her ambition. The information about her was difficult to sort out. The only widely available book, a suspiciously sensational biography called *The White-Boned Demon* by Ross Terrill, painted her as a political gold digger, a former movie actress who had chained her wagon to the young and enormously charismatic Mao, becoming his girlfriend, accompanying him on the epic Long March, and as age weakened his grip on internecine politics, taking over the controls and pointing the ship of state into the turbulent waters of the Cultural Revolution. Among Peter's first impulses upon conceiving the opera was to stage one of the lurid, agitprop ballets that Madame Mao had sponsored in the hope of creating a new genre of people's art. These ballets, first performed in theaters and then later made into films, usually featured peasants in a victorious struggle against villainous landowners, and they were meant as vehicles to carry the revolutionary message in a form of accessible dance, song, and theater.

On their visit to Peking, the Nixons had been treated to a performance of the most famous of Madame Mao's ballets, *The Red Detachment of Women*. It tells the story of Wu Ching-hua, daughter of a poor peasant, who is chained to a post by a sadistic tyrant from the south. She escapes his evil clutches, almost dies in doing so, and falls under the spell of a handsome Red Army cadre, Hung Chang-ching. From him she learns the virtues of communism and self-sacrifice. The peasants revolt. There is a tropical storm, a fight, revenge, victory. The handsome cadre is wounded and dies, but the young girl takes up his cause and, under the banner of Chairman Mao, she does away with the wicked tyrant and leads her fellow soldiers on to the bliss of proletarian triumph.

Act II of *Nixon in China* climaxes with a surrealist reenactment of this same ballet. The Nixons are seated in an audience to the side, and when the curtain rises they are visibly shocked by the sight of a shapely young peasant girl, dressed in red pajamas, lashed to a stake while a leering and priapic landowner cruelly taunts her with his whip:

> Oh what a day
> I thought I'd die!
> That luscious thigh
> That swelling breast
> Scented and greased,
> A sacrifice
> Running with juice
> At my caress.
> She was so hot
> I was hard-put
> To be polite
> When the first cut
> —Come on you slut!—
> Scored her brown skin
> I started in,
> Man upon hen!

The Nixons are scandalized, especially when Pat begins to notice an alarming likeness between the heavy-breathing tyrant in the play and Secretary of State Kissinger, who is strangely missing from the presidential party. "Doesn't he look like you-know-who!" Pat nervously whispers to Dick.

At the crucial moment in the ballet, Madame Mao unexpectedly appears from behind the audience and starts screaming stage directions at the dancers: "That is your cue! . . . What are you gaping at? Forward, Red Troupe! Annihilate this tyrant and his running dogs!" A whirl of confused activity follows that is brought to a sudden standstill by Madame Mao's grand coloratura aria in B-flat major, "I am the wife of Mao Tse-tung."

In the third and final act, the main characters all appear alone in their bedrooms, each lost in his or her own recollections of the past, enervated, vitiated of strength. They are undressed, both literally and figuratively. Pat and Dick reminisce about the war and their early lives. Mao and Chiang Ch'ing do the same, she singing an erotic aubade while he remains to end the implacable Marxist and philosophical mass murderer:

. . . We recoil
From victory and all its works.
What do you think of that, Karl Marx?

It is left to Chou En-lai, the introvert, the only one of the leaders who appears to have a grasp of the human cost of history, to sing the final elegiac words:

How much of what we did was good?
Everything seems to move beyond
Our remedy. Come, heal this wound.
At this hour nothing can be done.
Just before dawn the birds begin,
The warblers who prefer the dark,
The cage-birds answering. To work!
Outside this room the chill of grace
Lies heavy on the morning grass.

The two-year period I spent composing *Nixon in China* was a steep learning curve, but I reveled in it. I found I loved creating character through my choices of harmony and rhythm. To begin, I asked myself, "What kind of music would best describe the psyche of Richard Nixon?" The answer seemed obvious: white big-band music from the Swing Era. It was the music of my parents, of Winnipesaukee Gardens, and with its admixture of sentimentality and reminiscence it conveyed to me the ideal of Nixon's imagined Middle America. Thus a big band became the nucleus of the orchestral sound for *Nixon in China*, a sound heavy on brass and winds and further padded by the addition of four saxophones. But jazz was only one of many elements in the score. For our reenactment of *The Red Detachment of Women* my goal was to create ballet music that would sound as if it had been composed not by a single composer but by a committee. I'd noticed when watching films of these Chinese Communist ballets that the music, rather than being indigenous Chinese music, faithful to the sources of the stories, had sounded instead like very bad imitations of Russian and French ballet music.

There are moments in the score to *Nixon in China* that are among my favorites of all the music I've ever composed: the landing of Air Force One and Nixon's "News" aria; the banquet toasts and "Cheers" chorus; and the final tender and melancholy minutes of the last act. Something about the story and the characters granted me a sense of freedom to write an American opera, an opera that is rooted in our peculiarly skewed political image of ourselves, an opera that aims to be both theatrically entertaining and psychologically acute. I have seen productions of it that have misunderstood and coarsened its humor, or worse, have made stiff cartoons of its characters. Staging the opera requires enormous subtlety. One can be too easily drawn in by its pageant-like imagery and its all-too-familiar historical characters. Too often directors and singers will yield to the urge to satirize and vamp, ignoring the complexity and ambiguities of its words and music and turning it into a heavy-handed comic strip.

The premiere was in October 1987 at the Houston Grand Opera. The company's young general director, David Gockley, had taken a big risk commissioning a composer who'd never written a note for solo voice much less a full-length opera. A talented cast performed it with grace and humor and was largely responsible for the opera making the impact it did. The roles of Nixon and Chou En-lai were created by two

Boston-area baritones, James Maddelena and Sanford Sylvan, both of whom had been active in local productions of Bach and Handel. They were singers with clear, unforced diction, free of the noxious vocal affectations so typical of operatic singing. And they were also deep and thoughtful actors, able to respond to the enormous subtleties that Peter demanded of their characters.

Carolann Page, a soprano with experience in Broadway as well as in classical music, gave genuine poignancy to Pat Nixon. Her act II soliloquy, "This is prophetic," sung in the late-afternoon winter twilight in front of the Gate of Heavenly Peace, brought shadings of Whitman, Wallace Stevens, and Norman Rockwell together in an image of middle-American peace and plenty.

My vocal writing could strain the limits of even the most talented singer. There was nothing especially wild or shocking about it, but I had a penchant for keeping the voice pinned to a high tessitura for long periods without giving a pause for rest. The writing for Mao was especially cruel, demanding that the tenor stay at maximum altitude bar after bar and phrase after phrase. Nevertheless, tenor John Duykers found a way to make the Chairman's music sound inevitable. My impression of Mao as a self-made media event, an artificially constructed peasant hero, required that he sing much of the time with a voice of Siegfried-like strength.

The orchestration, with its gangbuster brass, soaring saxophones, and Yamaha synthesizer, was burly beyond belief, requiring amplification of the voices in order to be heard above the din coming from the pit. At the time I did not understand the necessity of working closely with a sophisticated sound designer. In Houston, the house sound engineer, unable to read a musical score, operated the mix and amplification from a booth behind a glass window at the back of the hall where he could make no useful judgments whatsoever. As we'd neglected to request supertitles to aid the audience in understanding Alice's poetry, it is unlikely that many listeners gleaned more than a fraction of what was being sung. But just the idea of an opera called *Nixon in China* was enough to galvanize the classical-music community, and people who came from all parts of the country were generally disposed to like the work, regardless of the severe drawbacks of the sound and unintelligibility of the text. The set, designed by Adrienne Lobel, took every advantage of the colors and iconography of Chinese Communist political art. The first act featured a huge pasteboard replica of Air Force One that taxied onstage to the accompaniment of my stuttering brass tattoos and fractured version of "The Star-Spangled Banner." When Jimmy Maddelena stepped out of the door of the plane and waved presidentially to the audience, one of the memorable coups of operatic staging was instantly achieved.

As a backdrop for Madame Mao's blistering act II coloratura aria, Adrienne provided a gigantic portrait of a placid, omniscient Mao. His iconographic face had in its center a small door through which, at a key moment in the final act, John Duykers as Mao himself emerged and descended to the stage—Mao emerging from his very image. Mark Morris choreographed his own take on *The Red Detachment of Women*, a version that was at once extremely funny and, in its fidelity to the original, fastidiously accurate, even down to the young Chinese girl dancers on pointe, brandishing rifles as they salute the Chairman and give chase to the capitalist running dogs.

A convention of the nation's music critics was timed to open in Houston the same week. Our opera, conducted by John DeMain, alternated in the large, newly constructed Worthem Theater with another opera featuring elephants—*Aida*, starring Placido Domingo. The Houston theatergoers cheered both productions loudly, especially the arrival of Air Force One. But I suspect that the melancholy detumescence of our final scene, with its deflated characters all lying on their solitary beds like corpses, may have puzzled and dismayed those Texans who had gathered in a blitz of diamonds, Stetsons, and white ermine for opening night. The critical response was not exactly a slam dunk. *Nixon*, with its verse libretto, Minimalist score, and postmodern choreography, all directed by the young upstart from Boston, had already received an inordinate amount of pretrial publicity, so it was only natural that our cheeky endeavor would get its just deserts from the national press. "That was it? *That* was *Nixon in China*?" began the review in *The New York Times* by the bewildered Donald Henahan. In retrospect, had I been an uninitiated member of the audience on that opening night, I may well have been hard put to give the opera a passing grade. It took many performances and much tweaking of its inner workings to make *Nixon in China* what we'd hoped it would be.

The musical language of *Nixon in China* is difficult to summarize. Perhaps inspired by the primary colors of our American political campaigns and by the garish, oversaturated photos in contemporary Communist publications, I opted for my own version of Technicolor orchestration. The score is emphatically triadic in a way that no other work of mine ever dared to be. At times, the orchestra functions like a giant ukulele underneath the vocal lines, chugging along with its pulses continually tripping up the listener's expectations. This technique worked best in the setting of high-energy monologues like Nixon's first-act "News" aria. Other moments are more patently Minimalist in texture and procedure, and in these—parts of the "Chairman's Library" scene in act I, and the interlude in the storm scene of the act II ballet—the debt to Philip Glass's *Satyagraha* is unmistakable. But I had the good fortune to understand one important thing even at that young age: that a good opera composer needs to be flexible and must learn to make his musical language capable of the slightest shift of mood or psychology on the part of his characters. Modernism, with its obsession for purity and rigor in musical rhetoric, had proven to be a debilitating artistic ground for effective music drama. My natural suspicion of orthodoxy and stylistic rigidity had given me a leg up when it came to writing for the stage.

8.

SINGING TERRORISTS

ixon in China received more than the usual number of performances for a new opera, and the original production moved on to Brooklyn, Amsterdam, Edinburgh, Los Angeles, Paris, and Frankfurt. I watched Peter's vision of the staging grow in depth and subtlety over that time. By the time it reached Los Angeles he had added a deeply affecting image of Chou En-lai's funeral to act III. There was nothing in the libretto that specifically mentioned this, but the tone of the final moments of the opera is grave and suffused with an awareness of mortality. Peter's sudden inspiration was typical of the way his images evolve over time and generate new subtleties and previously undiscovered threads in the narrative.

An original cast recording, conducted by Edo de Waart and made in the old NBC studios in midtown Manhattan during the Brooklyn run, helped to spread the word. The Houston production had also been videotaped for PBS's starchy, self-conscious *Great Performances* series, and in an attempt to make this unfamiliar work more palatable, the nervous PBS producers brought veteran newscaster Walter Cronkite out of retirement to act as host for the nationwide telecast. Later I had a chance to see outtakes of Cronkite's videotaping session that showed him staring intently at the teleprompter as over and over he stumbled on the phrase "coloratura aria." Again and again his tongue wrestled the slippery syllables as the delighted ghost of Madame Mao hovered malignantly over his microphone. Even though the major opera companies of Europe and the United States cast a wary eye on *Nixon*, public awareness of the work exceeded the norm for a serious piece of contemporary music theater. I was written up in *People* magazine, and the opera's title even appeared as an answer in one of the *New York Times* crossword puzzles.

In the spring of the year following the Houston premiere I accepted an invitation to be a resident at the American Academy in Rome. A change of pace and location seemed an excellent idea, and my interest in Roman history had been sparked by a newfound pleasure in the work of Gibbon, whose *Decline and Fall of the Roman Empire*, with its Mozartean perfection of phrase and witty, even droll expository style, made me anxious to see that vast and endlessly surprising city. The two months in Rome were difficult. The children, Sam and Emily, were very small and our living situation with no child care left us little time to absorb even a fraction of what the city had to offer. I was suffering from a bad back injury that made walking difficult. Even so, the Italian ambience had a similar restorative and creative effect on us then as it had on me twelve years earlier when I visited Florence.

While still in Rome I received an unexpected telegram. It was an invitation to attend the Third International Music Festival for Humanism, Peace and Friendship Among Nations to be held in two weeks in Leningrad. The telegram was signed by the president in charge of the Soviet Composers Union, Alexander Tchaikovsky, a name that hinted he might possibly be Russian. The telegram gave no information other than that I should appear at the Soviet Aeroflot offices in Rome to pick up my ticket. A few phone calls to New York revealed that I had been invited to this huge international festival of orchestra music to represent the United States along with John Cage (who had accepted) and Elliott Carter (who had declined). After a ridiculous comedy of errors trying to obtain a Soviet visa from their embassy in Rome, I picked up my ticket at the last moment and found myself on a Soviet jet heading toward Moscow, where I would transfer to a domestic flight to

Leningrad. In the Leningrad hotel I found composers from a staggering number of countries, among them Outer Mongolia, Laos, Japan,
Nicaragua, Chile, Italy, East Germany, and the Baltics. I was informed
that the Lithuanian State Philharmonic Orchestra would play my *Harmonielehre*. The eerie Leningrad Hotel was a Westerners-only hotel,
straight out of John le Carré, set off on a peninsula apart from the rest
of the city. Local Soviet composers that I met and invited back for a
drink would decline to come in, or if they did, they would sit anxiously in the lobby, their eyes furtively looking around to see if they
were being spied upon. The hotel's cash-only bar accepted only foreign
currency, its cavernous dining hall seemed never to be open, and one
very lonely and melancholy young Russian woman with a distracted
look on her face roamed the halls late at night, looking like a specter.

The Soviet Composers Union had huge resources and considerable
power within the Eastern bloc. All of these Soviet countries would be
well represented, although, sadly, the chosen composers were more often than not the top bureaucrats in each delegation. So in the course of
five days and nights of concerts, I heard a great deal of official symphonic music, some of it rivaling *The Red Detachment of Women* for
pompous bluster and stylistic confusion.

Several old-time European Communists were given an especially
warm reception, chief among them Luigi Nono, the Italian serialist
composer and contemporary of Berio and Boulez. Nono may have
been a Socialist in his political life, but his music was not in the least
condescending to the masses, adamantly maintaining its avant-garde
pedigree and commitment to post-Webernian compositional principles. The Soviet composers welcomed him largely because he'd been
coming to Russia for many years, even during the bad old days of the
cold war. In his mid-sixties, tall, with an elegant profile and sweeping
forehead, he looked handsome and patrician, a far cry from the Bol-
shevik model of people's artist that I'd always had in mind when I
thought of Socialist art.

During the weeklong festival, John Cage befriended me, and we
ended every night with the guilty pleasures of a bottle of the local
vodka, draining it in a corner of the vast lobby of the Leningrad Hotel.
Upon arrival in Leningrad, John had been greeted by the younger generation of composers as a long-awaited hero. The deep split in Soviet

musical life, between the party-line official composers and the suppressed experimentalists who followed the latest trends in the West, became obvious as soon as Cage arrived. One hot, stuffy evening we were taken to the official headquarters of the Composers Union, a large, elegant house that surely must have dated from before the Revolution. There, hungry and thirsty, we sat shoulder to shoulder through an interminable symposium on contemporary music. Cage was the celebrity. It was clear that the composers wanted him to act the role of Perfect Fool, and to prepare for this they had placed placards with Dadaist questions all around the large room, and they called upon John to give Zen-like answers to each one. Next to me sat my translator, a tired young Russian woman with thick glasses who struggled to make sense out of something that was already senseless. We had just sat through an exceptionally long concert, including a dreary symphony by an Italian Marxist—Symphony No. 3 "Lenin," it was called—and Cage was extremely fatigued, but he courteously played the part expected of him, answering each absurd question ("If a tone sounds alone in the air and no one is there to hear it, is it music?") patiently and with whatever gentle wit he could still summon. I would lean over to my exhausted translator and beseech her for a translation of some Russian phrase I'd just heard. She would twitch uncomfortably, shrug her shoulders, and mutter, "Mmmm . . . too deeeficult to explain."

I hoped that Cage would no longer be in town by the night *Harmonielehre* was performed because we'd become good friends, and I knew that my explosive, pounding triads and throbbing climaxes would most certainly discomfit him. The performance turned out to be surreal, taking place in that same Great Hall of the St. Petersburg Philharmonic where Shostakovich and Prokofiev had witnessed the premieres of so many of their symphonies. With its ivory-and-white Corinthian columns and elegant plush red seats, the hall possesses one of the most volatile acoustics for symphonic music anywhere in the world. The loud passages of *Harmonielehre* were like heavy metal, rattling the floor and making the curtains shudder. No wonder the Communist Party took a Shostakovich premiere seriously and monitored the potential political repercussions of his thunderous endings. One cannot sit calmly and indifferently in that hall while powerfully emotional music is being performed.

The Lithuanian orchestra had learned my difficult piece bar by bar. No tape or compact disc had reached the conductor, Juozas Domarkas, so he had only the printed score to work from. In the Soviet world, the Moscow and Leningrad orchestras appropriated all the good instruments—strings, brass, or winds. Orchestras in the satellite countries like Lithuania got the bottom of the barrel—cheap and coarsely made violins and trumpets that in United States not even a school band would put up with. Nevertheless the sound this Lithuanian orchestra produced was terrifyingly loud. Their manner of playing was to wildly exaggerate dynamic differences, especially fortes. All the details came across as amped to the max, as if each and every one of my phrases ended with four exclamation points. But there was an unmistakable feeling of commitment in their playing. It was passionate and powerful. One simply could not be in Russia without being swept away in the waves of emotion that greeted live music. Even in those optimistic days of perestroika and the incipient collapse of the Soviet system, life for these people was drab and cut through with pessimism and failed hopes. The exchange of music, no matter how official the sponsorship, was heartfelt, and to be a part of it was unforgettable.

n a twelve-month period not long after the completion of *Nixon in China* I wrote two orchestral works that couldn't have been more different in mood and intent, *Fearful Symmetries* and *The Wound-Dresser*. Begun during my stay in Rome, *Fearful Symmetries* was a thirty-minute industrial-strength boogie scored for essentially the same instrumentation that I'd invented for *Nixon in China*, including a quartet of saxophones, a double manual synthesizer, and, something new in 1989, a keyboard sampler that played raunchy, garish samples of pop percussion sounds. The title phrase comes from the poem "The Tyger" by William Blake. It was not so much the content of Blake's poem that stirred me but rather the key phrase, "fearful symmetries," that I was drawn to. As I worked on the piece, I found that ideas were coming to me in almost maddeningly symmetrical packages of four-, eight-, and sixteen-bar harmonic units. This was not far removed from the back-and-forth harmonic alternations of "On the Dominant Divide," the final movement of *Grand Pianola Music*. Rather than try to deconstruct the obviousness of these harmonic structures, I did the opposite: I amplified their predictability and in so doing ended up composing an insistent pulse-driven juggernaut of a piece that has continued to prove useful to scores of choreographers and dancers.

The Wound-Dresser began as a plan to set prose cameos from Walt Whitman's account of his Civil War days in *Specimen Days*. In a Berkeley bookstore I'd found an edition of the Whitman book that included graphic and disturbing photographs of Confederate and Union field hospitals, wounded soldiers, and the long rows of cots filled with the broken bodies of young men lying in stunned stillness. These images, along with the gentle homoeroticism of Whitman's texts, made me think of the stories I heard from San Francisco friends, many of them gay, who had lost partners and loved ones to the plague of AIDS that, in 1989, was still devastating the country.

As I began to work seriously with the Whitman texts I found myself plunged into the memory of a more personal story, that of the long, slow decline of my father from Alzheimer's disease. My first indication that something was wrong with him came on a trip home around 1983. He'd met me at Logan Airport in Boston, and upon going back to the parking garage he couldn't remember where he had parked the car. This was disturbingly out of character for him, as he was the kind of orderly man who took pride in his attention to details. I began to receive letters and phone calls from my mother, who described alarming quirks and attempts at deception on his part. He would try to cover for a new memory lapse by pretending that he was "just seeing if she was paying attention." Not long afterward a neurologist gave her the diagnosis of Alzheimer's, and although it was what my mother had surmised, upon hearing the awful news, she began to convince herself that it was in fact a misdiagnosis. "He's done two packs a day for all his adult life, and I think he's just lost some brain cells to all that smoke," she said at one point.

But the reality was unavoidable. Over the next four years he slipped into that oft-documented netherworld of mental confusion and physical deterioration. My mother was heroic in caring for him. She had no siblings who were willing or able to help her. Even her few close friends in Concord shied away. The changes wrought by this disease that attacks the personality are so alarming and devastating that even the closest family can find it unbearable to witness. Phone conversations with my father became surreal as he lost his control of speech. What had once been soft, wry, loving quips of Yankee wit was now a choked bleating into the phone, like a wounded animal. I was afraid to return home to New Hampshire. I had an atavistic terror of having to see him naked or of having to clean his soiled sheets or underwear. When I did summon the resolve to fly back home I took three-year-old Emily with me, perhaps in the hopes of shielding me from the horror of his condition, perhaps just as a living reminder of youth and health and wholeness.

On one of those rare, suffocating New England summer days in August 1987 I turned the rented car into the yard of the house where I'd grown up. My mother greeted us emotionally, and then I saw Carl, emerging slowly from behind the kitchen screen door, the muscles of his face now loose and slack and his legs and arms wobbling in that strange puppet-on-a-string dance common to Alzheimer's sufferers. He had tears in his eyes, so overwhelmed was he at the sight of his son and little granddaughter. But the attempt to communicate was foiled by his clouded brain, and the best he could do was emit little inchoate squeaks of gratitude. In the middle of the night I heard my mother yelling at him in desperation. The next morning she told me that he had fallen out of bed. The drug prescribed to keep him from having violent physical movements was so potent that it rendered him an inert mass on the floor.

Elinore Adams performed the ultimate act of caritas by caring for this man whom she had loved since the day they met fifty years earlier on the floor of her stepfather's dance hall. "The thirty-six-hour day," a phrase familiar to spouses of Alzheimer's sufferers, proved to be all too true an expression. Not long after my visit, without warning to either my sister or me, she abruptly sold the house and drove my father to Florida where, with the help of a friend, she bought a small house in a retirement community. Carl Adams died the following year. I saw him a few days before as he lay in the hospital bed, comatose, thin, and sallow, almost unrecognizable with his false teeth removed. All I could find comfort in were his hands, which still bore the vestigial bumps and calluses from his years of driving around New England and from playing the clarinet.

When I came to write my Whitman piece I kept thinking about my mother's struggle and the devotion with which she nursed him. Instead of setting *Specimen Days*, I chose "The Wound-Dresser," a poem that is both graphic and tender, perhaps the most intimate recollection of what Whitman experienced in his years of selfless work as a nurse and caregiver in the hospitals that surrounded wartime Washington.

．　．　．

ven before *Nixon in China* had premiered Peter Sellars proposed another idea for an opera, this also with its story from recent history. He mentioned to Alice Goodman and me an event from 1985 that had drawn the world's attention to the Middle East in a particularly lurid way. An Italian cruise liner, the *Achille Lauro*, carrying a group of European and American tourists, had been hijacked off the coast of Egypt by a small group of Palestinian men who had boarded the ship carrying false passports and concealed weapons. Their plan to gain entry to Israel and win the freedom of some fifty fellow Palestinians held in Israeli jails had been ruined when one of the ship's maids saw their rifles, and the ensuing hijacking was resolved only after rounds of tense negotiations at the highest levels of international politics. Only then was it discovered that, contrary to what everyone had believed was a peaceful ending to the crisis, a single passenger, a retired handicapped American named Leon Klinghoffer, had been executed, shot in the head and his body thrown overboard in his wheelchair. Peter, whose first impulse was to call this nascent opera *Klinghoffers Tod*, saw in the story a powerful drama that touched on a host of issues and assumptions that permeated our American way of taking in the news and responding to its images. I knew that this subject would inevitably be a hot potato and likely draw us into any number of heated controversies with all sides of the Middle East conflict. But I found myself instantly drawn to the story, principally because the murder of this man, Leon Klinghoffer, possessed a strange, almost biblical feeling. On the one hand, having come to our attention through the strident medium of television, it had the nervous, highly charged immediacy of a fast-moving media event. On the other, the man's murder, played out against a background of impassioned claims of Jews and Palestinians alike, touched a nerve that went deep into the body politic of our lives as comfortable, self-satisfied Americans.

Alice, Peter, and I talked about it and agreed to begin research and collect material, knowing that we were treading on very dangerous ground. Of the three of us, I probably knew the least about the Middle East, and I had the daunting task of educating myself in the history of the Israeli-Palestinian conflict, the roots of Zionism, the Balfour Declaration, and the long history of British, French, and American meddling in the complex demographics of that region. I reread the Old Testament for the first time since I was a teenager and found myself alternating between enchantment and alarm. Just as I was embarking on my course of study, Robert Alter and Frank Kermode's important scholarly work *The Literary Guide to the Bible* was published, a book that helped redirect some of my readings of Old Testament texts. I read some of the Koran but found it difficult going, and in retrospect I would have done better to find someone well versed in its tradition to guide me through it. I read several books by Noam Chomsky, but I found this philosopher turned activist implacably one-sided. His Manichean explanation for all the problems on the planet never failed to lay the blame on American greed and power-mongering. Chomsky would not, probably *could* not, acknowledge a single example of right action or right attitude on the part of America or Israel. To him they were always rogues, and on the world stage they never failed to play dirty.

The work of the Palestinian American literary scholar and social critic Edward Said sounded a more reasonable note, but I could sense in Said's writings the deep, inconsolable melancholy of an expatriate who knew he would never see his native land whole again. Perhaps the only "visible" Palestinian in the United States with a deep knowledge of American culture and the ability to make an eloquent defense of his people, Said had spent a lifetime futilely trying to gain an adequate podium from which to make his case in the most powerful national media. Another voice of intelligence and reason was Rabbi Michael Lerner, editor of *Tikkun* magazine, whose essays and dialogues spoke for what I gleaned was the American liberal slant on Jewish issues. Reading these and similarly educated authorities was enlightening, but I would soon learn that the Israeli-Palestinian issue was the most carefully controlled and fastidiously managed debate in American political life. Organizational watchdogs and lobbies like the American Israel Public Affairs Committee (AIPAC) and the Simon Wiesenthal Center, although they preached tolerance in the public dialogue, monitored the dissemination of information and opinion about Arab-Israeli affairs, and their considerable clout in Washington often smothered attempts from the other side to gain a hearing on American television and other media.

Work on the new opera proved difficult from the start. Neither Alice Goodman nor I could fall back on the vernacular wit or dramatic irony that had given us so much pleasure in *Nixon*. She made a unilateral decision not to compose the libretto from start to finish, but rather to write all the choruses first, a choice that left me waiting months for her to fill in the narrative. We started with much too grand a plan. The first inspiration was an opera in two parts with a prologue. The first part would reenact the hijacking and the murder of Leon Klinghoffer. Part two would be devoted to the world's response to the event and would include the last-minute appearance of the U.S. Air Force, whose jets, choreographed from Washington by Oliver North, diverted the plane taking the four hijackers to sanctuary in Algiers and forced it to land at an American air base in Sicily. This second half would feature politicians like Ronald Reagan, Margaret Thatcher, Yasser Arafat, and others, all trying to score political points off the tragic outcome of the hijacking. It was hard not to imagine such a second act being a dark comedy.

But when Alice delivered two choruses to begin the opera, one for the exiled Palestinians and one for the exiled Jews, the entire shape of the opera immediately changed for me. The depth of feeling in these choruses was suffused with the exile's longing for home and the pain that memory evokes. In the case of the Palestinian chorus, there was in her text an implied crescendo of rage as the imagery grew in intensity, culminating with the violent oath:

Let the supplanter look
Upon his work. Our faith
Will take the stones he broke
And break his teeth.

Ultimately our opera dealt only with the *Achille Lauro* hijacking and the murder of Leon Klinghoffer. Peter had as usual found an enormous wealth of factual information. Most valuable of all was a book written by the Italian captain of the hijacked ship, Gerardo de Rosa. His book was available only in the Italian original, and a translator had to render it into English for us. From this personal account Alice created a long verse narrative, the nautical imagery of which reminded me of Joseph Conrad's moody ruminations on fate and mortality. Interspersed with the hijacking story were seven choruses. Six of these came in pairs of opposites: a chorus for each of the two exiled peoples, Palestinians and Jews; an Ocean chorus and a Desert chorus; a Night chorus and a Day chorus. The seventh chorus, which opens the second act, relates the story of Hagar and the Angel, and thus within it contains its own duality, embodying the myth of the birth of both the Jewish and Arab peoples.

The dramatic structure reflected my initial impulse about the story. It was as up-to-date as this morning's news, yet it also was tethered to mythic moorings as old as recorded history. The mixture of reflective choruses and faster-paced narrative suggested the Bach Passions. I would not go so far as to compare my Leon Klinghoffer with Bach's Jesus, but I did think that Klinghoffer's murder was carried out not because of who he was as an individual but rather because of what he represented to his killers: a bourgeois American and a Jew. Nevertheless, one had to wonder why, of all the passengers on the ship, this seventy-year-old man in a wheelchair was the one chosen to be sacrificed. Had Klinghoffer, possibly believing his handicap would protect him from violence, spoken his mind too openly to his abductors, saying something that the other passengers might not have dared articulate?

I spent two years working on the opera: first sketching it at the piano; then, utilizing for the first time the new computer-controlled MIDI technology, making a synthesizer mock-up of the imagined orchestration; then doing a rough piano/vocal draft; and finally the fully orchestrated score. The musical language was far removed from the bright, triadic palette of *Nixon*. In *The Death of Klinghoffer* meditative passages in relatively stable harmonic areas suddenly explode with violent eruptions of dissonance. I never attempted to incorporate Middle

Eastern scales, but the flowing arabesques of the melodies were without a doubt influenced by traditions from Semitic cultures.

B y the time I finished, on February 12, 1991, Saddam Hussein, until recently an ally of ours, had been chased out of Kuwait, and the first Palestinian intifada had come to a raging boil. Radical Islamic fundamentalism, founded on a seething hatred of Western intrusion into the culture and economies of the Middle East, was taking root from Morocco to Bali. I was no different than most Americans in being appalled and frightened by terrorism, but I also found myself asking why the mainstream American media inevitably presented the Palestinians as delusional and self-defeating, unfailingly committed to nihilistic violence. Everyone seemed to enjoy repeating the oft-quoted remark of Abba Eban that "the Palestinians never fail to miss an opportunity to miss an opportunity." America's staunch support of Israel was the gold standard of a determined moral staying power in a world otherwise full of cynical Realpolitik. What I read about Israel and heard from Israeli friends was largely inspiring. I liked the fact that the Knesset was a big, fractious chamber of wildly diverse factions not unlike a noisy, contentious family with all sorts of opinionated in-laws. I thought the Israeli kibbutz tradition of community welfare and social responsibility was something we Americans could learn a lot from. And Israel's pluck and determination to survive during its early years when it could not be certain of American support was surely a story of grit and courage.

One might ask why I, an American non-Jew living in California, far from the Middle East, would be concerned about the Israeli-Palestinian issue when the world was already so full of troubles. The answer is that for American goyim the Jewish experience, the Holocaust, and the founding of Israel have become a tale of exemplary moral history, one of suffering, heroism, and redemption. Through constant exposure by means of films, books, plays, music, and mass media, Jewish culture and Jewish history have gained a position of special meaning, even of special privilege, in American life. Their suffering and courage have granted the Jews a unique moral status. But with this special status comes a problem: Israeli behavior on the world stage is off limits to criticism, at least in the United States. No American politician can hope to win a campaign if he or she does not speak the received wisdom about Palestinian "terrorism" versus Israeli "security." For all the public hand-wringing over the Middle East crisis, the major U.S. media barely ever acknowledge the lamentable fact that Israel has pushed the Palestinians into the most arid and least productive corners of the land. No one can acknowledge without being labeled anti-Semitic that, as members of a democracy, Israelis nevertheless live according to a constitution that gives special status to one religious and ethnic group at the expense of another. The unspoken rules of the public dialogue forbid us to acknowledge the fact that terrorism as practiced by the Palestinians is, as the historian Stanley Hoffmann describes it, "the weapon of the weak in a classic conflict among states or within a state."

I was puzzled and eventually infuriated by how the Middle East was presented to the average American who reads a newspaper or watches television. As the world's most flagrant energy consumers, the United States continued to suck the teat of the oil-rich nations, cynically indifferent to who exactly was accepting our cash so long as the barrels kept rolling and the oil kept flowing. If Iran had a popular Islamic revolution, as it did in 1979, we'd put them on our enemy list and back our good friend Saddam Hussein in the ensuing war. If either Iran or Iraq had ambitions to develop nuclear capacity we'd roundly condemn them and threaten them with embargos or, failing that, a military invasion. But we could never seem to answer them truthfully when they asked why they were forbidden a nuclear arsenal while Israel could maintain one. No wonder we appeared to the average Muslim as irrational and capricious and thoroughly dishonest. I felt that journalists, lobbyists, and many intellectuals in the United States were too ready to invoke the Holocaust and charges of anti-Semitism to short-circuit the debate about the Palestinian question. The pro-Israeli lobbies like AIPAC had a huge influence on members of Congress and were heavily funded while Palestinians, vastly underrepresented in the United States, were forever scolded or ridiculed for their violence and self-defeating refusal to accept what Israel deemed right to offer. I thought it was a noble thing for Americans to show solidarity with the Jews of the world, but Israel's behavior, its appropriation of the choicest land and water rights, its discrimination against non-Jews within its borders, and its deeply provocative settlements in Gaza and the West Bank all struck me as arrogant and ultimately destructive to the cause of peace.

In Alice Goodman's libretto Rambo, the loudmouth bully terrorist, mocks Leon Klinghoffer, saying, "America is one big Jew!" His words are disgusting, but is that not precisely how so many hopeless and disenfranchised poor in the Middle East feel about us?

The Death of Klinghoffer premiered in March 1991 in Brussels at the Théâtre Royal de la Monnaie. A large consortium of companies was involved in the production: the Brooklyn Academy of Music, the Glyndebourne Festival, the Los Angeles Opera, the San Francisco Opera, and the Lyon Operal, along with the Monnaie. The central figure in making this very complicated business arrangement was Gérard Mortier, the general director at the Monnaie. He would soon move on to shake up the Salzburg Festival, then to Paris as director of the Bastille Opera, and eventually became general manager of the New York City Opera. Mortier was a highly cultivated and artistically sensitive Belgian who, having been educated as a Jesuit, had a passion for the arts that was superseded only by his love of media attention. I am sure that he did not lend his intelligence and prestige to our *Klinghoffer* project out of a desire to provoke a scandal. He already had an enormous regard and deep personal affection for both Peter Sellars and Mark Morris, and he had been instrumental in bringing Peter's highly controversial Mozart productions to Europe. *Nixon in China* he regarded as a cartoon, but he seems to have had enough confidence in its creative team to make the six-company coproduction plan for our second opera a reality.

I arrived in Brussels with a badly injured right shoulder, the result of too many months of feverish work on the orchestration. On the second day of rehearsals I tripped and fell into the orchestra pit, further exacerbating the pain. My hotel was upstairs above a fishmonger's shop, and every morning on the way to rehearsal I would pass by the front window and see the owner slitting the bellies of shiny black eels and tossing them into a bucket, an image I tried not to take too symbolically. I spent countless hours trying to tame the complicated array of synthesizers and samplers that I had included in my orchestration. The resulting sound gave the *Klinghoffer* orchestra a completely unique color, but getting the bulky keyboards and temperamental electronic modules to behave reliably was infuriating. The conductor, Kent Nagano, spent countless hours patiently prodding the uncertain Belgian orchestra and chorus through my difficult score. European orchestras were familiar with their own contemporary music, much of it of the stop-start, rhythmically disjunct kind. But they found my long, pulse-driven structures extremely difficult to maintain. The Monnaie chorus had such difficulty with the final scene that some of the singers had to scribble mnemonics on their hands to remember the metric changes.

The Brussels *Klinghoffer* production was as different from *Nixon in China* as it could possibly be, substituting the latter's user-friendly Americanisms with a theatrical atmosphere of almost religious intensity. Composing it, I had imagined a ship's deck with images of the sea as a background to the captain's ruminations and to the long, predawn confession of the young Palestinian, Mamoud, who had formed a bond with him. Instead of having a ship, Peter asked the Russian-born designer George Tsypin to create a huge steel tower of planks and girders that thrust some forty feet up from the stage floor. It was built and lit so that the audience could see straight through its four floors. With gangplanks and metal staircases it could look like the interior of a large ocean vessel. But it was nonspecific enough in design to also suggest a mosque, a synagogue, a prison, or a fortress. The stage action, including the violent hijacking scene, was largely carried out on the remaining floor space, empty of props or furniture. No one was dressed either as a terrorist or as a pleasure-seeking tourist. Given that we had doubled up on some of the roles—the same singer would play an Italian ship's officer and then later be one of the terrorists—this non-specificity of costuming left the audience frequently puzzled as to who was impersonating which character. Added to this was the gender confusion (nothing new in opera, of course) of having the role of the youngest hijacker, Omar, sung by a female mezzo, Stephanie Friedman, the same mezzo who had earlier in the opera sung the role of a Jewish housewife from New Jersey.

Leon Klinghoffer, however, was unmistakable in his wheelchair. Sanford Sylvan, with his voice of intense lyricism and deep, dark colorations, gave the title role a real personality. Alice wanted to invest his character with more shading than the media accounts had routinely provided. Already two made-for-television movies about the event had featured a Leon Klinghoffer of pretty much spotless moral attributes, brave and defiant in the face of his abductors and loving to his cherished wife. One, *The Hijacking of the Achille Lauro*, released in 1989, starred Karl Malden. A year later came a second, *Voyage of Terror: The Achille Lauro Affair*, with Burt Lancaster.

Amazingly enough, our Leon Klinghoffer does not sing a note until well into the second and final act. But when he does, he voices both the indignant rage of an innocent hostage as well as letting slip some of the typical condescension that Americans, Jews and Christians alike, hold about Arabs and Palestinians:

We're human. We are
The kind of people
You like to kill.
Was it your pal
Who shot that little girl
At the airport in Rome?
You would have done the same.
There's so much anger in you.
And hate. I know how
Children in the Promised Land
Learn to sleep underground
Because of your shelling.
Old men at the Wailing
Wall get a knife
In the back. You laugh.
You pour gasoline
Over women
Passengers on
The bus to Tel Aviv
And burn them alive.
You don't give a shit,
Excuse me, about
Your grandfather's hut,
His sheep and his goat,

And the land he wore out.
You just want to see
People die.

The four hijackers were young Palestinians who had sneaked onto the *Achille Lauro* carrying false Norwegian passports and concealed rifles, a testament to the congenial screening methods of Italian customs agents. The master plan, designed by Muhammad Zaidan, whose nom de guerre was Abu Abbas, called for the four men to remain on board undetected until the ship reached the Israeli port of Ashdod, where they were to disembark and seize Israelis to exchange for Palestinians in Israeli jails. Almost immediately the plan went awry. A maid walked into their stateroom while the four were cleaning their rifles, their cover was blown, and they were forced to hijack the ship, demanding that the captain take them to the Syrian port of Tartus. The hijacking became headline news around the world almost instantaneously. Syria refused them sanctuary. For several days, under a broiling Mediterranean sun, the ship wandered aimlessly on the high seas while the hijackers, frustrated and feeling increasingly abandoned by their sponsors, warned that they would begin systematically executing the passengers. During the tensest phase of the negotiations, Leon Klinghoffer was wheeled off to a remote part of the ship, shot in the forehead, and dumped into the ocean. About the decision to kill Klinghoffer, Abu Abbas later said in an interview with *The Boston Globe*, "He created troubles. He was handicapped, but he was inciting and provoking the other passengers. So the decision was made to kill him."

The news of Klinghoffer's murder was not conveyed to the outside world until after the hijacking. Nor did Klinghoffer's wife, Marilyn, suspect that anything amiss had happened. When the ship safely docked in Port Said it was the captain's difficult duty to inform her of her husband's murder.

The opera ends with the anguishing moment when Marilyn Klinghoffer hears this terrible news, made even more awful by the fact that she had arrived in the captain's quarters full of relief and joy at the thought of being reunited with her husband. What follows is a final aria for her, an outburst moving from rage to grief and ultimately to a bitter regret that it was not she who had been killed.

If a hundred
People were murdered
And their blood
Flowed in the wake
Of this ship like
Oil, only then
Would the world intervene.
They should have killed me.
I wanted to die.

The premiere, on March 20, 1991, attracted an inordinate amount of attention, perhaps in part because of the opera's theme and the fact that the Gulf War was still in its final phase. John Rockwell, covering the event for *The New York Times*, remarked that the "audience was overflowing with critics—they filled the foyer for an intermission reception, glowering at one another suspiciously—from seemingly every corner of the Western world and, perhaps, the Middle Eastern world as well." The response to the Brussels production was neither wildly effusive nor vehemently negative. If any in the audience had expected a graphic stage rendering of a hijacking and the execution of an innocent American Jew in a wheelchair, they were surely let down. The production was highly symbolic. Peter had so thoroughly integrated the dancers of Mark Morris's company into the stage action that at times it was difficult for a first-time viewer to know which body on-stage represented which person. Nevertheless there were moments of overwhelming beauty, as when Leon Klinghoffer's body is slowly wrapped in a long, canvas shroud and gently drawn away to the gymnopedie of the "Aria of the Falling Body." Another unforgettable scene was Mark's choreographic narrative of the legend of Hagar and the Angel, which opens act II and for which I composed a chorus in the dry-bones, matter-of-fact style of an Old Testament story.

The production went to Lyon a month later, where it played not in the magnificent opera house of that city, which was unfortunately undergoing reconstruction, but in a hideous, multifunction *maison de culture* with dreadful acoustics and located way off on the outskirts of the city. But the climate for *The Death of Klinghoffer* changed abruptly when the opera reached the United States in the Brooklyn Academy of

Music performances the following September. Even before opening night there were indications that it was going to get a difficult reception. An opera that took as its theme a recent event still burned into the public's memory was liable itself to get singed by current events, and so it was. Only a month before opening night, Brooklyn had suffered through a bitter racial and religious controversy when a car in the entourage of Rebbe Menachem Mendel Schneerson ran a red light and killed a seven-year-old African American boy, thereby causing a race riot and the eventual murder of a visiting Jewish rabbinical student, Yankel Rosenbaum. Emotions were high. I must have been out of my mind to think that an opera that opened with a "Chorus of Exiled Palestinians" would be received in Brooklyn with placid equanimity. No matter that the "Chorus of Exiled Jews" was to my mind every bit as deeply felt. The opening lines of the opera, sung by the exiled Palestinians—

My father's house was razed
In nineteen forty-eight
When the Israelis passed
Over our street

—were received by more than a few in the audience as a slap in the face. The following scene, one that featured a fictitious Jewish family in New Jersey—Harry and Alma Rumour and their son, Jonathan—only magnified this anger. Harry, a Reagan Republican, sits in his easy chair, watching the news while Alma, stylish and fifty-something with liberal views, fusses with lunch preparations while chiding their son and occasionally sneaking a glance at the TV. "Reagan? That asshole?" she comments acidly. The Rumours know the Klinghoffers and mention the fact that their friends are about to undertake the same kind of Mediterranean cruise that they themselves had taken last season.

The Klinghoffers
Will never manage all the stairs.
Those little ladders! Marilyn
Is so brave. She's a saint.

There is a premonition amid this comic scene. Suddenly, in the middle of all the banter, Alma's expression turns troubled as she looks at a headline in Harry's newspaper: she's seen something, perhaps an item about a terrorist act. "They're vile!" she says. "Who's vile?" asks her son. Harry mocks her:

> Just about everyone.
> This time I think she's got a bone
> To pick with Arafat.

Many in the Brooklyn audience were offended by the Rumour scene. Both Jewish and non-Jewish listeners experienced it as a back-handed slap at the Klinghoffer family, especially given its artificially bubbly sitcom music. Some even suggested that the humor of both text and music revealed an only thinly disguised anti-Semitic agenda on our part. Certainly the inclusion of the Rumour scene proved destructive to what followed next. By the time the Rumour scene gave way to the following "Chorus of Exiled Jews" all emotional power had been compromised. For some in the audience, it was impossible to recover.

After the Brooklyn performances I deleted the scene from the prologue. In truth I was glad to see it go. I had no problem defending other ostensibly "offensive" lines in the opera such as Rambo's "America is one big Jew" or Molqi's

> We are soldiers
> Fighting a war
> We are not criminals
> And we are not vandals
> But men of ideals.

As brutal and hard to hear as these lines may be, they would be true expressions of the feelings of the characters that sing them. But the comedy of the Rumour family now seems in retrospect to be inappropriate and served only to obscure the seriousness of the rest of the opera.

The Death of Klinghoffer remains a flashpoint of bitter contention

Elinore Coolidge with the Ross Cole Band, circa 1934

Carl Adams (seated, third from left), Winnipesaukee Gardens, circa 1935

LEFT Young composer in New Hampshire snow, 1959

BELOW The "white hat" portrait, made for first LP recording of *Shaker Loops*, with San Francisco city lights in the background, 1980
(Photograph by Mark Drury)

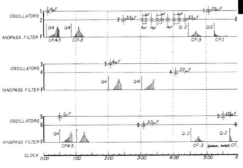

LEFT A score from the faulty wiring era for homemade electronic circuits, 1975

LEFT Harmonic progression mapped out in advance of composing "Negative Love" movement of *Harmonium*, 1981

BELOW With Carl Adams, who didn't really know Charles Ives, but would have liked to, 1983

(Photograph by Deborah O'Grady)

LEFT In rehearsal with Los Angeles Philharmonic, Royce Hall, 1989

(Photograph by Betty Freeman)

With composer Conlon Nancarrow during one of Nancarrow's rare visits outside Mexico. Beverly Hills, 1982 (Photograph by Betty Freeman)

With Peter Sellars, stage director and collaborator for *Nixon in China, The Death of Klinghoffer, El Niño, Doctor Atomic,* and other works (Photograph by Betty Freeman)

RIGHT "I am the wife of Mao Tse-tung." Trudy Ellen Craney, coloratura, at the Brooklyn Academy of Music production of *Nixon in China*, December 1987 (Photograph by Martha Swope)

BELOW Molqi (Thomas Randle), an *Achille Lauro* hijacker, is led off in handcuffs by Egyptian police in Penny Woolcock's 2003 film of *The Death of Klinghoffer*.

BOTTOM The plutonium sphere hangs menacingly over the stage action of *Doctor Atomic*, 2005. Gerald Finley sings and acts the role of the complex genius, J. Robert Oppenheimer. (Photograph by Terrance McCarthy)

JOHN ADAMS EL NIÑO
Lorraine Hunt Lieberson   Dawn Upshaw   Willard White
Conducted by Kent Nagano

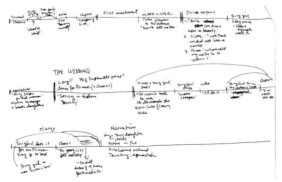

LEFT *A Flowering Tree*: Kumudha (Jessica Rivera) is surrounded by three Javanese dancers (Eko Supriyanto, Rusini Sidi [behind the mask], and Astri Kusama Wardani). Berlin, 2006 (Photograph by Andreas Knapp)

BELOW A family self-portrait: Emily, John Adams, Debbie, and Sam. Berkeley, California, 2004

RIGHT With violinist Tracy Silverman and composer Terry Riley. *The Dharma at Big Sur*, written for Silverman's electric violin, pays homage to Riley. Santa Cruz, California, 2005

(Photograph by Deborah O'Grady)

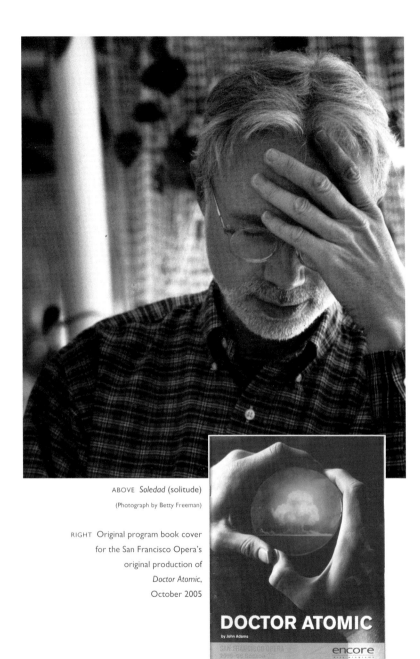

ABOVE *Soledad* (solitude)
(Photograph by Betty Freeman)

RIGHT Original program book cover
for the San Francisco Opera's
original production of
Doctor Atomic,
October 2005

and shows little sign of losing its power to provoke. New productions—and there have been many outside the United States—are almost routinely condemned by Jewish information groups. On some occasions performances have even been picketed, as were those in San Francisco in 1992. Fourteen years after the premiere, a rabbi at the Simon Wiesenthal Center, Abraham Cooper, condemned the Edinburgh International Festival's 2005 production, saying, "I would hope the people of Edinburgh would respond appropriately by allowing these moral midgets to do their opera to an empty house." When asked, he admitted to a BBC interviewer that he had never seen the opera but had only read extracts.

Of the reviewers who have written favorably of the opera, many have praised its "evenhandedness," a characterization that puzzles me. Such a judgment seems irrelevant. I didn't start out with the idea of being evenhanded, and I suspect that neither did Alice Goodman. How can one say it? Neither of us was trying to parse out judgment in equally measured doses, and neither was attempting to make of the drama a political forum. The tragic results of this act of terrorism permeate the end of the opera. What I emphatically did *not* do was tally up the number of bars assigned to one side or the other, and I did not keep a running account of how much "noble" or "beautiful" music was accorded to the hijackers as opposed to how much was given to the hostages or to the Jews. A common complaint was that the hijackers were treated at times like heroes and that the Palestinian cause was evoked in especially stirring music while Marilyn Klinghoffer's first aria is a laundry list of her medical problems, making her sound like just another cranky, complaining retiree. In fact, the cruise for the Klinghoffers was a gesture of fortitude for both. He was handicapped but otherwise in good health. She, however, was dying of cancer and knew that this would be the last trip they would ever take together. Marilyn's oft-repeated references to physical infirmity and decay were to me a moving acknowledgment of her sense of frailty and mortality. And it is the image of Marilyn Klinghoffer, grief-stricken, alone, and bereft on the empty stage, that the audience takes home after the final curtain falls.

The Death of Klinghoffer is a difficult opera to stage. The large role for the chorus lends an oracular tone to the events, placing the work in an area between opera and oratorio, something I know I had in mind from the start. The original Sellars production bent over backward to avoid sensationalism and accentuate the hieratic elements in the text, music, and dance. The staging had moments of great beauty and gravitas, but it could also be extremely confusing for an audience actually trying to follow a story line. Ten years after its premiere, a British filmmaker, Penny Woolcock, a director with no experience whatsoever in opera, made a searing and deeply disturbing movie of the opera, taking the action off the stage and placing it in real-life locations—including a Mediterranean pleasure ship—and staging graphic reenactments of Israeli-Palestinian violence, the latter scenes of which were shot on Malta. I was so impressed by the screenplay that Penny had sent me that I willingly accepted her invitation to collaborate. This collaboration involved two responsibilities: one happy, conducting the London Symphony and Chorus for the soundtrack; and one less happy, having to find more than twenty minutes of cuts in the score in order to make the film fit the requirements of its producer, Channel Four Television in London. One cut in scene 2 of act I did not bother me a bit. This is a moment when the captain muses about his role as a host to all the various souls on board. If anything, I think tightening that long, generally slow scene helped it a lot. Other cuts I found only expedient for the movie and would not want to approve in any future stage productions.

Penny Woolcock turned out to be exceptional in every way, and to this day her friendship remains dear to me. A modest woman, nervous and intense, with a dry, self-deprecating wit, she was born in an English enclave in Buenos Aires and ran away from home as a teenager, becoming a single mother before she was twenty and only beginning to work in films in her late thirties. Her previous films such as *Tina Goes Shopping* and *Tina Takes a Break* and *Macbeth on the Estates* used for actors and actresses actual working-class and unemployed families from the tough, blighted inner-city areas of northern England. She had a special grace for gaining an actor's confidence, and I thought her work with poor children, many of them from families with drug-addicted parents, was the closest thing to Dickens I'd ever encountered. Her film of *The Death of Klinghoffer* was more provocative than the Sellars stage version. Instead of allusive uses of dance and ritualized gesture, Penny employed graphic cinematic reenactments of the events. There was nothing at all symbolic about this murder, and little left to the imagination. She elicited a disturbing intensity from the singers. Watching them on-screen one forgets that they are opera singers at all.

To solve the problem of how to deal cinematographically with the long choruses, Penny invented an ancillary plot of two different families. One was a Holocaust couple whom we first see as young lovers newly arrived in Palestine in 1948. Later we discover them, now in their sixties, huddled among the hostages on the deck of the *Achille Lauro*. The other newly imagined story involves a beautiful young Palestinian woman, a lover perhaps of one of the terrorists, who is attacked by an angry mob of jihadists and, because of her crime of wearing stylish Western clothes and not covering her face, is showered with acid and suffers horrific scars. Most controversial, however, was Penny's reenactment during the opening chorus of the violent eviction of a Palestinian family by a band of Israeli homesteaders. Some Jewish friends who saw the film denied that such kinds of forced appropriation of land at gunpoint ever happened during the creation of Israel. Others said that if it did happen, it was rare, and that the film erred by not immediately showing equivalent Palestinian violence against Jews. But I believe Penny's treatment is well thought out. The point of the story, as she chose to depict it in this scene, and the point of the "Chorus of Exiled Palestinians," is that it comprises the Palestinian version of the narrative. The Jews' version will come in the following chorus.

he controversy over the opera's content continued for years. In 2001, not long after the attacks on September 11, I received an e-mail from the Boston Symphony Orchestra, telling me that they had decided to remove choruses from *Klinghoffer* from their November concert calendar. They explained that, given the nearness of the terrorist attacks both in time and in geography—the planes had taken off from Logan Airport in Boston—they felt it inappropriate to present the choruses during a period when what audiences needed from music was "comfort and solace." They proposed substituting *Harmonium*. I did not agree with this substitution and asked them not to program a

different piece of mine if they could not perform the *Klinghoffer* choruses. It bothered me that they were making an implicit connection between the Palestinians and the Al Qaeda–planned attacks of 9/11. The
Boston Symphony management did not actually specify in their
e-mail what in the *Klinghoffer* choruses necessitated their removal from
the program. Presumably it was simply the theme of a terrorist act. Only
later, when news of this cancellation and my unwillingness to cooperate
with it became a media event, did the orchestra's press department come
forth with the information that a member of the Tanglewood Festival
Chorus, the BSO's regular chorus, had lost her husband on one of the
planes that crashed into the World Trade Center. Now they said that
asking the chorus to sing music from an opera about terrorism was an
unfair imposition, given that the tragedy was still so fresh in the chorus members' minds. But this fact had not been communicated to me
earlier. Indeed it was not made public until the cancellation had
caused a news boomlet, with music critics and even editorial writers
around the country weighing in on one or the other side of the matter.
Opinions stretched from outright condemnation of the Boston Symphony's "censorship" to indignant accusations of grandstanding on the
part of a composer who would do anything, say anything to keep his
name in the news. In truth, no one came out of this controversy looking very good, and I felt myself reaping what I'd sown by having
leaked the contents of the BSO's e-mail to some members of the press.

With September 11 only a month in the past, classical music reviewers were hard put to make their columns seem relevant when all
that people wanted to read about was terrorism and national security.
The overblown BSO cancellation story gave these reviewers an opportunity for moralizing or scolding, or both. I contributed my own hot
air in several interviews. The loudest thunderclap came on the front
page of *The New York Times* Arts and Leisure section a month later
when the noted Stravinsky scholar Richard Taruskin contributed a
long article, "Music's Dangers and the Case for Control," that provided
a lengthy, historically based argument on why certain music, including *The Death of Klinghoffer*, should never be performed under any
circumstances. Accompanied by a disturbing cartoon of a hand, the
fingers of which are nailed crucifixion-style to the keys of a flute,
Taruskin lost no time in immediately setting a jeremiad tone by invok-

ing the prophet Muhammad's warning that "on the Day of Judgment molten lead will be poured into the ears" of "those who listen to music and songs of this world." Taruskin's thesis was that music is too emotionally powerful, is literally a subversive force, and therefore, as all clever tyrants have always known, needs to be controlled, especially during times of social crisis or unrest. As examples of those who in the past had keenly understood this need for "control," he lists Plato, the Ayatollah Ruhollah Khomeini, Saint Augustine, Leo Tolstoy, Joseph Goebbels, and Andrei Zhdanov, the Soviet bureaucrat who hounded both Prokofiev and Shostakovich. He goes on to make a distinction between censorship ("a mandated imposition on people's rights") and what he calls "voluntary abstinence out of consideration for people's feelings." Daniel Barenboim's insistence on programming Wagner in Israel was by this measure a blatant violation of "voluntary abstinence." According to Taruskin, Barenboim's principal motivation for breaking the ban on Wagner in Israel was nothing more than sheer personal opportunism. The conductor having to honor the feelings of the Holocaust survivors apparently posed "an intolerable infringement on his career," wrote Taruskin.

But Barenboim (the same who'd won about every humanitarian award in the book) and his supposed cynical self-aggrandizement was nothing compared to the mindlessly romantic creators of *The Death of Klinghoffer*, who were guilty of trading in "the tritest undergraduate fantasies." The unforgivable transgression of this opera was that it made the intolerable mistake of going beyond the condemnation of terrorism to question the motivation of those perpetrating it. "But isn't it time for artists and critics to grow up with the rest of us, now that the unthinkable has occurred?" Taruskin testily asks in that classic preemptive tone of exasperation so dear to the neoconservative talk-show bullies. The only way to defeat terrorism, he goes on, is to turn public opinion decisively against it, and the only way to accomplish that "is to focus resolutely on the acts rather than their claimed (or conjectured) motivations . . ."

"Why should we want to hear this music now?" Taruskin asks. All the "beautiful" music in the score is given to the Palestinians. The composer, he reveals, has in fact given the Palestinians the same musical "halo" that Bach gives Jesus in his Passions. The only such "halo" or "aureole" accorded a Jew in *The Death of Klinghoffer* is given to Klinghoffer's dead body. "Only after death does the familiar American middle-class Jew join the glamorously exotic Palestinians in mythic timelessness," writes Taruskin. The reader of his analysis thus has no trouble in drawing the obvious and inevitable conclusion that the message of this opera is "the only good Jew is a dead Jew."

"What is called for is self-control," Taruskin concludes. The management at the Boston Symphony "laudably exercised" that self-control on behalf of its audience by canceling the performance, and it only follows that the work should in the future be similarly "controlled" by sensible arts administrators and management who understand the danger this opera, with all its subversive music, poses to their audiences. This opera, he opines, expresses a "reprehensible contempt for the real-life victims of its imagined 'men of ideals,' all too easily transferable to the victims who perished on September 11."

Alice's response, given in an interview with the British writer Rupert Christiansen in *Opera* magazine, was that Taruskin's interpretation of the "Aria of the Falling Body" revealed his own personal preoccupations.

> His idea that I am implying that the only good Jew is a dead Jew is not just a bad reading of what I wrote, but a case, I believe, of pathological Jewish self-hatred on Taruskin's part . . . I think what upset a lot of people was that the libretto violates certain taboos, common to all minority groups, such as the taboo on washing one's dirty linen outside the community. People didn't like the way that I presented Klinghoffer as an ordinary, touchy, vulgar bourgeois—there's this Jewish fantasy that our heroes and our victims are always either highly cultured or pious. Well, some of us can be very vulgar—we aren't all Nathan the Wise. And we have behaved very badly towards the Palestinians, they have justifiable grievances, and we and they are very, very much alike—temperamentally, culturally, in family dynamics and in ultimate origin. At which point I should add that by origin, upbringing, and education I am a Jew. I'm Jewish by nearly every definition. I converted to Christianity between writing the choruses and arias for *Klinghoffer.*

9.

MONGREL AIRS

ith its psychological tensions, somber choral meditations, and sudden bursts of outright violence, an opera about terrorists and their victims could not possibly speak in the same bright, extroverted musical language as *Nixon in China*. What one writer called the "chugging minimalist" engines of *Nixon* was inappropriate for the emotionally complex mood changes of *The Death of Klinghoffer*. I was confronted with having to find a new voice to express these darker sides of the human condition, and although *Klinghoffer* still retained a distinctly tonal grounding in its harmonic language, it departed emphatically from the Day-Glo colors and upbeat energy of its predecessor. I discovered how composing for the operatic stage could have a hugely beneficial effect on the evolution of a composer's musical language, a realization that was even further confirmed over the coming years with works like *El Niño*, with its gentle marriage of European medieval music and Latin American texts, and *Doctor Atomic*, for which I was challenged to find musical expression for an atomic bomb detonation in a remote desert landscape.

I put *Klinghoffer*'s chromaticism and melodic sharp edges into a comic spin in the work that followed, Chamber Symphony. Written in

1992 while the political controversy stirred up by the opera still simmered, the Chamber Symphony was to its operatic predecessor as a fool is to a brooding king. It could not have been more different temperamentally. Its eponymous ancestor, the Opus 9 by Schoenberg, had long fascinated me for its manic intensity and hyperactive athleticism. Listening to it and conducting it, I was made to think of an entire Strauss tone poem or a Mahler symphony compressed into a trash compactor, squeezed down and spring-loaded into a tightly wound mass of volatile energy. I began to wonder what my version of such a piece would be. Around the same time I'd also become aware of the brilliant music written in the 1940s and 1950s for Hollywood cartoon films. Some other adventurous musicians, including the composer John Zorn and the Kronos Quartet, had been rediscovering cartoon music by Carl Stalling and Raymond Scott. Although Scott had never composed specifically for cartoon films, his music had been liberally adapted for them during the 1950s and his name was inextricably linked to the best of them. More recently, in the early 1990s, a sly and scabrous television cartoon show, *Ren and Stimpy*, a favorite of my young children, had brought back Scott's music, mixed together outrageously with old classical chestnuts like *Peer Gynt*, *Swan Lake*, and *The Carnival of the Animals*.

My mind began to conflate the compressed intensity and abrupt mood shifts of cartoon music with the not dissimilar ambience of the Schoenberg symphony. Added to that was the image of Schoenberg himself, a central European of deep, probing seriousness, forced by fate and history to make a new life in Southern California amid the garish commercialism and vacuousness of Hollywood culture. And thus my own Chamber Symphony, dedicated to the seven-year-old Sam, devotee of *Ren and Stimpy*, came to life as a result of these strange but not irrational connections. The piece opens with the clang of a cowbell, as if it were a tin can banged by a boy bent on annoying everyone within earshot. The fifteen solo instruments shriek and pile on, leaping over one another, yelping, shouting, each trying to drown out the other. It is the densest polyphony I ever wrote, and the piece is hugely risky to perform, not so much because of the individually difficult parts but because of the challenge of achieving acoustical balance within its endlessly competing inner voices.

Like the Schoenberg Chamber Symphony, which also suffers from nearly insurmountable balance problems, my work is a virtual hive of contrapuntal activity. Scored for an ensemble of solo instruments that was similar to the Schoenberg with an additional keyboard sampler and drum set, it gives all players special moments to shine as soloists, often in melodic lines of finger-twisting complexity. A lot of gnarly music that I'd long had a fondness for—pieces by composers as different as Nancarrow, Milhaud, Hindemith, Stravinsky, Birtwistle, and including Stalling and Scott—helped to set the tone of this twenty-five-minute essay in fauvist colors and raucous sonorities.

The Chamber Symphony went to the edge of comprehensibility and clarity. After finishing it I wasn't certain that I wanted to push the envelope much further. Although the title of the first movement, "Mongrel Airs," happily acknowledged the work's confused genotype, there was a problem lurking beneath the surface. The piece's in-your-face, jester-like tone obscured the fact that the musical rhetoric had been prodded almost to the point of imploding. An inspired performance was both entertaining and breathtakingly virtuosic. But a bad performance—and I heard many—sounded like undifferentiated noise, fifteen instrumentalists loudly and aggressively riffing as if casually indifferent to one another. The work that followed, the Violin Concerto, shows that impending crisis acknowledged and then painstakingly diverted.

As a musical vehicle the concept of the violin concerto is unique. The instrument itself, when posed against the background of even a delicately scored orchestra, presents an acoustically small profile—*vox clamans in deserto*. More often than not the sound of the solo violin struggles to be heard above the mass. If it succeeds, it results in a heroic scenario, a David-and-Goliath setting in which the violin might win our sympathy and involvement through the force of its tenacity and the lyrical intensity of its small but commanding sound.

In our time LPs and CDs have given us a false impression of the great concertos of Beethoven, Brahms, Sibelius, Tchaikovsky, Berg, Prokofiev, and Shostakovich by heavily manipulating the relationship of the soloist to the orchestra. Studio engineers position the solo violin in the foreground in a balance that is essentially a lie, an idealized proportion between soloist and orchestra that does not reflect the actual acoustical reality of the concert hall. Who has not gone to a concert hall to hear a familiar concerto only to be confounded by the disappointing reality of the actual sound, with a tiny violin barely able to maintain itself against the fabric of the full orchestra? Yet the violin concerto continues to retain the position of privilege on classical music programs exactly because of this heroic scenario. The solo violin at full throttle projects a lyrical intensity that instantly focuses the listener's attention. Composing a concerto that takes advantage of this quality, that keeps the violin from being submerged in the orchestral mass (a challenge not always met in the concertos of Berg and Stravinsky), and that creates a supple relationship between the solo instrument and the massed sonority of the orchestra—all of this is no small responsibility.

My concerto, begun in 1992 and premiered in January of the following year in Minneapolis by Jorja Fleezanis—when the winter temperatures outside were a bone-brittle thirty degrees below zero—created its own acoustical conflicts. The first part is constructed upon a constantly recirculating staircase motif, a rising figure of evenly spaced eighth notes that is virtually omnipresent throughout the movement. Above this gentle staircase the violin intones long, lyrical melodies, floating above the orchestral body as it slowly turns and shifts direction. The orchestral music is by and large modal, moving among various scalar patterns that I would later refine into a modulation technique called the "earbox." The writing for solo violin, however, is free, spontaneous, improvisatory, referring harmonically to the underlying tutti music much as a jazz artist embellishes according to the chord structure of a song. A satisfying performance of my concerto lives or dies on how sensitively the solo voice is balanced against the orchestra. Such balance is extremely difficult to achieve because the orchestra is constantly playing, its sound continuous (a relic of my Minimalist past) and, with the inclusion of two keyboard samplers, often thickly scored. Performances can also be affected by the acoustical qualities of the concert hall in which the piece is being heard. The conductor must ride herd mercilessly on the orchestra to keep the orchestra's dense low and middle registers from suffocating the solo violin voice.

I coined the term "hypermelody" to describe the violin music. Indeed, the soloist plays almost constantly throughout the thirty-five-minute concerto with only a handful of four- or eight-bar moments of rest. This gives the piece its strange intensity, an intensity that, in the hands of a truly inspired performer, can result in a cathartic release at the end of the toccata third movement. The central movement, a rare flirtation with an archaic musical form, is a chaconne, a slow, stately, dreamlike dance based on an eight-bar closed-circuit bass line in D major. In the course of that movement I pass this familiar-sounding ground bass through a structural and harmonic hall of mirrors, warping its contours and shifting its modality. Some of these manipulation techniques were suggested by algorithms in a music software program I was using at the time, algorithms that were originally invented to help film composers squeeze or stretch music to fit the needs of a screen image. I, however, used them for fundamental creative purposes.

The first movement, while essentially tonal, is nevertheless contrapuntally complex with many forays into chattering dissonance and textural density in the manner of the Chamber Symphony. The second and third movements are tropes on two musical artifacts from the past, the chaconne and the toccata. The chaconne bears a title that I borrowed from a poem by Robert Hass, "Body through which the dream flows." That seemed like a perfect image for the music: the orchestra as the "body" and the solo violin as the floating, disembodied "dream." The toccata finale, "Toccare"—I used the Italian infinitive form of the word—is based on scales that flip back and forth between modes. Its virtuoso writing hints at the high-energy early Minimalist pieces of the 1970s like *Shaker Loops* and *Phrygian Gates*, but does so without the earlier Minimalist "gradual" treatment of material. The concerto seems to be of two minds about what it is, at times hinting at a stylistic crisis that would not be resolved for several years. I am sometimes puzzled by how the first movement seems to exist in an entirely different expressive world from the succeeding two. Whatever its internal contradictions, it remains one of my most often-performed pieces, a serious work and one that continues to attract some wonderful virtuosos—Gidon Kremer, Vadim Repin, Leila Josefowicz, and Midori among them. Leila especially took the concerto to heart, playing it from memory in cities all over the United States and Europe, finding rhythmic shadings and expressive possibilities that even its composer had never realized were implicit in the music. The concerto is Leila's signature piece, and her mesmerizing performances became a model for how a serious new instrumental work could indeed achieve repertoire status through the determined advocacy of an exceptionally talented artist.

No longer interested in mining the depleted ore of Minimalism yet uncertain about the directions implicit in *Klinghoffer* and the Chamber Symphony, the composer of Violin Concerto made a detour through old Italian musical archetypes, finding perhaps an attractive if not entirely rigorous way around the problems posed by the first movement.

.   .   .

n the spring of 1991, a large, rambling, four-story house in south Berkeley appeared on a list of city probate sale offerings. The previous owners, who died after occupying it for nearly sixty years, had left the eighty-year-old structure in a state of what could only kindly be called "deferred maintenance." On first inspection the kitchen was covered in a coat of dust and decade-old grease, a Miss Havisham's museum of broken 1950s appliances and ugly light fixtures surrounded by stale, prison-green walls with broken blinds and shades. The top floor still had a call-box intercom system from the 1920s, and under the dining table, concealed beneath a ratty carpet, was what remained of a foot buzzer for discreetly summoning servants. A contractor friend inspected the house, optimistically proclaiming it "a diamond in the rough—very rough." He also strongly suspected that the structure was playing host to an infestation of termites. Urban folklore had it that a savvy homeowner might get around the high cost of a full-blown pest extermination by hiring a special service that provided trained dogs to sniff through every inch of a building and identify whether or not the wood was bug-infested. For me, a lifelong dog lover, this was too good a gambit not to try. On a warm May morning a man in a banged-up pickup truck arrived with a pair of ancient beagles, two of the oldest canines I'd ever seen, both of whom promptly went to work, scratching surfaces, sniffing, and listening with cocked ears, only later to apprise their handler of the fact that our house was richly inhabited by vermin. Eventually the big green house on El Camino Real was sealed inside an enormous tent and pumped full of toxic gas. A week later, not without some trepidation, we moved in and thus began a new life in the house's spacious rooms, its five bathrooms, hidden closets, and long-neglected backyard. A large music room with windows facing west was so generously designed that it would over time become the site of chamber music gatherings, student recitals, and, on a night ten years later, a party for three hundred sweaty teenagers, dancing, mating, and mixing to the bone-crushing throb of a disco jock with imported sound system.

A top-floor studio for me and an entire basement photography studio for Debbie made the house not only a home but also a cheerful work space for our two careers. I arranged my studio so that from my desk I could look out over the tops of the high trees of neighboring properties. In the distance lay the San Francisco Bay and, to the north, Mount Tamalpais in Marin County.

Life began to alternate regularly between periods of intensely introverted creative work at home, surrounded and leavened by a noisy and musically active young family, and trips away, often to conduct orchestras in the United States and Europe. I worked to mesh schedules with Debbie's trips to the Nevada desert or to the Sacramento River delta where she would spend days alone with her large-format field camera, staying nights in small-town hotels and gaining an intimate knowledge of the rural West. In February 1992, at the age of forty-two, Debbie was diagnosed with invasive ductile breast cancer and had to undergo surgery and months of uncomfortable chemotherapy. Emily and Sam, eight and six, were at a vulnerable age. Explaining the cause of the disease, its dangers, and the reasons for such drastic treatment was something to be done sensitively yet honestly. My wife, still very much a young mother with two young children, handled the sudden emergency unflinchingly, obtaining the best advice, treatment, and support she could find. But even with the medical data and statistics so strongly favoring full recovery as they fortunately do in our time, there is no minimizing the terror of the first diagnosis and the trauma, both physical and psychological, of the surgery and the chemical treatment that follows it. When the first round of chemo took effect, the whole family sat during an early-summer evening on the back stairs of the Berkeley house and took turns ceremonially cutting the remaining hair off Debbie's head until she looked like a Nubian princess. Her photographic work, always lyrical and serene, took on an even deeper tonality. Images of the desert, of flat riverbeds and rock-strewn lava beds spoke or even sang quietly with a serene reflection that may well have been the fruits of her encounter with a life-threatening disease. Our house has ever since been populated by large prints of her landscapes, first of the West and then later, as she traveled, of Guatemala, France, Rome, and even India. I was inspired deeply by her way of seeing, and there is little doubt that the landscape quality of some of my music owes a debt to her photography.

I traveled less during her recovery, but I eventually went back on the road, the composer-conductor I'd fantasized in such careful detail as an early adolescent. Programs usually included at least one Adams work, and I would round them out with pieces ranging from Debussy, Copland, and Stravinsky to Haydn, Reich, Zappa, or even Wagner. I was fortunate enough to work with the very best orchestras— Cleveland, Chicago, Los Angeles, the New York Philharmonic, the London Symphony, and the Amsterdam Concertgebouw, among others. In one two-week period in 1999 I led the Chicago Symphony Orchestra in eight concerts, including music by Ives, Copland, and Harrison as well as my own, all but one of the works never before having appeared on that orchestra's programs. I found orchestras in the United States and England generally very quick to absorb unfamiliar material. More traditional Continental orchestras like the Santa Cecilia Orchestra in Rome or the great Concertgebouw Orchestra in Amsterdam required more time and patient repetition of intricate passages, but the results could be no less impressive. Some orchestras responded enthusiastically to my programs and to my presence, while others would treat their week with me as something to be endured. American classical music was inevitably a hard sell in most foreign countries, and probably for good reason. The canon of great symphonic music, one that ranged from Bach and Haydn to Messiaen and Ligeti, was a European creation, and Continental audiences had every right to feel proud and proprietary about it. Although American pop music, from show tunes, to jazz, to rock and Motown, is omnipresent in other parts of the world, our country's concert music has been slow to gain a foothold elsewhere.

istorically, Americans came late to classical music. As the social historian Frank Rossiter points out, during its first hundred years of independence the country was simply too raw, too absorbed in pushing its frontiers westward and taming its wilderness to foster the kind of artistic climate that might produce a Schubert or a Mahler. Classical music is essentially an urban experience. Concert halls, symphony orchestras, opera companies, manufacturers of instruments, sheet-music publishers, and music conservatories all thrive in cities, and American cities throughout the nineteenth century were rough and disorganized collision points of mostly poor immigrants struggling for survival. Culture in the cities, as we learn from descriptions by Melville, Whitman, and Dreiser, was coarse and vulgar. What passed for refinement were more often than not secondhand versions of novels, plays, paintings, and sculpture from Europe. The Henry James American, wealthy, perhaps educated but still intellectually uncertain, looks to Italy, France, or England for refinement and Culture with a capital C. For the small segment of the leisure class that could afford the adornments of fine art and literature, indigenous themes were treated exotically, evoked in a misty Romantic glow, such as in the anglicized stanzas of Henry Wadsworth Longfellow, whose *Hiawatha* and *Evangeline* suggest Tennyson-style verse epics transposed to the New World more than they represent something genuinely native. All the more credit, then, must go to Emerson for identifying the real traits of the New World sensibility. His admonishments to individualism and personal independence signaled a turning point in American self-awareness, a change that would be felt first in literature and poetry and much later in painting and music. Thus a homegrown, truly indigenous American poetical expression, most provocatively embodied by Whitman, gradually began to take hold shortly after the Civil War. That war in itself was so devastating to the national psyche that it may have precipitated a new maturity in the minds of the country's artists.

Charles Ives, a solitary visionary, a committed "philosophical" artist in the mode of his idol, Emerson, left as his legacy a problematic body of work about which even he was ambivalent. I conducted his music often, not only his many small pieces for chamber orchestra, but also the bigger ones like the impressionistic *Three Places in New England* and the mysterious, "transcendental" Fourth Symphony. These are works that are both radically new in their compositional ideas while at the same time curiously steeped in a type of New England Indian Summer nostalgia that was popular at the turn of the century. I enjoyed solving the performance problems these scores presented, especially those rhythmic conundrums in the Fourth Symphony that in some cases I charted out and made more realistically playable with the aid of computer software. There are rhythmic ideas in Ives's mature music that are so far ahead of their time that one is left both humbled and amazed. We think of Stravinsky as the great rhythmic innovator and point to his fracturing of the conventional phrase structures and his use of irregular stresses and accents as the fountain of new rhythmic resources for the twentieth century. But in matters of rhythm Ives, writing at almost the same time, actually was more widely innovative, utilizing polyrhythms, simultaneity of tempi, and complex layerings of pulsation that other composers didn't catch up with for another forty or fifty years. The difficulty of performing these pieces was such that even the most adventurous of musicians rarely tried to take them on during the composer's lifetime. On the few occasions when someone did attempt a performance the results were more often than not confusion and misapprehension. Only in the last twenty or thirty years have performers begun to approach a comfort zone in tackling the gnarlier of Ives's compositions.

For all my love and admiration of Ives, I confess to going back and forth in my opinion of his music. The symphonies, for all their flavor of local color and Yankee eccentricity, more often than not seem like special cases, snapshots of an earlier America, quirky and ingenious but ultimately reticent and imperfect when played alongside the great European masterpieces of his contemporaries, Mahler, Debussy, Sibelius, or Stravinsky. The first two of his symphonies are nineteenth-century orchestral essays spiced with Ives's unpredictable wit and penchant for rule-breaking, and colored by the frequent use of American musical artifacts. The Third Symphony, deeply nostalgic while at the same time much less beholden to European models, is a sincere creation in which Ives really succeeds in making something confidently original out of the musical found objects of his past without sounding in the least derivative. In the hands of a sensitive and sympathetic conductor like Michael Tilson Thomas this surprisingly quiet and reserved piece cannot fail to move those of us who are attuned to Ives's spiritual universe. Hearing it brings back memories of the small-town life of my childhood.

The Fourth Symphony gladdens the heart with its Emersonian optimism just as it maddens one's aesthetic senses with its uneven formal design and its often murky, unbalanced orchestration. Ives was doing something very bold in his treatment of the orchestra in this symphony. He wanted to create the effect of hearing sounds simultaneously from both near and distant locations. In theory, a trumpet playing fortissimo three hundred yards away might sound at precisely the same decibel level as three flutes playing pianissimo only a few feet away. In his treatment of the orchestration Ives tried to find ways to achieve that physical fact in the hope of creating a new art of acoustical perspective. But because he never had the chance to hear proper performances of his large-scale works and know what worked and what didn't, pieces like the Fourth Symphony remained speculative, at least insofar as they represent an attempt to make the orchestra behave as a very different animal compared to how the Europeans traditionally deployed it.

I always hope Ives's grander pieces will carry me away, but they so often let me down a little at the end. I want the Fourth Symphony to be *the* great testament of American musical imagination. I want it to be the *Moby-Dick*, the *Leaves of Grass* of American music. Perhaps this is an unfair expectation, or perhaps, even after a lifetime of exposure to it, I am still missing its essence. But something about the shape of this and other of his larger pieces, together with Ives's own deep ambivalence about himself and his place in the world, always prevent this cathartic experience from occurring. In its lofty aspirations and visionary theme, the Fourth Symphony desires to go where no symphonic work, either American or European, ever ventured. And indeed, on many technical levels, it does cross a brave new musical and philosophical frontier. But as a complete, satisfying statement of the kind we hear from other great composers of the same era, the Fourth Symphony never quite achieves the wholeness that one demands from the very best of the best.

n those years, in addition to much Ives, I frequently programmed works by other Americans, Copland, Cage, Nancarrow, Feldman, Reich, Glass, and Zappa, in concerts that I presented with orchestras throughout the United States and in Europe. This was in part an attempt to forge a connection among our native works, but I often had to admit that some works were less than successful, largely because of the fact that, for many of these unique and inventive composers, the symphony orchestra was not their real chosen medium. Copland understood the orchestra well enough to forge a personal style with it, characteristically simple and free of the excess and ner-vous, over-wrought detail of much European fin-de-siècle symphonic practice. In comparison to a Strauss tone poem, with its swirling currents of inner voices, mercurial shifts of mood, and constant upending of harmonic stasis, Copland's orchestral works are like pieces of Shaker furniture, simple to the point of being humble, but sturdy and effective and free of excess emotional baggage. They are typical of the American grain, not unlike the prose of Ernest Hemingway or the poetry of Robert Frost. I was especially fond of the very young Copland's work, particularly the Piano Concerto of 1926, which I conducted with Garrick Ohlsson with both the Chicago Symphony Orchestra and the New York Philharmonic. This is a youthful work full of brash cheekiness, along with Gershwin's *Rhapsody in Blue* the first "urban" piano concerto, with a brassy, bold sense of jazzy American rhythms that Leonard Bernstein would later mine for fun and profit thirty years later when composing *West Side Story*.

Copland had meant much to me as a boy. My parents had taken me to Tanglewood around 1960 to see him conduct the Boston Symphony in a program he shared with music director Charles Munch. Seated far in the back of the Tanglewood "shed" I saw him conduct *Appalachian Spring*, his thin Ichabod Crane body jerking awkwardly with the music. As a young composer Copland was adept at playing the role of provocateur, particularly in his gift of melding the leanness

and angularity of Stravinsky with the demotic energy and raucous timbres of twenties jazz. Before Copland's conversion to Depression-era
populism and social awareness, he had produced a number of works—
Piano Variations, *Statements*, and *Symphonic Ode*—in a pungent and
dissonant Modernist mode that demonstrated a willingness to be less
audience-friendly and more in line with his radical contemporaries
like Varèse, Cowell, and Schoenberg. Sometimes the impulse toward
the hortatory, toward a stilted grandiosity, could creep into his large-
scale works, but more often than not Copland, like his compatriots
Robert Frost, William Carlos Williams, and Edward Hopper, managed
to locate that quintessence of the American "grain," a deeply expressed
sentiment couched in a Lincolnian simplicity of utterance. This is an
American trait so deceptively plain and ordinary that European or
Asian audiences are frequently nonplussed by it. How can one explain
the profoundly moving artlessness and emotional restraint of a work
like *Quiet City*, with its simple trumpet tattoos, its open-spaced string
chords, and pensive cor anglais melodies? Even in his most over-the-
counter populist works of the thirties and forties Copland maintained
an unfailing intuitive sense of rightness, producing works of great
appeal and immense popularity—*Billy the Kid*, *Fanfare for the Common Man*, *Appalachian Spring*, *Lincoln Portrait*—while almost never
crossing the line into bathos or caricature. He was able to summon
America's best image of itself without yielding to the sentimentality or mawkishness of a Norman Rockwell, a Frank Capra, or a Steven
Spielberg.

During the early 1980s, while I was doing concerts in San Francisco, a friend who had been copying music for Frank Zappa sent
me several large orchestra scores by Zappa with the hint that perhaps I
might lobby for performances of them with the San Francisco Symphony. They were part of a rapidly growing number of Zappa's compositions for conventional classical orchestra. Although they still bore
the familiar mocking, in-your-face Zappa titles like "*Bogus Pomp*," "*Mo
'n' Herb's Vacation*," and "*Penis Dimension*," they also included passages
of dissonant, thickly orchestrated material, sometimes featuring per-
versely difficult rhythmic groupings that all but dared a big-time or-

chestra to take them on and wrestle with the knots and tangles of their polyrhythms. Nothing came of my perusal of those orchestral scores, but ten years later I began to program some of Zappa's works for smaller orchestra, and over a period of time I did performances of his works in many cities throughout Europe and the United States, both on symphony orchestra programs and with special virtuoso ensembles like Frankfurt's Ensemble Modern and the London Sinfonietta.

Zappa's admiration of Edgard Varèse was deep, genuine, and oft proclaimed. Even my own wife had said that *Freak Out!*, Zappa's first best-selling album with the Mothers of Invention, had changed her life, introducing her to Varèse and launching her on a long voyage of discovery in the world of experimental music. Varèse himself was a lonely outsider, an émigré composer whose visionary futurism and stubborn individualism had kept him apart from the conventional classical music community, a community that Copland so expertly navigated. Varèse's outlaw persona coupled with the radical constructivism of his music provided the perfect model for Zappa, who himself played the role of outlaw, angry individualist, and musical radical within the context of American pop music. But unlike Varèse, who seemed to care little for public notoriety, Zappa was an immensely clever self-promoter gifted with perfect pitch when it came to identifying the absurdities and vulgarities of American popular culture. The music he made with his bands was advanced by the standards of rock music, but in comparison to what was being accomplished at the same time by other contemporary composers, it was hardly more advanced than what had been around already for half a century. Zappa the snarky social critic, the taunting homunculus who ridiculed the vacuousness and stupidity of American culture, was very much in the lineage of our best social satirists—Mark Twain, Ambrose Bierce, H. L. Mencken, and Hunter S. Thompson. With his snarling, potty-mouthed titles and song lyrics he had a gift for appealing to the eternal six-year-old in all of us. "Don't Eat the Yellow Snow," "Alien Orifice," "G-Spot Tornado" were musically interesting enough to beg multiple listenings, more at least than most of what was being produced at the time.

Zappa's engines were driven by his savagely critical animus against commercial pop and the market-oriented, image-conscious, media-driven world of rock. Shortly after the 1966 release of *Freak Out!* he broke with the money-driven corporate world of commercial music, took control of all aspects of his work, and from then on entirely self-produced his music. Everything, the composing, recording, editing, mixing, packaging, marketing, and licensing, was under his personal direction. This of course gave him enormous creative freedom, and with the knowledge that there was no corporate middleman to answer to, his individuality flourished. He stayed outrageously productive, almost manically so, right up to his early death at the age of fifty-two.

I was always uncertain about Zappa and remain puzzled by him. His autobiography, *The Real Frank Zappa Book*, is one of the best of its kind written by a composer. Only Berlioz's memoirs give such a delicious taste of the life and times of its writer without resorting to pomposity or self-promotion. What other composer would feel compelled to begin his memoirs with a statement denying the long-standing rumor that he had once taken a shit onstage? How can one not be impressed by his outgrowing the imaginative poverty of a childhood in the bleak desert town of Lancaster, California, where the signal cultural events were sock hops and car thefts?

Zappa's creative life played out during the same time as the birth and flowering of rock, and much if not most of his work was a commentary on it. Having educated himself in contemporary classical techniques, he introduced phrase and metric irregularities to the boilerplate symmetries of pop music. In the 1980s he was one of the first, or possibly the first, to compose works exclusively on electronic instruments, in his case the Synclavier, a precursor of computer-controlled technology, and the experience appears to have even further liberated his creativity. Zappa's cool yet curmudgeonly persona and his hard-won maverick status brought him a huge and appreciative audience. He was a hero in the USA, but his fame was even larger in Europe, where his image as cultural icon continues to occupy a status not unlike that granted to Charles Bukowski in poetry.

I knew I ought to be grateful to Zappa for his going head-to-head with the worst vulgarities in American popular culture and satirizing them with a flair worthy of Panurge. But I struggled to stay involved when I listened to his music, whether it was his canonical early Mothers of Invention songs, his Synclavier compositions, or the "avant-garde" instrumental works of his late *Yellow Shark* compositions. Too often the butt of his humor turned out to be something I didn't much care about—bad pop music, Los Angeles car culture, or adolescent complexes of not being popular. What one of his fans acknowledged as an "aggressive defensiveness concerning 'high art' " sounded right to me. Zappa's vein of wary, almost paranoid suspicion of cultural elitism runs very deep in the American psyche and often for good reason. But what he ridiculed as bogus pomp was also something he deeply desired to possess, a cachet in the world of serious art music, although strictly on his own terms. Curiously, despite their composer's huge name recognition and popularity, Zappa's "classical" works have yet to be taken up as part of the regular repertoire. They are difficult and require much rehearsal time. But so are the works of Ives, Carter, Ligeti, and Adès, and conductors—at least some conductors—will accept the challenge of those composers. There seems to be a quality issue with Zappa's "serious" works that cannot be gotten around.

■ ■ ■

he more I found myself leaving home to spend weeks in distant cities to conduct orchestras or attend productions of my operas, the more I came to envy the old masters like Bach or Rembrandt who kept their creative and public life confined to a small geographic locus. I am not an enthusiastic traveler, and I find the compulsion for globetrotting, so much a requisite of contemporary life, not only psychologically jarring but also ecologically disturbing. I wonder often if a time of scarcity will come that will require the human species to stay put in one place and confine travel to a virtual activity.

The exigencies of having to jump on planes and appear in distant cities created an internal tension that I came to identify as characteristic of a duality between the creative life and the life of the performer. Having to move back and forth from the inward, hermetic world of daily creative work and the extroverted, people-oriented activity of conducting was not then and never will be easy. Days or even weeks before a trip to work with some orchestra in a faraway place I would suffer anxiety dreams, images of jetliners malfunctioning or of my being caught in traffic while an orchestra on the other side of town waited onstage for me to begin the concert. The schism between creative life and performing life is not unbridgeable, but it requires psychological preparation and a full awareness of what can be achieved and what cannot. As painful as it may be to jerk oneself out of creative solitude and plunge into the nervous activity of rehearsals, concerts, interviews, and general public life, the yin and yang of the experience is ultimately salubrious. Too much hermetic solitude can divorce one from the realities of music-making, causing one to forget that music is ultimately an act of communication that requires a complex web of personal interactions.

Western classical music from the Renaissance to the present evolved as an ever-more controlled and prescriptive activity. Over time, musical notation became increasingly determinate, its parameters allowing for greater and greater precision in performance, especially in the coordination of large ensembles. A student of classical music in India might spend years mastering the inflections in pitch and timbre in the singing or playing of ragas, but the moment of performance always involved on-the-spot creative improvisation. In the classical tradition of the West, however, notation prescribes roughly 95 percent of the performer's behavior. One rarely stops to reflect on how immense a gap exists between these two worlds of music-making, the one grounded on theory and systems but ultimately spontaneous and creative (as it is also with jazz), the other almost slavishly obedient to the printed page, to the precise prescriptive data of the composer's notation. Even so, and in spite of the printed page's circumscribing the performer's freedoms, the Western tradition of notated music still manages to allow for singularities among performances, at least enough for a knowledgeable listener to distinguish between two or more different performances of a Chopin prelude, a Verdi opera, or a Shostakovich symphony.

Simply put, there are things that notated music can accomplish that would be impossible in the tradition of improvisation. The organization of multiple voices in an orchestra requires a highly evolved degree of notational specificity. The complex polyphonic web of a Bach fugue could not be produced in an improvisational setting (although there are maddening but probably true stories of the Bach family spontaneously improvising a fugue while sitting around the dinner table). Curiously, once musical notation evolved sufficiently to enable sophisticated instrumental ensemble playing, improvisation in the Western classical tradition rapidly disappeared. We have contemporary descriptions of Beethoven mesmerizing his audiences with his keyboard improvisations and doing so within an otherwise fully notated concerto. But even that tradition died out within another generation or so. Descriptions of Chopin's composition practice describe him freely improvising his pieces and then spending countless hours painstakingly finding the exact notation to permanently freeze that initial impulse onto the page. In the twentieth century, jazz brought free and spontaneous improvisation back into the public awareness, and that fed the imagination of the bolder and more adventurous of rock performers like the Grateful Dead, several of whose members were keenly aware of Indian and East Asian musical traditions.

Free improvisation in the context of contemporary classical music has always been a problematic matter. In the 1970s we frequently encountered pieces in which the composer had provided rudimentary ideas but had left much of the critical decision-making up to the performer. There were all kinds of degrees of liberty, ranging from the tightly controlled, not at all spontaneous *liberté* of Boulez to the cosmic improvisations of Stockhausen's *Aus den sieben Tagen*, where the notation is simply the verbal directive to "play a sound . . . for so long until you feel that you should stop." I well remember doing long improvisations with my friends, often going late into the night, with results that could be illuminating. Ideas occasionally occurred that might be construed as having meaning. By "meaning" I say that there was a semblance of formal unifying factors that gave the music structural coherence. Unfortunately this kind of extemporaneous jamming—improvisation not based on a longstanding and communally understood set of rules but rather free-form and without any kind of critical filter—was unlikely to produce anything of lasting value. What made the best jazz so thoroughly satisfying was the same principle that made the enduring traditions of Indian raga singing: a complex and subtle constellation of rules of style that governed all aspects of the music's harmonic, melodic, and rhythmic workings. One comes to that great tradition of improvisation only after years of training and exposure to the canon of past masters of the art, nowadays fortunately preserved on recordings. But free improvisation for classically trained performers in the West is usually based on no tradition other than that of the players following a composer's specified notational commands. Moments of free improvisation inserted into pieces of contemporary music rarely achieved anything more than producing a fleeting, anecdotal effect. The results only amplified the gulf between the two traditions of making music.

What does a composer do? From where do the images and sounds originate and how are they organized into a coherent statement? There are probably as many answers to these questions as there are individual composers. Anxious graduate students often ask me about the "right" way to compose, as if there were a correct way to be creative. I tell them that you do whatever you can and whatever you must and that there is no one proper way to be creative. Some composers are laboriously methodical, painstakingly logical in building a new musical structure. For them the composing act is as conscious and aboveboard as humanly possible. Nothing is left to chance. Others are more like spontaneous improvisers or Expressionist painters, trusting implicitly their subconscious instincts. All composers are fundamentally intuitive. There is no such distinction as "intuitive versus rational" for us. The difference among creative types is in *how* one responds to those intuitions, whether one fastidiously organizes, compartmentalizes, and schematizes, or whether one is confident enough to let instinct and an animal sense of rightness be the guide and ultimate judge. The former method can result in a cold, abstract art with strained expressivity; the latter runs any number of risks, ranging from distended, indifferent formal structures to expressive overindulgence.

Beethoven's sketchbooks reveal what for me is a thoroughly individuated creative process in the act. They are Exhibit A of how the rational mind collaborates with the irrational feeling function to produce an artistic statement that combines reason with expressivity, producing in the listener a sensation of profoundly unified energies.

For Beethoven, that process of discovery could be wonderfully messy and circuitous. Examining his sketchbooks, you see him veering into infertile blind alleys or going in wrongheaded directions, only to grope toward the final, authoritative realization of a gesture or musical image. You see the composer struggling to know the potential of his own material. His first versions can be amazingly crude or if not crude, at least strangely bland. One is astonished that he even bothered to write down some of these ideas. But then you watch the refining process kick in, the unifying of melody with its harmonic underpinning, and you witness the gradual elevation of the material to its ideal status.

Sometimes I liken the creative act to that of being a good gardener. The musical material itself, the harmonies, rhythms, timbres, and tempi, are seeds you have planted. Composing, bringing forth the final formal arrangement of these elements, is often a business of watching them grow, knowing when to nourish and water them and when to prune and weed. Morton Feldman once likened musical tones to people. "I don't think you should push them . . . they're very much like human beings—if you push them, they push you back. So, if I have a secret it would be: Don't push the sounds." This doesn't suggest that composing is in any way a passive act, but rather that the alchemy of rhythm, pitch, and timbre requires that the composer heed the implications of what he's written and not try to force an arbitrary solution. The discomfort one so often feels when listening to schematically composed music is the result of the musical elements being forced to behave according to principles that are arbitrarily imposed by the numerical scheme, where the tones have been too aggressively "pushed" in order to fit a predetermined plan.

When I was quite young I read *A Composer's World* by Paul Hindemith, a book in which he laid out his theories on how music ought to be composed. For Hindemith everything must be known about the piece before the first note is committed to paper. Such precompositional certainty was for him indispensable in order to begin. In a vivid metaphor, he likens that moment of inspiration to the way a darkened landscape is instantaneously illuminated during a lightning storm. For a split second we see all the minutest details surrounding us in complete clarity. This is the vision of the completed piece that the composer holds in his mind during the ensuing labor of committing it all to the manuscript paper.

I find Hindemith's image evocative, but it bears little resemblance to the way I compose. Instead, I often plunge into a new work like an explorer navigating uncharted waters, with only a rough idea of what is lying out there just beyond the visible horizon. And I suspect I am not alone in doing this. When I consider the first version that Sibelius made of his Fifth Symphony and compare it with the final product, I am impressed at how the first attempt reveals a composer not fully aware of the potential of his own materials. The rudiments are there, and the piece's genetic code has been established, but Sibelius has yet to discover where and how the pieces might best fit together, as if he were still groping around in a dark room, fumbling for the light switch. The mythology of classical music has promoted an image of the genius composer hearing all the sounds in his head and simply writing them down, as if by automatic writing. I strongly doubt this is the case, even with a quick, laser-sharp mind like Mozart's. Composers certainly have the gift of internalizing the gestalt of a piece, of being able mentally to move chunks of material around in musical space, imagining any number of formal arrangements. But this abstract ability can't exist entirely in a vacuum. One needs the stimulation of the tactile contact with sound. That is why so many composers have received their best inspiration improvising with some sort of instrument, be it a piano, a synthesizer, a guitar, or a room full of percussion instruments. We know that Beethoven, even in his period of most advanced deafness, still used the piano as part of the compositional process, even if he had to lay his head directly on the sounding board of the instrument to receive the vibrations through his bones.

For me the most difficult moment is always the beginning of a new piece. Even if I'm lucky enough to have come up with a striking opening idea, the first attempts at developing the material and making coherence often sputter and implode. I like to think that this is because I have yet to identify the piece's DNA, that I'm still unaware of what's buried within its strands of information. Often the "code" of a movement, if not an entire symphony or opera, is encapsulated within the first page or two, albeit in fractal form. Beethoven and Wagner packed an abundance of information in their opening motifs and harmonies, investing them with exceptional potential to generate large and complex expressive structures. But who knows how much effort it cost them to fully realize the potential of what their first ideas contained?

Who knows for sure whether, after the full work was completed, the composer didn't revisit the opening and tweak it to more perfectly mirror the course of later events?

We composers often are at a loss to explain how we made something. Oftentimes I will be singularly unable to remember the route I took to arrive at some unusually satisfying musical moment. A more methodical composer would probably have a drawer full of schematic flowcharts that would show the step-by-step evolution of the piece's growth. But I suspect that most composers work in a state of semitrance, a creative state that is precariously balanced between conscious, logical decision-making and the unknowable instinctual workings of the freely associating brain. I have a deep respect for my own subconscious apparatus, for that part of me that is unknowable. Over the years I've taught myself to remain open to any unexpected inspiration, virtually to relearn a child's state of mind. I remember sitting in the architect Frank Gehry's studio in Santa Monica, while he made pencil sketches of the patterns of scales on a fish. On that particular day he was obsessed with the way fish scales fit together. Sooner or later that playful obsession would transform itself into an architectural inspiration. But had Gehry suffered from the usual self-canceling impulses that most "mature" creative artists eventually acquire, the utter simplicity of his discovery, so pregnant with possibility, would have been nipped in the bud.

A compositional idea may come from any source. The composer's mind is like flypaper, ready at any moment to attract and trap an idea, a single sound or a complex of sounds. It may be the rhythms of a group of people chattering in a restaurant, or the Doppler effect of a passing train, or three notes from someone else's song, be it Mahler's or Otis Redding's. Or an inspiration might arise from half-consciously diddling with some piece of technology. We need to foster and jealously protect the "what if" mode of creative play, taking delight in moving sounds around just for the pleasure of seeing and hearing what might happen. The point is to maintain a childlike openness, not to foreclose on a possibility because it does not immediately fit your preconceived notions of what the piece you wish to compose *ought* to sound like.

Any truly inventive artist brings to the act of creation abilities that are on the one hand playful, intuitive, and open to any possibility, and on the other hand powerfully self-critical. Both capacities are indispensable. If one lacks a free, uncompromised sense of play, ideas will arrive (if they arrive at all) stale and stillborn. But once the good idea arrives it must be handled expertly and critically. If the composer's critical sense is not acute enough to judge the rightness of an idea, the possibility of it growing and blossoming into a fully satisfying form will be compromised by what we call, for lack of a less blunt term, a failure of taste. The creative act is a balance of positive and negative forces, the yin and yang of a subconscious artistic invention that goes hand in hand with a keenly attuned, conscious power of discrimination.

10.

THE MACHINE IN THE GARDEN

ne afternoon in the spring of 1968 a mysterious-looking device with blinking red-and-amber lights, dials, meters, and a cat's cradle of thin gray cables was wheeled into an empty attic room in the Harvard Music Department. In a building otherwise devoted to worn-out grand pianos, blackboards with musical staves, and stacks of printed music, it contributed an anomalous and eerie presence like a piece of medical technology or an experiment from a nearby physics lab.

The machine sat on a large bench top, and with its three panels suggested a space-age triptych of buttons, switches, jacks, and a tangle of multicolored cables. It was one of the first modular electronic music synthesizers, made by an eccentric and brilliant inventor in California, Don Buchla. Even before my first encounter with it, the sound of the synthesizer was well on its way to becoming familiar to anyone listening to popular music in that era. Its metallic, shiny, futuristic timbre would soon enchant a whole generation of listeners who would automatically associate its sound with the psychedelic experience, its timbres emblematic of the love generation, suggesting—wink wink—"alternate" states of consciousness. The modular synthesizer was the newest and most accessibly prepackaged advance in the slow but steady evolution of musical instruments powered by electricity rather than by muscle and tissue—the hands, arms, lips, or diaphragm—of the performer.

    y life, both as a composer and as a performer, has been dominated by the confrontation of naturally produced acoustical sound with that which is electronically produced and reaches my ears via a loudspeaker. The marriage of these two means of making and reproducing music has been a fact of life since Thomas Edison first recorded his voice onto a tin-foil disk in 1877, only a year after he introduced the first commercially available microphone. The invention of sound reproduction is *the* historical dividing line between the Old World and the New World of music. Recordings, radio transmission, microphones, and loudspeakers radically changed how music is consumed and facilitated the rise of what we now know as popular culture. Absorbing a new piece of music could become a much easier, more passive activity. As a young boy growing up in the 1960s, I learned Beethoven's Ninth Symphony first by hearing it on an LP recording by Toscanini. Even though I heard live concerts from time to time, 90 percent of the virgin experiences I had with the classical canon, not to mention the great works of American jazz, came through the small speakers of a hi-fi set, later replaced by a stereo system. By comparison, an adolescent Aaron Copland, living at the time of the First World War, could only have heard a symphonic work by attending a live concert, and chances were slender that the performance would be at the level of my Toscanini recording. The only alternative to live concerts would be to get hold of the printed music and play it on the piano. This was indeed how most curious musicians learned the repertoire in the days before recorded music. When Brahms finished one of his symphonies, the first order of business was to arrange it for piano, either for solo or for four hands. The act of absorbing the work in this manner required skills and effort far beyond the passive involvement of a record collector sitting in front of a stereo console. Musical sophistication or "literacy" was the exception rather than the rule, and in a frontier culture like America's in the nineteenth century, it was a rarity shared almost exclusively by the upper classes. The musical education of the young Charles Ives, living in small-town Connecticut in the 1880s, was a chaotic seat-of-the-pants affair that included everything from the obligatory piano lessons to playing organ in the local church, watching his father's marching band rehearse, learning Beethoven and Schumann by laborious hours spent at the keyboard, and composing pieces that might never be performed live except by himself at the piano. The future visionary composer of the Fourth Symphony and the "Concord" Sonata took in music firsthand, but with real effort and without having easy access to what I, growing up eighty years later, had gathered in my burgeoning record collection.

Recorded music had an impact on twentieth-century musical culture so profound that historians have not even begun to analyze its effect. There is little doubt that its easy availability created a more passive listening audience, with many learning the repertory from LPs or CDs. On the other hand recordings, especially in the era of compact discs, increased our awareness of and familiarity with a vast range of styles. What began in the 1920s as mass-marketed 78 rpm disks that could barely contain more than a few minutes of scratchy, tinny sound evolved within the following eighty years to digitally compressed sound files that could contain an entire Wagner opera and allow it to be transmitted in a matter of minutes over an Internet connection. By the year 2000, the pressing issue for music consumers was no longer one of accessibility or availability, but rather one of discrimination. How did one find something new and of true value amid the blizzard of recordings currently available? Even more serious was the question "How can one make the public aware of your own creations amidst the din and chaos of what is already out there?"

Each new advance in technology has brought with it a generalized anxiety over the quality of the essential musical experience. Serious musicians worried that recorded music, with its emphasis on pristine technical perfection, would be to music what prepackaged food is to fresh organic produce. But this fear doesn't seem to have been confirmed. If anything, recorded music may have actually been a stimulus to performers, prodding them to even higher levels of technical accuracy.

One need only listen to an archival recording of the New York Philharmonic or the Concertgebouw Orchestra from the 1920s to hear how standards of ensemble playing and rhythmic precision have evolved since that time, much of which is due to the expectations that recorded music has nurtured in us. It is as if the recorded version of a work acts like a mirror in harsh light, threatening to expose the slightest wrinkle or blemish on the surface. Classical musicians today have to assume this kind of clinical perfection in their live performances. It is part of the job description, and the rare artist who can join technical perfection to absolute spontaneity and unpredictability—a Martha Argerich or a Yo-Yo Ma—has managed a peculiarly personal triumph over what has become too literal and too rigid an art form.

he union of technology and *live* performance, however, has always been an agonistic struggle fraught with colliding aesthetic values. For purists, that collision comes down to a single choice: Do we listen to music through loudspeakers or do we experience it directly from the human source, whether it be someone singing, playing a violin or guitar, or a hundred-piece orchestra performing in a concert hall? Popular music has never troubled itself with these decisions. Amplification and electronic manipulation have gone hand in hand with the invention of new styles. Rock would be unthinkable without amplification. I have long thought that great moments in the evolution of musical style are often the result of some new technological breakthrough. The emphatic, percussive language of Beethoven could never have been imagined in the previous era of harpsichords and viols. The invention of the electric guitar enabled a new expressive style based largely on that instrument's ability to sustain sound and vary its timbre by distortion and modulation. Jimi Hendrix understood this better than anyone.

One frequently cited definition of music is that it is "organized sound." Most of what is commonly considered music involves tones or pitches. Musical tones are the result of air molecules being pushed and pulled in a regular, periodic movement. Air itself is an elastic medium. (There could be no music in outer space because there is no air to transport the vibrations.) Any regularly vibrating body, be it a Stradivarius, a singer's vocal chords, or a humming air conditioner, produces an identifiable pitch. But we can identify it as such only if that vibration remains stable long enough for the psychoacoustic capacity of the brain to recognize its regularity. Much of what surrounds us in everyday life is noise—that is, disturbances in the elastic medium of the air that are *not* periodic, that do not produce a recognizable pitch. The anatomy of the inner ear and its interface with the brain is a miraculous and mysterious structure that is only partially understood. Aural cognition is an intricate interplay of consciously and unconsciously analyzed data. I can answer a telephone and hear the voice of an old friend from many years past and recognize within a split second who is talking. How does my brain, otherwise so easily distracted, make such rapid and accurate calculations well in advance of a willed response?

When I was still in graduate school a professor teaching a class in acoustics gave us a test. He made tape recordings of several different instruments all playing the same pitch. One was a piccolo, another a trumpet, another a violin, and another a clarinet. But before playing us the sounds of each instrument he took a razor blade and cut off the attack of each instrument's note, so that all we could hear was the sustained sound, not its attack. It was surprising how much of each instrument's individuality and identity had been lopped off. I could tell that all the instruments were playing the same note and that each was coming from a different instrument, but I had to struggle to recognize which instrument I was actually listening to. The lesson was that most of the characteristic information in a musical sound is in the onset, or the "attack." Strange but true: the attack is largely characterized by noise rather than by pitch. Each instrument has highly complex attack characteristics, and it is from here, in this split second of the beginning of a sound, that we derive the lion's share of the information. Of course there are many other contributing features to sound recognition, including resonance and formants, those special areas of characteristic frequency that help us to recognize words without having to painstakingly parse each sound. My professor's little demonstration revealed to me how much subtlety is embedded in the beginning of any sound and how vastly evolved is the anatomical and neurological network of the ear-brain network.

The science of psychoacoustic perception alone cannot explain the emotional power of a vibrating string or air column. Pulsation, whether it's the throbbing kick drum of a rock band or the much faster pulsation of a musical tone, has an immediate effect on the emotive structures of the brain and is capable of producing a palpable change of mood in the listener. What we generally understand as music is an organization of these sounds into a coherent pattern. The simplest children's song is in fact a subtle matrix of periodic frequencies (the tones of a scale), the acoustical phonemes or noises made by the tongue and other organs and tissues of the singer, all strung together by some form of architectonic organization involving repetition and formal symmetries. Tonality is a sensation of hearing musical pitches in hierarchical arrangement, giving us the feeling of a gravitational pull toward an all-powerful center. It is an ordering of sounds at a higher psychoacoustic level, specifically a human urge, although predicated on the naturally occurring ratios of a vibrating system, otherwise known as the harmonic series. Animals do not appear to have cognitive equipment to recognize tonal organization, although birdsong seems to involve rhythmic and intervallic cognitive factors.

Thinking about the listening experience on these most rudimentary levels has always been second nature for me. The problem with conventional music education, whether it be piano lessons for a five-year-old or a full-blown conservatory curriculum, is that the listening experience is inevitably presented as a closed system, confined to the twelve tones of the tempered scale as represented by the white and black keys of the piano. Mastering an instrument or becoming an accomplished singer is such a daunting task that one usually plunges in without first stopping to question what are the real essentials of the listening experience.

I didn't begin to ask these questions until I was well along in my college education. But I received stimulus to change my thinking from three very different sources. The first glimmer that there might be a different world out there happened on that day I first entered an electronic music studio. As clumsy and primitive as the early "tape music" studios of the sixties and seventies could be, they still could shake up one's notions about musical perception. Working with raw and primitive sound sources like sine wave oscillators or recorded snippets of ambient sound, I experienced how sound could be organized differently from the conventional tonal scheme I'd been spoon-fed since childhood. The tape recorder and the synthesizer not only produced sound differently than a live instrument but also suggested new and radical formal structures. Steve Reich's early tape pieces, *Come Out* and *Violin Phase*, were cast in completely novel musical forms that could never have been dreamed of without the aid of the tape recorder. Other machines, whether sequencers or random voltage generators, made their own musical forms, and these forms were new and never-before-imagined by any composer. It's common to hear about how the advent of moving pictures, with its techniques of fast edits, montage, and flashbacks, profoundly affected novelists and prompted a transformation of the narrative form. It's no less important to understand how the tape recorder and mixing board and digital sequencer have suggested new musical structures and new approaches to musical form and syntax. My own musical forms owe much to these new machines. As far back as 1977, in *Phrygian Gates*, I composed a piece as if the piano was the generator of waveforms. Rather than base the musical surface on small compact motifs, melodic fragments, or cells, I set out to build long architectonic structures of rippling wave motion. Being waves, the music by definition had to be repetitive and generate a perceptible pulse. I designed *Phrygian Gates* so that its undulations and slow transformations of mode would avoid producing a hypnotic monotony (although hypnotic monotony can have its own enchantments). Sudden, arbitrary changes in the mood, texture, tempo, and harmony would keep the listener continually poised to expect surprise or even shock. These characteristics begin to add up to a description of the features we associate with musical Minimalism. In fact, much of the aesthetic of Minimalism seemed to me to be a response to the precise, regular, periodic behavior of machines, and particularly of electronic machines. Certainly the early, pure process works for amplified organs and winds by Philip Glass give the impression of an autonomous electronic circuit passing back and forth over a grid of regular tones and periodic rhythms. This at times unnerving analogue of an impassive piece of technology both enchanted and disturbed listeners. I well remember the scorn that was heaped on Minimalist composers at the time of its first blossoming, how their use of seemingly endless, machinelike repetition and their supposed rhythmic obtuseness was deemed an affront to sophisticated listeners, a reduction of the musical experience to the most atavistic of principles.

Another source of viewing and hearing things differently came from my first encounters with non-Western music. Even in the 1960s it was rare to hear music that did not originate in the European systems of tonality and the musical forms that were derived from it, be it a Bach fugue, a Beethoven symphony, or a pop song. In the late sixties, influenced like so many of my contemporaries by George Harrison's sitar playing on several of the later Beatles albums, I began listening to recordings of the great North Indian sarod player Ali Akbar Khan. The world of Asian, African, and Middle Eastern music suddenly opened up my ears in a radical way. I realized for the first time that there were other ways to tune a scale than the default black-and-white tuning of the piano keyboard. I also realized that "through-composed" music, in which every note is written down by an "auteur" composer, was actually *not* the norm in the rest of the world. Indeed, the real standard is *not* written notation but improvisation based on rhythmic and melodic patterns and structures. Skilled, carefully inflected improvisation is a tradition with a long-standing pedigree in cultures as different as those in Java, India, and Turkey, or the jazz of the United States. Perhaps because of its very evanescent nature and the absence of written documentation, improvised music has had to struggle to be accorded canonical value in the minds of Western classical scholars. During my six years in college we students were never offered a course in a musical tradition that wasn't based on notation. Any music that did not present itself via the five-lined stave with accompanying notes and clefs was relegated to the disciplines of anthropology or ethnomusicology.

I also discovered that inflection in intonation, especially as it's done in the raga-style singing and instrument playing in the Indian subcontinent, could embody immense emotional force. Years later, when I composed *The Dharma at Big Sur* for the electric violinist Tracy Silverman, I did so with the keen awareness that in non-Western music the expressive power lies *in between the notes*, in the meaningful slides, glissandi, and portamenti that are the norm in so many other cultures.

In the European classical tradition, the piano, with its twelve precise divisions of the octave—inflexible, immovable—has dictated musical thinking for several centuries. Once developed, the piano quickly became a machine of almost tyrannical influence throughout the Western world. Its division of the octave into twelve intervals, each mathematically equidistant from its neighbors, forces one to regard pitches as discrete entities, like nations with strictly policed border. A piano-generated melody goes from point to point with no expressive sliding in between. This is not a fault—Bach and Mozart built their entire work on the notion—rather, it is a stylistic choice. Since the advent of the black-and-white keyboard (which of course is the concrete representation of the equally divided octave), Western music, particularly Western instrumental music, has had to state itself according to the twelve discrete, individual pitches of the scale, resulting in a more limited universe of emotional expression.

The perfectly equal division of the octave was a long time coming. J. S. Bach's "well-tempered" scale was not in fact a perfect democracy of intervals, but it began the process by which a single musical structure would no longer be bound to its one tonality.

In previous tuning systems, most of which were derived from a more natural resonant property of vibrating bodies, some intervals were more satisfying than others. Modulation to remote key areas was considered an unpromising expedition because the farther one got away from the tonic, the less consonant the intervals became. The tempered tuning of Beethoven's time allowed forays into more distant keys and with it came an explosion in expressive possibility, surprise, shock, and any number of new approaches to form. By the time of Wagner and Brahms true equal temperament, allowing for a potential overthrow of the tonic by any one of the other eleven available contenders, was assumed. To this day equal-tempered tuning holds a position of almost total hegemony in the Western world, being the source for everything composed and performed for the past 250 years. Wagner discovered that the perfect equanimity among pitches produced a lack of fixity that could be used to great emotional and psychological purpose. With this insight he developed the tools of harmonic detour and postponement as a means of maintaining formal and dramatic tension.

Schoenberg, Webern, Babbitt, and others saw in the neatly symmetrical division of the octave a group of integers, and they designed systems to make the pitches behave according to new principles that had little or nothing to do with the laws of harmony, laws which had evolved out of intuitive aesthetic judgment rather than mathematical principles.

But this tempered tuning system, so vividly embodied in the image of the black-and-white keys of the piano, does not encourage a way of treating pitch as something flexible and fluid. In the music of other cultures, and of course in the great tradition of African American music, the expressive slide constitutes the heart of the music's emotional power. In the ecstatic Qawwali singing of Pakistan, in melancholy Scottish folk songs, in the soaring saxophone of Johnny Hodges or Eric Dolphy, or in a bending and sliding electric guitar solo by Jimi Hendrix or Eric Clapton, the greatest expressive power lies in the bending of the tones. It lies in *how* one goes from one pitch to another. The archetypical blue note (technically a flatted seventh of the seven-tone scale) is usually approached via an expressive slide. Modern electric guitars, instruments that are defiantly indifferent to the neat, orderly black-and-white world of the piano keyboard, usually come equipped with a lever that allows the performer to bend the pitch this way or that.

This approach to melodic "shaping" couldn't be more different from that in a work by Bach or Stravinsky, where pitches are separate and there is no expressive space around them. A glissando in the middle of a Bach aria would be a positive indecency, whereas in an Indian raga it might be an expression of utmost devotion. This "sliding" or "keening" was doubtless discouraged long ago by the Church, who must have felt that it was *too* expressive, too much like a human in great pain or in great sexual ecstasy. Of course both of these qualities are what make us love a great jazz saxophonist, a Billie Holiday, or a master rock guitar player. But for a culture that was devoted to propriety and religious piety, the ordered division of the octave into stand-alone pitches represented a more appropriate image of divine law, and wailing was firmly discouraged.

John Cage was also instrumental in making me feel comfortable and in tune with new technology. His playful yet disciplined approach to objects of twentieth-century life like radios, loudspeakers, microphones, tape recorders, and even computers had for me the effect of empowerment. He gave me the courage to see technology as a fertile terrain for creativity. Cage celebrated the fact that we could accept the entire world of available sounds, including noise itself, as the base material with which to mold our new compositions. For a while this extravagant liberty seemed almost too good to be true. Even in the 1940s Cage himself had created performance works using radios, tube oscillators, kitchen appliances, and other unorthodox sound sources. Later, he and David Tudor had produced pieces like *Cartridge Music*, heavily amplifying the sound of a phonograph cartridge as it scraped against surfaces of wood, paper, metal, cloth, and other materials, producing a brave new world of aural experience. I suspect that these first experimental pieces of Cage's were the spiritual progenitors of the grunge aesthetic of the 1990s. It was under Cage's influence that I made my first experiments with electronics, including my first tape composition, *Heavy Metal*.

ventually I had to acknowledge the hard fact that while it may be possible to have meaning without pitch or without tonality, these possibilities are severely limited. Even Varèse, uncompromising futurist that he was, seems to have been cognizant of this limitation, because after he composed *Ionisation* in 1931, scoring it for percussion orchestra, he rarely if ever again attempted a work without some kind of pitched instruments, his late electronically conceived *Poème électronique* being a rare exception. *Ionisation*, a six-minute essay in making sonata form behave without the gravitational pull of a tonal center, is a first-of-its-kind invention. With its nervous snare-drum tattoos, anxious sirens, and sudden eruptions of lockstep violence, it evokes a nervous scenario of militaristic activity. It might be a perfect accompaniment to an old film of a dictator's afternoon. But, Varèse's and Cage's optimistic proclamations notwithstanding, composing with noise alone proved difficult. In *Ionisation* Varèse was able to achieve coherence and intelligibility only by creating small identifiable motifs and recirculating them throughout the piece, hinting at classical forms like the rondo and sonata. In the end he reverts to pitched sounds with the entrance of the piano and chimes, the arrival of which produces a startling and dramatic effect because they fill the air with resonance and color after so many minutes of unpitched noise.

While I gradually lost interest in making compositions out of pure noise, I continued to be enchanted by the new world of electronically produced sound—in fact I have never lost this sense of enchantment, even though the music that made my reputation was largely written for the traditional instruments of the orchestra or for voice. The overwhelming obstacle for composers of electronic music is one of the setting: For whom are you making this music and how will your listeners take it in? The options have never been very promising. Sitting in a dark room surrounded by loudspeakers has never had much appeal for even the most committed of audiences unless the music is combined with film or some other form of visual activity. Commercial releases, LPs or CDs of studio-produced electronic music, have proven a hard sell over the past four decades. Even the most inventive and imaginative electronic compositions by Stockhausen, Berio, Xenakis, Subotnick, Wuorinen, and Marshall have long remained niche items, seldom if ever emerging from their obscurity in the back bins labeled "electronic music." In the 1980s the appearance of a new genre of "soft" electronic music called New Age briefly hinted that there might be a younger and larger audience for electronically produced music. Listeners brought up on a diet of digitally produced music seemed more willing to accept a compact disc as the end result of the creative process. But there exist composers who have made an impact by inventing new genres of studio-produced music. Brian Eno, originally a rock performer with the band Roxy Music and a clever, imaginative studio producer, coined the term "ambient music" around the end of the 1970s to describe his smooth, dreamy, opiated sound washes. Virtually acknowledging the passive nature of consuming recorded music, Eno described his exquisitely engineered *Music for Airports* as if it were a Cageian utopia of equanimity among the sounds. "Ambient Music," he said, "must be able to accommodate many levels of listening attention without enforcing one in particular; it must be as ignorable as it is interesting." A few years later Nine Inch Nails began producing a body of work as dark and disturbing as Eno's could be sleek and becalmed, taking us to a new region of expression that further opened up the range of what electronically produced and engineered music could encompass.

By 2005 an even newer genre dubbed "electronica" had captured the attention of many serious listeners. My son, Sam, introduced me to the British composer Aphex Twin, aka Richard David James, who uses sophisticated computer programs, many reputedly of his own design, to create a style of music that could not possibly be rendered by live performers. Aphex Twin's nervous, insect-like pulses and sharp-edged timbres suggested a nonhuman world that can be as sinister and robotic as the androids of William Gibson or the Wachowski brothers.

Electronic technology that first entered my composing stream with *Heavy Metal* has continued to add color and texture to my orchestral palette. Most of my works involve one form or another of electronic instruments, sometimes only in the form of a keyboard synthesizer or sampler in the orchestra, at other times, as in *On the Transmigration of Souls*, as a fully realized sound environment, completely integrated into the orchestral setting. After the "faulty wiring" period of my first San Francisco days, I began using more reliable instruments. The advent of digital synthesizers in the early eighties was a mixed blessing. The digital synth behaved predictably and kept the tuning and wave modulations exact and constant. No more wandering, screaming feedback loops from overcooked oscillators or burned circuit boards. But the downside of the introduction of digital was that all the synthesizers came hardwired to the conventional black-and-white piano keyboard. You opened the box, plugged in the synth, and the first thing you did was play the keyboard, producing the same old version of the notes of the tempered scale, long familiar to us since the time of Bach. This of course made conventional musical organization along tonal lines very easy, but as a default mode it also made one less apt to stumble upon truly novel, futuristic discoveries. For all the bulkiness and ornery stubbornness of my homemade Studebaker of the seventies, that clumsy instrument was a real "black box" waiting for me to tell it what to do. The sleek digital synths of the next decade, those made by Yamaha, Korg, and Roland, were preprogrammed with colorful timbres, but their musical essence remained locked to the traditional tempered scale that was already hundreds of years old.

Nevertheless, I took quickly to the newer instruments. The long electronic symphony I created for Lucinda Childs, *Light Over Water*, was made with a simple Casio keyboard that produced only several organ-like timbres, timbres which I passed through an effects processor and recorded on a multichannel tape recorder. *Light Over Water* was admittedly compromised by the crudeness of its technology. Many of the spontaneous musical impulses that came to me were oftentimes impeded by the clumsiness of the instruments. All the gear used to make it could fit into the backseat of small car. As music it aimed high, an attempt to compose a Brucknerian symphonic form, projecting long vistas of sustained harmonies building over fifty minutes to a final, majestically ramped crescendo. But the tools at my disposal were too primitive to make a polished, aurally satisfying whole. Laptops were still a thing of the future, so all the fruits of my labor lived on a single, easily damaged, three-quarter-inch four-channel tape. The recorded sound was compromised by my medium-priced tape deck, and internal balances were hit or miss.

But I persisted. In *Nixon in China* I wrote for a two-manual Yamaha synthesizer, the Electone. This instrument was one of the first synthesizers to incorporate the technique of frequency modulation, a synthesis technique invented by the engineer and composer John Chowning at Stanford University. The Chowning algorithms were clangorous, crunchy, and colorful, and for a period of five or more years in the mid-eighties they were the emblematic sound of new music, especially after Chowning sold his patent to Yamaha, who turned it into the ubiquitous DX7, the most popular synthesizer of all time.

For *The Death of Klinghoffer* I went much further, virtually basing the orchestration on an ensemble of four MIDI-controlled synthesizers, a total of five keyboards, and one mallet-controlled synthesized percussion instrument. The problems arising from this heavy technical requirement have plagued me and the piece ever since. Synthesizers and samplers are not like violins and pianos. They are not generic instruments that basically stay unchanged over many years. Beethoven might compose for pianoforte, but he would certainly recognize his music played two hundred years later on a modern Steinway. The new electronic instruments, however, are like software operating systems. They morph on an almost yearly basis, requiring constant upgrading and modification. My music publisher, Boosey and Hawkes, a company accustomed to licensing and selling sheet music, was now having to cope with floppy disks, sound files, and the constant headache of keeping abreast of the ever-evolving digital music industry. Even so, for all the daunting challenges it entails, the incorporation of electronic instruments into the orchestral palette of my operas and orchestral works has enabled me to deeply enrich the nature of my sound world.

It is an immensely complex undertaking to successfully marry the sound of natural acoustic instruments with those that come from a synthesizer, sampler, or computer-generated program. The setting in the concert hall or opera house is often fraught with discontinuities. Over time I have come to realize that a generalized sound design is required to make a completely unified and satisfying experience. Ideally, when electronic sound sources are involved, the entire listening space should be organized and acoustically prepared. Around 2005 the acoustician and loudspeaker manufacturer John Meyer, of Berkeley, California, began working on a sound system called Constellation that he installs in a performance space after having minutely measured every resonant nook and cranny with computer-aided listening instruments. Meyer's technology is able to improve a dead, acoustically unresponsive space into something resembling a live, resonant performance area. This is a major advance from merely sticking a public-address cluster in the ceiling of an auditorium and hoping for the best.

By 2000, with all my stage works I was requiring that every aspect of the production be subject to sound design. This extended not only to the performers—the singers, chorus, orchestra, and electronic sounds—but to the actual room itself. The confidence I had in doing this was bolstered by the growing collaboration I was enjoying with an exceptionally brilliant and creative sound designer, Mark Grey, who proved that sensitive and subtle use of technology can be a major artistic element in the listening experience.

I found that I sometimes needed nerves of steel and an iron will to effect my desires. Most orchestras and opera companies were reluctant to support the expense. And even if proper sound design could be achieved, it would inevitably be followed by objections from musical purists, certain that the use of microphones heralded the corruption of the art form. The day after the world premiere of my opera *Doctor Atomic*, an opera with any number of thought-provoking artistic and moral issues, the music critic of a major U.S. newspaper chose to devote a sizable part of his otherwise thoughtful article to complaining about what he called "amplification." And he returned to the subject a week later with another article, warning of the incipient damage this practice was threatening to wreak on the natural human voice. By utilizing sound design with its multiple microphones, speakers, and mixing boards in my stage works I certainly was not proposing it ought to be the norm for the next run of *Figaro* or *Traviata*. I was seeking to create my own individual acoustic environment. This environment is as much a part of the originality of my music as the notes and harmonies and timbres. The music critic, having anxiously exported his concerns about the potential corrupting of Mozart or Verdi into the way I wanted my own operas to sound, was doing me a disservice by not judging my work on its own, as an entirely new sound world.

I understand now the gale-force winds of tradition that a composer like Wagner encountered when trying to introduce a millennial change in the way his audiences experienced music drama. The marriage of the machine to the musical experience is no more and no less a provocation and a stimulus to our normal modes of behavior than the machine's intrusion into all other parts of our lives. It can, as is often warned, be a source of corruption of the art form. Anyone suffering through any recent Broadway musical with its horrifically overamped vocals and shrill, unbalanced microphones will know this lamentable truth. But at the same time new technologies can be a stimulus for new modes of aesthetic experience and novel creative impulses. Artists should take each new step in the evolution of these machines and turn them into instruments of divine play. It's what we do.

11.

TECHNICAL DIFFICULTIES

At the age of four I made my first appearance as a performer in a production of Jean Cocteau's *Les Mariés de la Tour Eiffel*, standing next to my mother on the stage of the Woodstock Playhouse in Woodstock, Vermont. I perched on a chair and threw make-believe paper bullets from a basket at the assembled cast, most of whom were wearing berets and monocles. Six years later I again appeared with my mother in Rodgers and Hammerstein's *South Pacific*. I played the role of Jerome, the little French-Polynesian boy who, along with his sister, opens the show with the song:

Dites-moi porquoi la vie est belle,
Dites-moi porquoi la vie est gaie.
Dites-moi pourquoi,
Chère Mad'moiselle,
Est-ce que
Parce que
Vous m'aimez?

I wore a knee-length sarong and my otherwise naked torso was daubed a deep café au lait to suggest that the Polynesian sun was smiling on what in reality was the frigid and drafty stage of the Concord, New Hampshire, municipal auditorium in midwinter. When I was not onstage, I sat in the pit next to the pianist, following the score, learning all the songs by heart. Later seasons brought other musicals into the circle of my acquaintance, many of which featured Elinore Adams in the contralto "mature woman" roles: *Carousel*, *Oklahoma!*, *The King and I*, and *The Sound of Music*. The radio airwaves were full of famous singers doing covers of songs by Cole Porter, the Gershwin brothers, Lerner and Loewe, and of course, the Leonard Bernstein–Stephen Sondheim collaboration I thought was the summit of the art, *West Side Story*. It is hard to describe how, during the era before rock began to exert its hegemony over radio and television, the songs of these immensely talented composers and lyricists, almost all of them second-generation American Jews, saturated the country's collective musical memory. What began in the first decade of the century with the simpler harmonic practice and shallower psychological shadings of Irving Berlin, Victor Herbert, and Jerome Kern by the late twenties had grown more subtle and ambiguous. Ira Gershwin's rhymes reveled in an urbanity and sophistication that managed to be both cosmopolitan and slyly vernacular at the same time. His brother George's harmonic genius and the Mozartean fecundity of his melodic gift transported these lyrics, uniting verbal phrase to musical motif in an inseparable and perfect epoxy. That generation of composers had grown up learning music by playing the great nineteenth-century piano music, particularly Chopin, Schumann, and perhaps a little Liszt, Brahms, and Debussy. They brought to their songwriting an intuitive sense of harmonic balance, a gift for the piquantly sustained dissonance, and a shared taste for the half-diminished chord, that Tristan harmony so beloved of anyone looking to summon up an aching heart.

The Richard Rodgers songs I learned at a young age were of a sunnier variety than those that he had written with his first partner, Lorenz Hart. The songs of the Oscar Hammerstein period were more attuned to the mythically imagined Middle America of Norman Rockwell or Frank Capra. Like Aaron Copland, another New York Jew, Rodgers, during the 1930s, had made a similar stylistic voyage out of cosmopolitan Manhattan into the imagined American heartland. In the thirties Copland had abandoned his Modernism of the previous decade in favor of the "common man" aesthetics of the Depression and war era. Rodgers took the popular song in a similar direction. What he composed in *Oklahoma!*, *Carousel*, *South Pacific*, and *The Sound of Music* might lack the harmonic ingenuity of Gershwin, but his songs had a freshness and uncluttered simplicity that earned them instantaneous folk status. Americans may have welcomed the operas of Mozart, Verdi, and Wagner to their stages, but when it came to cultivating a native tradition of music theater they favored the Broadway musical for its easier, more familiar connection to the vernacular.

After I left home for college, I lost touch with theater music and only thought about those songs when I heard them in a version by Miles Davis or Bill Evans. But the notion of writing a Broadway-style music-theater piece lingered in the back of my mind. Then, in 1993, I conducted Kurt Weill and Bertolt Brecht's *Mahagonny Songspiel* at the Ojai Festival and in Minnesota with the Saint Paul Chamber Orchestra. A mordant precursor of the wildly popular *Threepenny Opera*, the *Songspiel* appealed to me because of its skillful mixing of period jazz, cabaret songs, and the "new" music of composers like Hindemith and Stravinsky. The Brecht/Weill collaborations—*Threepenny Opera*, *The Seven Deadly Sins*, *Rise and Fall of the City of Mahagonny*—were the bitter harvest of a broken Germany, a society whose culture and economy had bottomed out, crushed and humiliated by defeat in a war it had initiated out of pure hubris. Compared to the sunny palaver and cheeky repartee of the Broadway musical of the same time, what the Germans in the 1920s were making was dark and acerbic theater that cut close to the bone, saying something deep and troubling about the human condition. The songs were cast in a tonality of despair and cynicism with a morbid humor that would have been unbearable had it not come from the mouths of such appealing characters. These were Brecht's downtrodden, the drunks, prostitutes, and wandering street people who in spite of it all managed to maintain a defiant humanity in the face of life's most brutal obstacles.

For years I'd kept a mental cache of musical and theatrical ideas thinking that I might someday write my own piece of musical theater. It seemed only logical that I should be able to produce something of that genus, given my childhood exposure and my love for the repertory. I talked about it circumspectly with Peter Sellars, knowing that one of his first professional experiences, a staging of a Gershwin revue called *My One and Only*, had ended in his being fired by the show's producers. I wanted to make something that had the wit and social percipience of Brecht, but I wanted to couch it in the American musical vernacular. I'd loved American pop music, particularly that of the late 1960s, almost as much as I'd loved the classical canon. I didn't feel that being good in one field precluded success in the other. Both Gershwin and Bernstein had moved freely within the two disciplines, although admittedly not without their share of misfires.

I searched high and wide for a librettist. Friends in New York suggested setting up meetings with famous theater stars like John Guare and Tony Kushner. Thom Gunn, the brilliant San Francisco poet, at the time one of the best of our living writers, proposed a libretto about Jeffrey Dahmer, the infamous Midwest necrophiliac and cannibal who had murdered seventeen young boys. Gunn thought that an opera, the main character of which not only had sex with his victims but ultimately ate their flesh, was the logical progression from Isolde's *Liebestod*. It wasn't quite what I had in mind.

And then Peter and I both began reading the work of June Jordan, poet, essayist, and political activist who was a professor of African American Studies at the University of California in Berkeley. June was a socially committed artist with a rich and complicated past, having survived a difficult upbringing in Brooklyn and Harlem and having come of age during the heat of the civil rights movement. Her Jamaican-born father, determined to see his daughter excel in a world of white indifference and hostility, had treated her harshly in the hopes of making her tough and resilient. Although fortunate enough to attend private schools and graduate from Barnard College, she still felt the brunt of racism throughout her younger years, especially when she married another student, a white man, and experienced firsthand the sting of recrimination and discrimination from both blacks and whites. Separated from her husband, now a single mother, she eked out an existence by writing journalism and an occasional book review. She wrote poetry and children's books and eventually became one of the country's most impassioned and eloquent essayists with a range of concerns that touched on almost every social and political hot point confronting the country over a thirty year period: the civil rights

movement, Vietnam, black power, Nicaragua, Northern Ireland, Palestine, women's rights, and sexual freedom. Trapped with hundreds of
others in the terrifying mayhem of the Harlem Riot of 1964 when
white police fired indiscriminately into crowds of unarmed blacks,
she developed, as she later wrote, "a hatred for everything and everyone white." But she had resolved not to succumb to that embitterment
but rather "to use what I loved, words, for the sake of the people I
loved . . . This was self-interest, to be sure. As Mrs. Fannie Lou Hamer
said, years later, as she stood on her porch in Mississippi, 'Ain' no such
a thing as I can hate anybody and hope to see God's face.' "

June's poems appealed to me because they spoke with the authority of personal experience, yet they were full of humor, warmth, and a
generous eroticism. By the time I met her she had moved from New
York to Berkeley and had already attained heroic status among grass-
roots activists for any number of progressive causes. The FBI must
surely have had a vault full of information on her, because she had
never ceased to be at the forefront on the most intensely debated social
issues of our time. But June was never a poseur, never an opportunist
who jumped from one noble cause to another in search of self-
validation. All her commitments were from the heart, and although
emotionally and physically drained by the demands made on her by all
these causes, she never lost a lightness of touch that was the precious
complement to her iron will. The extraordinary durability of her character came accompanied by a warmth and gentleness that was punctuated by a wry and hearty laugh that always managed to throw life's
multiple indignities into perspective.

We were soon gathering in her sun-filled bungalow on Carlotta
Street in north Berkeley, gradually evolving a theatrical story that
would become *I Was Looking at the Ceiling and Then I Saw the Sky*. The
spacious and alluring title was a survivor's quote that June had found
in a newspaper account of the 1994 Northridge, California, earthquake. I have forgotten how that earthquake, at the time of our writing
only a year in the past, became the focus of our piece. The three of us
were all California transplants, June from Brooklyn and Harlem, Peter
from suburban Pittsburgh, and I from rural New England. But each
had found something privately meaningful about his or her West
Coast experience—we were grateful immigrants. June had initiated a

significant project at UC Berkeley called Poetry for the People, an imaginative program to make poetry a vehicle for self-expression and empowerment among all types of people, young and old, in the extended community. People's poetry was greeted with skepticism and not a little condescension among the academic literary community, some of whose members viewed Poetry for the People more as a social welfare project than as a valued artistic activity. But I liked the Whitmanesque democracy of language and expression that inspired June to invent this program. To me, what she was doing and saying was a fresh and spontaneous alternative to the precious obscurities of the contemporary poetry coming from the East Coast establishment.

What transpired was a multivectored love story, an "earthquake/romance," situated in the ethnic bouillabaisse of urban Los Angeles. The libretto's potentially harsh themes of racism, immigration, homophobia, and sexual harassment were leavened by June's humor and her natural feel for the rhythms of inner-city speech. The characters are all twenty-somethings, sensual, impulsive, full of self-doubts and insecurities, rocked and buffeted by the tedious impositions of adult authority and the daily insults of the police, the government, the media, and even their contemporaries. But this is a love story, not necessarily one with a perfect happy ending but one in which feelings are ultimately positive and optimistic. It must have been a balm for June to compose poetry so full of youthful energy and wit, because at this same time she was suffering from a wrenchingly painful form of breast cancer that eventually took her life. *Ceiling/Sky* allowed her to express in a less confrontational manner than she did in her essays the deep feelings that she'd long experienced about gender, race, discrimination, and violence. It was no small thing that a woman who in her earlier years had been raped and forced to flee naked into the night from her assailant could, thirty years later, still celebrate with humor the joys of heterosexual love as she does in "Song About the Bad Boys and the News," when the three girls sing:

and then there's The Absolute Sleeper
The flower
The fish
and the bone

and the bone on the throne
and the delicate flesh on the bone
on the Throne
the pen on the pillow of sperm
the penis stretched out for Venus
the Thunderbolt
long as it's firm!

The tense, brittle social and racial confrontations that constitute *Ceiling/Sky*'s foreground all melt away amid the warmth and engaging sexuality that permeates the seven characters' mutual attractions. David, the charismatic black Baptist preacher (modeled in part on the Harlem congressman Adam Clayton Powell Jr.), can't keep his roving eyes and roving hands off the younger ladies of his parish. But he's met his match in Leila, a smart, attractive black graduate student who works in a family-planning clinic, trying to educate young teenage couples about birth control. Leila may be blunt and clinical in her lectures on hygiene, but she is cautious and vulnerable in matters of the heart. She feels the electric pull of David's male energy, but she is not about to be just another station in his rake's progress.

Dewain, the sweet but hard-luck gang member trying to straighten out his life, is pursued by the young white rookie cop, Mike. After an altercation in a corner convenience store, Mike slaps the handcuffs on Dewain, charging him with a trumped-up felony—he's stolen two bottles of beer and then argued with the arresting officer when caught. But Mike's anger is not because of Dewain's petty crime; it's because his secret infatuation with Dewain is only getting a busy signal. Tiffany, a grown-up Barbie doll of a woman, a roving correspondent for a "crime as news" television show, has her own problem, an aching and unrequited crush on the handsome Mike. As clueless about his sexuality as he is, she thrills to be taken around in his squad car as he cruises the various ethnic neighborhoods of Los Angeles. "How far can I go in a car (driven by a cop)?" she sings to herself, puzzled over her hero's frustrating inability to read her hints.

A counterpoint of small and large plot elements comes to a climax when the earthquake suddenly jolts everyone's life. The walls of Dewain's prison cell break asunder, and he is able to walk away to free-

dom. David, having finally convinced Leila of the purity of his intentions, takes her for a tryst in the sanctuary of his church. When the
earthquake hits, a falling pillar fatally injures her. As Leila's life ebbs
away, David, in shock and remorse, finally understands how precious a
thing real love is.

The piece's three creators were not always in full agreement about
the nature of the characters or the flow of events in the story. Consuelo, a Salvadoran refugee and teenage mother of two, was difficult to
limn. According to our plan, she would be Dewain's girlfriend, hence
the Latina "novia" of a young black man. She would be beset by two
simultaneous crises. Her four-year-old son is kidnapped by the Immigration and Naturalization Service, and she is thrown into a panic
because she fears that if she goes to rescue him she, as an "illegal
alien," will be immediately arrested and deported. But Dewain can't
come to her aid because he's once again run afoul of the law (the arrest for stealing the beer) and, since it's his third felony, he's facing
a mandatory prison sentence. Consuelo may be a political refugee
from the right-wing death squads of her homeland, but to the police
and to the bilious talk-radio hosts, who fill the airwaves with merciless
immigrant-bashing, she is nothing more than an undocumented Hispanic. As commentators like Lou Dobbs would so quickly point out,
simply by having crossed the border without permission, Consuelo is
a lawbreaker, a criminal.

June Jordan could speak from painful personal experience about
the toxic racial tensions that permeated relations between white police
forces and the black, Hispanic, and Asian communities they patrolled
and routinely harassed. Only a few years earlier the videotaped beating
of an unarmed black man, Rodney King, at the hands of LAPD officers
had set off the most destructive urban race riot in twenty years. An
emotional California ballot initiative, recently approved by the state's
voters, had instituted an arbitrary "three strikes and you're out" law,
requiring that a third felony conviction, regardless of the nature of the
crime, result in a mandatory prison sentence. The state's prisons, already teeming with young, undereducated, unemployed black and
Hispanic men would now have to absorb a huge surge of new inmates,
most of whom would be returned to society with little or no hope of
making a successful reintegration. Dewain, whose three felonies have

been victimless, is thus facing hard time for what are in fact minor offenses.

Of all my stage works, *Ceiling/Sky* took the most lumps upon its initiation and has had the hardest time establishing itself. People who might normally be disposed to like it felt its politics were too close to the surface, too much a case of preaching to the converted. And, as I soon learned, fending off charges of political correctness is a futile task. Labels have a way of boring in like ticks. Once you're stuck with a tag, your only recourse is to wait it out.

The more conservative critics saw the show as an affront to moral decency, an example of the typically liberal romanticization of criminals and scofflaws, a similar charge to the one that had been leveled at *Klinghoffer*. For them, *Ceiling/Sky* made light of serious issues of law and order—graffiti on public property, illegal immigration, drug abuse, and abortion—and instead of condemning these lawbreakers, we the show's creators appeared to be letting them go scot-free. And Peter's extreme sense of delicacy and respect for the ethnic backgrounds of the characters prevented some of the bawdier and raunchier suggestions of the text and the music from coming to the fore. Consuelo, for instance, an eighteen-year-old Latina, was made to dress with a demure modesty that I doubted any present-day L.A. inner-city teenager would even dream of. There were no bustiers, no high-heeled lifts, no flashy jewelry or Afro "dos," no tattoos, tinted hair, or significant body piercings. Instead, all of the characters dressed as if they were turning out for a job interview or to canvass for their favorite congressman.

The themes of the show were timely, perhaps uncomfortably so. I had argued with Peter about the veracity of the INS actually kidnapping immigrant children and using them for bait to capture their frantic parents, but he insisted this was standard operating policy for policing the border. This I strongly doubted at the time, but twelve years later, in 2007, while Congress was yet again wrestling with an immigration bill, an article in *The New York Times* by Nina Bernstein described the "boom" in immigration detention, what she termed "the nation's fastest-growing form of incarceration," a program that "ensnares people for dubious reasons, denies them access to medicine and lawyers and sometimes holds them until they die." My collaborators had indeed been right about this. The only difference was that the situation had become worse in the intervening years.

To a lot of otherwise willing enthusiasts *Ceiling/Sky* may have felt overly hectoring and issue-driven. Many who came to the performances prepared to be entertained left three hours later visibly stunned and annoyed. After each performance Peter mounted the stage and held a Brechtian postmortem with what was left of the audience. There was no doubting the sincerity of his impulses, but I was uneasy with the wholly political spin he was putting on the piece, turning it into a civics lesson, a *Lehrstück*.

I composed twenty songs to June's lyrics. I quickly discovered that a good pop song needs to get to the point immediately. You want that "hook" within the first thirty seconds. For a composer who'd found his voice in 1970s Minimalism and who was used to taking at least a half hour or more to get his musical jumbo jets off the runway, the demands of a five- or six-minute pop song presented a wholly new challenge. Fortunately I already had some experience in terse, compacted pieces. I'd composed the four-minute *Short Ride in a Fast Machine* in 1985, and I'd also done music for several sixty-second television commercials, a challenge I accepted less for the money than for the unique demands it made on my composing processes. But none of that prepared me for the task ahead. I found that, although I loved doing it, turning out one song after another was hugely exhausting. I worked hard for a solid year on *Ceiling/Sky*.

June's libretto was cast in very free verse, with some lines being short and concise followed by others in a different rhythm that could be two to three times the length of their predecessors. Although we were living in the same town, communication between the two of us very rapidly grew distant and difficult. She and Peter had bonded like electrons, and I often found myself on the outside looking in. As was usual in our collaborations, during the creative phase Peter was physically present for only a tiny fraction of the time, although he was available by phone to help solve dramatic and structural issues. But the libretto often bewildered me, not because of the quality of its imagination or its inventiveness but because I found the rhythmic and formal design of June's verse extremely hard to put to music. It was not the sort of criticism I could easily voice, least of all to a widely respected and much published woman of letters like June. Instead, I assigned the blame to myself, thinking that the problem of not being able to come up with good solutions to the text-setting was a fault of my own stubborn ways.

Some songs came easily, and I finished them in a matter of days, even hours. With others I struggled for much too long, and instead of asking June to make changes, I simply avoided contact with her, which was of course tremendously counterproductive. Eventually I began to play the songs for her, and the two of us took real joy in what we'd done. But there was a crushing number of them to set, the show was getting longer and longer, and no one seemed to want to yield ground. Things were further stressed by June's decision to publish the entire libretto as a hardcover book of poetry in advance of the premiere. With the libretto now published, chances of retooling the story or altering the structure appeared to recede further and further into the distance. At one point June bopped me with the criticism, "There have been altogether too many libretto violations in this project." At another point, in an interview she gave for a newspaper article, she referred to me as "privileged," a code word that I had little trouble deciphering.

Some thought that my notion of composing pop songs was bound to misfire since I had not arisen from that tradition but was only taking a tourist dip in the waters. Others felt, perhaps accurately, that although the story was about young, hip inner-city kids in their twenties, the music I'd composed for them was hardly the kind of cutting-edge stuff that they would actually be listening to. *Rent*, a Broadway show with similar themes, wisely kept the musical language more consciously contemporary, and in so doing became a hugely popular and commercial success while our show struggled to fill the house as it limped from California to Montreal to New York and then on to Europe.

The ingenious set for *Ceiling/Sky* was a sequence of several dozen colorful graffiti backdrops, each one keyed to the title of a particular song. These backdrops were painted by tag artists, the best of whose graffiti skills had evolved to the point of being bold expressions of a new urban art form. The casting was done the old-fashioned way, by holding auditions in a series of small, cramped studios in Manhattan.

Our singers were young and talented, but they were versed only in pop and Broadway styles. Several could not read music without difficulty and could only learn my tricky rhythms by means of endless repetition. But this did not prevent them from finally internalizing their roles and their songs and giving, at least in some cases, absolutely memorable performances. Darius de Haas, an excellent musician who had no trouble absorbing the written score, played the role of David, the randy preacher. He could catapult his thrilling tenor voice into a stratospheric falsetto that brought immediate goose bumps. Welly Yang, in the role of Rick, the love-struck young public defender, dazzled with a flawless machine-gun delivery of his courtroom scenes.

I composed for a band of eight players—at the premiere it was the excellent Paul Dresher Ensemble—all of whom had to be multitalented in styles of rock and jazz and be skilled readers. For the first production I made the mind-boggling requirement that each character act and sing everything using a hand-held microphone, à la Mick Jagger or Aretha Franklin. Thus, Mike, the young cop, arrests, handcuffs, and frisks Dewain, all the while singing into the microphone in his left hand. Couples grappled with each other, fought, kissed, and made love, and somehow managed to do it all with only one free hand. It was a virtuoso staging feat, but it was ultimately awkward and discomfiting. In later versions body mikes were employed to the cast's great relief, and the band, which had started out performing onstage right next to the actors, was moved to the pit.

The problems that *Ceiling/Sky* encountered may really have been more artistic than political. To begin with, there was the nagging issue of what exactly to call this piece of music theater. No one could quite find the term that best described it. I proposed "songplay," which was accurate, but it didn't catch on. It wasn't exactly a "show" by Broadway definition. Its three-hour duration indicated that weighty matters must be in play. But then, it certainly wasn't an opera. I believe that the public's inability to define this piece in its own mind created yet another obstacle to its reception.

Artistic collaboration is never easy. On occasion it has occurred to me that, next to double murder-suicide, it might be the most painful thing two people can do together. Genuine creativity requires of the soul and the psyche that they be wide open. This extreme position leaves one vulnerable on all fronts. Each artist yearns to have his or her work represented at its peak of perfection. Compromise is out of the question. What's at stake here is not a political negotiation or a lawsuit; it's a work of art. In making an opera the librettist invariably feels cheated or disrespected. But the composer is responsible for so much more than the librettist. The music is what determines the ultimate form and feel of the piece. Music, because it is so psychologically precise, requires that the composer take on the role of ultimate arbiter, the one who sets the emotional tone of the drama.

Over and over in the course of making six stage works I have found myself having to tweak, torque, expand, or delete text in order to make it fit the formal demands of the music. It is nearly impossible to know in advance what the dramatic and structural necessities are going to be. They are dictated by the way in which musical and dramatic time evolves. Often I'll need to make a character repeat a phrase, not for purposes of emphasis, but because the musical rhetoric demands it. There are situations where I'll have to delete significant amounts of the text because the musical statement has already culminated. To continue on for the sake of inclusion would only damage that special feeling of rightness, that critical zone between "not enough" and "too much." Of course my seemingly arbitrary refusal to include all of the given text can cause immense grief to the librettist, especially when he or she has taken great care to construct something elegant and poetically unified. "Whose sense of rightness?" they may justifiably ask. Even so, I never change the text without the permission of the writer or casually substitute easier-to-set words—that is an ethic that has to be honored between librettist and composer. But I often have to leave unset some of the best lines of text because the musical statement has already reached closure. "Bleeding chunks" is what Alice Goodman called the many lines in her *Nixon in China* poem that ended up on the editing-room floor. "All I seemed to hear from John when I was writing the libretto was 'More! More! More!' And when I gave him more he responded, 'Less! Less! Less!' "

Setting June Jordan's texts posed new challenges. Her poems were full of wit and sensitivity. Her goal was a simulacrum of natural, uncluttered, spontaneous street dialect, as far away from the biblical gravitas and nested complexities of Alice's *Klinghoffer* meditations as one could imagine. But as lyrics for pop songs they were like bucking broncos. In the opening ensemble I had to find a way to make natural long lines such as:

> I was searching for a reasonable reason for my smile
> I was finding what I want washed out completely in denial.

In fact, lines like these were no more daunting than those Alice had provided me for the *Achille Lauro*'s captain as he meditates on the solitude of a life at sea:

> In the interminable hours
> Of navigation, thoughts take shape
> And the same skill that steers the ship
> Makes intellect an animal.

But with an opera one has more leeway to stretch music and text so that they eventually marry each other. The best pop songs, on the other hand, are those that state themselves in the most natural manner possible, free of artfulness and embellishment. My goal in setting words is always to render the natural rhythm of speech so that its musical setting has a sense of rightness, of unforced spoken English. When I set a text I speak it out loud line by line, repeating it over and over until I have internalized its inner rhythms, found its most effortless expression. Then I search for the most precise musical notation to reproduce those rhythms and the contours, the ups and downs of its inflections. In *Ceiling/Sky*, for the lengthy courtroom defense that Rick presents to the judge, "Your honor, my client, he's a young black man," I recorded myself, speaking the text like a rap artist to the beat of a metronome click, and then with minute attention to every slight turn of phrase, every rhetorical pause or emphasis, I carefully notated the rhythmic contours of what I had just improvised.

I am astonished at how rarely the union of music and text succeeds in English-language opera. People invariably point to Benjamin Britten as the gold standard of setting texts in English. But to my (admittedly American) ear, his vocal settings can produce a sensation uncomfortably stilted and oddly archaic. They may satisfy the needs of the English dramatic sensibility, but they are not a comfortable fit for an American ear brought up on everything from George Gershwin and W. C. Handy to Joni Mitchell, Bob Dylan, and Stevie Wonder.

Ceiling/Sky gave me the chance, in the context of the popular song, to expand on some rhythmic and harmonic ideas that had been brewing for some time in my concert works. In the overture to the first act each character offers short, melodic cameo phrases describing his or her amorous predicament while beneath them a rolling ostinato of keyboard figurations that hark back to the techniques of *Phrygian Gates* provides a slowly evolving sequence of wave patterns. The overlapping phrase-lengths and rhythmic elusiveness of the duet for De-wain and Consuelo, "Este País," still gives me pleasure when I hear it. The charging, punchy "Mike's Song About Arresting a Particular Individual" and the polyphonic passacaglia-like finale show two different ways of creating forward movement by means of a chromatic manipulation of the harmonies.

I have no idea how the future will treat this work, whether it will pale next to the best contemporary pop music of its time or whether it will eventually, like the early Kurt Weill pieces, summon up a peculiar time and place in our culture's history. Shortly before her death, June and I met on a warm Berkeley afternoon near her home and talked about fixing what we thought needed to be fixed, but soon she was gone, and *Ceiling/Sky* was locked in its form forever.

I n the mid-1990s I had close encounters of the best kind with the music of Charles Ives and Conlon Nancarrow that left lasting effects on my own compositional language. From Nancarrow I learned about the counterpoint of different tempi within a single continuum. I had known about Nancarrow since the first LP of his player-piano music had been released by Columbia Records in the mid-1970s. Two good West Coast friends, Peter Garland and Charles Amirkhanian, had done much to bring the music of Nancarrow, a crusty expatriate then living in obscurity in Mexico City, into the larger public awareness. Nancarrow had been the first composer to receive a MacArthur "genius grant," and he'd spent a portion of the proceeds living briefly in Berkeley—his first trip to the United States since having left during the

McCarthy purges of the early 1950s. On occasion I would see him walking down Solano Avenue with his Japanese-born wife, Yoko. I'd also met him at one of the Sunday afternoon musicales held at the Beverly Hills home of the arts patron Betty Freeman. He was characteristically terse and cryptic, and with his pencil mustache and clipped manner of speaking, his appearance suggested more sheriff of Dodge City than radical composer.

Although I'd listened intently to the recordings of the player-piano studies that Amirkhanian had brought back from Mexico City, I didn't get the full impression of Nancarrow's originality until I began conducting the instrumental versions of his studies made by Yvar Mikhashoff. The Ensemble Modern in Frankfurt asked me to add several of these arrangements to programs we were doing in concerts throughout Europe and the United States. The brittle, spiky edginess of the original Nancarrow piano-roll sound was of course missing from the versions for instrumental ensemble. There was no way that a group of ten or a dozen players could re-create the mechanical precision of the player piano. But Mikhashoff found a way to make Nancarrow's multiple tempi coexist so that, for example, the bassoon would travel at quarter = 88, while the double bass and cello traveled at an arbitrarily different rate (say, eight = 82) and the upper woodwinds scurried along prestissimo at half = 132. The appeal of the Mikhashoff arrangements was that the various lines of Nancarrow's canons now had human personality and an individual color. They were, compared to the player-piano originals, totally different pieces, but that didn't diminish their value.

I was especially enchanted by the earlier Nancarrow studies, those like numbers 1, 3A, 6, 7, and 12 that held close to their vernacular roots, be it funky jazz, big-band riffing, ragtime, boogie-woogie, tango, or flamenco. To me these seemed to be an ideal integration of radical technical ideas with the familiar tropes of everyday musical language. The later studies, those composed in the 1970s and 1980s, felt to me exactly that—studies. It was as if, after Ligeti and Carter and other established contemporaries acknowledged his importance, Nancarrow started to become ever-more self-consciously modern. I missed the insouciance and punchy wit of the earlier studies, although I recognized that he was searching for denser, more layered forms of polytemporality. There is no disputing the value and originality of the later studies, even if they don't produce quite the tickle of pleasure that the earlier ones do. Nancarrow's work almost always expressed itself in a familiar form that features one or another kind of contrapuntal interplay among multiple melodies, each traveling at a different speed.

The pinging, ultraprecise metallic timbre of Nancarrow's music comes of course from the action of the player piano, his instrument of choice. Those of us who grew up watching old Westerns on film and television can never quite disassociate the sound of a Nancarrow study from the classic saloon piano of that genre and the ever-present possibility of a good chair-smashing, table-turning fistfight.

As a matter of personal preference, I do eventually tire of the fact that Nancarrow's musical discourse is forever couched in canonic imitation and that he shied away from the creation of extended structures that would produce music of much greater expressive variety. After a while, the brusqueness of tone and the de rigueur contrapuntal behavior of the inner voices begin to burden the listening experience.

But the fact that Nancarrow achieved this level of precision and complexity in the days before personal computers is one of the great stories of twentieth-century music. That he did so in the obscurity of political exile in Mexico City makes his life history even more memorable.

I found my own way to make independent tempi coexist by means of a software program that allowed me to stretch or compress material. The program, Digital Performer, had originally been developed to help film and television composers tweak their music to fit the exact demands of the frames of imagery. But, beginning with my Violin Concerto, I began subjecting melodic material to arbitrary time compression or expansion. In so doing, I found that I could take a melody that was originally fifty beats long and shrink it 10 percent so that its duration would be only forty-five beats. This of course gives the impression that the tempo is increasing, although in fact the tactus, or original tempo, remains the same. The resulting effect was not unlike what Nancarrow had laboriously achieved by first mathematically calculating the tempo differentials, measuring them onto the blank paper of a piano roll, and then painstakingly punching the notes into the paper. However, I was not looking for as rhythmically layered a sound as can be found in the later Nancarrow studies; I was searching for a way to make the musical surface varied and unpredictable yet keep the divisions of the pulse to larger integers. My goal was forever to keep the dance-like roots of my style inviolate.

Ives too continued to feed my imaginative processes. Close exposure to several of his large-scale pieces suggested ways to make the sound images of my orchestral works richer and more complex. A weakness of the Minimalist aesthetic was its tiresomely uniform surfaces. To be sure, in the best of Glass's and Reich's works the uniformity of texture could produce in the listener an ecstatic, trancelike state. This was the Minimalist doctrine of order and precision, the clean machine, the answer to the chaos and jarring unpredictability of post-serialism. But I wanted something less sleek and orderly than the orthodox Minimalist sound, something less predictable, capable of evoking multiple layers of atmosphere and activity.

I had already remarked that in both the Fourth Symphony and *Three Places in New England* Ives had hit upon something very special, his own kind of Impressionism that was in part achieved by constantly emerging and receding levels of musical activity. I found in these works a highly refined sense of foreground, middle ground, and background, an ordering of musical ideas according to their imagined placement in a perspective, just as a painter might fill a canvas with a mix of images, some of which appeared very close and in photographic clarity, while others grew more vague and less defined as they receded into the background. In my mind, Ives was the first composer to approach the orchestral setting as if it were a giant mixing board. Objects, be they fragments or tunes, atmospheric effects, or enormous blocks of sound, appear on the listener's radar as if the composer were moving faders in a grand mix. This is a radically different way of treating musical material from the traditional rhetorical procedures of European art music, where the discourse is far more linear and logically spun out. What I also liked about Ives was his quest to keep the vernacular roots of the art alive within the context of his formal experimentation. The postwar Modernist aesthetic, whether the European version of Boulez, Xenakis, Birtwistle, or Lachenmann, or our homegrown American academic composers, had made the fatal error of super-refining their ideas, following self-imposed protocols that robbed the experience of its cultural connectivity. Ives, for all his experimentalism, kept the commonplace roots of his inspiration largely intact, a gift he shared with Bartók, Shostakovich, Stravinsky, Copland, and Britten.

In 1999 I toured seven European cities with a huge orchestra and chorus that had been put together by the Ensemble Modern, doing a program that began with the complete Fourth Symphony of Ives and ended with my own forty-five-minute symphony, *Naive and Sentimental Music*. In between we played a mind-bendingly intense fifteen-minute work in micro-tuned intervals, *Sunshine of Your Love* by Michael Gordon. I'd performed two other pieces by Michael in previous years, *Yo Shakespeare* and *Love Bead*. The newest piece, written for me to conduct with this very large orchestra, bore a title copped from a famous song by the 1960s British rock trio Cream. Of all the American composers in the generation ten to twenty years younger than I, Michael possesses the most unique voice, one that is radically visionary and full of personality and imagination. With roots in both experimental rock and the hard-edged Minimalism of his mentor, Louis Andriessen, this music has a sense of inevitability that can at times alarm, even frighten the listener. Rhythmic cells are launched as if they were robotic juggernauts lurching across an alien landscape. The sound images are industrial-strength—big, insistent, at times very aggressive. This is not elegant music. Played at rock-volume levels, Michael's micro-tuned timbres are shrill and thrilling and full of phantom artifacts that fool the ear, playing tricks with one's cognitive faculties. Conducting the hundred players of the Ensemble Modern Orchestra in *Sunshine of Your Love* was like putting one's head in a blast furnace or standing behind a jet engine. Compared to an elegant Reich ensemble piece or a delicately attenuated tapestry by Feldman, this is a world of banshees and dybbuks, of screaming highs and throbbing lows, a classical composer's response to the assaultive sonic environments of experimental rock and grunge aesthetics. Part of the thrill of performing this work was in knowing that the visceral emotion it produced could only be attained in a live performance. No recording or compact disc representation could hope to re-create the sensory overload of hearing it played by a large orchestra with its added component of four synthesizers, each tuned a quarter-tone different, and thrashing electric guitars. Not long after Michael composed *Sunshine of Your Love* the English composer Thomas Adès made a not dissimilar evocation of rave-induced acoustic *ekstasis* in the central movement of his orchestral work *Asyla*. Adès's cleverness, his subtlety with the orchestra, and his enormous rhythmic sophistication (some of which reveals his deep absorption of Nancarrow's discoveries) may have produced a music of greater intricacy than Michael Gordon could hope to achieve, but for me the sheer strangeness and implacable intensity of *Sunshine of Your Love* conjured a physical and emotional out-of-body experience quite unlike anything I could remember. I was grateful for the chance to bring such a work into the world, and I only regret that its huge forces and complicated intonational scheme have prevented it from being performed more often.

I drew much from my firsthand experience with Ives. *On the Transmigration of Souls*, written in 2002 for the New York Philharmonic, shows how much of an impression Ives's "mixing board" technique of handling the orchestra affected me. In that piece's immediate successor, I made public my homage to him in a piece of musical autobiography, my own Proustian madeleine with the mischievous title *My Father Knew Charles Ives*. Of course my father did not know Charles Ives, but there was so much about the symmetries between me and my father and Charles and George Ives that it seemed a reasonable assumption, given the right time and place, that the two men would have become good friends. Both fathers were artistic and not particularly successful in their conventional business lives. Both were dreamers, perhaps not fully disciplined or motivated, but capable of inspiring their sons. Both loved small-town New England life and aligned themselves with the individualist, skeptical philosophy of Thoreau. While still an adolescent I'd played in a marching band with my father during the summer months. Ives's father was a band conductor. Drawing attention to this symmetry was a fanciful act, whimsical and certainly not to be taken too literally. My piece, which Michael Steinberg wryly described as "Three More Places in New England, Only a Little to the North," is a very obvious homage to my Yankee predecessor, although I avoided the extreme gnarliness of Ives's rhythmic design. The density and irregularity of Ives's rhythmic texture, so ahead of its time in 1915, impressed and exhilarated me, but it was not something I was drawn to integrate into my own Minimalist-inspired, pulse-driven personal language. Of the three movements in *My Father Knew Charles Ives* the first, "Concord," is the most Ivesian in its impressionistic tone-painting and use of anecdotal signals, such as a quotation from a little ditty by Beethoven that I used to play with my father; the bugle call, reveille; the faint wisp of Ives's totemic hymn, "Nearer My God to Thee"; and of course my faux march tunes.

The second movement, "The Lake," is a summer nocturne, a memory of the sound of a lakeshore late at night, with the quietly repeating rhythms of objects gently stirred by a light breeze or of the lapping of water on the shore or against a pier. From far in the distance disembodied fragments of dance music come floating over the lake surface. Is it the ghost of Winnipesaukee Gardens in the summer of 1935? The music drifts in and out of hearing, while a long plaintive oboe intones a melody made of bending micro-intervals.

The final "place" in my triptych is simply called "The Mountain." It is no specific mountain but rather an archetypical one. From earliest childhood granite peaks with names like Chocorua, Monadnock, Kearsarge, Moosilauke, and Passaconaway had imposed themselves on my imagination and become numinous, expressive of a transitional realm between the material world and an other less knowable one, populated by spirits and primitive energies. The music begins with the same distant trumpet that announced the opening of "Concord," an Ivesian trope for certain, even down to the questioning intervals of the rising major seventh and falling minor third. But from there the Ivesian models disappear and the piece departs on its own voyage, eventually locking on to a feverish rush of skipping trochees that press ever higher, rising and falling with enormous effort and ultimately breaking through into a surprise ending, where the energy suddenly vanishes, and the air is clear, with a stillness prevailing. On a trek in the Trinity mountains of northern California with Sam and some friends I'd gone high up the bald face of Mount Eddy on a cool summer afternoon in 1999. Sweating and huffing, and unaware of how close the summit was, we emerged from a crag onto the windswept summit to see the snowcapped vista of Mount Shasta looming in the shimmering air across the expanse of a blue-green valley. It was a moment of "the shock of recognition," a transitional instant between the earth and the ether.

Another American composer who influenced me, but in a very different way, was Lou Harrison. Lou—and he was always known by his first name to everyone who came in contact with him—was in some ways the quintessential West Coast composer. He was born in Portland, Oregon, and grew up in the San Francisco Bay Area. His early musical influences came as much from the Orient as from Europe, and that awareness of things Asian colored every aspect of his creative life. Although he had studied with Schoenberg at UCLA and could compose knowledgeably in the twelve-tone style, as he did in part of his *Symphony on G*, his most original music showed his absorption with Balinese, Korean, Chinese, and Japanese music. Some Eurocentric critics mistakenly dismissed Harrison as an ethnomusicological dabbler, an Orientalist who mixed Eastern and Western styles in a kind of hippie one-world ethnic stew, complete with texts in Esperanto. But these same critics failed to see how exceedingly sharp Lou's intellect was, how widely read and deeply informed he was about all kinds of musical theory, not just East Asian theory but that of ancient Greece and the European Middle Ages as well. He was the first major composer in the Western world to seriously incorporate alternate tuning systems into his music, composing pieces in a variety of just-intonation systems and bringing back long-forgotten temperaments, as he did in his Piano Concerto (written for the jazz pianist Keith Jarrett), in which he calls for the solo piano to be tuned in an archaic mode called "Kirnberger 2" that is subtly different from our garden-variety equal-tempered scale.

I did not love all of Lou Harrison's music uncritically. In a BBC documentary on West Coast music, he once joked: "We California composers don't mind being pretty." I sometimes found that "prettiness" cloying, and too many of his instrumental pieces seemed strangely lightweight, out of touch with the emotional complexity that our contemporary experience requires. Lou was a devout believer in systematic composing, and in that sense his musical rhetoric could at times bear resemblances to the methodical *Durchkomponieren* of Hindemith. But, unlike the oftentimes-pedantic Hindemith, Lou was capable of spinning a web of sheer gossamer delicacy, making melodies that wound gracefully and sinuously like garlands of jungle flowers. He could also kick out the jams when he felt like it, producing his own unique brand of sassy up-tempo dances that filled me with a sense of pure giddiness. A movement in his Concerto for Organ with Percussion Orchestra, which I conducted both with the Chicago Symphony and at the BBC Proms in London, calls for the organist to flail the keys with a felt-covered wood block, producing big chunks of funky sound clusters, while the accompanying orchestra of clangorous metal, wood, and skin resonators cheerfully bangs along in sync. In the "stampede" movement of his Piano Concerto, the pianist whacks the keys with his or her fists in a jubilant frenzy. And how could one not find delectable a title like *Jahla in the Form of a Ductia to Pleasure Leopold Stokowski on His Ninetieth Birthday*?

As Lou grew older I began to realize his utter uniqueness, and I became more and more grateful for his way of being in the world, for his freedom from the tyrannies of style and orthodoxy that held sway over musical politics in Europe and on the East Coast, and for his openness to influences from the most unexpected sources—ancient Greek modes, Elizabethan keyboard music, Balinese gamelan, and the Chinese *pipa*. He and his longtime partner, the instrument builder Bill Colvig, would appear at concerts looking like a couple of mountain men, Lou in his customary red corduroy shirt and bolo tie and Bill, even as he approached eighty, always in shorts and hiking boots. A Santa Claus of a man in appearance with his generous belly and full beard, Lou spoke in a gentle, precise, slightly schoolmasterly manner. He and Bill lived in a small house on a ridge above Aptos, several miles south of Santa Cruz. The house was full of unusual instruments, many of which had been built by Bill according to Lou's specifications. Their "California gamelan" included deep resonant gongs made from sawed-off oxygen tanks suspended from redwood frames. When the annual summer Cabrillo Festival in Santa Cruz took place, Lou and Bill customarily invited the festival director, who one time was me with my young family, to move into their Aptos house, and the two of them, although already nearly eighty years old, would spend the two-week period in an old Airstream trailer behind the house, enjoying an annual rustic honeymoon.

Most of all I appreciated Lou's delight in being indigenous, in being the authentic West Coast composer. He was a living example of what the nineteenth-century California-born philosopher Josiah Royce termed Provincialism with a capital P. Royce used the term in the most positive sense of the word, meaning it to be "any one part of a national domain, which is, geographically and socially, sufficiently unified to have a true consciousness of its own unity, to feel a pride in its own ideals and customs, and to possess a sense of its distinction from other parts of the country." Royce, like Bartók, felt that true culture thrived in these pockets of focused self-identity, that uniqueness and originality lay in the local rather than in the global. In an era of instant communication, compulsive globe-trotting, and cultural cosmopolitanism, Lou Harrison possessed that "true consciousness" of his West Coast birth, and he reveled in what made the local culture deliciously different.

paid homage to Lou and to another indigenous California composer, Terry Riley, in a piece called *The Dharma at Big Sur*, which I composed to celebrate the opening of Disney Hall in Los Angeles in 2003. The debut of that hall, designed by Frank Gehry, promised to be a signal event in the history of West Coast culture. Gehry was already world-famous, most recently for the Museo Guggenheim Bilbao in Spain. Disney Hall, with its sweeping stainless-steel curved sails on the outside and its warm and inviting Douglas fir interior, was to become the new home for the Los Angeles Philharmonic. After a visit to Frank's Santa Monica studio where I was able to see a large model of the planned hall, I had become convinced that over time Disney Hall would be for Los Angeles what the Eiffel Tower was for Paris and the Sydney Opera House was for that city. Together with Richard Meier's recently completed Getty Center perched on a cliff overlooking the west end of the city, the new downtown orchestra hall was without doubt going to attract international attention to a city that for so long had suffered the disdain of East Coast and European tastemakers who persisted in ignoring its significant artistic achievement in favor of mocking associations with Hollywood, Mickey Mouse, swimming pools, and surfboards.

I wanted to compose a piece that embodied the feeling of being on the West Coast—literally standing on a precipice overlooking the geographic shelf with the ocean extending far out to the horizon, just as I had done thirty-two years before on my arrival at the Pacific's edge. A year earlier I had been in an Oakland jazz club, listening to an ensemble that included Tracy Silverman, a free-spirited Juilliard-trained violinist who did improvisations on a custom-made six-string electric violin. Tracy's manner of playing was a fusion of styles that showed his deep knowledge of a variety of musical traditions, ranging from North Indian sarangi playing to that of jazz and rock artists like Stefan Grappelli, Jimi Hendrix, and John Coltrane, and even to Appalachian fiddling. The instrument itself was small, a solid piece like an electric guitar with no hollow resonating space. The two extra strings took the tessitura down into the deep cello range, and Tracy had perfected a wonderfully gritty manner of attacking these strings with a small, student-size violin bow, drawing forth an explosive stutter of upper partials that gave sparkle and uncanny expression to the sound. The instrument, because it shared the same amplified properties with the electric guitar, could sustain long, bending portamenti, allowing slides between notes that mimicked a great jazz vocalist, a Hebrew cantor, or a Qawwali mystic singer. I was enchanted by this instrument and by Tracy's manner with it. I determined to compose my California coastal-trance piece for him. I named it *The Dharma at Big Sur*, a title that could easily have been invented by Jack Kerouac. In fact, Kerouac's elegiac California novel, *Big Sur*, was certainly in my mind as I composed the piece.

At about the same time that I began work on the piece, I happened to conduct a concert in New York that included Lou Harrison's little concerto for violin and chamber ensemble, *Concerto in Slendro*. This charming piece in just intonation for solo violin and an accompaniment that includes tack pianos, celesta, upside-down trash cans, washtubs, and large ranch triangles is built on two Indonesian scales. Each scale has five tones, with the tuning adjusted so that the seconds are wide and the thirds are small. It is impossible to find a celesta that is tuned in such a manner, so I made a version that could be played on a keyboard sampler, retuning the samples to match Harrison's requirements. The intonation, all in the key of B, charmed me greatly, so much so that when I began work on my own concerto, I based it on a similar just-intonation scale on B, although I expanded my scale to seven pitches.

I wrote for an orchestra with a large string section, a full brass complement, two bass clarinets, harps, piano, percussion, and two keyboard samplers. The tuning specifications of this large ensemble were laboriously worked out, to the point where I even indicated every single overtone that each brass instrument would play, all in an attempt to create a perfectly "just" sonic universe for the piece. For months I had all the instruments in my home studio completely retuned to this B just-intonation tonality. The effect on my retuned synths and samplers produced a magical sound world, dreamlike and delicately clangorous, unlike anything I'd ever imagined. Tracy came often to my Berkeley studio and improvised on small motivic fragments I'd written for him. Together we made a genuinely collaborative piece with a form that loosely mirrors the Indian raga models, beginning with a long, dreamlike opening, similar to the *alap*, without pulse and with a feel of unpremeditated improvised lyricism (although everything is precisely written out in the score). This *alap* opening is followed by a lightly rhythmized *jor* section that gradually expands into a final, pulse-throbbing virtuosic *jhala*. The solo part is painstakingly notated, but the intent is to achieve the opposite—to give an impression of purest spontaneity, as if the solo violin were a seabird, riding the air currents as they shift direction and elevation in a high wind.

At the very first rehearsal with the Los Angeles Philharmonic the realities of professional orchestral practice came into immediate conflict with my imagined brave new world of just intonation. Even though I'd consulted with brass players via phone and e-mail about my tuning ideas, the truth was that every individual brass instrument has its own resonant peculiarities. I had made infinitely detailed decisions about intonation, sometimes a matter of no more than a few hundredths of a step that could easily be achieved in the controlled environment of my studio but that was impossible to duplicate in the real world, where the tightly coiled tubing of trumpets, trombones, horns, and tubas produced unpredictable nuances of sharpness and flatness. Even more impossible to attain were the intervallic subtleties I'd asked from the string section. Thirty-two violinists gave thirty-two differing opinions of what a slightly flatted perfect fifth ought to be. The result was a chaotic first rehearsal under circumstances that were already tense due to the huge pressures surrounding the opening night of the new hall. The premiere of *The Dharma at Big Sur* was not a success. On the night of the first performance the tuning issues still remained unresolved, and the proper amplification of the violin, so essential to achieving an attractive sound in a large public space, had never been adequately sound-checked. Listeners who knew my music were kind enough to give me the benefit of the doubt, but I was distraught, driven into a state of shock by the grating unbalanced sound emerging from Tracy's amplifier and by the unfocused, confusing intonation of the orchestra. In an opening week of otherwise triumphant musical performances, many of which revealed the new hall to be an acoustical marvel, *The Dharma at Big Sur* was a sonic bomb, a victim of its own technical difficulties, and an embarrassment for its composer, who had aimed high for something far out of the ordinary but had run aground through the incorporation of two unpredictable elements—tuning and amplification—into the realities of conventional orchestral practice.

Nonetheless I loved the piece, and I eventually found a compromise, a kind of hybrid tuning that produced for me a tremendously satisfying impression in live performance. The fixed instruments—piano, samplers, and harps—could be retuned into just intonation, the brass and strings, however, remain in their normal intonation. Intonation purists—and they are legion and messianic—might be bothered by the compromise, but the mix of "tempered" and "just" resulted in an expressive world that had its own unique beauty.

The conventional orchestral setting is simply too full of multiple voices to accurately reproduce the subtle gradations of just intonation. That would seem to be a realm best left for smaller ensembles of individual solo instruments or for studio-produced music, as was the case with my first synthesizer mock-ups of this piece. My misfortunes aside, the move away from conventional tempered tuning was a venture into an enchanted garden, into a new expressive realm that I am determined to return to before my compositional life has run its course.

12.
HOW COULD THIS HAPPEN?

or unto us a son is born . . ." The words from Handel's *Messiah*, set to the ecstatic shuddering and quivering of violins and jubilantly exclaiming voices, long expressed for me the certainty of spiritual renewal. It was a certainty that with the passing years would be increasingly challenged and thrown into doubt. In my preadolescence I'd been a fervent churchgoer, zealously taking to heart the message of the conservative New England Episcopalian Christian theology, imagining Christ and his apostles exactly as they were pictured in the standard Sunday school texts—handsome thirty-something WASP-looking guys with excellent hair and gentle, earnest faces. The anthropomorphic Episcopalian God, looking down on me with beneficent indulgence—or looking the other way when I slipped into venality—was for an eight-year-old boy a reasonably unintimidating entity. On some Sundays we children would be shown movies of stories from the Gospels, black-and-white films produced by the ministry and featuring actors representing Jesus in a variety of defining moments, standing on the waters of the Sea of Galilee, officiating at the Last Supper, confronting Judas, and calmly accepting the verdict of his accusers. A film about Saul's conversion on the road to Damascus and another featuring Christians being fed to the lions spooked me. Religion and violence, even in these watered-down Episcopalian narratives, seemed inextricably linked. As I grew older I began to grapple with the finer, more complex points of theology. I found an ardent defender of the faith in a mysterious and seductively attractive Catholic girlfriend who enjoyed crossing swords with me on philosophical and spiritual issues, winning all arguments with her mathematically logical reasoning and confident command of the Church's catechism.

Then my mother, who had been born a Catholic, decided to move her affiliation yet again, from the Episcopalian to the Unitarian church. The Unitarians tended to be the most socially and politically liberal people in the community, and in the Concord parish they had the best choir, which my mother very much wanted to sing in. The Unitarian theology, if it could be called that, was about as close to secular philosophy as one could get and still call it religion. In 1960 the community had one of the few gay ministers in the region. He not only preached in the church but also acted in the local theater group with my mother. When he stood at the lectern on Sundays—"pulpit" was too brazenly clerical a term for the Unitarians—he spoke more often than not of Emerson and Thoreau, Gandhi and Krishnamurti than of Jesus or Paul. The reasonable and reasoning Unitarians eschewed the eerie mysteries of transubstantiation, bleeding stigmata, wafers, wine, hell, and purgatory. They even had scruples about allowing a cross to be displayed in the sanctuary. The Catholic Church, with its shadowy rituals of confession and Communion and its chilling emphasis on sin, damnation, and judgment, provoked in me an uneasy feeling. I had no idea of its long and complex ideological history nor of the many different tributaries that fed the mainstream of its worldview. All I saw were suffering scenes of crucifixion, the serenely untouchable Mary, an unknowable Father, and the impenetrable mystery of the Trinity, more often than not represented by a ghostly pale Jesus pointing demonstratively to his exposed, bleeding heart.

In place of the Catholics' disturbing symbols of man's pain and vulnerability the Unitarians offered Enlightenment values of civic morality and philosophical ecumenicalism. At its best it could be the catalyst for inspired gestures of public spirit, the New England liberalism so eloquently articulated in Emerson's essays. At its worst it begged comparison with the self-help movement of the 1970s and

'80s. Being with Unitarians was good moral and intellectual training, but it didn't satisfy my need for mystery. I was an impressionable adolescent, and the Unitarian vision, although humanistic and comforting, seemed barely different from secular philosophy of the kind I'd been reading in Plato, Voltaire, and Bertrand Russell. I couldn't find a port in which to drop anchor, so I gradually lost interest in churchgoing and religion and, by the time I was sixteen, I had ceased being a practicing Christian of any sort. "Art is my religion," I told my skeptical friends.

n college, while studying ancient Greek, I'd read some phrases from Saint Paul in the original. The words, so strange and so different from the King James English I'd known from childhood, gave to Jesus' words a powerful numinosity. I went back to the English translation and read again with renewed interest, realizing that the Gospel of the New Testament is told through a sequence of miracles. The barren, menopausal Elizabeth unexpectedly finds herself pregnant with the baby who will grow up to be John the Baptist. An angel appears before a frightened and astonished teenage virgin, Mary, and tells her that she will bear a child without having first been with a man. The baby is born, causing immense joy for the poor and humble while provoking extreme paranoia among the powerful. The baby, God's own flesh-and-blood son, preaches humility and forgiveness, has superhuman powers but suffers acute human pain. He brings the dead back to life, turns want into plenty, shames the powerful (both the church and state), is persecuted, betrayed, tortured, and dies only to reappear as Holy Ghost. The miracles are there to show the divine power of God manifested in the human form of the Son. These miracles are what Jung called "spiritual truths," different from physical truths, but no less real, at least in the mind of the beholder.

The miracle to which I reacted most profoundly was the initial one, that of birth. I did not require a "virgin" birth in order to make evident the miraculous nature of the event, an event that repeats itself thousands of times every minute throughout the planet and that is never any the less astonishing and inexplicable.

When our daughter, Emily, and then our son, Sam, were born, I was there, witness to the miraculous. "How could this happen?" I asked myself, shocked and amazed, as the brightly lit, sterile hospital delivery room suddenly became the scene of a profound mystery. At one moment there were four people in the room, and a few seconds later there were five, as a new spirit entered to share my realm of existence, a bud, a template of a future consciousness.

Fifteen years later I got my chance to express this event in music and drama in the form of a request from the Théâtre du Châtelet in Paris to compose a work to celebrate the millennium. I proposed to the Châtelet that I compose an oratorio about birth in general and about the Nativity in specific. I called Peter Sellars and asked him to help me compile a libretto. We settled quickly on the idea of a work that could exist either in a fully staged version with the orchestra in the pit or as a simple unstaged oratorio. The process of assembling texts for a libretto for what came to be called *El Niño* was sheer pleasure. We would meet periodically at the same coffee shop on Bancroft Way in Berkeley, each of us arriving with a backpack full of poetry books. There, to the sound of hissing espresso machines and among Cal students hunched over their laptops, we developed our text for the piece. Working with a narrative that was already familiar to our listeners gave us a great freedom not to have to concern ourselves with plot exposition. In fact, we could feel at ease to do the opposite by taking detours from the traditional Nativity narrative. Thus our libretto was able to absorb sources that spanned millennia and geographical continents from the Old Testament prophet Isaiah to the twentieth-century Mexican feminist poet Rosario Castellanos. What makes this libretto significantly different from other versions on the Nativity is the presence of the woman's voice. As beautiful as the telling is in the New Testament, it is nevertheless an imagined secondhand experience, written by men. But our texts have at their core poetry by women, and the intensity of their imagery and feeling imparts a special authenticity to the work.

I have forgotten how the piece gradually assumed its Hispanic flavor. Perhaps it was because Peter had been recently working with Latino actors, poets, and muralists in the Los Angeles area, and through them he'd become aware of the great tradition of poetry from Central and South America. Apart from the familiar works of

Jorge Luis Borges, Mario Vargas Llosa, and Gabriel García Márquez, I was largely ignorant of Hispanic literature. I'd never heard of Rosario Castellanos or Sor Juana Inés de la Cruz, a blindingly intense seventeenth-century Mexican nun whose alternating flashes of darkness and light, searing spiritual pain, and sudden transports of ecstasy had never appeared in any of the usual collections of canonical poetic texts I'd seen in the United States.

Nonetheless, the mention of including Hispanic texts aroused my interest because I realized that, after nearly thirty-two years of living in California, the moment had finally arrived for me to master Spanish. Although not a naturally gifted linguist, I had long felt an almost seductive power of speaking and thinking in other languages. I was taught high-school French by a small, nervous Quebecois, Monsieur de la Pointe, who wore polyester suits with padded shoulders and sported a pencil mustache and greasy pompadour. I later read *Swann's Way* in the original, or most of it, and eventually gained enough confidence with it to do a live interview on one of those late-night Parisian talk shows so popular with Radio France. (The other guest on that interview program was none other than William Burroughs, who wisely stuck to his Kansas-inflected English.) I'd had a smattering of Latin in junior high and had suffered through a brutal semester of ancient Greek during my first semester at Harvard. Later, in my forties, I learned German, working with a private tutor, and after four years of effort I was able to appreciate the hard-won pleasures of Goethe's poetry and Thomas Mann's short stories in the original. I also discovered that German was the ideal language for running an orchestra rehearsal because it most naturally lent itself to the imperative voice. But of all the languages I have learned, Spanish has afforded me the greatest enchantment and was the one that most radicalized my worldview. It unlocked for me the cultures, sensibilities, and long histories of Latin America, making me more aware and more sensitive to what it means to *not* be a part of the dominant culture. On an almost daily basis I read (and continue to read) news and opinion from Mexico, South America, and Spain, learning to see my own country and culture through the eyes of those who have an equally long and complex history but not the material wealth or the unquestioned economic presumption that we have. For several years I met regularly with a brilliant tutor, Judith Berlowitz, reading texts by Cervantes, García Márquez, and Vargas Llosa, and studying the scripts of Pedro Almodóvar. This immersion gave a color and vibrancy to my life that was almost like turning over a new leaf, leaving for good the muted, sedate tonalities of my New England upbringing and ushering in a new Latin warmth of spirit and spontaneity.

My first impetus was to call this oratorio about birth *How Could This Happen?*, a phrase I'd found in one of the traditional church antiphons sung on Christmas Eve. But as the Hispanic theme grew and took center place, I changed the title to *El Niño*. Only a few years earlier, in 1997, the Pacific coast had weathered one of the most violently stormy winters in history, an event of almost supernatural force that had drenched California in heavy rains and caused large-scale disruption and even death in the poorer regions of Central America. The oceans were abnormally warm, and strange things happened. Tropical fish were sighted as far north as southern Alaska and rains of unimaginable intensity poured forth day after day in what seemed like a never-ending sequence of drenching storms. That meteorological phenomenon gained the name El Niño—"the little boy," presumably a mischievous one. I thought that the advent of the Christ child had caused its own kind of spiritual storm, blowing away the corruption and cynicism of the previous world order and offering a new and radically altered vision in its place.

I determined that I would set the most important of these poems not in English translations but rather in their original language. The final version of the libretto thus became a multilingual mix, so richly evocative of our present-day life in California. Poems by Sor Juana and Rosario Castellanos formed the expressive core. I set other poems in English translations by the great Chileans Gabriela Mistral and Vicente Huidobro and by the Nicaraguan Rubén Darío. The emotional and sensory power of these Latin American poets is abundant. The poems are always about the spirit, about the deepest matters of our existence, but they are cast in webs of imagery that is unlike anything I've read in North American or European texts. Huidobro's "Dawn Air," for example, is an encomium to "the Queen of Heaven," drawing on his "creationist" techniques of seemingly incongruous juxtapositions that evoke a dreamlike, psychedelic awareness:

Ah sky blue for the queen in the wind
Ah herd of goats and white hair
Lips of praise and red hair
Animals lost in her eyes
Speak to the skeleton combing its hair
From the tip of the earth to the end of the ages
Tunic and scepter
Amplification of memories
Sound of insects and highways
Speak to the land as the ocean flows

The Nativity story is one of the simplest and most sincere in the Bible. Images of the scene in the stable of Bethlehem, with Mary and the infant surrounded by astonished peasants and placid farm animals, emphasize the humble circumstances of this particular birth. I pinned to the wall above my worktable several images by Giotto and other medieval and early-Renaissance painters to remind me of the power of simplicity in rendering this myth. Peter drew my attention to several little stories, virtually fairy tales, that are now classified as Apocrypha, miraculous events having to do with the birth and childhood of Jesus that had been written in the century after his life but which the Church fathers had expunged from the official canon. One of these Apocrypha tales tells of the relationship of Joseph and Mary in much greater psychological detail than anything in either Mark or Luke. In this version, Joseph is a much older man than his teenage bride, a widower not much interested in her, marrying her more out of a sense of tribal obligation than for love. He is away on a long trip when his young wife, still a virgin, is visited by Gabriel and conceives her child. When he at last returns to find her pregnant he immediately fears himself a cuckold, and in his violent rage he nearly does her serious physical harm. In another tale, this attributed to the Gospel of "Pseudo-Matthew," Joseph and Mary take refuge during their flight from Herod in a cave in the desert where they are suddenly accosted by "many dragons." The baby Jesus stands down from his mother's lap and calms the dragons, who then bow down to worship him. "Do not be afraid, nor consider me a child," the infant Jesus says to his parents. "I have always been a perfect man and am so now."

El Niño opens with a polyphonic choral setting of an early English poem that I'd first spied in a poster on the interior of a London Underground train:

> I sing of a maiden
> a matchless maiden
> King of all Kings
> for her son she's taken
> He comes there so still
> His mother's yet a lass.
> He's like the dew in April
> that falleth on the grass.

That lovely image of the dew raining down on Mary set the tone for the work, although later on the music, like those thrashing El Niño winter storms, would be capable of conjuring great violence and destruction.

Once the opening chorus winds down, a terrifying flapping of wings announces the apparition of the angel Gabriel. Gabriel's voice is intoned by three countertenors singing in perfect homophony a text from one of the English Wakefield mystery plays. The genderless purity of the countertenor voices lends an air of archaic mystery and devotion to the music, making it resonate in curious ways with music from the Middle Ages. The three of them carry the narrative weight of the work, although at times they embody character roles—the angel Gabriel at one point, and the three Magi kings at another. These countertenors, Daniel Bubeck, Brian Cummings, and Steven Rickards, with their perfectly tuned and blended three-part harmonies, gave the work an aura of unforced grace and Giotto-like simplicity. I was reminded of the sound world of Guillaume de Machaut's *Messe de Nostre Dame* that had made such an impression on me in my early experimental music days and had figured in my very first new music concert in San Francisco nearly thirty years earlier. Now, in *El Niño*, Machaut's strange and alien beauty had resurfaced in my own music.

The first performances took place, appropriately enough, in the weeks before Christmas 2000, in the Théâtre du Châtelet in Paris. It was indeed possible to walk out of rehearsal and cross the bridge onto the Ile de la Cité and wander into Notre Dame cathedral to stare in wonderment at the medieval statuary and pictures of Mary with her newborn on her lap.

The Châtelet world premiere of *El Niño* featured an American soprano and American mezzo, a Jamaican-born English baritone, a German orchestra conducted by a Japanese American from California, a British chorus, a Portuguese dancer, six Chicano actors from Los Angeles, and a French children's chorus singing in Spanish. Perhaps never again in my compositional career would I have a cast of vocalists so ideally suited to their roles as I had for the Paris premiere of *El Niño*: soprano Dawn Upshaw, mezzo Lorraine Hunt Lieberson, and baritone Willard White.

The production, however, was not without its obstacles and self-imposed challenges. This staging was even more busily detailed than other of Sellars's works. At times the activity onstage could be daunting in its physical polyphony. Three dancers, two female and one male, wove their bodies in and out of the clusters of singers and chorus, sometimes amplifying the implications of the text, other times freezing into positions that subtly recalled archetypical configurations from religious paintings and sculpture. Although the choral music of *El Niño* is rhythmically demanding of the singers, Peter nevertheless devised a densely contrapuntal plan of stage movement for the thirty-six members of the London Voices. There was always a lot going on onstage, with three solo singers, three countertenors, and the full chorus, everyone moving in one of several simultaneously spinning orbits.

Putting *El Niño* together for the first time was, as it always was with my stage pieces, a staggering assignment for everyone involved. The German orchestra began rehearsing in Berlin at the same time as the stage rehearsals in Paris and the chorus preparations in London. Kent Nagano, the consummate Euro-traveler, shuttled back and forth, sometimes arriving from the airport only minutes before a grueling eight-hour day of work. At times tempers ran raw. Finding the middle path between lyrical ease and rhythmic accuracy took patience and discipline and mutual trust. Everyone was working extremely hard to make the best possible performance, but the pressures could burden one's spirits on a bad day. I had first encountered Kent in San Francisco in the early 1980s, when he held the lowly position of assistant conductor of the Oakland Symphony. From there he proceeded with unflappable determination to become conductor of the Berkeley Symphony, and then one of Boulez's successors with the Ensemble Intercontemporain, associate conductor of the London Symphony, and eventually music director of the Hallé Orchestra in England, the Deutsches Symphonie Orchester in Berlin, the Montreal Symphony, and the Bavarian State Opera. For more than a decade Kent was the most dedicated conductor of my music in Europe, giving the world premieres of *The Death of Klinghoffer*, *El Niño*, and *Slonimsky's Earbox*. He conducted the first recording of my Violin Concerto with Gidon Kremer and led a memorable production of *Nixon in China* in Los Angeles. I am much indebted to him for his devotion to my work and for the several excellent recordings he made during that time.

With his good looks, chiseled Ralph Lauren profile, and samurai hair, Kent projected a carefully polished persona, part modest, laid-back Californian and part globe-trotting, aristocratic maestro, heir to the von Karajan throne. In his desire to obtain the most accurate results, Kent could at times be cool and unbending during rehearsals, especially with singers. Even artists as innately musical and vocally secure as Dawn Upshaw and Lorraine Hunt Lieberson failed to meet his exacting demands for rhythmic precision. As a result, there was an uncomfortable air of stress backstage throughout the preparation period of *El Niño*. Lorraine, also a native northern Californian, having known Kent since her early days as a violist in the Bay Area, had some issues adjusting to what she construed as Kent's maestro demeanor. So there in Paris, on the stage of the Châtelet, these two former residents of Berkeley and San Francisco, now nearing the pinnacles of their international musical careers, butted heads as if they were still in high school.

In truth, both Dawn and Lorraine were capable of performing with an expressive force that left one stunned. I later conducted the same piece with them in a concert performance in Amsterdam with both of them standing only a few feet away from my podium. My memory of the performance was one of standing in a circle of a burning feminine fire, of being in the midst of the same all-consuming flames that Rosario Castellanos evokes at the climactic moment of her greatest poem, "La Anunciación."

Of Lorraine much has been said and written. She was a unique, profoundly charismatic performer, combining an enigmatic mystique with a concentrated emotional power that drew the listener into her orbit and held him mesmerized. I first encountered her in 1979 when she played viola in *Shaker Loops* with a local new music ensemble in Berkeley. Rehearsals were at ten on Sunday mornings, and she would arrive sleepy and sexy, hastily dressed, barely awake, totally alluring. She was a good instrumentalist, but there was nothing that might hint at what she would become over the following twenty years. I believe Peter Sellars was influential in unlocking those forces, as he was with so many other singers. As she rapidly rose to the status of vocal superstar, Lorraine felt the conflict between her public and private lives more and more. She knew keenly the discord that comes from wanting to practice one's art at the highest level while simultaneously yearning for privacy and solitude. She was not the kind of stage personality who thrived on being the center of attraction or who cultivated a coterie of fawning admirers. Lorraine never felt impelled to make the obligatory crossover album. She declined the blandishments of promoters and managers who would try to entice her into lowbrow recording projects or splashy gala concerts. I was always impressed with her great seriousness of purpose, a seriousness that ran in a perfect flow with her free laughter and slightly ditzy California-native manner that surfaced in her moments of ease and release. She carefully measured her time between her high-profile engagements and her home life in the New Mexican high desert with her husband, the composer Peter Lieberson. Even in the year 2000, while learning *El Niño*, she exhibited a quiet melancholy that surely was rooted in the awareness of her own physical vulnerability. Anyone listening to her recordings will immediately understand the uniqueness of her voice, with its dusky low register and its pure, unforced upper notes. But the recordings cannot convey the sense I always felt of being captured in her peculiarly feminine emotional space. Three years later I composed the role of Kitty Oppenheimer in the opera *Doctor Atomic* expressly for Lorraine. The parallels of the two women were uncanny. Both were complex, highly intelligent, mercurial, sensual, and visionary women. Both passed through high and low points of their lives among the numinous vistas of the New Mexican landscape. I gave to the character of Kitty Oppenheimer the same kind of Cassandra-like intensity that I found in Lorraine. But the match never could happen. Lorraine had to cancel the San Francisco premiere in 2005, and not long afterward she died at an absurdly young age.

While Lorraine bided her time and chose her commitments only after long deliberation, Dawn Upshaw was forever willing to give herself unconditionally and unselfishly to long, time-consuming projects, sometimes at great personal sacrifice. In *El Niño*, and in the many other roles both classic and contemporary that she assumed, the warmth and generosity of her being was mirrored in her manner of singing, which conveyed a sense of openheartedness and emotional sincerity rarely encountered in the world of divas and extravagant flower-strewn curtain calls. At the start of her career Dawn's pure unforced soprano, crystal-clear diction, and note-perfect pitch made her the ideal American classical singer, almost to the point of typecasting. She struggled to break free of being stereotyped as the "girl next door," the sweet, winsome voice that one associates with the Samuel Barber–James Agee nostalgia of *Knoxville: Summer of 1915*, the recording of which helped launch her career. In 1989, not long after her emergence, I had arranged for her five songs by Charles Ives, and together we recorded them with the Orchestra of St. Luke's. Her singing was fresh and pure and radiated a kind of eternal youthfulness, particularly in the hushed stillness of Ives's "Serenity," in which her voice floats effortlessly over a pair of slowly oscillating diminished chords.

Over time, however, Dawn revealed a depth and emotional range that put the lie to her earlier simple-girl image. Her Angel in the Salzburg production of Messiaen's *Saint François d'Assise*, while still employing the purity and clarity of her voice, probed new levels of expression, taking her into realms of rapt devotion and spiritual ecstasy. By the time I began to compose a major part for her in *El Niño*, it was clear that Dawn had become a singer and an actress of astonishing vocal and dramatic intensity. I took advantage of both sides of her gift. In the setting of Gabriel's announcement to the young Mary, a setting of a text from the early English Wakefield mystery plays, I wrote for the earlier "virginal" Dawn, a voice that is as spotlessly pure as those familiar images of Mary from medieval iconography. But later in the piece comes a scene of violence and terror, the "Memorial de Tlatelolco," a setting of a poem of outrage by Rosario Castellanos that categorizes with caustic irony and harsh imagery the massacre of hundreds of young students by Mexico City police during a political protest in 1968. This is El Niño's "slaughter of the innocents" moment. Rising to the challenge, Dawn threw herself fearlessly into the mood of bitter lament that this setting requires, and in so doing she revealed layers of vocal and dramatic power that no one, not even its composer, had imagined possible.

A full-length, wall-to-wall silent film made by Peter Sellars accompanied every performance of the Paris El Niño. Shot in Los Angeles and outside of Joshua Tree, in the Southern California desert, the film retold the Nativity story as a drama of a Los Angeles Latino gang member and his teenage girlfriend as they escape, not from Herod but from the LAPD. The film had an innocent beauty that touched on the same simple truths that I'd drawn from the anonymous medieval paintings. Joseph, played by the Los Angeles community activist Pete Galindo, and Mary, played by the serenely beautiful Latina teenager Martha Carrillo (with her real-life child in her arms) flee into the desert in a Toyota truck. One of the policemen, profoundly disturbed by a religious vision he's had while sitting in a fast-food restaurant, begins to weep quietly. As onstage Joseph relates the Apocrypha description of Mary staring in rapture at the heavens, the audience watches the onscreen cop's tear-streaked face in close-up as he bends over his Pepsi and french fries.

The union of film and live orchestral and vocal music presented a serious challenge of focus for audiences in Paris and in later productions in San Francisco, Los Angeles, and Brooklyn. No matter how commanding or compelling the singers were, and no matter how active or brilliant the live onstage choreography was, the eye of the audience member was irresistibly drawn to the movie. Even when the film action was nearly static and uneventful it still dominated the viewer's attention and, to my mind, compromised the stage action. The music defaulted to an accompaniment role as the listener's attention remained implacably directed to the onscreen activity. This was disappointing for the production overall, because the film in itself is full of charm, particularly in the closing moments when the dragons that Jesus subdues appear through a rainy windshield as overhead streetlamps, while Mary lies curled up asleep on the front seat of the Toyota in an abandoned parking lot. Having been shot and edited before I'd composed most of the score, the film corresponds with the music only infrequently—like a John Cage–Merce Cunningham collaboration. Coincidences were largely matters of chance, and in the end, for all its tenderness and beauty, the film seemed to me always a problematic element in the staging. I felt a similar competition and sensory discord several years later when I saw Bill Viola's video interpolation of *Tristan und Isolde*. Viola's creation was a thing of intensely felt emotion and unforgettable imagery, in itself a masterpiece of video art. But as an added element to the music and the stage action, it too had the effect of reducing the music to an accompaniment role, no small achievement when the score is one of the greatest musical works of all time.

There are two birth scenes in *El Niño*. The first culminates with the long mezzo aria "La Anunciación," my setting of Castellanos's moody and impassioned monologue that seems to speak from the deepest, most intimate part of the feminine consciousness. The poem begins with a pre-creation scenario:

> before the ages of wheat and larks
> and even before fishes
> when God had nothing more than horizons
> of unlimited blue and the universe
> was a will not yet pronounced

It is cast in the form of an apostrophe spoken by a mother to her child. What I love about Castellanos's writing is her brutal honesty about being female, about carrying a fetus inside her body, about the frequent, unwelcome tangle of emotions—anger, guilt, need, and repulsion that accompany pregnancy—and finally about the searing physical pains and sudden tidal waves of exhilaration that herald the moment of childbirth. *Desprendimiento*—the "loosening" or the "detaching"—is the multilayered Spanish word the poet uses.

I took great care in my setting of "La Anunciación" to follow the curve of Castellanos's emotional ascent, from the bleakness and solitude of the beginning to her union with the soul of her newborn, a moment in which she sees herself surrounded by flames of ecstasy:

> Your gaze,
> benevolent, transforms
> my wounds to fiery splendors.
> And now you approach and find me
> surrounded by prayers as if by high flames.

The intimate confessional style of these Castellanos poems, so intensely personal, so much a part of both the darkest as well as the most sublime experience for a woman giving birth, is utterly absent from the canonical Nativity texts, all written by men. Those men, most presumably celibate, could only have abstractly imagined the experience. In Matthew and in Luke there are no detailed descriptions of Mary's emotional or physical state either before or after the birth.

The second representation of birth, or the Birth, occurs in the final number of part one, a setting for the entire ensemble of two poems by women of emphatically different backgrounds, the twentieth-century Chilean Gabriela Mistral and the twelfth-century German mystic, poet, and composer Hildegard von Bingen. Within the fevered, almost manic impetus of Mistral's "Christmas Star," with its charged imagery of a little girl running and holding a star that sears the flesh of her hands, I wove the serene Latin of Hildegard's delicately sensual text:

> O how precious is the virginity
> of this virgin
> whose gate is closed
> and whose womb
> holy divinity infused

with his warmth
so that a flower grew in her.

In part two, Herod, sung in Paris by the awesomely imposing
Willard White, has his attack of paranoia. He tells the Magi to go and
find the child "so I may come and worship him too." While he's bid-
ding the wise men to make this journey, the chorus, accompanied by a
pounding boogie beat, intones the admonition of Isaiah, "Woe unto
them who call evil good."

El Niño ends with Joseph, Mary, and Jesus fleeing into the desert to
escape Herod's assassins. In a final scene, also taken from the Apocrypha Gospel of "Pseudo-Matthew," the exhausted family takes momentary refuge under a palm tree. Mary, parched with thirst, wonders
out loud if she could have some of the fruit from the top of the tree.
Joseph, cranky and equally exhausted, chides her, reminding her that
they already are out of water and that the top of the palm tree is impossible to reach. The infant Jesus then commands the tree to bend
down and refresh his mother. The palm bends down, shares its fruit
with the family, and then produces from its roots fountains of water
"very clear and cold and wet." Into this image of relief and plenty I in-
terpolated another poem about a palm tree, this one in Spanish by
Castellanos, sung by a children's chorus that suddenly, almost miraculously, appears onstage in the final minutes of the piece:

Lady of the winds,
heron of the plains,
when you sway
your waist sings.
Gesture of prayer
or prelude of wings
you are the cup into which the skies
pour one by one.
From the dark land of men
I've come kneeling to behold you.
Tall, naked, alone.
A poem.

.   .   .

l *Niño* was a message for the millennium. The first performances, in December 2000 while Paris was decorating its streets and shops for Christmas, heralded not only this landmark date in the history of Western spiritual life but also marked the beginning of a new epoch. The world in the year 2000 seemed, if not exactly in a state of balance and stability, at least on a better path. I could perceive a certain feeling of Enlightenment optimism that manifested itself in the newly evolving "green" consciousness and in the sudden, never-before-imagined interconnectivity and accessibility that the digital age and the Internet were enabling. The Bill Clinton era, while not as progressive or as radically imaginative as that of FDR, had at least brought about a shared sense of social responsibility after years of our government's increasingly mean-spirited, trickle-down domestic policies. But then the bitterly disputed presidential election of 2000 put another Bush in the White House, and only a few months later, September 11 instantaneously changed the mood of the country. The nation as a whole experienced a different kind of "how could this happen?" moment. Overnight we became Fortress America, wary, suspicious, paranoid, unilateral in our actions. The key changed abruptly from major to minor. The disturbing themes that in 1991 had swirled through the text and music of *The Death of Klinghoffer* now rose out of the depths like a sea monster, and the world found itself in the grip of its own shadow. One spoke in darkly prophetic utterances of "asymmetrical warfare," of the "clash of civilizations," of "preventive strikes," "shock and awe," and "overwhelming force." Ten years earlier Alice Goodman had given me the words for Omar, the youngest and most dangerous of the *Achille Lauro* hijackers, who yearns for self-immolation and martyrdom:

> May we be worth
> The pains of death
> And not grow old
> In the world
> Like these Jews.

My soul is
All violence.
My heart will break
If I do not walk
In Paradise
Within two days
And abandon my soul
And end the exile
Of my flesh from the earth
It struggled with.

Suddenly Omar's intoxicated death wish had become a reality. One could no longer ignore the fact that there was a sinister alienation growing like a tumor between the modernized, secular culture of Western globalization and the profoundly conservative world of fundamentalist Islam. This sense of being threatened, of being alienated, of being rendered second class and disrespected had long been simmering through centuries of colonization and economic exploitation by European and American markets and military forces. Now it was exploding into scenes of uncontrollable violence, inescapable on television and in the newspapers. The implacable, insoluble Israeli-Palestinian conflict lay like an open, festering wound, a never-ending crisis that provided a constant flash point for volatile emotions and daily images of degrading violence. To many in the West and particularly to the United States, Israel represented an island of representative democracy, of reason and the rule of law in a sea of autocratic, corrupt, inefficient, incompetent Arab countries. To the Islamic world, and also to many non-Islamic but poor and weak countries, the Palestinians were the living examples of a society robbed of its land, crushed and oppressed by the massive economic, political, and military hegemony of the largely secular, pro-Israeli American government. There are many reasons for the disenfranchised to resent the wealthy, overbearing culture of the West, but the Palestinian failure was the one sure to anger Muslims the most.

I must have had an unconscious premonition of something unsettling about to happen, because I had followed *El Niño* with a twenty-five-minute orchestral piece called *Guide to Strange Places*. This began in my mind as something along the lines of those graphically pictorial orchestral works from the latter part of the nineteenth century in the manner of *Pictures at an Exhibition*, *The Sorcerer's Apprentice*, or *The Golden Cockerel*. My initial inspiration had been a traveler's guidebook, *Guide de la Provence mystérieuse*, that I found while staying in the French country home of a friend. This specialist French guidebook featured a long list of strange locations in the Provençal countryside, sites of long-forgotten, bizarre occurrences, murders, disappearances, miracles (both pagan and Christian), ghost stories, apparitions, weird topographical configurations, and the like. *Guide to Strange Places* starts with a furious buzzing of strings, and it plunges headlong into a journey, the form and style of which repeats some of my "travel" music of earlier pieces (*Hoodoo Zephyr*, *Common Tones in Simple Time*, *Road Movies*), but the ambience is more unsettling. It is an intense, at times exhausting, unbroken "guide" to inner spaces that culminates in a violent sequence of hockets between the jabbing strings, pounding timpani, and bestial brass. Although I composed the piece in the months leading up to September 11, 2001, I conducted the first performance in Amsterdam a month after the attacks. I made the trip to Amsterdam in that menacing post-attack climate of fear and trepidation, passing through nearly empty airports and being eyed by wary security personnel. As soon as I heard it, I realized I'd unconsciously composed a piece of music that embodied that same unsettling mood of crisis anxiety.

Guide to Strange Places was only one of a sequence of orchestral pieces that I would write between work on the operas and other stage works. In addition to *Century Rolls*, a piano concerto written in 1996 for Emanuel Ax and the Cleveland Orchestra, I composed in 1998–99 what turned out to be the longest of all my orchestral pieces, a symphony in all but name called *Naive and Sentimental Music*. This piece was inspired by hearing a rehearsal of Bruckner's Fourth Symphony, conducted by Esa-Pekka Salonen. I had been a Bruckner fan in my adolescence, but apart from a few encounters with his seventh and ninth symphonies, I'd not thought about him much until I heard Esa-Pekka's interpretation. I was struck by the long, leisurely accretions of mass and energy, the huge climaxes that surged up and then faded into the mist only to gave way to even bigger ones. They suggested mountain ranges in the distance. Their form, although in one sense quite textbook conventional, was nevertheless strange and mysterious, reminding me of certain slow-motion cinematic techniques.

At forty-eight minutes, *Naive and Sentimental Music* hardly compares for lengthiness and scale with the behemoths of Bruckner and Mahler, but in performance it nevertheless establishes a similar feeling of slowly evolving, almost seismic events. I wrote much of the piece in a studio carved out of an enormous agricultural warehouse surrounded by high redwood trees, part of a forty-acre plot of deep forest on the Sonoma coast that we'd acquired in 1997 after years of searching. The land lay about five miles inland from the Pacific in an ideal location that was neither too chilly and foggy in the winter nor too searingly hot during the summer.

There was a rumor that the property had been used earlier for cultivation of a notoriously popular weed. Indeed, the thousands of feet of leftover irrigation pipes and growbags I found hidden deep in the dense undergrowth seemed to corroborate that rumor. However, by the time we had moved in and I had set up my workplace there was no product to be found anywhere. I told inquiring friends that the only dope on the property was its new owner. The coastal climate, so variegated and so capable of producing palpable mood changes in the person who inhabits it, must surely have played a role in the creation of this music. I was keenly aware of how this same California landscape could elicit dramatic changes in the tone of the many writers and poets who passed through it or, as in my case, resolved to make it their permanent home. Robinson Jeffers, Jack Kerouac, Allen Ginsberg, Gary Snyder, and Lawrence Ferlinghetti were only a few of those whose work showed the unmistakable influence that these surroundings have on a receptive and responsive sensibility.

In composing the symphony I returned once again to the Friedrich Schiller essay that had caught my attention years earlier, "On the Naive and Sentimental in Poetry," thinking much about his thesis that creative types were of either one or another of opposing sensibilities.

There are all sorts of problems and paradoxes that crop up when one takes Schiller's dichotomies too seriously. But I found a fanciful portrait of myself lying somewhere amid the contrasting types that he posited. My own personal narrative was about extricating myself from what I felt to be the cold, dead hand of the academic avant-garde, from the theory-bound orthodoxy that held sway in the sixties, and from the fealty paid to European serialism and its offshoots. All of this seemed to me, in looking back, the ne plus ultra example of Schiller's "sentimental" attitude. The image of the young Boulez railing against almost all music except the tiny slice of repertoire that fulfilled his demand for progress by now seemed shrill and off the mark. His historical pronouncements had not come to pass. One could make the point that being naïve in our time is simply not possible, that to be naïve, one would have to feign innocence at a time when all is known about everything: "Been there, done that." Indeed, a symphony informed by symphonies of Bruckner, themselves informed by the operas of Wagner and the symphonies of Beethoven, could not hope to claim any truly naïve ground. But then I thought about Proust or Ravel or Mahler evoking their own childhood. I thought of the mixture of innocence and violence in the Nativity story I'd soon be using for a subject in El Niño. And I thought of the balance of light and darkness in the songs of the later Beatles albums or of Laura Nyro or Joni Mitchell, and I realized how the search for the naïve, the struggle to reclaim it, is one of the great gestures in the history of all artistic endeavor.

Naive and Sentimental Music does not take its title too literally. The essence of the piece is the presence of very simple material—the "naïve" tune in the first movement, the long meditative steel-string guitar solos in the second movement, and the chain of little Minimalist cells of the last movement—which exists in the matrix of a larger, more complex formal structure. It is, like so many of my large-scale pieces, a long journey with stopping points along the way. I dedicated the symphony to Esa-Pekka, a modest, reserved Finn who, like myself, had come to California only to experience a similarly radicalizing change in his creative and philosophical outlook.

The Los Angeles Philharmonic gave the premiere of this, my longest orchestral work, in February 1999. The first performance nearly derailed in the opening bars, but Esa-Pekka righted things and from there on conducted a performance that became increasingly confident. The orchestra played the piece many times after that, touring it in New York and recording it.

A recovering Modernist whose compositional training had centered on the postwar avant-garde styles of Ligeti, Lutoslawski, and late Stravinsky, Esa-Pekka had been hired to take over the Los Angeles Philharmonic at a young age. He had an enviable technique on the podium, a quick intellect, an easygoing manner with his players, and knew how to thrill an audience with dazzling physical gestures that elicited brilliant orchestral playing, especially in his favorite early-twentieth-century repertoire that centered on Bartók, Stravinsky, Messiaen, and Ravel. Conducting seemed an effortless activity for him, but like many European-trained musicians who suddenly found themselves at the helm of an American symphony orchestra and thus by default a spokesperson for that city's culture, Esa-Pekka was challenged to integrate himself and his artistic ideals with the surrounding community. This he did perhaps more genuinely than any other foreign-born music director in the history of American orchestral music. He befriended Frank Gehry, another Angelino, and together they collaborated on the creation of Disney Hall, one of the few thoroughly satisfying new concert halls to be built in the past fifty years. Gehry's playfulness and freedom from formalist ideology had been an inspiration for my own creativity, and there is no doubt that he had an even deeper effect on Esa-Pekka's outlook. Esa-Pekka's music began to ease off from the steely rigor of his earlier style and adopt a more luxurious sensibility, much informed, of course, by his firsthand understanding of what the modern orchestra is capable of. He brought up his young family as Californians and familiarized himself with the same American pop music, the same movies, and the same computer games his children knew. In so doing he shed his former cautious reserve, acquiring an increasing openness, both as an artistic thinker and as a person, although never losing his characteristic and endearing Finnish tendency toward self-deprecation. He tuned into my music in a special way, intuiting its musical architecture and reveling in its rhythmic inner life. He conducted exciting, exemplary performances of my Chamber Symphony, *El Niño*, *Slonimsky's Earbox*, and *The Dharma at Big Sur*. And in turn I conducted performances on the East Coast of his *L.A. Variations* and his cello concerto, *Mania*. Esa-Pekka made going to concerts of contemporary classical music an exciting and appealing activity, and when Disney Hall finally opened after years of political and financial cliff-hanging, California culture could no longer be pegged to the usual risible stereotypes. By the time he announced in 2007 that he would step down after nearly two decades of leading musical life in Los Angeles, the city and its orchestra had become a model of how classical music could thrive amid the colliding cultural values of modern urban life.

n January 2002, only a few months after September 11, I received a call from the other coast—from the New York Philharmonic. Their artistic administrator, Jeremy Geffen, asked if I would compose a memorial piece for the victims of the World Trade Center attacks. The Philharmonic had been much involved in the immediate aftermath of the catastrophe. Its musicians had on their own initiative formed ensembles and gone to Ground Zero to provide live music for the workers and the many traumatized family members and area locals who clustered around the site. Kurt Masur had performed the Brahms Requiem in Avery Fisher Hall that, by all accounts, had brought a sense of consolation and momentary tranquillity to a grateful audience, reminding the world that classical music has the capability to speak to the deepest parts of our spirits that other forms of music are powerless to reach. Nevertheless, I was appalled by the idea of a piece of music that would take as its theme the events of 9/11. It seemed like a fool's errand, trying to make musical or poetic expression of an event that continued to ache like a raw nerve in the national psyche.

The Philharmonic was asking for a piece that would open the orchestra's first concerts of the 2002 season, which also coincided with the official start of Lorin Maazel's tenure as music director. Curiously, the previous music director, Kurt Masur, had begun his era eleven years earlier with a program that also started with music of mine, *Tromba lontana* and *Short Ride in a Fast Machine*. For this proposed 9/11 piece, a chorus was available, since Maazel had originally planned an opening program of Stravinsky's *Symphony of Psalms* followed by the Beethoven Ninth.

I found myself in a situation of serious self-conflict. On the one hand I was impressed and humbled that the New York Philharmonic, the orchestra whose radio broadcasts with Leonard Bernstein had been so formative for me as a youth, would now choose me, rather than a

New York composer, to make such a piece. I knew how the members of the orchestra had responded so willingly and selflessly to the needs of the community in the days immediately after the attacks. I recognized that the request for this piece was virtually a call to civic duty and that the orchestra was reaching out to an American composer, asking him to give voice to complicated, communally shared emotions, but I could not imagine what such a piece would be. Worse, I feared that my status in the public's mind as a composer of "current event" operas, the mindless and pejorative tag that the media often pinned to me, would arouse suspicion in cultural circles. Most of all, I was concerned that my own private thoughts about the nature and reasons for the September 11 terrorist attacks might fall afoul of the lockstep, unquestioning patriotism that the Bush administration was so successfully cultivating throughout the country.

I had been in London on September 11, rehearsing the cast of singers for a film version of *The Death of Klinghoffer*. A more disconcerting coincidence between art and life is hard to imagine. The *Klinghoffer* rehearsals were leading up to a recording sessions with the London Symphony Orchestra in the famous Abbey Road Studios. Members of our cast included an Egyptian Arab, Kamel Boutros, and Tom Randle, an American-born African American, both of whom played the roles of Palestinian hijackers. In the title role was Sanford Sylvan, a New York–born Jew, who had created the role ten years earlier. The emotions among the cast upon receiving the news from New York and upon seeing those by-now iconic images of the falling towers were, to say the least, turbulent. Kamel, who lived in New York, was immediately concerned at the thought of having to travel back to the United States. There was a momentary thought of canceling the sessions, but then a collective sense of commitment to the project took over, and the recording sessions went forth in a mood of intense determination and the sober realization that the themes embedded in the opera were no longer simply abstractions to be suffered only by people in the Middle East.

The same week of the London *Klinghoffer* recording sessions and the news of 9/11 also featured a planned performance of *Short Ride in a Fast Machine* on the Last Night at the Proms concert in the Royal Albert Hall. Last Night is the traditional classical music blow-out of the London season, the most popular concert of the year, and normally an occasion for the faithful Proms audiences to take a sentimental bath in familiar (and mostly British) orchestral and choral pieces, wave their Union Jacks, sing patriotic songs, and generally act just a little bit goofy. The 2001 Proms season had featured an unusual amount of American music, doubtless because the American Leonard Slatkin was leading the BBC Symphony Orchestra that year. Opening-night audiences heard him conduct *Harmonium*; Copland, Ives, and Bernstein were liberally sprinkled throughout the rest of the season; and *Short Ride* was given a place on Last Night, a rare honor for an American. In fact, my piece had already been the victim of a last-minute cancellation several seasons earlier when a few days before that concert Princess Diana had died in a high-speed auto crash. With the news of Diana's death so present in everyone's mind, the BBC presenters had felt that the title *Short Ride in a Fast Machine* was uncomfortably suggestive. Now with the news of the September 11 attacks dominating all conversations and concerns, this Last Night program also would have to be reconsidered.

British citizens exhibited an exceptional sense of solidarity with Americans in the days and months following September 11. Whatever anxiety and frustration we stranded Americans felt at not being able to board a plane and return home to our loved ones was mitigated by the spontaneous expressions of sympathy and good feeling that we received from any number of Londoners passing us in the street or overhearing us in a restaurant. I remained in London for almost a week beyond my original return date. In the days following the attacks, air travel was nearly impossible, and many travelers found themselves learning to live with their temporary holding patterns. The Last Night concert, one that was to have been festive and celebratory, had to be changed to reflect the somber mood felt by all. My rowdy and high-energy *Short Ride* was replaced by the quiet orchestral fanfare *Tromba lontana*, a work I'd composed fifteen years earlier for the Houston Symphony. Samuel Barber's evergreen *Adagio for Strings* was added to the concert's first half. There are times when I can feel affection for Barber's emblematic piece of Americana. But that night I found it too heart-on-sleeve, especially in comparison to the noble simplicity of El-gar's "Nimrod" from the *Enigma* Variations, to which Slatkin, in his spoken remarks to the audience, compared it.

Most disturbing to me, though, was the solution to how the concert ought to conclude. The BBC presenters, who included not only Slatkin but also the imaginative and widely knowledgeable Nicholas Kenyon, were unable to find an American orchestral work that they felt could respond with the gravitas that this historic emergency had made indispensable. In the end, they defaulted to Beethoven, ending the program with the last movement of the Ninth Symphony. That decision brought to light a distressing reality about American classical music, almost an irony. America, quite possibly the world's most fertile and creative musical culture during the twentieth century, did not have a single orchestral work that could satisfy the need for collective emotional experience that a seriously traumatized public maintained in those jarring days after the attacks. Even in New York City, the musical event that received the greatest outpouring of appreciation in the days following September 11 was not of an American piece but of Masur's performance of the Brahms Requiem.

For once our popular music, so highly esteemed throughout all layers of the culture, fell flat. And our classical composers apparently were equally unable to meet the challenge, or so it would seem from the repertoire that orchestras chose to mark the tragedy. In our canon of more than a century's worth of American orchestral music, there apparently was not a single work that had the power or pride of position to answer to the needs of that peculiar moment in history. Shorter, more intimate works we had—Ives's *Unanswered Question*, Copland's *Quiet City*, the Barber *Adagio*. But we could not contribute anything on the level of a grand public statement of communally shared hope and idealism such as Beethoven or Mahler would satisfy. (I also recalled that at the time of the JFK assassination in 1963, the two musical tributes I saw on television were performances of the Beethoven "Eroica" and the Mahler "Resurrection" Symphony.) Was this simply a fault of history? Were the kind of Enlightenment ideals of Beethoven or the yearning spiritual quests of Mahler simply relics of the past, no longer possible in our more ironic and painfully self-conscious contemporary climate? Were listeners forced to go back to an earlier era to find expression for such idealized emotions as are expressed in Beethoven? Or was Beethoven simply a greater artist who spoke in a language of the sublime that no American composer could hope to rise to? Music is above and beyond all else an art of feeling, and in the days after 9/11 intelligent people were in need of an experience that spoke to those wounded feelings. Yet our musical tradition, for all its energy and vitality and fundamental optimism, seemed unable to respond to this need. It disturbed me greatly to realize this awkward fact.

Statements of grand-scale nobility are not particularly an American trait, are not typical of our artistic utterance. When we raise the roof we do it with a discharge of physical energy, more often than not to the accompaniment of a pounding pulse. That special gravitas of European concert music, while we may love it to death and demand it every time we go to a symphony concert, is not a tonality in which we Americans normally speak.

One thing is for sure: I did not accept the commission to compose *On the Transmigration of Souls* in order to fill the void that I detected during that week in London. The truth is that I responded to the request from the New York Philharmonic with reluctance. Orchestra music is by definition a public art form, and I had great difficulty imagining anything "commemorating" 9/11 that would not be an embarrassment. In the intervening months after the attacks the images of the collapsing World Trade Center towers, of dust-covered survivors, of valiant firemen, and of the smoking pile of toxic rubble dubbed Ground Zero had saturated our consciousness. There was no escaping the iconography of the event and its aftermath. Composing any kind of music to amplify these tortured emotions could only be an exercise in the worst possible taste. I also privately felt a nagging unease about the way Americans had reacted to the event. Were we truly shocked and grieved by the loss of life? Or were we more disturbed by the temerity, the outright flamboyance of the attacks? I had been keenly aware of what the novelist Philip Roth called the "kitschification" of 9/11, the way in which the event had almost immediately been distorted by the media and by politicians eager to capitalize on its imaginative potential. During World War II, the "good" war, our bombers had rained fiery death on hundreds of thousands of civilians in cities like Tokyo, Hamburg, and Dresden. But that was "warfare." September 11 was, we were told, "terrorism," something substantively different. Once George W. Bush had seized the moment, standing on the pile of rubble at Ground Zero and mouthing into his bullhorn a John Wayne oath of vengeance, the country as a whole began to buckle, yielding up decades of hard-won civil rights and allowing itself to be manipulated by cynical appeals to patriotism, xenophobia, and paranoia. What had begun as genuine shock and trauma devolved into that "orgy of narcissism" and collective victimization that so repelled Roth.

t seemed an impossible assignment to compose a piece with a subject like this. I agreed to do it in large part because I felt that a serious artist ought to be able to rise to the occasion and fulfill a need for a public statement that went beyond the usual self-centered, auteur concerns of his own personal individualism.

I worked hard against a deadline that was ridiculously tight, given the importance of the occasion. For the first month I did nothing but surf the Internet, looking not for the public, political face of the event but rather searching for its effects at the most intimate, most personal level. I found a willing and sympathetic collaborator in Barbara Haws, the archivist of the New York Philharmonic, a historian of New York City whose attorney husband, Bill Josephson, had coordinated the 9/11 frontline charity services. Barbara showed me photographs that she had taken around Ground Zero in the days immediately after the attacks. They were mostly of hand-lettered missing-persons signs placed on walls by the desperate families of those who had disappeared when the towers collapsed. The little signs were unbearably poignant, usually no more than a photocopied picture, a name, physical characteristics, date last seen, a contact number, and then frequently a little tag-end phrase like "We love you Chick." I took some of these phrases and began to make a text of them that would be part sung and part spoken, like an interior monologue. I also found text material in *The New York Times*'s "Portraits in Grief," a daily column that the newspaper ran for more than a year, providing small anecdotal histories of each of the nearly three thousand victims who had died on that day:

"I am so full of grief. My heart is absolutely shattered."

"He used to call me every day. I'm just waiting."

"I loved him from the start . . . I wanted to dig him out. I know just where he is."

I found, much to my surprise, that in choosing the World Trade Center towers to destroy, the terrorists had picked the most high-profile target imaginable, but that their victims were not the wealthiest of the wealthy, the Wall Street financiers who control the global economy and represent the long arm of American influence throughout the world. Of the thousands who died that day, most seemed to be mid-level employees, people in their thirties and forties, just starting their careers. But there were others: service workers, many of them Hispanic and Asian, who were in the building as janitors, restaurant workers, and the like. The CEO alpha males with the $100 million salaries and generous stock options worked elsewhere in Manhattan. The huge, homely WTC buildings turned out to be not the nexus of the world's richest power brokers but rather the annex, the mid-level office buildings where, for the most part, the financial industry's data crunchers and the many immigrant workers who serviced them labored away in relative obscurity.

On one of my many trips to New York I recorded onto a mini-disc player the sounds of the city late at night, and I noticed how it is never silent. No matter how tranquil the streets may seem at 3:00 a.m., there is always the sound of traffic, of distant sirens, idling vehicles, passing groups of pedestrians, footsteps, quiet conversation, brief laughter. I made a collage of these city sounds, intertwining them with quietly spoken texts—a long list of the names of the victims, some of the messages found on the missing-persons signs, and other fragments of words and phrases, all acting like little fractals of information, emotionally charged cues that stood for larger, longer personal narratives that one could never completely know but might imagine. I decided that the only way to approach this theme was to make it about the most intimate experiences of the people involved. Shortly after deciding to do the piece I visited an exhibition at the New-York Historical Society, where I witnessed a quietly disturbing video exhibition of footage taken by amateurs who were at ground level during the moments between when the first plane struck the towers and when they eventually collapsed. The videos were silent, eerily disturbing, pervaded by an air of uncertainty and confusion. Pedestrians in the street all were looking up, and the sky slowly rained down a floating blizzard of paper. Millions of pieces of what looked almost like confetti drifted gently amid the clouds of dust and smoke. People on the ground could not have been certain of what had happened, but their faces registered anxiety and unease.

That image of those millions of particles eerily, silently floating from an immense height was the generating idea of the piece. The orchestration, itself refracted and rendered into particulate matter, mirrors the impression I took from those home videos. The guardian angel of my piece was Ives, whose *Unanswered Question* hides within my scrim of sonic imagery, every once in a while making itself known with a chord change or a distant trumpet call. Ives was also influential in suggesting the density of material—my firsthand experiences of conducting both *Three Places in New England* and the Fourth Symphony came to fruition here.

On the Transmigration of Souls is a problematic piece for concert audiences. Even those disposed to like the work have had a difficult time situating themselves within its peculiar sonic environment. The "soundtrack" that I made with spoken voices and ambient city sounds surrounds the audience from all sides. For the New York premiere Mark Grey designed a computer-controlled network of forty small loudspeakers located throughout the immense space of Avery Fisher Hall. He also placed microphones over the orchestra and the two choruses and subtly added their sound into the general house mix. In cavernous Avery Fisher the mix of live and recorded sound struggled with the hall's unfriendly acoustics. Some listeners found themselves uncomfortably close to a loudspeaker while others, being too far from the nearest one, barely could make out what was coming from them. Nonetheless, the musicians took the piece to heart and performed with absolute care and utter sincerity. The venerable Lorin Maazel, at age seventy making his first appearance as newly named music director of the Philharmonic, knew the piece securely, and he conducted a sincere and authoritative performance, the tone of which was set by the

Brooklyn Youth Chorus, singing my difficult rhythmic hockets from memory, and by the magnificent New York Choral Artists. I could not have asked for a more committed first performance of a new piece, but still, it was an imperfect experience, due largely to the clash between technology and live music-making. In later performances in different halls, the piece fared both better and worse. I found myself oscillating wildly between loathing it and loving it. A distinctly unsatisfying performance of the piece in London with an amateur British chorus in 2007 left me thinking the piece was a dud. But not long afterward I experienced a revelation with the very same music and texts when I heard first the Atlanta Symphony Orchestra Chorus and then the Cincinnati May Festival Chorus sing the piece with an understanding and empathy that I'd never before suspected was lying inherent in the texts. The pure American quality of their enunciation and their perfectly balanced sonorities lifted the matter-of-fact plainness of the words to a transcendental level, and for once the piece did not seem as compromised and uneven as I had previously thought.

13.

A SWIRL OF ATOMS

n the predawn darkness of a summer morning in July 1945, on the harsh pebble-strewn floor of a remote New Mexican desert, a group of exhausted and jittery young physicists and engineers, working under the watchful eyes of the U.S. Army, exploded the world's first atomic bomb. The blast was created by forcing the surface of a small sphere of the artificially created element plutonium to "go supercritical," to compress its heavy load of neutrons to the point where the atomic mass suddenly became energy. In a microsecond enough heat was generated to turn the desert rocks to glass and to bathe the surrounding landscape in a purplish glow, full of lethal radiation capable of killing organic life for a radius of a mile or more. It was the most dramatic laboratory proof of Einstein's forty-year-old formula that revolutionized Newtonian physics by equating mass and energy.

The event leaped to instant mythological status with the deadly follow-up of the bomb's use on two Japanese cities three weeks later. The bomb was the symbol of the American dream. It projected awesome power the likes of which no previous empire in history—not Augustinian Rome, nor imperial Spain, nor Victorian England—had ever approached. By bringing the agonizingly destructive Pacific war to an abrupt conclusion it announced with reassuring certitude that Yankee ingenuity, the same ingenuity that had brought forth the telephone, the lightbulb, the automobile, and the airplane, might also prevent future wars of global scale. Although the discovery that made the bomb possible, that the atom could fission and in so doing give off energy, had already been accomplished a decade earlier by Europeans, the actualization of that knowledge in the form of a weapon of immense destructive force was a typically American accomplishment, suffused as it was with patriotic zeal and a unique strange-bedfellow collaboration between tight-lipped military bureaucracy obsessed with secrecy and the free-form scientific inquiry of college professors. The story, compelling and even romantic from the start, became even more iconic over time, especially when the main characters and their personal narratives became public. Chief among these, of course, was J. Robert Oppenheimer, a scientific and literary prodigy from a wealthy New York Jewish family, who while still a teenager had found in the study of physics a perfect expression of his worldview. Oppenheimer had been doubly blessed. Not only was he gifted with one of the quickest and most comprehending intellects ever known among scientists, but he also had the fortune to come to his profession just at the time when physics as a field of knowledge was in full bloom with the revelations of Albert Einstein, Werner Heisenberg, Niels Bohr, and others. After postgraduate work in England, Holland, and Germany, Oppenheimer arrived in Berkeley, where he quickly became a star on the University of California campus, a brilliant and at times arrogant cynosure who rapidly collected a clutch of adoring young disciples who followed his every word.

Almost from the start Oppenheimer led a life of dizzying complexity. Shortly after arriving in California he was holding simultaneous professorships at UC Berkeley and at CalTech in Pasadena, collaborating with his Berkeley colleague Ernest Lawrence, helping to lay the groundwork for what became the cyclotron. When World War II intensified, he was chosen by the U.S. Army to lead the development of the atomic bomb. He did so with astonishing imagination and success, so much so that within a few years of the war's end, he had become a virtual media star, second only to Einstein in the public's image of the "genius" scientist. But after seeing his creation used to destroy two Japanese cities and transform warfare into a theater of potential human annihilation, he became a passionate spokesperson for the open sharing of information on nuclear technology. Ultimately, with the cold war at full tilt and the volume turned up on anti-Communist propaganda, people in the U.S. government, which had so aggressively sought out his services to help win the war, made Oppenheimer the target of a sinister, backstabbing smear campaign. Deemed a security risk because of personal associations he'd maintained twenty years earlier, he was forced to leave public service and to return once again to academic life, but he never fully recovered from the personal damage that his very public chastisement cost him. If one were to take seriously Aristotle's requirement of a tragedy—that its characters be persons of consequence, of exalted station—Oppenheimer would be an ideal choice.

America loves its heroes and savors the most intimate details of their lives. We consume every scrap of information about them and thrill at their triumphs. But we love even more to bear witness to their weaknesses, to see them fall from their pedestals, suffer humiliation, even degradation. In this way their eventual rehabilitations can be all the more bittersweet and inspirational for us. If they die before they are forgiven, we raise them up posthumously. It is part of the national psychic drama, the dark, nether side of fame. Oppenheimer, like Richard Nixon, was publicly disgraced, ousted, and tried on what was essentially a technicality. Unlike Nixon, he was a noble character, one who, although enjoying his prestige and position as the country's most highly regarded expert on nuclear policy, had no Machiavellian pretensions to power. He was brought down largely through vendetta because he bruised the vanity of some Washington politicians and because his moral scruples about America's behavior on the world stage posed an uncomfortable ethical challenge for the U.S. government at a time when the country was caught up in an arms race.

By the year 2000 I didn't think that the idea of composing another grand opera of the size of *Nixon in China* or *The Death of Klinghoffer* was likely to appeal to me ever again. Even though *Nixon* had made me famous and *Klinghoffer* had made me infamous, the idea of immersing myself for two or more years in a labor-intensive project of that scope held little appeal. People completely unknown to me continued to send draft libretti or elaborate proposals for new operas, many of them pegged to some contemporary event or public figure. Meanwhile American composers were busy writing operas with themes from popular culture or news events. Many of them were keyed to the lives of well-known personalities or hot-button topics like political assassination, racial politics, homophobia, or the death penalty. I'd seen some of them and was not encouraged.

I thought that the musical dramatic style of *El Niño*, with its modest theatrical demands and emphasis on symbolic storytelling, would be the standard for me from now on. The reluctance of our major American opera houses to accept either of my operas also discouraged me, although I was aware that in the opera world acceptance into the canon is slow and grudging, and that only in very recent times had the dramatic works of Janacek, Britten, Shostakovich, Berg, and Schoenberg been granted repertory status in American opera houses. Indeed, as a college student I'd played with the Boston Symphony Orchestra in the 1966 American premiere of Schoenberg's *Moses und Aron*, an opera that had waited nearly thirty years to be heard in this country.

n 1999, while still working on *El Niño*, I received a call from Pamela Rosenberg, who was just beginning her tenure as general director of the San Francisco Opera. She had a provocative suggestion, that I compose an "American Faust" opera. Her historical figure of choice to embody that character was none other than J. Robert Oppenheimer. In Pamela's mind, Oppenheimer's decision to accept the U.S. Army's invitation to lead the Manhattan Project and develop the atomic bomb had a latter-day "pact with the Devil" implication. Oppenheimer's eventual fall from political grace and public humiliation mirrored the Faust myth.

I might have been a little uncomfortable with the thought of taking on a myth as familiar and universally celebrated as Faust, but Pamela's mention of Oppenheimer rang a bell with an urgency I'd not felt since Peter Sellars had popped the Nixon and Mao question to me nearly twenty years earlier. The atomic bomb had been the overwhelming, irresistible, inescapable image that dominated the psychic activity of my childhood. The mushroom cloud was a sinister consort to my young thoughts, a source of existential terror that seemed permanently factored into every one of life's decisions, the ultimate annihilator of any positive emotions or hopes. I had come of age during the era of heated rhetoric and skittish paranoia that typified the cold war, and the small-town, rural idyll of my childhood was always clouded by the absurdities of air-raid drills, "family" bomb shelters, arsenals of nuclear warheads, and the chatter of politicians invoking the evils that lurked behind what Churchill with his gift for epithets had so evocatively dubbed the "Iron Curtain."

Despite my misgivings about the Faust connection, I answered Pamela's request in the affirmative almost immediately, and within a few days I was plunged deep into what would become nearly four years of research and thinking about the topic. Besides being the American myth par excellence, the story of the bomb's creation had its roots right in my backyard, in Berkeley, where many of the principal scientists, Oppenheimer among them, had lived and taught in the decade leading up to World War II.

My first portal of entry was the massive, 850-page *The Making of the Atomic Bomb* by Richard Rhodes. Rhodes, whom I eventually met and became friends with, had that rare and exceptional ability to weave difficult technical theories and detailed descriptions into a narrative that had both dramatic tension and historical sweep. His book, despite its title, turned out to be a history of nuclear physics during the fifty-year period from 1895 to the moment when Oppenheimer's plutonium sphere detonated near Alamogordo, New Mexico, in July 1945. The story included names, some of which were familiar to me—Einstein, of course, and Niels Bohr, Richard Feynman, Enrico Fermi, and Edward Teller. But my formal scientific education had ground to a halt with high-school biology, and most of what I read about atomic theory was utterly new territory. I knew roughly the structure of the atom, the principles of ionization, and the behavior of electrons whirling in their prestissimo orbits around the nucleus. Years earlier, while still in college, I'd worked, with the help of books by Bertrand Russell and Buckminster Fuller, to internalize the meaning of $E=mc^2$, trying to absorb Einstein's revolutionary discovery that matter and energy are essentially interchangeable. But my mathematical skills were woefully underdeveloped, and I had to settle for analogy rather than working through the actual equation-verified proofs.

What did eventually impress me was the realization of how much energy even the smallest lump of humble matter contained. Just to contemplate that famous equation was enough to give a hint: the "E" stands for energy. Thus, the energy contained in the tiniest speck of matter was equivalent to the mass of the matter times the square of the speed of light (299,792,458 meters per second). With this equivalence we are suddenly catapulted into the realm of imponderable quantities. A gram of uranium, for instance, contains what Richard Rhodes called an "absurdly large" number of atoms: 2.5×10^{21}, or 2,500,000,000,000,000,000,000 atoms.

A homely analogy in one of the many books I read in preparation for composing the opera was more explicit. It said that if the energy contained in a small glass of water could be liberated, if the immense force that kept its atoms together could be sprung, the result would be sufficient to power the *Queen Mary* across the Atlantic and back. For centuries scientists had known about these adamantine nuclear forces, but it was not until 1938, when Lise Meitner, Otto Hahn, and Otto Frisch discovered that the nucleus could be split, that the possibility of unleashing and utilizing this mind-bendingly enormous potential was actually realized.

There was something about the unlocking of these forces by human intellectual effort that was ripe for a mythic treatment. Mythology abounded in stories of hubris, of the arrogant human or god who through cleverness makes an invention that unleashes powers that eventually turn on their inventor and destroy him. The manipulation of the atom, the unleashing of that formerly inaccessible source of densely concentrated energy, was *the* great mythological tale of our time. It touched on every possible theme of our lives as modern inhabitants of this planet. Above and beyond all, it was a parable about ecology. In fact it was the ultimate parable: Were we as a uniquely evolving species able to take responsibility for preserving our nest? Or would we succumb like one of those vainglorious Greek or Norse gods, overcome with our imagined sense of power and unable to measure its destructive potential until it was too late to pull back from the brink?

Oppenheimer, known as "Oppie" to his friends and students, was certainly a magnetic figure for dramatic treatment. In life he possessed qualities we don't usually associate with scientists. He was highly cultured in all the arts; immensely literate; able to speak fluent German, French, and Dutch; and had a reading command of half a dozen more languages, including Sanskrit, which he learned so that he could read the Bhagavad Gita in its original form. He collected paintings—there was a van Gogh among the family's artworks—and he listened exclusively to classical music. Among his favorite pieces were the late Beethoven quartets, and it is said that in his last years, while living at Princeton, he met Stravinsky and became a fan of that composer's twelve-tone *Requiem Canticles*. This was not your standard playlist for a physicist. At Harvard, as an eighteen-year-old taking advanced graduate courses in physics and chemistry, he unwound at night by composing sonnets. Some twenty-five years later, in the anxious hours leading up to the test firing of the bomb, he is rumored to have calmed his shattered nerves by reading from a tattered copy of Baudelaire's *Fleurs du mal*, which he kept as a kind of spiritual vade mecum. He and his younger brother, Frank, had the benefit of an elite education, the finest tutors, travel, and exposure from a young age to high culture. The family's wealth, the result of their immigrant father's successful import business, gave them a certain sense of independence and ease in social circles.

Reading Oppenheimer's letters I sensed a soul of labyrinthine complexity, one that in its youth had found an almost sensual satisfaction in the laws and behavior of particles and force fields. His was very much the kind of character that could have stepped out of a Goethe play or novel—brilliant, romantic, arrogant, irresistibly attractive to women, and moody, alternating between morbid introspection and charming conviviality. At the young age of thirty-eight he was chosen by General Leslie Groves to lead the intellectual expedition that would produce the atomic bomb. It was, as many of those who worked on the project would later admit, essentially an engineering feat. The scientific basis was already well understood; the real challenge was turning theory into practice, making a weapon that would actually work.

Oppenheimer was gifted with the kind of quick intellect that allowed him to grasp almost instantaneously the essence of a problem. Hans Bethe, one of the many German- or Hungarian-born physicists whom Oppenheimer invited to the remote high mesa of Los Alamos, said of him, "Simply put, he was intellectually superior to all the rest of us." To Bethe, himself one of the most accomplished physicists of the twentieth century, Oppenheimer was in the unique position to lead because his intellect had a much broader reach. It was, in fact, his "taste," his ability to identify immediately what were the most important problems, that made him so special. That taste, combined with a unique confidence and charisma, made him the ideal leader of a project so daunting in its complexity and so delicate in its demands for secrecy.

There were any number of ways to treat the story. In some respects Pamela Rosenberg's Faust analogy was very apt. Certainly Oppenheimer and many of his coworkers suffered remorse after the war when they witnessed the devastation wrought by the weapon they had made. And Oppenheimer himself had traded scientific independence for great political influence. But this was wartime, and the young physicists and engineers that Oppenheimer assembled in Los Alamos outside of Santa Fe all rightly considered themselves in a race with the Nazis. There was every reason to believe that the Germans, who had Werner Heisenberg working for them, were well on their way to developing a similar weapon. Had they done so—and after the war it was discovered that they'd tried but were far from achieving their goal— the history of the next hundred years could have been radically different for the free world. Oppenheimer had many left-wing friends, and he had dabbled moderately in Socialist causes during the 1930s. His brother, Frank, had joined the Communist Party, and his wife's first husband had been a Communist union organizer in the Pennsylvania coal mines. For Oppenheimer to sign on to be the principal player in the army's most secret weapons program had some aspects of a Faustian bargain. He pledged loyalty and obedience in exchange for which he was allowed to assemble the most stellar cast of scientific geniuses ever to be brought together to solve a single problem. But in the end, there was no reason not to believe that their efforts were anything other than patriotic and devoted to saving civilization as they knew it.

A more cogent parallel might have been *The Magic Mountain*, because the Los Alamos mesa became a kind of intellectual hothouse, not unlike the collection of brilliant and eccentric characters that populate Thomas Mann's novel. Several of the physicists were European born and educated and brought Old World cultural values with them. Edward Teller, still a young man of thirty-four, somehow managed to arrange for a small piano to be hauled up the long, muddy road to his tiny Los Alamos cottage so that he could spend his few leisure hours playing Bach and Mozart. Conversations about literature and the arts were mixed in with speculations about uranium separation and neutron capture.

Once I'd decided to make this opera I contacted Peter Sellars and asked if this might be a project that would interest him. Alice Goodman had not written a libretto for a dozen years, but the story seemed ideal for her penetrating historical gaze and her canny way of bringing real historical characters to life through language. The three of us met for several days in Santa Monica, fleshing out a synopsis and focusing on characters. As with the earlier operas, we started with plans that were much too grand, projecting a design that would begin with Los Alamos and culminate eight years later with Teller betraying Oppenheimer at a hearing of the Atomic Energy Commission, of which Oppenheimer had been a charter member.

But by the time this opera reached the stage several years later, in October 2005, almost all of this had changed. I had given it a name, *Doctor Atomic*. Peter had proposed calling it *The New Atlantis*, after an essay by the sixteenth-century English philosopher Francis Bacon, but I wanted something that had more of a populist ring to it, as if it were a story title out of *Life* magazine, circa 1950. It was a title that resonated with science fiction and the American middlebrow impression of scientific geniuses. And in a nod to Pamela Rosenberg's initial inspiration, it also hinted a backdoor reference to Mann's *Doktor Faustus*. The libretto for *Doctor Atomic* was unlike anything the opera world had ever encountered. Alice Goodman, newly ordained as an Anglican minister with her own parish in the English midlands and overwhelmed with her church responsibilities, had withdrawn from the project. Rather than search for a different librettist I had prodded Peter to assemble a libretto from the huge amount of documented material that we'd already compiled. This was a radical but actually workable idea. Instead of writing an original text from scratch, we would give the historical characters the very words they had said, either by quoting them verbatim, as we did by utilizing Edward Teller's and General Groves's memoirs, or by using recollections by and interviews with the scientists and military personnel who had participated in the project. The filmmaker Jon Else, director of the classic Oppenheimer documentary *The Day After Trinity*, generously offered us the transcripts, already twenty-five years old, of interviews he'd done with many of the surviving participants in the Los Alamos project. Obtaining permission for these texts was not always easy. Teller's estate, upon receiving our request to use passages from his memoirs and several of his other books, at first declined, probably assuming that anything having to do with Teller and Oppenheimer would damn the former while lauding the latter. In fact the young Edward Teller of Los Alamos in the mid-1940s was not yet the Strangelovian advocate of thermonuclear weapons and betrayer of Oppenheimer that he became a decade later. He was a man of overflowing intellectual ideas, devoted to his family, and upset after his time in Los Alamos that he wasn't given more credit.

I had a brief correspondence with Teller's daughter, Wendy, whom I'd known slightly while we were in college together. She read the libretto and pronounced it "anti-science," but in the end she gave us permission to use her father's words. She was the only scientist I encountered who would see the opera in that light. In conferences and symposia in San Francisco and Chicago at the time of the local premieres, many physicists, including several Nobel laureates, would praise the opera, saying that it made a profound impression on them and succeeded in bringing to the fore matters, both political and ethical, that had largely disappeared from the public dialogue during the intervening decades.

Peter made the libretto by photocopying several hundred fragments of text, cutting them, and arranging them in a sequence that had real dramatic flow, especially in the scenes where the back and forth between scientists and military officials became dangerously heated. In addition to the quotations, he incorporated other text elements. The opening chorus, which I set to a busy, propulsive ostinato like the newsreel music of the 1940s, is taken verbatim from a 1945 book titled *Atomic Energy for Military Purposes*:

A weapon has been developed
that is potentially destructive
beyond the wildest nightmares
of the imagination;
a weapon so ideally suited
to sudden unannounced attack
that a country's major cities
might be destroyed overnight
by an ostensibly friendly power.
This weapon has been created
not by the devilish inspiration
of some warped genius
but by the arduous labor
of thousands of normal men and women
working for the safety of their country.

But the expressive high points in *Doctor Atomic* are those set to real poetry, poetry that Oppenheimer had a special affinity for. In both acts I set passages by his beloved Charles Baudelaire, dreamlike evocations about time and space, about the keenest of sensual pleasure on the one hand and the bleakest of existential dread on the other. Later in the opera, the eerie silence that accompanies the final countdown is interrupted by a pounding, violent choral vision of fiery holocaust set to Christopher Isherwood's translation of the Bhagavad Gita:

At the sight of this, your Shape stupendous,
Full of mouths and eyes, feet, thighs and bellies,
Terrible with fangs, O master,
All the worlds are fear-struck, even just as I am.

A fourth poetic voice, that of Muriel Rukeyser, an American who lived and wrote at exactly the same time as Oppenheimer did, gave a special contemporary intensity to the opera. Rukeyser—like Oppenheimer born into an affluent and cultured New York family, educated at the same Ethical Culture Fieldstone School in New York—produced wartime poems that spoke in veiled imagery of the hope and desperation prevailing in those uncertain years. I set the bittersweet love poem "Am I in your light?" for Kitty in the act I bedroom scene, when the Oppenheimers are alone late at night. The short poem gives voice to the mix of sexual frustration and emotional longing of a partner who has long been denied affection and cannot get the attention of her lover.

> only my fingers in your hair, only, my eyes
> splitting the skull to tickle your brain with love
> in a slow caress blurring the mind,
>   kissing your mouth awake
> opening the body's mouth and stopping the words.

Other Rukeyser passages could be alarmingly obscure, and I had to open myself to their multiple meanings and to the confusion of responses they prompted. But poetry offers that possibility of multiplicity and ambiguity in a way no other art can, presenting images that have their individual potency but may not elicit in the reader a logical progression of reasoned thought.

Our grand plans for an epic story line stretching over nearly a decade ended up drastically compressed. Instead of spanning eight years, the timeline of *Doctor Atomic* was pared down to an evening in June 1945 in Los Alamos and then the single night of July 15–16, 1945, when the first bomb was detonated at the Alamogordo Test Range several hundred miles to the south.

The drama is twofold. Of immediate concern was the implacable deadline set by the White House and the scientists' extreme anxiety about whether or not their experiment would actually work. The pressure from Washington came because Truman was just arriving in Potsdam, where the victors in the European war, including Stalin, were set to draw the outlines of postwar Europe and decide which countries would fall under Soviet influence and which would ally with the West. Even more pressing was the news that the Russians had announced their intentions to join in the final attack on Japan. The Americans, already heavily engaged in an intense bombing campaign of the Japanese cities, did not need and did not want Russia's help. Had Russia joined in, Stalin would have demanded a share in the division of spoils there, too. So Truman was in great haste to end the war before Russia made it official. It was essential for Truman to know confidently that he had a workable atomic weapon at his disposal. It would be an ace up his sleeve, and his plan was to obliquely mention it to Stalin at the appropriate moment, little suspecting that Stalin already knew everything about the bomb thanks to espionage going on right under Oppenheimer's nose.

But threats from the Pentagon and the White House were only surface ripples compared to the slowly ripening moral conflict that was beginning to grip the Los Alamos laboratory in the weeks prior to the test. Several of the young physicists and engineers had been sympathetic to Socialist and even Communist causes in the years leading up to the war, and all must surely have known that Oppenheimer, their leader and idol, had hosted fund-raisers for Russia in Berkeley and that his wife, Kitty, had been married to a Communist Party member. With the defeat of Germany already accomplished, these young scientists began to wonder why and how this bomb that they had labored so hard to create would be used on the Japanese. The end of the Pacific war was all but assured, but the cost in American lives required to bring it to a conclusion was unknown. The slow crawl of our forces across the western Pacific toward mainland Japan was one of hideous attrition, with each conquered island or atoll costing thousands of lives, both military and civilian. Oppenheimer was called to Washington to consult about targets for his soon-to-be-completed weapon. He had returned to Los Alamos having bought into the harsh logic of aerial bombing. The decision had been made to drop the bomb on Japanese cities with an aim that had less to do with strategic damage to their matériel than with wreaking terror on and intimidation of the civilian population. Most of the major Japanese cities by August 1945 had been thoroughly demolished by the Air Force's conventional bombing. In fact, as I later learned by talking with several of the surviving physicists who had participated in the Manhattan Project, Hiroshima and Nagasaki had been deliberately spared from bombing so as to leave them virgin targets for the atomic bomb. In the end, of the 225,000 killed in Hiroshima and Nagasaki, 95 percent were civilians, most of them women and children.

The younger scientists at Los Alamos, led by the idealistic Robert Wilson, got wind of these plans to bomb civilian areas, and they were outraged. Much of the first scene of *Doctor Atomic* centers on this moral conflict, the question of whether a scientist should bear responsibility for the ultimate use of his inventions. In scene 1, Teller reads Oppenheimer a letter he has just received from their friend, the physicist Leo Szilard. Szilard's letter is actually a petition that he hopes all the scientists "working in atomic power" will sign. It is a protest against the use of the bomb on an already devastated Japanese population. The Szilard letter notes that Americans were now holding individual Germans responsible for not having spoken out against Hitler, saying that those Germans who kept silent must share the guilt for what their country had done, even though they would have risked losing their lives just by saying so. Similarly, Szilard felt that scientists working for the American government had a moral obligation to speak out against the use of the atomic bomb at a time when its use was no longer necessary to win the war.

Szilard was not optimistic that his petition would make much of a dent in Washington's determination to use this new weapon, but it would be "a matter of great importance" if a large number of scientists working in the field "went clearly and unmistakably on record as to their opposition on moral grounds to the use of these bombs in the present phase of the war." Teller, accompanied by grave harmonies in the strings and trombones, sings the actual words of Szilard's petition:

We scientists, working on atomic power, are in a position to raise our voices without such risks, even though we might incur the displeasure of those who are at present in charge. The people of the United States are unaware of the choice we face, and this only increases our responsibility in this matter.

Oppenheimer answers by deferring the ultimate decision on the bomb's use to "the best men in Washington . . . it is for them to decide, not us." Furthermore, he is genuinely concerned that allowing political discussions of this sort on the property of the Los Alamos laboratory could get everyone into very serious trouble. Wilson, one of Oppie's prize students, is shocked by what he senses is Oppenheimer's unwillingness to confront the moral implications of using the bomb on civilian populations. Wilson reads from another Szilard petition, one that describes the position of those scientists who felt that an unannounced nuclear attack by the United States would not only be ethically intolerable but would ruin any chance of a postwar campaign to place a moratorium on the bomb's development. Even as early as 1945 scientists were aware of what the future would likely bring, that it would be impossible to contain the genie now that it had been released from the bottle, that sooner or later our enemies would have the bomb as well. (Paradoxically, Harry Truman, after having been briefed on the technological complexity of building nuclear weapons, announced confidently that the Russians "would never" develop the bomb.)

The Japanese, says Wilson, should be told of what might happen to them. The bomb should be demonstrated so that their leaders can see what might be in store for them, and then they should be given a chance to surrender. This was the position of the scientists from the University of Chicago who had signed what became known as the Franck Report, a petition to President Truman pleading for a demonstration of the bomb rather than an unannounced attack on Japan. The Franck Report reasoned specifically:

> From this point of view a demonstration of the new weapon may best be made before the eyes of representatives of all United Nations, on the desert or a barren island. The best possible atmosphere for the formation of an international agreement could be achieved if America would be able to say to the world, "you see what weapon we had but did not use. We are ready to renounce its use in the future and to join other nations in working out adequate supervision of the use of this nuclear weapon."

Perhaps Truman's military advisers misled him into thinking that Hiroshima and Nagasaki were military rather than civilian targets. A year after composing the opera I found this quote from his diaries, written during that contentious period when targets were being selected:

> I have told the Sec. of War, Mr. Stimson, to use it [the atomic bomb] so that military objectives and soldiers and sailors are the target and not women and children. Even if the Japs are savages, ruthless, merciless and fanatic, we as the leader of the world for the common welfare cannot drop that terrible bomb on the old capital or the new.

Somehow these concerns were forgotten, and even Oppenheimer advocated an atomic attack on cities. The official decision in Washington was that the bomb should be used on the Japanese to make "as great an impression as possible," in other words to strike terror sufficiently in the minds of the military authorities, and presumably those informing the emperor, that an immediate surrender would be effected. This is indeed what happened, although many historians now argue that the Japanese were already seriously signaling their desire for a surrender, but that the Americans, intent on using their new weapon, were not interested in hearing the terms until after the bomb had been used.

In scene 1, I set to music Oppenheimer's words (taken from the transcript of the Interim Committee meeting he attended) when he describes what the bomb's effect will be:

> I explained that the visual effect
> of an atomic bombing
> would be tremendous.
> A brilliant luminescence
> rising to a height of up to
> twenty thousand feet.
> The neutron effect
> of the explosion
> would be dangerous to life
> for a radius of at least
> two-thirds of a mile,

On the night of the scheduled test, while the plutonium sphere was already hanging from its scaffold-like tower, a freak electrical storm blew into the test site, bringing rain, high winds, and lightning and further amplifying the mood of extreme stress among all the scientists and military personnel. The gusts of wind lashed the plutonium sphere as it hung ominously from a high tower. Robert Wilson was assigned to climb the tower and attach canisters to measure the bomb's chain reaction, and he had to do this while thunder and lightning threatened to set it off prematurely. To add to the collective case of nerves, a rumor circulated that some of the physicists, including the much respected Enrico Fermi, were taking bets as to whether the bomb's chain reaction might set fire to the entire earth's atmosphere.

The third scene of act I starts in the midst of this storm. General Groves rails at the Army's chief meteorologist, Jack Hubbard, as if the bad weather were somehow Hubbard's fault. There are only three people who can call off this immensely important test: Oppenheimer, Groves, and Hubbard. Hubbard thinks testing an atomic bomb in the middle of an electrical storm with its grave potential for uncontrollable fallout is pure folly. In the original production the role of the harassed meteorologist was played by James Maddelena, who eighteen years earlier had created the unforgettable characterization of Richard Nixon. Groves, who triumphantly wrote later about his management of the Manhattan Project, "I interfered with *everything*," fumes and barks orders at everyone. When a medical specialist informs him that plutonium is proving to be far more lethal a substance than anyone had imagined, and that a plan for emergency evacuation of the test site ought to be devised, the general retorts, "What are you, a Hearst propagandist?"

When I first saw Peter's draft libretto I wondered if sufficient dramatic tension for a three-hour opera could be built and maintained on such matters as scientists circulating a petition or a crisis over an unexpected storm. But these issues turned out to be stepping-stones to the much deeper matters that lie at the core of *Doctor Atomic*. The weather's unwillingness to cooperate brought home the fact that, no matter how sophisticated humans may consider themselves, nature always holds the trump card. Likewise, the deepening sense of moral conflict weighing down the conscience of the young scientists is the first murmur of an ethical debate that will dominate our lives for decades if not centuries to come. The moment Oppenheimer's bomb exploded, the relationship between humans and the planet they inhabit changed unalterably. Man's evolving technological know-how now included the potential to destroy all life on Earth. This was the chilling realization that the writer Jonathan Schell made so starkly in his book *The Fate of the Earth*, an ecological doomsday scenario so unsettling that I was troubled with nightmares when I first read it in 1982. Wagner could not have imagined a moral and psychological dramatic conflict as potent and complex as this.

In an inspired decision, Peter placed the famous John Donne Holy Sonnet, "Batter my heart, three-person'd God," at the very end of act I. Oppenheimer was much drawn to the metaphysical poets Donne, Andrew Marvell, and George Herbert. The "three-person'd God" of Donne's poem provided the stimulus for Oppenheimer's whimsical naming of the test site: Trinity. The image of the physicist, alone at last, contemplating his dark, destructive creation, drew from me a musically strange response, but one that in retrospect seems entirely appropriate. After a whole act of music that teeters on the cusp of atonality, "Batter my heart" appears as an archaic trope, its D-minor chord sequences projecting a slow, stately gravitas that to me spoke for the poem's content as well as for what most surely have been Oppenheimer's wildly conflicting emotions. How could this supremely intelligent and sensitive man not have peered into the terrible future of what this bomb would bring? How could he not have suspected the horrific, lingering pain and slow agonizing death that its radiation would cause for tens of thousands of innocent civilians? The Donne poem is an expression of the keenest spiritual pain, a beseeching, an appeal to God that He physically beat and batter the speaker in order that his divided self might rise up and be made whole again:

That I may rise, and stand, o'erthrow me, and bend
Your force, to break, blow, burn and make me new.

Oppenheimer sings these words in the depth of night while standing alone in front of the sinister plutonium sphere that has been swathed shroud-like in a canvas tent. It was one of the eeriest and most disturbing stage images I'd ever witnessed. When Oppenheimer is done singing and the orchestral coda batters the last of a sequence of D-minor chords, he unfolds a flap of the tent and disappears into it, like a man going back into the womb. Gerald Finley, the Canadian-born baritone for whom I wrote the role, sang this aria with an intensity of feeling that never failed to leave the hall rapt in awe. Rarely had I experienced a moment when the performance of a piece of mine brought so much more to the music than its composer had imagined.

s a counterpart to all the male energy we were blessed to have the figure of Oppenheimer's wife, Kitty, a woman who in real life was a person of manifold psychological shadings. Restless and unhappy in her imposed role of the project director's wife, full of resentment over the fact that her talents as an accomplished biologist were being ignored, Kitty spent much of her time in Los Alamos alone or in the company of other wives. She drank heavily, and she seems to have been a lightning rod of strong feelings among the other women in the community, with some adoring her and some openly despising her. But to be the soul mate of Robert Oppenheimer she must surely have been a deep and powerful being, and I kept that in mind constantly as I composed for her character. Apart from the quiet yearning of "Am I in your light?," Kitty's music is exclusively visionary, oracular. (This was most certainly given impetus by the fact that I was creating this role for Lorraine Hunt Lieberson, who by the time of the premiere was too ill to sing it.) Both Kitty and her Tewa Indian maid, Pasqualita, embody differing aspects of Goethe's *ewig Weibliche*. Both possess Cassandra-like powers, but their utterances are delphic, cryptic, ambiguous. For this the elusive and allusive Muriel Rukeyser was a perfect fit. By placing her poetry in the voices of Kitty and Pasqualita, my musical imagination was unlocked and given flight in strange ways that at times I was unable to explain even to myself. In her long opening soliloquy of act II, Kitty, invoking the myth of the Resurrection, sees the ritual death and indifferent destruction engulfing the planet as "our black honor and feast of possibility," a means of celebrating "casting life on life."

Lit by their energies, secretly, all things shine.
Nothing can black that glow of life; although
each part go crumbling down
itself shall rise up whole.

Composing this scene, drawn from a Rukeyser poem called
"Easter Eve 1945," I kept thinking of how a redwood tree thrives on
forest fires that leave the rest of the landscape scorched and charred,
but that are nonetheless salubrious for the redwood's growth and
health. Rukeyser summons an atavistic reasoning for the omnipresent
death that has seized the world in these bleak war-torn days. It is
"death of all man to share," a holocaust that will be followed by a
renewal.

This earth-long day
between blood and resurrection where we wait
remembering sun, seed, fire; remembering
that fierce Judean Innocent who risked
every immortal meaning on one life.

Pasqualita sings a Tewa lullaby to Kitty's infant. The four points of
the compass are ritually invoked in this lullaby. In the north, the east,
the south, and the west "a cloud-flower blossoms." Her words project
a wholeness that is profoundly lacking in the mood and behavior of
the men. But as the countdown approaches and the tension rises, even
Pasqualita is seized by the bad energy, and she too is possessed by
visions:

Then word came from a runner, a stranger:
"They are dancing to bring the dead back, in the mountains."
We danced at an autumn fire, we danced the old hate and
    change,
the coming again of our leaders. But they did not come . . .
News came on the frost, "The dead are on the march!"

Between the native Indians and the interloping collection of physicists and their military minders two vastly differing cosmologies peer

at each other across a gulf of culture and experience. The scientists are rational, materialist, verbal. Their relation to the physical surroundings is utilitarian. In their hands the material world is reduced to data. As far as their relation to the land is concerned they are visitors to it, here to carry out an experiment. The rocks beneath their feet are made up of atomic particles that obey the laws of cause and effect. The Indians are no less rational, but rather than being actors in this drama, they are the observers. They know that if they listen carefully enough, the rocks may reveal other secrets that science is powerless to explain.

The sheer intangibility of Kitty's and Pasqualita's utterances stands in stark contrast to the earthbound materiality of the men. Only Oppenheimer bridges the divide between the concrete imagery of the scientists and the mystic visions of the women. As the moment of detonating the bomb approaches, Oppenheimer begins to slide in and out of rational consciousness. The Baudelaire poetry that he kept in his pocket and read from on that fateful night comes rushing back to him, articulating both his blackest fear and his most inexpressible ecstasy.

> O beatitude!
> That which we generally call life,
> even when it is fullest and happiest,
> has nothing in common
> with that supreme life
> with which I am now acquainted
> and which I am tasting
> minute by minute,
> second by second!
> No! there are no more minutes,
> there are no more seconds!
> Time has disappeared;
> it is Eternity that reigns now!

As the countdown advances, the time onstage slows down. Individuals become wrapped in their own visions and fantasies. Teller enjoys injecting some dark humor in the general mood of angst, mentioning Fermi's wagers on just how destructive to the atmosphere the bomb might prove to be. General Groves is not amused by this, curtly reminding Teller that this is just the kind of loose talk that might paralyze the enlisted men with fear. Teller goes back over the calculations he'd made several years earlier. In this section I set Teller's exact words, taken from his postwar book *The Legacy of Hiroshima*: "Might we not be setting off a huge chain reaction that will encircle the globe in a sea of fire?" The truth is that by the time of the bomb's detonation in 1945, the possibility of an uncontrolled chain reaction had been satisfactorily disproved and none of the physicists considered it even a remote possibility, but its inclusion in the libretto seemed nonetheless appropriate. To me, it amplified the fact that, in splitting the atom and unleashing its immense energies, human manipulation of natural forces was finally at the point of destroying nature's equipoise. Indeed, seven years later, when "Mike," the world's first thermonuclear device, designed by Teller and Stanislaw Ulam, was detonated on the Pacific atoll of Eniwetak, the force unleashed was the equivalent of twenty billion pounds of TNT. That single explosion was roughly twice the amount of all the explosives utilized in World War II. While an individual explosion might not "encircle the globe in a sea of fire," the combined arsenals of our present-day nuclear-armed countries most certainly threaten to accomplish this.

The act II countdown proceeds, passing through stages of increasing musical tension. The libretto assumes that two locations are visible to the audience throughout. One is the Alamogordo desert test site, with the bomb hanging menacingly from its scaffold tower. The other is the cramped living room of the Oppenheimers' Los Alamos cabin, two hundred miles to the north, where Kitty sits awake through the long night, accompanied by Pasqualita, who comforts the children and drinks with Kitty. The audience watches the activity in both locations simultaneously. As the moment of detonation nears, time and space begin to blur. Oppenheimer's presence moves back and forth from one place to another. Women are forbidden from the test site, but Kitty is not unaware of what is going on there, and her visions begin to collide with those of Pasqualita's.

Teller, Groves, Oppie, and the assembled physicists all huddle in the drizzling rain, sipping coffee from thermos bottles and keeping themselves occupied by placing bets on the probable yield of the explosion. Most are pessimistic, with Oppenheimer predicting barely more than a fizzle. Teller mocks them by pointing to the bomb's "blackboard potential" of 20,000 tons of TNT. They will soon find out that the potential was realized almost exactly as Teller predicted.

The music fizzles almost to a standstill. Then a fiery apparition bursts out, a choral evocation of Vishnu, god of gods, creator and destroyer of all existences.

> When I see you, Vishnu, omnipresent,
> Shouldering the sky, in hues of rainbow,
> With your mouths agape and flame-eyes staring—
> All my peace is gone; my heart is troubled.

It is a premonition of the blast, of the immense mushroom cloud, "shouldering the sky," a vision both awful and awe-inspiring, that witnesses would later describe as filling the sky, first with a flash of white light (brighter than the sun at midday, in the words of one), and then passing into a rainbow sequence of reds, purples, and livid blue. Again, as with the Baudelaire and Donne verses, this fragment from the Bhagavad Gita was one of Oppenheimer's favorites. In a filmed interview made years later, Oppie rather stagily reminisced on his thoughts at the moment of the detonation by recalling another quote from the Bhagavad Gita, "I am become Death, destroyer of worlds."*

I struggled for months over how to treat the explosion. No operatic evocation of an atomic bomb could go head-to-head with the dazzling effects available to a Hollywood director. Trying to pull out the orchestral stops to approximate an atomic explosion would only produce a laughable effect for an audience inoculated by years of George Lucas space epics. Every ten-year-old boy had already seen and heard better son et lumière at the local movie theater. But avoiding the detonation entirely or treating it in the manner of Sophocles or Aeschylus,

---

Oppenheimer apparently mistranslated or misquoted the original, which should read: "I am Time, destroyer of worlds."

by having it verbally described by a third-party observer, seemed a perverse solution. Ultimately I chose to create an extended orchestral countdown, a panoply of clocks, some ticking, others pounding like pile drivers, each at its own tempo. Underneath the clock polyphony is a bone-rattling booming coming from loudspeakers that surround the audience. I made the sound from a sampled timpani roll, which I looped and processed with heavy resonant filtration. To this I added, at the peak moment, a cluster of recorded baby screams that shrieks across the physical space of the theater like a sonic knife, slashing the darkness. At the high point of this countdown, with the chorus singing frantic, wordless exclamations, the entire cast takes cover, lying prone on the stage, staring straight into the eyes of the audience. The audience members gradually realize that they themselves are the bomb. It was an exceptionally disturbing moment, quite unlike conventional operatic scenarios.

When the booming dies out, only a light shower of clock fragments, played by harp, celesta, and tuned gongs, remains. As their quiet tintinnabulation tolls, we hear the distant voice of a Japanese woman. She is repeating phrases spoken by several survivors of the Hiroshima blast that I'd found in John Hersey's famous account of the immediate aftermath: "I can't find my husband." "Kazuo, come over here!" (This spoken to her little boy.) "Mr. Tanimoto, please help us." "Please, may we have some water?"

Doctor Atomic was heartily received in San Francisco, even to the point that extra performances were added to the run. It continued to attract large and responsive audiences the following year in Amsterdam and Chicago, and the Metropolitan Opera added it to its 2008–09 season. Not everyone was in agreement about it. Some disliked the more obscure passages in the libretto, some thought the musical language not sufficiently succinct, while others had their expectations about the final moments let down. The choreographic element in the Sellars staging was controversial, with some viewers feeling it posed an uncomfortable fit. The sight of small, lithe female dancers dressed in U.S. Army uniforms and darting across the stage in dance slippers during the opening chorus caused some embarrassed titters in the audience. But the Corn Dance, an evocation of the traditional Tewa ceremony that Lucinda Childs provided to go with my most complex contrapuntal writing of act II, was for me one of the expressive high points of the entire opera.

In both San Francisco and Chicago members of the scientific community responded enthusiastically. Many physicists confessed to me their love of music. At one dinner party, arranged so that I could meet several famous Nobel laureates, I never got to exchange a single word about science because the guests preferred talking about Mozart and Stravinsky. Perhaps it was just as well. I had asked the venerable Donald Glaser, winner of the Nobel Prize for the invention of the bubble chamber (and also a violist), if he would explain the general theory of relativity to me. He responded without dropping a beat and in dead earnest, "Yes. It will take ninety minutes." Not eighty-nine, or ninety-one? I wondered just how long it might actually take in my case, and getting cold feet, I never took him up on his offer.

I was not able to persuade Wendy Teller to attend, but Nobel laureates from UC Berkeley, Harvard, Columbia, and the University of Chicago were in the audience and spoke about the opera and its scientific and historical background at symposia organized at the time of the various productions. The opera was discussed not just in the arts section of newspapers and magazines but also in those devoted to science and technology. "*Dr. Atomic*: Unthinkable Yet Immortal" was the title of an article in the Science section of *The New York Times*. The writer, Dennis Overbye, who described himself as an ex–physics major, sci-fi addict, science writer, and lover of apocalypse, who "long ago concluded that there was not much new to say about the atomic bomb," confessed that after seeing *Doctor Atomic* he had been wrong. "Talk about popularizing science, this is it," he wrote.

Another physicist, Marvin L. Cohen, a professor at UC Berkeley and president of the American Physical Society (and an avid clarinetist), found some theoretical problems with the text to our opening chorus and recommended correcting it (which I did). But he also said publicly that hundreds of years from now all that popular culture might know about Los Alamos and the Oppenheimer story could be from what happens on the stage of *Doctor Atomic*, the way most people know about Elizabethan England from the works of Shakespeare. This I found a bit hyperbolic, but I was nevertheless grateful that someone from Oppenheimer's world would see the value of a work of art based on these themes.

was reminded of how listeners will rarely express themselves about a piece of contemporary concert music, whereas in the case of opera, everyone has strong opinions and feels no compunction whatsoever in sharing them. Walking the dog in my neighborhood of Berkeley, people would slow their Volvos, roll down the window, and bark out a comment. "I liked your opera. Saw it three times . . . but I thought you were much too nice to Teller." I felt that, through a mixture of poetry, music, and science, I'd made a work of art that had penetrated the consciousness of educated and thoughtful Americans and made them feel strongly about a matter that touched them all.

But *Doctor Atomic* will never be an easy addition to the standard repertoire. The long, dreamlike second act will always present a challenge for directors and conductors. Where act I follows a more or less logical narrative thread, act II is a nearly ninety-minute symphonic arch that oscillates back and forth between a real-time event (the countdown) and a deliberately abstracted treatment of time and space that is part dream vision and part sudden, terrifying apparition. Moody soliloquies and alien electronic moonscapes give way to frantic scrambling, shrieking choral voices, and panicky orchestral stampedes. Sitting one night at a Chicago performance conducted masterfully by Robert Spano and with Gerald Finley again singing the role of the great physicist, I wondered how this complicated piece of music drama would fare in the hands of less caring or less informed performers. Some operas will survive a mangled or indifferent production, but others live or die on the devotion and intelligence of the performers. *Doctor Atomic*, because of its exceptionally risky formal scheme, is more vulnerable than most, and it will always require the most alert and sensitive treatment from conductors, singers, and stage directors if it is to make the impact it made in its earliest embodiment.

| 4.

TREE OF LIFE

t is early December 2005 as my plane circles the Aeropuerto Interna-
cional de Maiquetía Simón Bolívar just thirty miles south of Caracas
and prepares to touch down on a narrow strip of Caribbean beach
on Venezuela's north coast. In the dark, the ocean is a carpet of
black velour, but I can make out a necklace of tiny lights along the
shoreline. Behind that is more darkness, a rocky escarpment that rises
abruptly from the water's edge, jutting up two-thirds of a mile into the
sky. Once out of the plane and into the terminal I'm met by my friend
Maria Guinand, a petite, remarkably beautiful woman with a shock of
snow-white hair and the youthful, energized features of a woman
thirty years younger than her fifty-two years. Brazenly ignoring a phalanx of uniformed customs officials who stiffen visibly at the sight of
my blue American passport, she whisks me through a thicket of cus-
tom officials as if I were a visiting diplomat on a tight schedule. Maria
speaks flawlessly idiomatic English, but she's cutting me no slack
tonight, and her Venezuelan-tinged Spanish is coming at me full
speed. It is a lovely sound, this accent, although the local habit of
swallowing the "s" makes it markedly different from the Mexican and
Guatemalan intonations I am used to hearing back home in California.

The road from the airport to the city provides a dizzying ascent, enough to shake off any lingering jet lag. Once the sun has risen it reveals views of earthen-colored barrios, desperate slums without water or electricity, perched precariously along the looming cliffs. A critical viaduct that takes traffic across a yawning chasm on this, the only major route to the city, will collapse a month later, much to the embarrassment of the government. But tonight it is still in one piece as the car in which we ride passes over it and grunts up the steep incline.

In the morning, a light fog burns off to reveal Caracas with its tangle of overpasses, endless concrete apartment complexes, billboards, and palm-studded avenues. The city turns out to be a climate paradise, situated at 3,000 feet above sea level under the ever-present profile of the Avila, an imposing green mountain monolith that hovers high over the busy urban nexus below. Cars and trucks swirl wildly in every direction. Cheap gasoline, government-supported at absurdly low prices, prompts thick snarls of congested traffic. Street repairs appear to be slow or to have ground to a halt. An occasional dead animal lies near a gutter. Broken furniture and vandalized vehicles line the side alleys, while on the walkways men and women of astonishing physical beauty talk and laugh and move with that seductively casual air that only the tropics seem to invite. Music is everywhere. The beat is Caribbean, but it's frequently spiced with the elongated cadences of the local style that tempt but never quite achieve 5/8 time: *"café con leche café con leche café con leche"* is the mnemonic.

I am arriving in the middle of a vitriolic election campaign that will further cement the political power of President Hugo Chávez, a former paratrooper now turned Socialist hero. On the walls of tenement houses and on huge billboards in sight of every motorist and pedestrian hang garish political advertisements, crude caricatures of George W. Bush, and equally crude heroic profiles of the local Chavista party candidates. Being a gringo here is an exercise in extreme cognitive dissonance. You're profoundly embarrassed by the obtuseness of your own president and by the long lugubrious history of U.S. hegemony that has imposed itself on generations of South Americans. But Chávez, who favors Mussolini-style four-hour harangues on the local TV stations and immense political rallies that fan the flames of a feverish anti-Americanism, also grates, sparking a quiet resentment in your most private thoughts.

In a bizarre and delightful twist of unanticipated events I have ended up coming to Venezuela to meet the singers and instrumentalists who will perform my next opera, *A Flowering Tree*. Maria, long a major player in the musical life of her country and a choral director with an international reputation, is my guide, and she will introduce me to this country's vibrant musical culture. It is only a few months since *Doctor Atomic's* plutonium sphere went supercritical on the stage of the San Francisco Opera. After two intense years of handling radioactive matter and peering down the long dark tunnel to the end of the world, I ought to be ready for a rest, but instead I am already deep into another stage work.

Doctor Atomic was an opera about technology and the end of ecology. *A Flowering Tree* is its antidote, a parable about youth, about hope, and about the ecology of the soul. As Handel was the model for *El Niño*, the Mozart of *The Magic Flute* is the guiding spirit for this opera, an opera that has for its theme the magic of transformation, both physical and spiritual. Here in Caracas, visiting for the first time, I am about to launch a project that will end in my having written the libretto and composed the entire two-act opera in a little over nine months' time, from December 2005 to September 2006. The deadline is fixed. The premiere will be the opening event of the New Crowned Hope festival, one of several festivals in Vienna celebrating the 250th anniversary of Mozart's birth. While a number of other more conventionally programmed Mozart retrospectives will occur earlier in the season, New Crowned Hope will be decidedly different and off the beaten path. It will pay homage to the profoundly humanist themes of Mozart's last compositions by featuring a long list of newly created works by living artists, many of them from distant parts of the world. For the enlightened Viennese cultural officials who conceived this event, the obvious choice for artistic director was Peter Sellars, and Peter has taken the assignment to heart, to the point where only a single event in his entire festival actually includes music by Mozart. Everything else is given over to new work commissioned from artists, choreographers, filmmakers, and composers from Java, Iraq, Paraguay, the Pacific Islands, South Africa, and many other points of the globe. Peter has appropriated the name, New Crowned Hope, from that of the Masonic lodge that Mozart belonged to in the final year of his life: *Zur neugekrönten Hoffnung.* As a response to the depressing morbidity of much recent contemporary art and theater, New Crowned Hope has an optimist, Enlightenment-inspired agenda. It intends to give a jolt, a kick in the pants to Vienna, a city that has largely become a museum for its own past glories. The festival's monthlong series of concerts, theatrical and dance events, films, and exhibitions hopes to offer up the bright colors, high energy, and emotional directness of the Third World in place of a tired avant-garde mind-set increasingly beholden to irony, self-absorption, and the aesthetics of denial.

Not everyone involved is from Asia, South America, or Africa. Peter has invited the Finnish composer Kaija Saariaho and the Lebanese poet Amin Maalouf to create a monodrama based on the life of Simone Weil. Osvaldo Golijov, Argentine-born but educated in Israel and the United States, has been commissioned to compose a major piece. And Mark Morris, that most musical of all choreographers, will make an evening of dance to Mozart piano music, a creation that will turn out to be one of his most sublime achievements. The festival brochure is a riot of bright colors, inspirational essays, and images of handsome, youthful, and decidedly non-European bodies. In a display of extravagant modesty, Peter Sellars has declined to have his picture included in the brochure. Straight, white, middle-aged, male John Adams has somehow made it through the cultural screening process, and he is delighted, because it allows him the opportunity not only to collaborate with these marvelous Venezuelan musicians but to pay homage to Mozart in his own way.

The festival is keyed to those Mozart works composed in his last year, and it is a thrill for me to come back to them, as they have long held a special meaning for me. The Clarinet Concerto, the String Quintet in E Flat (K. 614), *The Magic Flute*, and the Requiem—all composed in that amazingly fertile year of 1791—were pieces that held a totemic significance for me as an adolescent. During my most formative years they constituted a universe of the sublime, models of the ideal union of form and expressiveness. As a young listener, I might have lacked the analytical tools to explain the reasons for their technical perfection, but I nevertheless could intuit the absoluteness of their beauty and design. I cannot imagine my life without this music, particularly the Clarinet Concerto, which I knew by heart and performed with local orchestras as a sixteen-year-old. I would not be the person I am today had not these pieces existed. So when the idea of composing something for this remarkable festival came up, I had answered yes instantaneously without even pausing to reflect on the absurdly short amount of time I would have to meet the deadline. I had wanted for a long time to compose my own *Magic Flute*, something that would share with the Mozart opera themes of youth and transformation. Suddenly the opportunity is available to me, not only to compose it but also to premiere it in the city of Mozart's maturity.

I had committed to making this new opera while *Doctor Atomic* was not even half completed. By the time of that piece's premiere in October 2005, barely ten months remained before the new one had to be delivered. I had the general feeling and tone for the new opera in mind, but finding the right story to embody it was not easy. It seemed that the simplicity and directness of folktales would be the right way to proceed. Together with Peter, I read through many, casting the net wide over both ancient and modern stories from cultures near and far. As usual, Peter's immense knowledge and limitless curiosity about traditions from unknown regions opened up completely new and unexpected vistas for me. A typical meeting might begin with him reaching into his backpack and pulling out a slim volume entitled *Watunna: An Orinoco Creation Cycle*, saying, "Now John, of course you're familiar with this, aren't you?" No matter how far my own reading might range, both in terms of time and place, Peter's would be exponentially wider. Ultimately he turned my attention to the work of the South Indian poet, scholar, and translator A. K. Ramanujan, a contemporary writer who had spent the latter part of his life living and teaching in Chicago. Needless to say, I had not heard of Ramanujan, just as I had heard of neither Rosario Castellanos nor Sor Juana before writing *El Niño*. Born in Karnataka Province in 1929, Ramanujan wrote original poetry as well as making translations of folk poetry and oral tales ranging far back into the remote origins of his native culture. He had command of five languages: Tamil, Kannada, Telugu, Sanskrit, and English. Of the many stories that he had transcribed after having heard them from storytellers and relatives in the region of his upbringing, we chose "A Flowering Tree," one that Ramanujan had offered in English, although its original roots were in his native Kannada.

It was a typically simple-yet-complex folktale about a young peasant girl in a "certain town" who wants to aid her sick, impoverished mother. With the help of her sister and a precisely performed ceremony, she transforms herself into a tree, the flowers of which her sister gathers up to be woven into garlands and sold at the marketplace to earn money for the mother. This carefully performed ritual, which requires two pitchers of water for the girl to turn into the tree, and two pitchers of water for her to turn back into human form, also demands of the person assisting that he or she treat the tree with great care and respect, not damaging or breaking its branches. A brash young Prince from the nearby palace spies on the two of them during one of these transformations. He becomes obsessed with the younger sister and demands of his father, the King, that she become his bride. On their wedding night, the Prince cruelly withholds affection from his new wife, refusing to speak to her or touch her until she agrees to perform the ritual for him. Shocked and ashamed by this request, she nonetheless complies.

The Prince's jealous sister hides in their bedroom and spies on the transformation ceremony. Overcome with envy at her new sister-in-law's powers, she plots her revenge. When the Prince is away from the palace, the sister forces the girl to perform the transformation for a group of her friends. But the friends botch the ceremony, breaking her branches and tearing off her flowers, and when a storm comes up, they run away, leaving the young girl in mid-transformation. Alone and abandoned, half tree and half human, a miserable stump of a being, she crawls into a gutter in shame and agony. The Prince, not knowing what has happened to his young wife, is distraught and full of guilt at her disappearance. He mortifies himself by shedding his royal robes and becoming a wandering mendicant. Time passes and the Prince, now haggard and wasted, wanders into a distant town. His wife, still in her hideous half-tree, half-human form, has also by chance ended up in this same town. The town's new Queen happens to be the Prince's long-lost sister. Shocked at her brother's deterioration, the Queen tries to help him, but to no avail. Finally, as a last resort, her servants bring the "hideous stump" of a woman to the Prince's bedroom, where he has been lying rigid and unresponsive. Alone at last, husband and wife recognize each other even through their drastically changed appearances, and with two pitchers of water he restores her to her human self.

All are ecstatic—the Prince, his bride, the King, and both families. Only the jealous younger sister is singled out for punishment, and in a curiously offhand and brutal coda so common to folktales, the King orders that this unfortunate sibling, his own daughter, be tossed into a pit of burning lime in retribution for her sins.

The story needed to be compressed in certain aspects while expanded in others. With input from Peter, who also suggested the inclusion of some 2,000-year-old Tamil and Kannada love poems also translated by Ramanujan, I shaped my own libretto out of the written text. I gave the young girl and her sister names, Kumudha and Kavanila, names that I'd found on a website called "A Hundred Favorite Tamil Female Names." I amplified some character traits, especially those of the Prince, whom I made more imperious and selfish during the first part. The tale had many darker themes lingering just below the surface that I wanted to make use of such as class privilege, sexual oppression, physical deformity, sexual impotence, and sibling hatred. I brought out the Prince's self-absorption, making him more psychologically unconscious, less sensitive to the feelings of the poor young peasant girl he marries. This made the moment when he realizes that she has disappeared all the more shocking for him. In the original story it is clear that the Prince uses his social position, his royal pedigree, to force the young girl into marriage. He further forces her, this time by withholding affection and sexual contact, to perform a ritual transformation that she presumably had thought she would never again have to undergo. When, in act II, his bride disappears, he assumes she has fled from him. He experiences a moment of the shock of recognition, and to express his grief and remorse he rejects his royal privilege, leaves home, and becomes a beggar.

The dozen poems that we injected into the body of the story come from 2,000-year-old Tamil sources. Of these, the *Kuṟuntokai* ("Interior Landscape"), a series of highly symbolic and deeply intimate love poems, had their own story: Ramanujan had literally unearthed them from their centuries-long obscurity when he found them buried in an archive at the University of Chicago in 1962 and made English translations of them. How these precious poems, composed more than two millennia ago, ended up in Chicago, I have yet to learn. I used several of these delicate and erotic *Kuruntokai* verses along with other classic Tamil texts that Ramanujan had translated under the title *Poems of Love and War*. More devotional poems, bhakti texts devoted to the worship of the God Shiva and dating from a slightly later period, provided a further intensity to the inner voices of my three characters. When the young Prince, hiding in a tree, beholds the beautiful Kumudha for the first time, he sings a poem from the *Kuruntokai*:

> Her arms have the beauty
> of a gently moving bamboo.
> Her large eyes are full of peace.
> She is far away,
> her place not easy to reach.
> My heart is frantic
> with haste,
>> a plowman with a single plow
>> on land all wet
>> and ready for seed.

Of the many marvels in this little story what attracted me most were the transformations that Kumudha would perform. The musical potential of these transformations was irresistible, and because she executed each one for a different reason, each could be musically unique. In the original story the young girl is rather matter-of-fact about her first transformation. There is a puzzling lack of mystery about this first enactment of an act of magic. Even though she has never attempted it in the past, Kumudha for some reason knows she can become a flowering tree. But I made her first transformation a scene of wonderment, far more emotionally powerful than she could possibly imagine it would be—she literally "passes over to the other side." When she and her sister begin the ceremony for the first time, neither has any idea of the depth of the experience that awaits Kumudha. Likewise, when in the second act the ceremony is botched by the sister-in-law and her idle young rich friends, Kumudha's horror at finding herself caught between two states of being is painfully intense.

I left the ancillary characters largely out of the story. The King, for instance, only appears in the scene in which he interviews the old woman. I also mercifully deleted the final punishment of the jealous daughter.

In the final version of the libretto I settled on just three singers: Kumudha, a soprano; the Prince, a tenor; and an all-purpose, omniscient baritone narrator, whom I call the Storyteller. This Storyteller moves in and out of the narrative, at times advancing the plot quickly and talking directly to the audience, as in the very first line, "Children, I want to tell you a story." At other times he is swept up in the passions and emotions of the events, as when he describes the mutilation that Kumudha's body suffers when she is abandoned in mid-ceremony. The original story is unclear about how Kumudha, with neither legs nor arms, manages to find her way to her sister-in-law's court in a distant city. I invented a band of beggar-minstrels who find her on the side of the road and incorporate her into their traveling troupe. She may be a freak, but she can sing, and her beautiful voice is what ultimately attracts the attention of the maids in the town square and leads to her being brought to the palace of her former sister-in-law. The beggar-minstrels provide the occasion for a high-energy, grotesque chorus in act II that is full of rude grunts, shouts, and vocal ejaculations from the male chorus (obviously inspired by the famous Balinese monkey chant). The Gypsy-like chorus of women, using a mocking, nasal whine, sing obscure, cryptic lines from a bhakti devotional text:

A running river
        is all legs.
A burning fire
        is mouths all over.
A blowing breeze
        is all hands.
So, lord of the caves,
for your men,
every limb is Symbol.

To add to the pan-cultural flavor of the piece, I set all of the chorus texts in Spanish. I did this in part because I knew that for our first Vienna performances I would have the luxury of Maria Guinand's famous Schola Cantorum de Caracas. I'd first heard of this vocal ensemble when they brought Golijov's *La Pasión según San Marcos* to the United States several years earlier. This was a vocal ensemble that could sing in a wide variety of styles, ranging from the chaste purity of Hildegard von Bingen to the raucous folk music of Cuba and the Caribbean. I also felt that Spanish had become virtually my second language, that its sonorities and particular rhythmic profile had become expressive of my daily life in California. While setting Castellanos and Sor Juana in *El Niño*, I'd learned that Spanish was nearly an ideal language for musical adaptation. The New Crowned Hope festival was planned to be a joyous celebration of global artistic miscegenation, and therefore it stood to reason that my piece would take pleasure in mixing even more colors into the rainbow of influences.

made two trips to Venezuela nine months apart. On the morning of my first day I was greeted at the Caracas Hilton by a group of young men dressed in suits and ties and dark sunglasses that made them look more like a team of Secret Service agents than representatives of a youth orchestra. They led me to a van in the backseat of which was a slight, balding man in his mid-sixties. He was dressed in a black coat and wore thick glasses that dominated his sunken eyes, eyes that were nonetheless alive with awareness and enthusiasm. This was José Antonio Abreu, the masterful initiator, architect, brain, and begetter of the grand Venezuelan program of musical education, El Sistema. Abreu was the man who had single-handedly brought about a revolution in the artistic culture of this eternally unpredictable country. Part Mother Teresa, part Godfather, Abreu not only had the capacity to dream large dreams about bringing the experience of classical music to even the poorest of children in his country, but he also had the political savvy to gain entry into the corridors of power, winning respect from the most influential of government officials. Trained as both an economist and a conductor, he had, over past decades, ridden the waves of successive administrations, straddling expertly both the left and right wings of political movements, always with the single goal of expanding the country's extensive program of music education. After years in obscurity, Abreu's most prized accomplishment, the Orquesta Sinfónica

Simón Bolívar, was making a name outside of the country, and rumors of its excellence were swirling throughout the music world in the United States and Europe. I had first heard about this 120-member youth orchestra from Simon Rattle, who had gone to Caracas, spent a week rehearsing and conducting a Mahler symphony with them, and come away humbled and astonished. Claudio Abbado, whom Simon would succeed as music director of the Berlin Philharmonic, had begun scheduling his vacations on an island off the Venezuelan coast so that he could divide his time between rest and relaxation and doing concerts with these young musicians. They were known to rehearse thirty to forty hours a week and could produce a commanding sound. It was also Simon who had mentioned my name to Abreu, and now I was here as their guest, introduced as *el estimado Señor Adams, gran compositor norteamericano.*

We drove to the outskirts of the city and passed through a security gate into a large concrete compound surrounded by razor wire. Once inside I saw hundreds upon hundreds of young musicians, ranging in age from four to twenty-five. I was taken into one large room where a hundred-member *orquesta de los infantiles* launched into a blazing, red-hot rendition of the bacchanal from Saint-Saëns's *Samson et Dalila,* a steamy old Second Empire potboiler I'd not encountered since my community orchestra days as a kid. Once we finished listening to the *infantiles* and Saint-Saëns's exotica, I was then ushered into a much larger auditorium, this time to see, much to my astonishment, some three hundred instrumentalists and singers all seated and ready to play. Introductions were made, and then Abreu said, "We have a little something to play for you." A slight, handsome young man of about twenty-five stood up, shook my hand, and went over to the podium. Dressed casually in jeans and a T-shirt, and with a thick mop of curly black hair, he looked more like a kid on his way to a ball game or to hang out at the beach with some lucky girls. This was Gustavo Dudamel, Abreu's protégé, a native of the western city of Barquisimeto, a former violinist in the orchestra, and, as I would soon discover in the course of the next eighty minutes, a conductor of immense talent, a "natural," gifted with the instincts and the charisma of a Bernstein. In less than three years this barely known youngster from Venezuela would become the most talked-about figure in the entire world of classical music and soon be named Esa-Pekka Salonen's successor as music director of the Los Angeles Philharmonic.

The "little something" that they had planned for me was the entire "Resurrection" Symphony of Mahler, which Dudamel conducted from memory. To me the players looked more accurately to be an orchestra of young adults than what we in the United States would term a "youth orchestra." Most appeared to be college age or only slightly younger. All played with enormous confidence, the product of their long hours of rehearsing and their many years of training. Members of the Berlin Philharmonic had been coming to Caracas for vacations, dividing their time between the Caribbean beaches and coaching the orchestra's young musicians. For a long time they had played only for audiences in Latin America, but now they had European management and were being invited to major festivals throughout the Continent. The Mahler Second that they knew so well had actually been shaped by Rattle during a previous visit, but Dudamel's own unique personality was evident in the interpretation as well. It was clear to see that the hundreds of young musicians in the room revered Abreu as if he were a saint. Even during difficult passages, they would sneak glances at him, and he would return their looks with a smile of benevolent pride and pleasure.

The plans for the premiere of *A Flowering Tree* had gone through a bewildering maze of changes since I'd first agreed to do it. At one point, before the Venezuelan element had come into play, Simon had pledged to bring the Berlin Philharmonic to Vienna for two weeks, rehearse the piece, and do all the performances. But this turned out to be unrealistic due to the high cost of housing and paying for this, one of the world's most sought-after orchestras. With the Berlin Philharmonic no longer in the mix, the idea arose of inviting Abreu's orchestra and Maria Guinand's chorus. This seemed like a felicitous solution, especially given my opera's theme and the pan-cultural flavor of the New Crowned Hope festival. It was for this reason I'd traveled to Caracas to meet and hear them. However, somehow, between the exhilaration of being in the midst of all those exciting young musicians, or perhaps due to some subtleties with the language, a misunderstanding of grand proportions was brewing.

After having been hosted so generously and being given my own private performance of a Mahler symphony, I returned home to begin work on the composing with the impression that Dudamel's Orquestra Sinfónica Simón Bolívar was the band for which I'd be writing. This in fact turned out not to be the case. Nine months later, with the opera composed and orchestrated, I returned to Venezuela to begin rehearsals and much to my surprise found waiting for me a different orchestra, an ad hoc group made up largely of adult professionals from Caracas and Barquisimeto. This orchestra had been contracted at Abreu's command, and they were being called Orquesta Joven Camerata de Venezuela. Thus *A Flowering Tree* started its life with a week of rehearsals in a tiny one-story concrete rehearsal hall in Barquisimeto, a city on the Lara plains near the Andes foothills, an hour's flight west of Caracas. This building was a recent addition to the local music conservatory, a school that each week serviced more than a thousand students of all ages (of whom one, only a few years past, had been Gustavo Dudamel). To use the bathroom you walked carefully across a dirt parking lot, skirting treacherous open trenches and potholes, until you reached the main building. *"Baño, por favor,"* addressed to the small group of old men who served as security guards, would win you entrance to the one functioning toilet on that side of the building. Through the walls one could hear folk songs sung by a chorus of preschool children or an orchestra of teenagers energetically having at *Scheherazade* or Tchaikovsky's Fifth.

The principal feature of our rehearsal building was a loud, malfunctioning air-conditioning system that thundered away like a B-29 on takeoff, making it nearly impossible for one musician to hear farther than the next stand. I soon developed a plan for rehearsing with the air-conditioner fans turned off for as long as we could possibly stand it. When I could see rivulets of sweat pouring down the faces of the players, we'd call for the fans to crank up, and I would rehearse only fortissimo passages, of which there were unfortunately not many. At night, the fans were shut off and the windows thrown open to let in the moist, cooling altiplano air. Soon local families were crowding around the open windows, peering in at the rehearsal, whispering among themselves, and taking pictures of us with their cell phones.

Some in the orchestra were memorably good players, and they filled me with admiration for their caring and considerate work ethic.

Others, including several section leaders, appeared to owe their appointments to reasons more political than musical. The overworked personnel manager, also our principal clarinetist, never seemed to have his cell phone off his ear. But the Abreu network would always mysteriously produce a new player in the nick of time. The personnel policy was never to fire anyone, but rather simply to add the replacement player to the section. The *camerata* (chamber) orchestra began to inflate like a blimp. Players were sharing hotel rooms and sleeping on sofas and rollaway beds. We arrived in Vienna to find the orchestra pit in the MuseumsQuartier (housed in an auditorium that was formerly a horse dressage rink) unable to hold what was by now a nearly seventy-five-player ensemble. The double bass section had to sprawl into the exit aisles, and for lack of space below, the woodwind and brass players ended up sitting onstage next to the solo singers and dancers.

For the performances everyone—soloists, dancers, chorus, orchestra, and even the conductor-composer—wore brightly colored costumes made from bolts of inexpensive fabric that our costume designer had purchased in bulk in New Delhi. The riot of reds, golds, greens, magentas, and violets gave the entire production the appearance of a Bollywood wedding. I conducted each performance wearing a hand-sewn red tuxedo jacket of Indian fabric covered with embossed gold-and-green flowers. Three Indonesian dancers, Rusini Sidi, Eko Supriyanto, and Astri Kusama Wardani, wove their graceful bodies like garlands into the movements of the three solo singers. Russell Thomas, a burly young tenor from Florida with a clear, ringing voice, sang the role of the Prince, alternating between youthful brashness and a tender vulnerability. Eric Owens, the big, powerful baritone for whom I'd earlier created the role of General Groves in *Doctor Atomic*, was the Storyteller. Eric was the commanding center of the opera, not just because of the scope of his role but also because of the charismatic presence that he brought to it. A singer of completely assured musicality—he had played the oboe professionally during his early years in Philadelphia—Eric never needed the constant prompting and endless safety cues that most singers working off book require. I needed only to give him a single glance on his first entrance and then didn't have to worry about him or even look at him until the end of a scene, so completely thorough was his intellectual command of the music.

Kumudha was sung by the soprano Jessica Rivera, a native of Los Angeles who at the time was barely known. Her voice was pure and unforced, but it also had color and, when needed, real dramatic weight. She sang and acted Kumudha's part while the elegant, diminutive Astri, dressed in jeans and a simple flower-print shirt, danced the role. When Kumudha was caught in the misery of her half-human, half-tree state, the two young women wove their bodies together like a knot of tangled branches. The ritual gestures of Javanese dance, ancient in their origins and often suggesting the mudras of Indian deities, conjured an atmosphere part contemporary love story and part very old folktale.

The Viennese press found *A Flowering Tree* symptomatic of everything that was wrong with American culture. One reviewer sarcastically likened it to an end-of-term student project at some multicultural Afro-Asian university. Indeed, "multi-kulti" was the preferred moniker for many of these critics, a dismissal that more often than not came hand in hand with a stern aesthetic scolding in which the name Adorno seemed to begin and end each paragraph. To their mind the fault with the piece was not merely our naïveté in making an undisciplined mélange of all these various cultural traditions (Indian folk literature, Indonesian dance, Venezuelan singing, European Enlightenment philosophy, Mozart, American rhythms, and so on), but that out of all these influences we'd come up with nothing better than intolerable ear and eye candy. Both the opera and its production were judged too pretty by a mile. And perhaps even more puzzling for many in the Viennese new music community, our creation had apparently been made from start to finish entirely without recourse to irony.

In the United States—the premiere was in San Francisco the following January—reactions were significantly less severe, but some still voiced a vague sense of discomfort over what seemed to be the opera's suspiciously accessible beauty and its enthusiastic drawing from world cultural traditions. The *New York Times* critic, reviewing the premiere, had joked about the production being "a big sloppy kiss to multiculturalism." This dubiousness and concern for cultural decorum was in complete contrast to the response of actual native-born artists who performed the piece. Eko Supriyanto, our male lead dancer and quite possibly the greatest living master of Javanese dance, ate up the transcultural mix of music, dance, and texts. He was an artist who thrived on moving back and forth between the highly disciplined traditional dance of his native Java and the crazy new universe of pop music, electronic technology, and indie rock. Evidently no Western anthropologist had gotten to Eko yet with a cautionary warning about the dangers of multicultural miscegenation. Already having toured with Madonna, Eko radiated star quality and thoroughly enjoyed exploiting it. Clad in only a pair of short knickers, he made a furious choreography to my Chorus of Beggar-Minstrels, literally letting his hair down (several feet of a jet-black mane looking like a stallion's tail) and going berserk to the shouts and pounding of the music.

For once I was not daunted in the least by such cranky critiques. Multiculturalism was the easiest of knee-jerk accusations to hurl at an artist who revealed (or reveled in) influences outside his or her supposedly prescribed social setting. Scholarly writers had recently been plowing up pay dirt in their sociological condemnations of what they called artistic "colonizing." I am fully aware of what is meant by "cultural appropriation," and I can talk the talk and walk the walk when fingers are pointed. But I do not suffer from what the literary critic Harold Bloom calls the "anxiety of influence." Of course I am cognizant of how, in the hands of an aggressive "dominant culture" like ours, any indigenous art form risks dilution, distortion, or even possible annihilation. Certainly by taking Ramanujan's version of the Kannada folktale out of its cultural context, I was subjecting it to distortion, adding my own set of meanings and either willingly or unwittingly robbing it of its original sense. But, to use another of Bloom's phrases, "to imagine is to misinterpret." Every reading of another work of art, whether it comes from a distant, unfamiliar culture or from one's own backyard, is a de facto misinterpretation. Appropriation is in fact *the* norm among societies. Since earliest recorded time one culture has intermingled its art with that of another, and that intermingling by its very nature must be subject to misapprehension, misappropriation, even misuse. Nevertheless, cross-fertilization more often than not is a willing, even enthusiastic act of mutual sharing. Like the strengthening of a species through genetic variety, a crossbreeding of artistic traditions, creatively engaged, can produce robust new genres. One need look no further than the absorption of African and Caribbean traditions into the mainstream of American music for proof of this. In our own time Maghreb singers from Morocco and Algeria have appropriated the rap music of urban American blacks and turned it into a persuasively expressive style that, while bearing the earmarks of its model, is nonetheless new and distinct.

I nonetheless acknowledge that political realities can exert irresistible pressures on smaller, more economically fragile cultures. There is little doubt that appropriation is as salubrious to the "colonizer" as it risks being toxic to the "colonized." The cultural traits of traditional societies have the enviable tendency to be more consistent, less subject to change over time than those of modern urban societies with their constantly shifting values and slavish vulnerability to fashion and style. We have seen over and over how indigenous art forms, when taken out of their societal setting, can lose their power as signifiers, lose their strangeness and their magic. But to argue, as some do, that an indigenous art form can only be appreciated in the context of its origin seems to artificially fracture and isolate the ultimate unity of the human experience. While the local—Josiah Royce's "provincial"—can possess a unique flavor, a special strangeness that, like certain wines or cheeses, doesn't travel well, the borrowing of an idea, even if it is a misunderstood or misapprehended borrowing, can nonetheless result in a vitally new artistic creation. "Creative misunderstanding" is what I sometimes call this habit of artists pilfering ideas across boundaries. We are put in mind of the famous apothegm attributed to Stravinsky that "the talented composer borrows, but the genius steals."

Some of the most shockingly original leaps in stylistic evolution have come about when a profoundly original artist like a Debussy or a Picasso or a Stravinsky raids an alien culture for his own selfish ends. The term "colonization" of course puts the distinctly negative spin on this activity. By today's unforgiving strictures, even Bartók would be deemed suspect for his incorporation of Hungarian, Slovak, and Romanian folk music. In fact appropriation is a decidedly two-way street, with many Third World cultures as wildly enthusiastic about appropriating American urban pop culture as we are about plundering theirs. But the argument persists nonetheless that the dominant culture, the one with the most economic and political power, ends up imposing its values on the weaker ones, ultimately crowding them out, suppressing their voices.

15.

GARAGE SALE OF
THE MIND

On a dark day I will become nearly overwhelmed at how little I have mastered in my life. Starting a new piece can cause me torment and can mean having to slog through a dismal swamp of indifferent ideas, pushing them, prodding them, often abandoning them in disgust or desperation. Many times I will have to launch a piece without any particular love for the opening material only to find the "eureka moment" many bars and many days later, forcing me to go back and re-form the beginning in light of what I have now learned.

The "next" piece ought to be the "best piece," the living proof that the disparate elements of my musical language, all the scattered ideas and half-formed mental images, have once and for all come together in a single statement of confident, unblemished perfection. But this is never the case. I wish I could calmly assure myself that Somerset Maugham was right in saying about perfection that it is a trifle dull and that it is better when not quite achieved. But I work in a profession where models of perfection really do exist. As a composer of orchestral works, I often witness my music sandwiched between a Mozart piano concerto and a Beethoven symphony. In the world of painting and sculpture independent space is customarily provided for exclusively contemporary work. There are museums of modern art in most large cities where the new creations stand in a harmonious context with other works of their own time or from the recent past. But my works, once completed, are immediately subjected to the most daunting acid test of all, having to precede or follow a masterpiece, a classic that not only is intimately known to the audience but also is most likely a creation of time-tested durability. At moments like these one has to work hard not to wonder if the act of composing in our time is a business of culling the slag left over from earlier virgin exploitations. From time to time when driving in the High Sierra I'll see amateur gold miners, panning in a river that 150 years ago gave up the best of its treasure to the first prospectors, and I'll be tempted to wonder if the image of these latter-day panners, hoping only for a tiny nugget, isn't an illustration of my own predicament as a composer.

The argument among evolutionary scientists is whether there is such a thing as progress. Darwin at his most candid said that species adapt and have the capacity to evolve in the direction of increasing complexity, but he had strong doubts about whether complexity constituted progress, or whether indeed there was such a thing as progress at all. In the arts it is even more difficult to say whether "progress" exists. Increasing complexity seems to arrive in periodic waves in all the arts, and when it peaks as a stylistic trope it almost inevitably expresses itself as mannerism. In almost all cases, every epoch of complexity is followed by a reactionary move toward a more direct, simpler form of expression. One need look no further than the contrast between the high German Baroque as exemplified by J. S. Bach and the pure Viennese classical era of Mozart to see how the pendulum can swing back and forth in barely a generation or two. Bach's music at its apogee was one of manifold polyphonic structures and a highly evolved system of decoration and melodic ornament. Mozart's language, no less subtle, represents a move in the direction of a more direct, song-based simplicity. Both composers are capable of the deepest psychological complexity. Only their rhetoric divides them.

Or complexity and simplicity might coexist, with neither owning the imprimatur for being the superior form. At the same time that James Joyce was taking literary allusion to the farthest reaches of intelligibility in *Finnegans Wake*, Ernest Hemingway was writing no less influential works in a style that was as direct and uncomplicated as Joyce's was packed with ambiguity and verbal legerdemain. In our own time we've seen the fiendishly detailed, labyrinthine mazes of Brian Ferneyhough's scores share the contemporary landscape with the grave, soft-spoken, monastic simplicities of Arvo Pärt.

I recall attending a festival of contemporary music in Huddersfield, England, in 1987 where several of my pieces were programmed cheek by jowl with those of several European composers who were writing in a style dubbed the "New Complexity." These composers, most of whom inhabited university music departments, had labored to evolve a creative signature featuring extreme examples of notational artifice. Specialist performers had arrived from Amsterdam and Paris to present these pieces, and I had overheard one of them talking about the hours, numbered in the high hundreds, he had needed to master one of these works. In concert, quite a few of these New Complexity pieces sounded not all that different from freely improvised music I'd been hearing from Cecil Taylor or from those resulting from coin-tossing by John Cage. However, the appearance of the music on the printed page had reached a level of extravagant detail, an adaptation of musical notation that had evolved into a technology unto itself. Visually these scores did indeed make an impact, but they also confirmed my suspicion that this compulsion to push the envelope to the extreme constitutes yet another example of mannerism. In comparison to the flamboyantly Baroque display of the New Complexionists, the matter-of-fact notation of my own music was like a pup tent squatting next to the Chartres Cathedral. I had to move away from this setup and remind myself of how the notion of "complexity as progress" is in fact a posture, an intellectual house of cards, and always has been. Writing in 1955 at the height of the postwar aesthetic power struggle over the future of art music, the French theoretician and champion of serialism René Leibowitz ridiculed the music of Sibelius, even going so far as to write an article titled "Sibelius, le plus mauvais compositeur du monde." This French savant may have enjoyed pricking the bubble of an immensely popular composer who, although still alive, was little more than a relic, having done his greatest work nearly half a century earlier. But in retrospect the critiques of Leibowitz seem little more than gnats swirling around the visage of a noble beast. How one of

Sibelius's symphonies looked on the page or how it failed to fit the au courant compositional style of the 1950s was of no importance at all to the grateful listener who continued to find in it the deepest emotional and formal meaning. Sibelius understood what his attacker didn't, that music is above and beyond all else the marriage of form and feeling. Even the ancient writers like Saint Augustine and Boethius, for all their attempts to treat music as a science or as a tool for moral elevation, tacitly acknowledged this fact.

In his book *Full House*, Stephen Jay Gould, the challenging thinker about evolutionary science, reminds us that our cultural legends include two canonical modes for trending. One mode is "advances to something better as reasons for celebration." The other is "declines to an abyss as sources of lamentation (and hankering after a mythical golden age of 'good old days')." Sitting among a classical music audience, I am much more likely to hear my neighbors mourning in the latter mode, the lamentation for the golden age, than I will hear them jubilantly celebrating an advance in the art form. Hearing such moaning, I'll find myself asking, "Is this the predicament of classical music? Is what I am hearing from the audience member the terminal expression of a dead art form, or have audiences always had this attitude?" Bless Nicolas Slonimsky for cataloging in his amusing (and, for composers, deeply consoling) *Lexicon of Musical Invective* the violent reactions of the public and of music critics over the years as one composer after another had the temerity to propose something new to the classical canon. It reminds us that of all audiences in the arts, those who follow classical music number among the most timid and least sanguine when encountering something new and unfamiliar. We composers can comfort ourselves in the knowledge that the classical repertoire aggressively resists absorbing new additions. A work such as the *Turangalîla-symphonie*, Olivier Messiaen's riotously colorful and ecstatic transcultural love fest, had to wait half a century after its premiere before the majority of concertgoers in the United States and Europe could receive it without the anxiety and foreboding they commonly bring to their encounters with an unfamiliar work. Conductors who place my big orchestral works like *Harmonielehre* and *Naive and Sentimental Music* on the second half of their programs run the risk of losing a third or more of their audience during the intermission. (I

have seen this happen more often than I care to remember.) The fleeing audience member may well be ignorant of me or my compositions,
but he'll nonetheless bet that the musical experience that awaits him is
unlikely to be as promising as an early ride home.

The frosty reception accorded major works by Debussy, so thoroughly chronicled in Slonimsky's book, confirms the unique resistance
that a musically radical idea must endure before eventually being understood and appreciated. Debussy was never impelled by the philosophy of épater le bourgeois. As far as we know he earnestly desired that
his music be accepted along with the other masterworks of Western
art music, and he appears to have suffered enormously when his work
was condemned or dismissed. Nevertheless, during his lifetime the
strangeness of his language and the mysterious, alien atmosphere it
evoked provoked outright hostility even from sophisticated listeners
who had learned to understand and love Wagner.

But one has to admit that we composers have not made things
easy, often adapting a de haut en bas attitude toward even the most
courageous and open-minded of listeners. Many composers, perhaps
too aware of the model of Thomas Mann's Adrian Leverkühn and
knowing the predictable resistance that a new work will likely encounter, have come to embrace the notion of the "prophet in his own
land," assuming that whatever they do will always be incomprehensi-
ble for all but the tiniest group of like-minded cognoscenti. This was
the mind-set typified by Milton Babbitt in the 1950s, an attitude toward art and culture that has endured in part thanks to a small but devoted church of listeners and performers.

In a musical world beset with uncertainties perhaps we can help to
orientate ourselves by taking a few hints from evolutionary science.
Rather than viewing "progress" as the paradigm for novelty in the arts,
we might be better advised to welcome the idea of "variation." This
way we might escape the tunnel vision that hobbles so much critical
reception of new work. If we hold fast to our prejudices, adhering to
strict stylistic orthodoxies, and if we are incapable of embracing variation as the normative standard in the arts, we run the risk of holding
to an impossible Platonic ideal of artistic perfection, an ideal that will
only result in endless disappointments as one creative artist after another fails to meet the standards set by the masters of the past. Under

such limiting circumstances the best we might hope for would be a plethora of smaller niche voices, famous perhaps for having reached a new extreme in one or another aspect of their expression, but forever imprisoned by the self-imposed exigencies of their personal style.

Gould, toward the end of his book on what he calls the "spread of human excellence," acknowledges that we understand ourselves as humans to be "uniquely complex," but he still insists that progress "truly does not pervade or even meaningfully mark the history of life." We in the Western world suffer from what he terms "our continued adherence to an ethic of innovation." He singles out contemporary music, attributing its apparent inaccessibility to the high premium we place on innovation in a new work. Unfortunately he draws the wrong conclusion from this otherwise acute perception: Were this destructive compulsion toward constant novelty not to exist, he muses, perhaps another generation of Mozarts and Bachs might arise in our own time. This is the fondly imagined hope of the musical amateur, the listener who wishes the present state of confusion in the arts would just go away and that an Arcadian creative paradise would prevail. Ironically, in voicing this complaint, Gould aligns himself with those who see history (at least the history of music) as in a state of decline. Pining for another Mozart, another Bach, he is no different from those who are, in his own words, "hankering after a mythical golden age of 'good old days.' "

If we can put aside expectations based on older models, we may not need to hanker for the good old days at all. The future for new music, not only in the United States but also elsewhere, looks remarkably promising. The so-called millennial generation, people born in the 1980s, appears to be full of young composers for whom the twentieth century is already the past and who seem to be blessedly free of the partisan orthodoxies and prejudices that dominated my generation. For these young men and women, most of them still in their twenties, the whole planet is a sounding board. They have grown up with instant access to musical cultures from all over the proverbial known universe. I read their blogs and home pages, and I am filled with admiration for the openness of their thinking and the wide range of their interest and curiosity. Their influences and their musical preferences are open to any number of possibilities, reflecting perhaps the fact that in the United States, for example, they are ethnically diverse, with nearly 40 percent being Latino, African American, Asian, or of mixed racial heritage.

But instant access and easy availability can have its downside. At times I may worry that for young Americans the urge to win approval and gain the kind of quick public acceptance that is common in the world of popular music threatens to produce a generation of composer lightweights unwilling or afraid to show their difficult or contrary side. Over the past thirty years the pendulum has swung so far away from the "angry young composer" model, that it now threatens to validate a mind-set more obsessed with immediate success and notoriety than with true imagination and daring. Indeed, in this new era of laptop composers and media-savvy multitaskers, a numbing amount of music is being cranked out, much of it on computer-assisted platforms that make the act of composing seductively effortless. These young composers are impatient and dream of enjoying the same success and same luster as their favorite indie rock idol. They forget that developing a real voice and finding one's muse takes time and effort and a truckload of misfires and embarrassments before the true and mature original emerges. But for those of the younger generation who refuse to be taken in by the thirst for quick recognition, the playing field is remarkably open and fertile for exploration.

recently spent a summer evening with my son, Sam, while he played me selections from the enormous library of music he carries on a small portable hard drive. In the course of several hours he took me through a sample of what on that particular day was at the foreground of his musical consciousness. The list included *Sonatas and Interludes* for prepared piano by John Cage; ritual gagaku court music from Japan; some Conlon Nancarrow studies for player piano; a work for chorus by Thomas Adès; part of an astonishing *Klangfarben* instrumental work called *In Vain* by the Austrian composer Georg Friedrich Haas; some Maghreb rap songs from Marseille; two recent compositions by the jazz composer and saxophonist Wayne Shorter; several "electronica" compositions by Aphex Twin and Squarepusher; and (a particular favorite) Sibelius's Seventh Symphony. That sampling seemed indicative of how broad a young musician's field of reference has become, a far cry from the limited universe that I was able to access as a twenty-year-old.

I have met other young composers in the United States, Great Britain, and Scandinavia who, still in their twenties and early thirties, reveal musical pedigrees that are refreshingly mongrel and as aesthetically liberated as my son's iTunes library. Of course having the most ecumenical playlist doesn't necessarily translate into being an imaginative or skilled creative artist, but if we think of culture in Arnold Toynbee's definition as "shared habits," we can take encouragement and great pleasure in knowing that the gene pool among composers is ever more varied and enriched by this open attitude toward music.

The evolutionary scientist's sentimental hankering for a return to a golden age in music may indeed be proven irrelevant by a new generation of composers who, while enjoying the option to creatively plunder (in the best sense of the term), give us something entirely new and fresh, thoughtful and pleasurable, and in so doing, confirm a more positive outlook: "advances to something better as reasons for celebration."

SUGGESTED LISTENING AND VIEWING

ACKNOWLEDGMENTS

INDEX

SUGGESTED LISTENING AND VIEWING

The official John Adams website is www.earbox.com.

THE JOHN ADAMS EARBOX *(Nonesuch 79453)*
A ten-CD box of most John Adams works written between 1973 and 1998, including *Harmonielehre*, *Harmonium*, *Shaker Loops*, Violin Concerto, Chamber Symphony, *Grand Pianola Music*, *Fearful Symmetries*, selections from *Nixon in China*, *The Death of Klinghoffer*, and *I Was Looking at the Ceiling and Then I Saw the Sky*.

NIXON IN CHINA *(Nonesuch 79177)*
Original cast recording with Edo de Waart conducting the Orchestra of St. Lukes, featuring James Maddelena as Nixon, Sanford Sylvan as Chou En-lai, John Duykers as Mao, and Carolann Page as Pat Nixon.

CENTURY ROLLS *(Nonesuch 79607-2)*
1996 piano concerto written for and recorded by Emanuel Ax and the Cleveland Orchestra, conducted by Christoph von Dohnányi.

THE DEATH OF KLINGHOFFER *(Decca 074 189-9 DH)*
Penny Woolcock's film version of the 1991 opera on DVD, with John Adams conducting the London Symphony Orchestra and Chorus.

HARMONIELEHRE, THE CHAIRMAN DANCES, 2 FANFARES FOR ORCHESTRA *(EMI 550151)*

The City of Birmingham Orchestra conducted by Simon Rattle.

HOODOO ZEPHYR *(Nonesuch 79311-2)*

1992 album of music created exclusively on synthesizers and samplers, with photos by Deborah O'Grady.

NAIVE AND SENTIMENTAL MUSIC *(Nonesuch 79636-2)*

1999 symphony written for and recorded by Esa-Pekka Salonen and the Los Angeles Philharmonic.

EL NIÑO *(Nonesuch 79634-2)*

Nativity oratorio for the millennium, featuring Dawn Upshaw, Lorraine Hunt Lieberson, and Willard White, conducted by Kent Nagano.

ROAD MOVIES *(Nonesuch 79699)*

An album of chamber and solo piano works, featuring Leila Josefowicz, Nicolas Hodges, Rolf Hind, and John Novacek. Includes *Phrygian Gates*, *Hallelujah Junction*, *American Berserk*, and *China Gates*.

ON THE TRANSMIGRATION OF SOULS *(Nonesuch 79816-2)*

Commissioned by the New York Philharmonic to commemorate the first anniversary of September 11, 2001. Lorin Maazel conducts the New York Philharmonic with the New York Choral Artists and the Brooklyn Youth Chorus.

THE DHARMA AT BIG SUR *(Nonesuch 79857-2)*

Concerto for six-string electric violin, inspired by Jack Kerouac. Performed by Tracy Silverman, with the BBC Symphony Orchestra conducted by John Adams.

A FLOWERING TREE *(Nonesuch 327100-2)*

Opera in two acts, inspired by Mozart's *Magic Flute*, with the composer conducting the original cast, the London Symphony Orchestra, and the Schola Cantorum de Caracas.

DOCTOR ATOMIC *(Opus Arte DVD)*

Original stage version of the Peter Sellars production on DVD, with Gerald Finley as J. Robert Oppenheimer, Jessica Rivera as Kitty Oppenheimer, Eric

Owens as General Leslie Groves, and Richard Paul Fink as Edward Teller in a 2007 production from the Netherlands Opera, conducted by Lawrence Renes.

JOHN ADAMS: A PORTRAIT *(Arthaus Musik 100322)*
DVD documentary about the composer, much of it devoted to the film and recording of *The Death of Klinghoffer*.

WONDERS ARE MANY *(Actual Films)*
DVD documentary by Jon Else follows the creation and first San Francisco production of *Doctor Atomic*, skillfully mixing science and music theater.

ACKNOWLEDGMENTS

Most of the people who have meant much to me are already mentioned in this book. For those who prefer to remain anonymous I will nonetheless risk their desire for privacy by extending my thanks for their help, and in many cases their delicacy in correcting my many errors and factual confusions.

Bob Hurwitz, my longtime friend and president of Nonesuch Records, first introduced me to Jonathan Galassi of Farrar, Straus and Giroux, and Jonathan became my editor in the course of writing the book. Belinda Matthews of Faber and Faber Limited in London enthusiastically supported the idea of a British release and also provided critical input.

Alice Goodman generously allowed me to quote extensively from her libretti, and Betty Freeman gave permission to reprint her photos.

Several close friends read chapters and made invaluable comments and suggestions. The list includes Emanuel Ax, Derek Bermel, Jenny Bilfield, Sarah Cahill, Jon Else, Matthew Gurewitsch, Ara Guzelimian, Philippa Kelly, Nick Kenyon, Craig Lambert, Ingram Marshall, and Ed Yim. Kyle Gann was instrumental in helping to clear up some misconceptions I'd had about intonation and temperament. My daughter, Emily Adams, did a deep reading of several of the early chapters, suggesting solutions to some of my more tortured constructions, and my wife, Deborah O'Grady, provided patience and encouragement and, when necessary, wisdom and caution. My aunt Dorothy Touart helped with some critical information about the early days of my grandfather in New Hampshire.

Alex Ross, although up to his ears in the creation of his own monumental history of twentieth-century music, still was able to find time to read some of these pages and help in the technical matters of book publishing, a new activity for me.

To them all I express my heartfelt appreciation for their support and enthusiasm.

INDEX